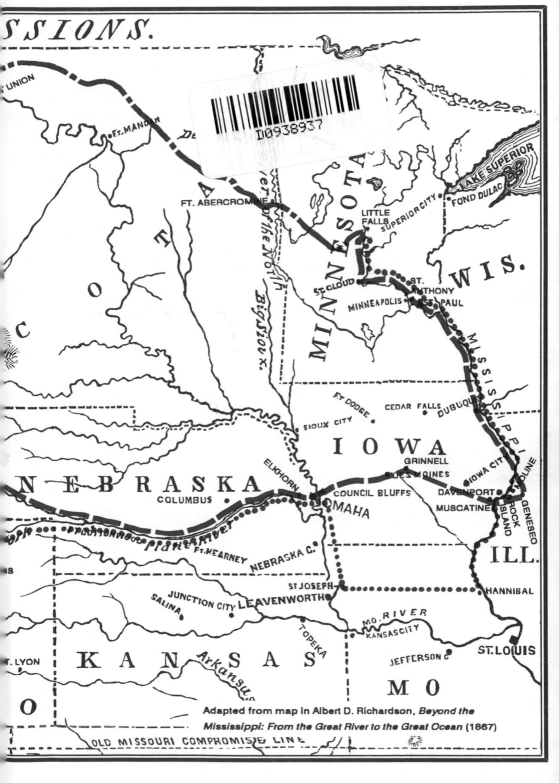

SSIONS.

FT. UNION

FT. MANDAN

River of the North

FT. ABERCROMBIE

DA

COTE

AU

MINNESOTA

LITTLE FALLS

SUPERIOR CITY

FOND DULAC

LAKE SUPERIOR

WIS.

ST. CLOUD

ST. ANTHONY

MINNEAPOLIS

ST. PAUL

MISSISSIPPI

BigSiou X.

FT. DODGE

CEDAR FALLS

DUBUQUE

SIOUX CITY

IOWA

GRINNELL

DES MOINES

IOWA CITY

MOLINE

ELKHORN

COUNCIL BLUFFS

DAVENPORT

GENESEO

NEBRASKA

COLUMBUS

OMAHA

MUSCATINE

ROCK ISLAND

ILL.

Platte River

FT. KEARNEY

NEBRASKA C.

HANNIBAL

ST. JOSEPH

SALINA

JUNCTION CITY LEAVENWORTH

KANSAS CITY

MO. RIVER

FT. LYON

KANSAS

Arkansas

TOPEKA

JEFFERSON C.

ST. LOUIS

MO

Adapted from map in Albert D. Richardson, *Beyond the
Mississippi: From the Great River to the Great Ocean* (1867)

OLD MISSOURI COMPROMISE LINE

THE

Gold Rush Widows
of Little Falls

THE
Gold Rush Widows of Little Falls

A story drawn from the letters of
Pamelia and James Fergus

Linda Peavy & Ursula Smith

Minnesota Historical Society Press
St. Paul

MINNESOTA HISTORICAL SOCIETY PRESS

St. Paul 55101

Manufactured in the United States of America

10 9 8 7 6 5 4 3 2 1

International Standard Book Number

0-87351-249-9 Cloth

0-87351-250-2 Paper

The paper used in this book meets the minimum requirements of the
American National Standard for Information Sciences — Permanence
for Printed Library Materials, ANSI Z39.48-1984.

Library of Congress Cataloging-in-Publication Data

Peavy, Linda S.
    The Gold Rush widows of Little Falls : a story drawn from the let-
ters of Pamelia and James Fergus / Linda Peavy and Ursula Smith.
        p.   cm.
    Includes bibliographical references.
    1. Fergus, Pamelia Dillin, b. 1824 — Correspondence. 2. Fergus,
James, b. 1813 — Correspondence. 3. Women pioneers — Minnesota —
Little Falls — Correspondence. 4. Pioneers — Minnesota — Little Falls —
Correspondence. 5. Pioneers — Colorado — Correspondence.
6. Pioneers — Montana — Correspondence. 7. Fergus family —
Correspondence. 8. Colorado — Gold discoveries. 9. Montana — Gold
discoveries. 10. Frontier and pioneer life — Minnesota — Little Falls. 11.
Little Falls (Minn.) — Biography. I. Smith, Ursula. II. Title.
F614.L58F477 1990
977.6'69 — dc20   89-49409
[B]   CIP

Contents

Foreword

A HUM OF EXCITEMENT ran through the 1984 conference on western women's history when Linda Peavy and Ursula Smith gave their first talk on "women in waiting"—the stay-at-home wives of westering men. This duo of enterprising independent historians had not only discovered important new source material—for the Fergus letters, to the social historian, are simply a treasure trove. They had also developed a way of approaching the material that broke with the old stereotypes of adventurous men and reluctant women, thereby providing insight into individual experience and personality and into the pioneering experience as a whole. Since they gave that first conference paper in 1984, the promise of the research has been abundantly confirmed in further talks by P.S., A Partnership (as Peavy and Smith call their collaboration); in this book; and, even more extraordinarily, in the opera *Pamelia,* which had its world premiere in Billings, Montana, in August 1989.[1] Unquestionably, the story of *The Gold Rush Widows of Little Falls* makes a major contribution to western history and, through the opera, makes a new and novel contribution to popular understanding of the pioneering experience.

Although the topic of women in waiting is new to western history, it is not new to historians of eastern and southern women in colonial and early-nineteenth-century America. What is distinctive about the western women described in this book may become clear if we look at some examples from those periods.

Perhaps the best-known "woman in waiting" in the eighteenth century was Abigail Adams, who was first left behind in 1774, when her husband John went away to represent Massachusetts in the Continental Congress, and was left again for six long years (1778–84) when John was chosen to represent America's interests in France and Britain during the Revolutionary War. Because most of their correspondence survives, we know that Abigail Adams, like Pamelia Fergus, initially took on her husband's business interests reluctantly and ignorantly, but rapidly gained a confidence and feeling of authority that did indeed make her more assertive within the marriage (although not enough to make John listen when she asked him to "remember the ladies" and enfranchise women).[2] Mary Beth Norton has identified a similar pattern in the correspondence between stay-at-home wives and their spouses who fought in the armies of the American Revolution. At first the husbands wrote giving detailed instructions about practically everything, as did James Fergus almost a century later, but as time went on the men's instructions got more general and the women managed more on their own.[3]

When we read the stories of Abigail Adams and her lesser-known sisters, we are most likely to focus on the way in which the husband's extended absence fostered the wife's sense of autonomy and self-respect, allowing her to overcome the limitations of the traditional domestic world of women. However, there are some underlying factors in the circumstances of women in waiting during the revolutionary era that must be recognized. The most important is that, although the wife might not initially know the details of her husband's business, she was not left helpless. Most women were not expected to act alone: they could — and did — get advice and help concerning their husband's business transactions or farm management from nearby male kin. If they had no one nearby to rely on and business went badly, most women knew that they could support themselves and their children at the subsistence level by the tried-and-true female methods of selling butter and eggs or taking in boarders. Furthermore, Laurel Thatcher Ulrich's careful and thoughtful look at the lives of colonial women shows us these early women in waiting in another framework. She argues forcefully and convincingly that the wife's role as "deputy husband" was well established — and limited. Although a wife acted as her husband's surrogate in his absence, it was still *his* business, just as it was *his* family. As the head of the household, the man had authority over everything: his business, relations with the community, decisions about children and child rearing, even day-to-day matters of household management. While the man usually gave responsibility for routine domestic operations to his wife and encouraged her to manage his affairs in his absence, when he was present in the household he expected to exercise his right to make decisions about everything. And when he returned from an absence, he expected to resume all of his decision-making authority. The power relationship between husband and wife did not shift permanently as a result of the temporarily expanded responsibilities that she had assumed in his absence.[4] That was the theory. The reality might be different, as in the case of Abigail and John Adams, but their experience may well have been the exception rather than the rule.

But these examples all date from the colonial period. What of later American history? Women's historians have documented a shift away from the patriarchal household, with its assumption of unlimited male authority, to a more complementary or "companionate" division of responsibility into separate spheres — the domestic for her, everything else for him — in the early nineteenth century. The shift occurred because industrialization and commercialization caused the separation of production from the household. The husband's business moved out of the household to the office or factory, while the wife remained behind at home. Consequently, she knew less about his business, and he was less involved in ordinary household decisions. The ideology of separate spheres was thus a reflection of reality — husband and wife each managed distinctly different operations, and to coordinate their activities they needed to cooperate more nearly as equals than as head and subordinate. The ironic result was that, although a woman gained more autonomy and respect within the domestic realm, she was less equipped than Abigail Adams had been to deal with her husband's business affairs in his absence.

How did this shift affect the eastern and southern women who were Pamelia Fergus's contemporaries? Henry and Elizabeth Cady Stanton, who were married in 1840, were frequently separated when he was away on political business, but she did not attempt to manage his law practice.[5] In their case, increased professionalism dictated that Henry entrust his business concerns to his professional colleagues rather than to the untrained Elizabeth. Many southern plantation women who managed estates in their husbands' absence, on the other hand, did so unwillingly and complained bitterly about the hardship and difficulty of the task.[6]

This brief historical background to the experiences of Pamelia and James Fergus and the other couples described in *The Gold Rush Widows of Little Falls* allows us to sort out our own assumptions about the effects of long-term separation from those held by James and Pamelia and by the other historical actors themselves. We need to try to see these mid-nineteenth-century people in their own terms.

The economy of the 1850s was, in twentieth-century terms, unimaginably insecure. An ambitious man like James Fergus took economic risks that most people living in the late twentieth century would never dream of taking. Failure was much more probable than success, and it was essential to know when to cut one's losses and move on. Although rushing off to Colorado in the hopes of striking it rich may seem the height of folly, it was not necessarily so foolhardy for the husbands of Little Falls. Once their first speculative venture—the gamble that Little Falls would become a prosperous, growing town—had failed, speculating on success in the goldfields was as reasonable a risk as moving on to another frontier town and hoping that it would succeed where Little Falls had failed. For the men of Little Falls, then, the trip to Colorado was not an irresponsible adventure but a serious effort to improve the family fortunes. Or at least it was for James Fergus; we may reasonably doubt whether Dr. Timothy Smith's sense of responsibility was much engaged! Nor did these men desert their wives. As we have seen, since colonial times it had been customary to leave wives behind in similar circumstances. James Fergus did not leave Pamelia helpless when he went west. Not only did he write often and in excruciating detail, he also left instructions with a business partner to help Pamelia in every way possible. Besides, he knew that if necessary she could get by on the money she could earn from selling butter and eggs or taking in boarders. None of this was novel; Abigail Adams would have understood completely. What *was* new was that, because Little Falls was a frontier town, Pamelia had no nearby kin to call on for emotional or economic support. And, because it was a failing town, Pamelia had more trouble collecting rents and debts than she would have had in an established town like Moline, Illinois. Clearly, then, Pamelia's residence on the frontier imposed some special hardships that made her "waiting" status more difficult. But her difficulties were surely less than they would have been if she had accompanied James to Colorado.

It is frequently hard for twentieth-century readers to believe that so many wives were willing to be left behind. Long separations are difficult for us, and we have a tendency to view historical separations as something close to abandonment. This, I am quite certain, is a misreading of the record. If the subject was discussed at all, James would certainly have argued that leaving Pamelia behind was a mark of his solicitude toward her—and she would have agreed. He faced a considerable period of uncertainty, economic deprivation, and frequent moves before he was reestablished financially. There is no reason to believe that Pamelia would have enjoyed the hardships of this migratory period. If we look at the question realistically, instead of through the haze of adventure that cloaks much of our thinking about the West, it is obvious that circumstances that were difficult for men would surely have been worse for women with small children. James Fergus did what responsible men did: he sent for his family as soon as his economic prospects were secure. Seen in this light, James Fergus's decision to go to Colorado without his family was evidence of his concern for them. Of course, it may also have been, at least some of the time, a challenging adventure that he and his fellow argonauts relished, but this in no way diminished his ties to his family. Studies like this should encourage us to modify the heroic and individualistic terms in which we have viewed many western male figures—explorers, gold rushers, and so forth. Family ties and responsibilities may have been much more important in the minds of the men in the goldfields and mining camps of the West than we have realized.

Readers may also have difficulty relating to the characters of James and Pamelia Fergus. James seems so officious, so constant, detailed, and niggling in his advice; Pamelia seems, in contrast, so passive and helpless when faced with the job of managing in his absence. James certainly was an autocratic, take-charge sort of person; Pamelia was younger, less well educated, less confident. But the key to understanding their relationship lies less in temperamental qualities than in structural ones. We need to see the Fergus couple, when they first separate, as closer to the colonial patriarchal family than to the emerging mid-nineteenth-century companionate one. James consistently wrote as though he had authority over everything: business, home, child rearing, and the rest. His assumption, like that of colonial couples, was that Pamelia was temporarily acting as "deputy husband," with all the responsibility but none of the permanent authority that the role implied. Pamelia's assumptions are a bit more difficult to ascertain, but it is reasonable to guess that her thinking was closer to the emerging separate-spheres approach, giving her a feeling of personal power and autonomy within the domestic sphere. She was unhappy about taking over James's business responsibilities, clearly feeling that her task was not only difficult, but inappropriate; she felt out of place in the male world of business. Undoubtedly her years of "widowhood" and increased responsibility enhanced her feelings of authority and ability. When James and Pamelia were finally reunited in Montana, however, the issue was not whether she would continue to be active in James's business, but whether she would allow him to continue to dictate to her in her own domestic sphere. The crucial episode occurred when James criticized her cooking: much to his amazement, Pamelia fought back. Her years of responsibility had increased her feelings of competence and authority, and she now resolutely insisted on managing the home without interference. In the aftermath of that battle, it seems that a bargain was struck: James relinquished control over household management (although not without protest), but control over the children, a basic prerogative of patriarchy, remained in dispute. Power had shifted, not massively, but nevertheless significantly. Women's historians have tended to portray the shift from patriarchal to companionate marriage as a natural result of more enlightened thinking, but it may be that many thousands of small domestic struggles, like that of the reunited Fergus couple, were the real engines of social change.

The story of Pamelia and James Fergus and of their acquaintances in Little Falls gives us a way to deepen our understanding of sex roles and family dynamics in the mid-nineteenth century. We see the ways in which the entire family was mobilized to deal with economic uncertainty. We see that even the most "rugged" individual needs to be considered in a family context. And we also see, at a microcosmic level, how marital relationships changed in small ways. In a broader context, the attitudes of Pamelia and James, so carefully explored in this study, give us insight into a basic polarity in the American identity. As Erik H. Erikson explained:

> The same families . . . were forced to prepare men and women who would take root in the community life . . . of the new villages and towns and at the same time to prepare these children for the possible physical hardships of homesteading on the frontiers. . . . Mothers had to raise sons and daughters who would be

determined to ignore the call of the frontier—but who would go with equal determination once they were forced or chose to go.[7]

James Fergus clearly represents the migratory tendency in the American identity, and Pamelia the sedentary. As they go their separate ways, they are at the same time working out compromises between the urge to go and the urge to stay. The small story of Pamelia and James, as this book so eloquently tells us, sums up a large part of the American experience. For the careful telling of this significant story we are all indebted to the loving attention of Linda Peavy and Ursula Smith.

Washington State University   SUSAN ARMITAGE

Notes

1. The Fergus letters were the basis for the libretto that Peavy and Smith wrote for *Pamelia*, which was composed by Eric Funk.

2. Charles W. Akers, *Abigail Adams: An American Woman* (Boston: Little, Brown and Company, 1980), 17–79.

3. Mary Beth Norton, ed., *Liberty's Daughters: The Revolutionary Experience of American Women, 1750–1800* (Boston: Little, Brown and Company, 1980), 216–24.

4. Laurel Thatcher Ulrich, *Good Wives: Image and Reality in the Lives of Women in Northern New England, 1650–1750* (New York: Alfred A. Knopf, 1982), 35–50.

5. Elisabeth Griffith, *In Her Own Right: The Life of Elizabeth Cady Stanton* (New York: Oxford University Press, 1984), 49–50, 64, 84.

6. Catherine Clinton, *The Plantation Mistress: Woman's World in the Old South* (New York: Pantheon Books, 1982), 74–76.

7. Erik H. Erikson, *Childhood and Society* (New York: W. W. Norton, 1963), 293.

Preface

IN THE LATE 1850s and early 1860s, the frontier town of Little Falls, Minnesota, struggled for survival in the face of droughts, floods, conflicts with Indians, and a failing economy. The struggle went on long after many of the men of Little Falls had left the town—and their families—behind, bound for the goldfields of Colorado and Montana in search of simple solutions to the complex problems at home. The women who were left behind drew together to weather the hard times and celebrate the good, pooling their resources, voicing their hopes, fears, and frustrations, and sharing their letters from the men in the mines. Through those letters—and through state and local histories, public records, and newspapers—the stories of these women and of the town in which they lived can be told.

The Gold Rush Widows of Little Falls is a chronicle of social disruption, of struggle to maintain a semblance of family life under extremely trying circumstances. Most of the women we write of here had had little or no experience beyond their roles as wives and mothers when they were called upon to add to their own duties those of their absent husbands. It is little wonder that they were initially reluctant to agree to plans that left them in the very situations their husbands sought to escape. With little more than promises to sustain them, these women waited months, even years, with no sure knowledge of when or where or even whether the promised reunion would take place.

One of the women, Pamelia Fergus, came to refer to herself and the other waiting wives of Little Falls as "the widows," an appropriate enough term, since only the death of a husband would normally have given a woman of that era such instant and complete autonomy.[1] Thus, though there was not an activist among them, the story of the widows might, by modern standards, be seen as a story of women's liberation—with an ironic twist. Independence, such as it was, came to these women unbidden, and, in most cases, unwelcomed. And the freedoms they gained hardly offset the hardships they endured. They were, for the most part, uneasy in their roles as surrogate heads of household and more than ready to relinquish those roles when their spouses returned. Little wonder, since their temporary control of business affairs brought with it few rewards and many problems. No matter how ably they carried on, they were still primarily viewed as wives carrying out the wishes of husbands. Though their duties increased, their status remained essentially unchanged. For those left with power of attorney, there was at least equality before the law. But it was, at best, a bastard equality, an equality of convenience, an equality by default. And it could be revoked as readily as it had been granted.

Difficult as their situation was, it was not unique. The experiences of the widows of Little Falls are representative of those of thousands of other "women in waiting" who were temporarily or permanently left behind when their husbands went west in search of gold, land, or excitement. The stories of the adventuring men have, by and large, been well chronicled in the lore of the American frontier, while the stories of the wives they left behind have largely been ignored.[2]

While recent studies have clarified much about the role of women in the westward movement, they have not dealt directly with the experiences of women in waiting. Perhaps because the contributions of these women to the settling of the American West were made outside western borders. Perhaps because the women themselves did not consider their accomplishments worthy enough of note to leave behind a full accounting. For any number of reasons, women in waiting left only scant evidence of their work as temporary heads of households. As Laurel Thatcher Ulrich has noted in the case of colonial women, it is extremely difficult to document the work women did in the absence of their husbands, since "female enterprise appears as the merest flicker on the surface of male documents."[3] The same difficulties pertain in documenting the roles played by nineteenth-century women in waiting. Often their work was only verbal—prodding a debtor or pleading with a creditor. Sometimes it involved pushing a male friend or business acquaintance to carry through on a project the absent husband had left in his care. Almost always their work was low key, behind the scenes, and seldom considered worthy of an entry in account books or business journals.

Even the personal records kept by women in waiting give little evidence of their day-to-day involvement in business affairs. The diarists among them wrote of their loneliness during periods of separation, yet said little about the everyday activities that ensured their survival.[4] It is the letter writers who have given us hints of the struggles they endured, probably because their letters were written at the request of absent husbands, many of whom expected a full and frequent accounting of life back home.

And it is the letters of one woman, Pamelia Dillin Fergus, that have given us the story of the widows of Little Falls. Her letters, together with those of her husband, James, not only reveal one family's story but also provide a rare glimpse into the daily lives of several other families who left virtually no written records of their own.[5] Without the clues given in the Fergus letters, our study of women in waiting would, like most social history based on personal records, have been limited to the examination of the experiences of a relatively elite group of people literate enough to write letters, diaries, and memoirs and perceptive enough to realize the wisdom of preserving such documents.[6]

With these clues we were able to reconstruct the stories of Amanda Smith, whose alcoholic husband, Dr. Timothy Smith, seldom wrote except to ask for money; Elizabeth Stone, a grandmother whose aging husband, Lewis, was among the first to head west; Agnes Russell, left first in her native Scotland and again on an isolated Benton County farm where she and her eight children barely managed to survive; Caroline Bosworth, nineteen and the mother of a baby boy when her husband, Daniel, joined James Fergus on the journey to Pikes Peak; Mary Paul, who left Platte River and went into St. Cloud in search of a job that would enable her to feed her six children; Rosanna Sturgis, a mother of seven whose skillful management of a sawmill and flour mill resulted in profits equal to those from her husband's ventures in the West; and Margaretha Ault, who supported herself by working as a cook and midwife while her husband, John, spent all he earned on the women who frequented his tavern in the Montana gold camp of Bannack.

In each of these cases, the women were struggling to hold onto whatever assets had been left in their keeping. They raised what money they could through traditional means, such as selling butter and eggs, and struggled to avoid going deeper into debt. Having been charged with carrying on the farming and business affairs of their absent husbands, they added those labors to their already substantial duties as housewives and mothers. Yet they received no salary and no recognition for their extra work, and they gained little status from their temporary participation in the business world.

While *The Gold Rush Widows of Little Falls* is not intended as a community study, the accounts of everyday life found in the Fergus letters give a fairly complete picture of a small town over a four-year period and offer a broad overview of a single decade in that town's history. In addition to details concerning the separated couples, the Fergus letters provide enough information about several other Little Falls citizens—including a dishonest sheriff, an enterprising shopkeeper, and a cowardly pastor—to enable us to present a cross section of Little Falls society, thereby greatly enriching our view of the circumstances under which the widows waited and enhancing our understanding of the obstacles they faced as female heads of household.

The richness and diversity of these stories defy any attempt to force from this study a single pervasive thesis. For example, while Pamelia's growth and development over the four years of James's absence might tempt one to suppose that life as woman in waiting served as a valuable apprenticeship for life as a frontier wife, the experiences of the other widows would hardly bear out that thesis. Since most of those women never went west at all, there is no way of assessing how well their experiences in Little Falls might have equipped them for new roles on the frontier. Furthermore, no two widows reacted in the same way to the crises they faced. Some grew more autonomous. Some held their own. Some faltered, then recovered. All managed to survive.[7]

By exploring the varied experiences of these women, *The Gold Rush Widows of Little Falls* reveals some of the immediate and long-range repercussions of the prolonged absence of westering husbands. By demonstrating the surprisingly high percentage of argonauts from a single community who were married and left wives and children behind when they set out for the West, the book suggests that the separated family might have been a far more common element of the westward movement than has heretofore been supposed. By detailing the added responsibilities women assumed in the absence of husbands who went west and/or in the course of their own migration and settling, this study calls into question the idea that the westward movement brought women the same freedoms that, by Turnerian standards, it afforded men.[8] And finally, by examining the successful networking accomplished by a diverse group of women whose major unifying factor was the absence of their gold-seeking spouses, the book seeks to heighten our understanding of the support systems developed by nineteenth-century women.

Acknowledgments

WHEN WE BEGAN our search for the widows of Little Falls, we had
no idea how controlling, how compelling the work would become.
For five years we followed the faint, 120-year-old trail, motivated
only by an insatiable curiosity about a group of women who had
learned impressive lessons concerning independence and inter-
dependence.

The letters of James and Pamelia Fergus were our starting point.
But we found there only the surnames of the women whose stories
we sought — Mrs. Russell, Mrs. Ault, Mrs. Bosworth — for women
of the nineteenth century were rarely referred to by their given
names. By comparing Pamelia's references to the widows with
James's references to westering men of the same surnames — Robert
Russell, John Ault, Daniel Bosworth — we came up with probable
pairings. Then, using territorial, federal, and state census records of
1857, 1860, and 1865, we searched for entries that matched the names
we had paired and also dovetailed with descriptive phrases in Pamelia's letters — for example, of Mrs. Russell, who had "seven children and looking for the eighth."

Armed with the names of the widows and their spouses, we expanded our search to include courthouses and town halls as we
sought the marriage, birth, death, probate, and land records we
needed to flesh out the skeletal stories that were emerging. We
visited state and local historical societies, university libraries, and
numerous archives in search of vintage county and community histories, newspapers, and Works Projects Administration genealogies
that could add color and substance to the facts we were accumulating about each widow. And, whenever possible, we interviewed
descendants and obtained from them the family histories and photographs we needed to complete our work.

The search that began with the last names of the widows and that
yielded enough material about these elusive women to enable us to
write this book was aided and encouraged by many. Our thanks go
first to Charlotte Quigley Orr, great-granddaughter of Pamelia

Fergus, for it was Charlotte who first told us about the Fergus Papers. She also introduced us to other members of the Fergus family — notably, Agnes Fergus Miedema, Pamelia Fergus Pittman, Andrew James Fergus, Stephen Fergus Gilpatrick, Margaret Maury Bristol, Thomas K. Hamilton, and Christine Kloezeman — who shared their memories, their papers, and their photographs and who patiently awaited the completion of our task and the publication of this book. Special thanks are due Hazel Akeley Fergus, daughter-in-law of Pamelia and James, for her perseverance in finding an archival home for the Fergus Papers and her generosity in allowing us to publish work based on those papers.

We thank, as well, Drs. Susan Armitage, Richard Roeder, and Lillian Schlissel — historians, mentors, friends — who helped us to believe in the worth of this undertaking and offered continuous support and guidance; Dr. William Lang, formerly editor of *Montana the Magazine of Western History,* who had enough faith in our women-in-waiting thesis to become the first to publish our work on it; and Dr. Paula Petrik, whose graduate class in research methodology gave us the skills we needed to make full use of the public records so crucial to our portrayal of the widows.

Dale Johnson of the University of Montana at Missoula and Susan Jackson, Delores Morrow, Susan Near, and Dave Walter of the Montana Historical Society in Helena made our archival work pleasant and productive, as did Minnie Paugh and Marlene Anderson of Montana State University's Special Collections. Jan Warner, Bruce Mellor, and Kim Hayes of the Charles A. Weyerhaeuser Memorial Museum in Little Falls not only answered our questions but went off on sleuthing missions of their own, enticed by the fact that the Fergus Papers held the clues by which the "lost" history of their town's early years could be recovered. Bonnie Palmquist guided our initial work in the research collections of the Minnesota Historical Society and introduced us to staff members Ruth Bauer, Steven Nielsen, and Ruby Shields, whose services were essential to the completion of this book. We also wish to express our gratitude to Dr. Robert Horne, whose dissertation was a key document in our work on the lives of James and Pamelia Fergus, and to Mary Logan Sweet, whose monograph on William Sturgis was a welcome discovery.

The Cedar Falls, Iowa, Historical Society and the state historical societies of Colorado and Illinois provided assistance, as did the historical societies of Todd, Benton, and Stearns counties in Minnesota; of St. Joseph County in Michigan; of Rock Island County in Illinois; and of Fergus, Beaverhead, and Madison counties in Montana. We appreciate the help of the staffs of the Bozeman Public Library and the Montana State University Library. Our search for public records was aided by clerks and officers in courthouses in Morrison, Todd, Benton, Stearns, and Hennepin counties in Minnesota and Gallatin, Lewis and Clark, Madison, Beaverhead, and Fergus counties in Montana. Doris Russell, Billie Batters Bennett, Mary Gabse, and Mary Phillips shared family memorabilia concerning descendants of early residents of Little Falls; Doris Youngs Sellers provided information on Pamelia's early environment; Shirley Rodman Lewison provided research assistance; and Ann Regan, managing editor of the Minnesota Historical Society Press, offered early encouragement and seasoned editorial advice. We thank as well Press editors Elaine H. Carte and Sarah P. Rubinstein, copy editor Patricia McKernon, and cartographer Alan Ominsky.

Upon the completion of our research, Centrum Foundation, of Port Townsend, Washington, provided us with a month-long residency that proved essential to the writing of this book. Equally essential has been the continued support of our families, who have more or less lived out the women-in-waiting experience in reverse during our researching and writing of *The Gold Rush Widows of Little Falls*.

THE
Gold Rush Widows
of Little Falls

Beginnings

PAMELIA FERGUS and her four children gathered about the south-bound stage on a March afternoon in 1860. They had come to say their good-byes, for James Fergus, husband and father, was bound for the goldfields of Pikes Peak. Fergus was a prime mover in the development of the Little Falls Manufacturing Company that had given the town its start, and his departure marked the end of an era as surely as his arrival had marked its beginning. Fergus was a dreamer who had set out to harness the Mississippi River by building a dam that would power a city he saw as potential rival to St. Paul. Having built that dam, he had watched the river tear out his handiwork and hurl it downstream.

Broke and discouraged, he had finally conceded that outside money would be essential if he was ever to alter either the town's fortunes or his own. Sure that the needed money could be obtained in the goldfields, Fergus was as optimistic about Pikes Peak as he had ever been about Little Falls, Minnesota. And the well-wishers who gathered about him the day of his departure shared that optimism.[1]

Although Pamelia hoped for a successful venture, she had her doubts—and her worries. The Fergus children, aged thirteen to three, were far less aware than their mother of the dangers that lay ahead for the father who promised to return in six months, laden with the gold they needed to set their lives on course. In the meantime, it was Pamelia who would be coping with the unfinished business James Fergus was leaving behind. With no prior experience to call upon, she would somehow have to learn to manage mortgaged lots, angry creditors, and a nearly bankrupt business. What she could not learn from the lengthy memorandum James had prepared for her would have to be gleaned through letters from afar.

But Pamelia was not the only Little Falls woman left behind by a gold-seeking husband. Nineteen-year-old Caroline Bosworth had already begun her stint as woman in waiting, for Daniel

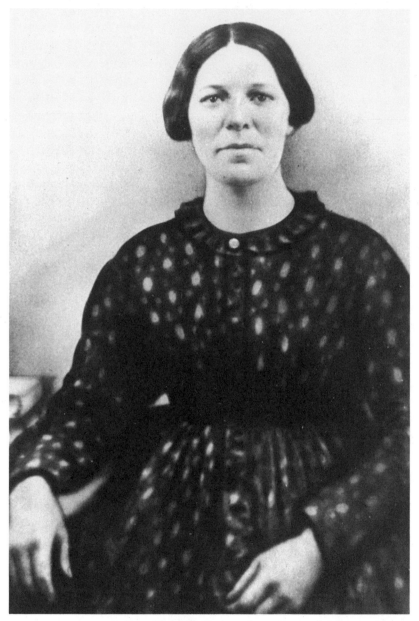

Pamelia Dillin Fergus, about 1860

James Fergus in the 1860 tintype that he sent to his father in Scotland

Bosworth had said his good-byes to wife and baby some two weeks earlier and was, by now, somewhere downriver buying wagons, oxen, and provisions for the trip west.

Somewhere in St. Paul, another Little Falls refugee whiled away the hours before beginning his trip down the Mississippi on his way to St. Joseph, Missouri, where he hoped to hook up with a wagon train in need of a doctor. Timothy Smith, an erstwhile physician who had moved his family to Little Falls four years earlier during the town's initial boom, had left Amanda and the children there to depend upon the kindness of friends and neighbors. For Amanda

Smith, Caroline Bosworth, and Pamelia Fergus, the future at home was as uncertain as the future in the mines out West.

Over the next few years, as the lure of gold proved increasingly irresistible to men in the Little Falls area, still other wives and mothers would be left behind. Indeed, most of the men who watched the stage pull away from John Ault's Northern Hotel and make its way down the rutted, thawing road toward St. Paul were already planning their own departures. As soon as James Fergus sent word of where and how the gold was to be found, they would make the necessary arrangements and set out after him.

There was nothing to hold them at home any longer. The dam, though partially rebuilt before the winter snows had set in, was likely to wash out again with the first spring freshet. Those who had hoped to become a part of the industry centered around the dam had long since abandoned their houses and their hopes and gone back to wherever they had come from or on to whatever new schemes had caught their fancy. Those less directly dependent upon the waterpower promised by the Little Falls Manufacturing Company still lingered. Lawyer James Hall had found there was as much money to be made in litigation over broken bonds as there had been in the daily transactions of more prosperous days. Farmers like John Workman and Benjamin Daggett held on to their land and prayed for good enough crops to make up for those they had lost to drought and grasshoppers.

Merchants Orlando Churchill, William Butler, and Francis X. Gravel stayed on in the hope that monied interests from St. Anthony or the East would buy out the company and bring in more laborers to purchase the goods that lined their dusty shelves. At present, they served only those who had been too broke or too tired to move on in December, when Fergus halted the work for which he could no longer pay them. Churchill, who had come to Little Falls to manage the company store, had long since found that whiskey made a man forget how much money he owed and how little chance there was of paying it. Butler and Gravel were both sober and hardworking, yet Butler had already made it clear to his partner that he was ready to leave everything behind and take his talents west, should James Fergus find a good place for him there.

Over the next four years, many Little Falls residents did, in fact, make their way west. That spring of 1860, when Fergus's departure triggered the exodus, the town's population had dropped to just over two hundred. While there is no record of the exact number of men from the area who went west between 1860 and 1864, it is known that more than a score of them took their leave and tried their luck in remote mining camps bearing such colorful names as Breckenridge Diggings, Gambol Gulch, and Grasshopper Creek. The first to leave were James Fergus, Daniel Bosworth, Timothy Smith, O. J. Rockwell, and James Dillin. Later, they were joined by others, including Lewis Stone, Alexander Paul, Robert Russell, Leonard and Lewis Randall, William Sturgis, John Ault, Johnny Johnson, James Hall, Charles Freeman, and Francis Gravel.[2]

Only two of the married men took their families with them when they first went west. Some of the men who set out from the Little Falls area eventually returned, no richer for their wandering. Some fared so well that they returned for their families or sent for them, intent on building a new home in the West. Some never returned at all.

The women left waiting in Little Falls came to depend upon one another, sharing their troubles, their provisions, and their letters from the West. Pamelia Fergus's letters to James frequently mention "us widows," a group that eventually included not only Caroline Bosworth and Amanda Smith but also Elizabeth Stone, Mary Paul, Agnes Russell, Rosanna Sturgis, Margaretha Ault, and Clara Hall.[3]

James Fergus was the most faithful correspondent among the absent husbands and his letters were the most frequent and reliable source of news from the mining camps of the West. In turn, Pamelia's letters contained news from home, including entreaties from wives who relied on James to deliver messages to husbands they could only hope were still "in the land of the living."[4] Thus the Fergus letters linked the mining camps of the West to the world back home, and Pamelia Fergus emerged as the central figure among the coterie of women who came to be known as the widows of Little Falls.[5]

Pamelia Dillin Fergus was a woman well accustomed to change in circumstance. A child of the frontier, she was born to Mahala and William Dillin on June 22, 1824, in Pamelia Township, a skeletal settlement near the shores of Lake Ontario in Jefferson County, upstate New York. She, like the town itself, was named for her maternal grandmother, Pamelia Williams Brown. The wife of General Jacob Brown, Pamelia Brown was grandmother by adoption, not by blood, having taken in Mahala Bellows [Dillin], the daughter of close friends, when she was orphaned in early childhood during a typhoid fever epidemic.[6] Like the Browns, the Bellowses had migrated to the edge of American civilization from New England, a move prompted by the same spirit that had caused the family to forsake its native Scotland for the new world.

Little else is known of Mahala's background and early life. Upon reaching maturity, she married William Dillin, whose roots, like her own, lay in New England. Over the next twenty years, the Dillins remained in New York, and several children were born to them. The first was Pamelia. There were at least three more girls — Mary, Elizabeth, and Jane or Jeannie — and three boys — Hiram, William Thomas, and James.[7]

As the eldest child of such a large family, Pamelia bore responsibility from an early age, learning the skills of housekeeping and mothering along with the lessons taught in the village school. Her formal education was not likely extensive, for in later years she lamented her lack of training in math and apologized for her poor writing and spelling. Unassuming but self-possessed, she moved from childhood into adulthood within the very small sphere of Pamelia Township.

Sometime during her eighteenth year, whether prompted by the lure of the frontier, the influence of friends, or the necessity of circumstance, Pamelia's parents loaded their household goods and retinue of children into several horse-drawn wagons and set out for Henry County, Illinois, a thousand miles distant. It was winter, and they made slow progress over the snow-covered roads and frozen lakes that lay between their old home and their new.[8] There are no reminiscences from which to reconstruct the events of that trip or Pamelia's response to them. Up to this point in her life, little is known of what she did, and nothing of what she thought and felt.

Shortly after the family arrived in Illinois, Pamelia made her way to Moline where she secured a housekeeping position in a hotel. That Christmas of 1844 she was a guest in the home of the George Stephens family. There she was introduced to another guest, an ambitious bachelor some ten years her senior, himself newly arrived in Moline. It would not have taken her long to find out that this loquacious little man shared her Scottish roots, for James Fergus was proud of his heritage. The son of Andrew and Agnes Bullock Fergus of Shawton, Glassford Parish, Lanarkshire, Scotland, James was born on October 8, 1813. In 1833, following the death of his mother and at loggerheads with his autocratic Presbyterian father, nineteen-year-old James had sailed to North America. There his determination and natural ability had served him well. Moving from Quebec to Toronto, thence to New York, Wisconsin, Iowa, and finally Illinois, he had made his way into the mainstream of American life.[9]

Pamelia's fascination with this self-made man is understandable. His experiences stood in stark contrast to her own. Widely read and widely traveled, James was a man who had dared to dream and do whatever it took to turn his dreams into realities. By his own account, he had acknowledged his inadequacies and had set about to make up for them. "To catch up with others I had to give it my whole attention," he later wrote to a grandson. "In place of going to theaters . . . I studied books."[10] And catch up he did. By the time he stood in the Stephens home talking to Pamelia Dillin that December of 1844, James Fergus had achieved his U.S. citizenship, had become a master carpenter and millwright, and was well on his way to partnership in the Moline Foundry owned by D. B. Sears, that city's founder.[11] He lacked only one thing.

That lack was filled some three months later, on March 16, 1845, when James Fergus married Pamelia Dillin. The wedding ceremony took place in the lobby of the hotel where Pamelia worked.[12] James's friends in Moline and elsewhere were somewhat surprised that the wanderer had finally taken root. "I herd that you have got mared," wrote an old acquaintance. "I suppose that she is verry hansom or else you wold not [have] . . . at enny rate I wish you much joy and a long life."[13] Fergus's bride was indeed handsome. A small, dark woman with a steady, even gaze, Pamelia Dillin caught the attention of any observer. While it was her no-nonsense manner that first attracted her serious-minded suitor, it was her warmth that held him.[14]

In a rare show of humor, James reported his wedding to his brother in Scotland, comparing his new union with the union he had made when he became a partner in the Moline Foundry: "I likewise had the misfortune . . . to enter into another partnership for life with Miss Pamelia Dilling who now calls herself Mrs Fergus to my no small annoyance Só you see I am finally married to an American thus by another tie uniting myself to the country of my adoption."[15]

There is truth, as well as humor, in this account of the Fergus marriage, for James did nothing without weighing the advantages. Little he did stood in the way of his pursuit of success. Thus, the day after the celebration of his wedding, he was back at work. If Pamelia was unprepared for such a honeymoon, it at least provided a forewarning of what married life would hold for her, for James was preoccupied with his work and routinely spent sixteen-hour days at the foundry.[16]

Though she lacked the company of her husband, Pamelia soon had that of his children. Mary Agnes was born a year after their wedding, on April 11, 1846. On November 23, 1848, Frances Luella arrived, and on July 3, 1850, Andrew was born.[17] Despite the time and energy she gave to child care and household duties, Pamelia found time to develop a wide circle of friends in Moline, notably Mary Ann Stephens, Harriett Berry, and Temperance Churchill, all of whom were also mothers of young children. She maintained close ties with her parents and siblings, most of whom lived nearby. Her youngest brother, James, occasionally lived in the Fergus household, attending school in Moline, running errands for Pamelia, and, by 1853, working in a nearby mill.[18]

In 1845, the year Pamelia married James, Moline, Illinois, was a town of 350 people.[19] Over the next decade rapid growth and industrial development brought many changes. With the coming of the railroad, James's foundry began to turn out parts for that industry. In the early 1850s, he sold to the Chicago and Rock Island Railway the right-of-way for the tracks that would soon link Moline and Chicago, a sale that necessitated the removal of a portion of the family's home.[20] A conscientious mother and an avid gardener, Pamelia could not have been happy with the decision that turned the children's backyard and her well-tended garden into a railbed. But James was not a man to let sentiment override an advantageous business deal.

Pamelia accepted the trade-offs, knowing that the family, as well as the town, prospered from the railroad boom. The Fergus account books reveal the purchases of a couple able to afford the finer things

Moline, Illinois, 1854. From a lithograph by J. C. Wild.

of life: ginghams and calicoes, linen thread, a palm leaf hat, children's mittens, yards of diaper material, infants' socks and shoes — and a butter mold that was destined to stand Pamelia in good stead in the years that lay ahead.[21]

As she watched her infants grow healthy and robust, Pamelia also watched her hardworking husband grow gray and bald, though he was not yet forty.[22] Her pleas that he get more rest, take time for meals, and give more of himself to his family went unheeded. She could not temper his relentless pursuit of success. Then, in 1852, a major illness did what she could not. It brought an abrupt, if temporary, halt to the frantic pattern of James Fergus's life. "Indigestion and nervous complaints" threatened "a softening of the brain," James himself recalled some years later.[23] Suffering emotional as well as physical trauma, he faced, for the first time, his own mortality. Life could not continue at such a pace. There were limits, even for James Fergus. After some months of recuperation and reflection, he sold his interest in the foundry at a handsome profit and became a partner in the firm of Wheelock and Fergus, paper manufacturers.[24] Within six months, however, that business proved as taxing as foundry work. Determined to find opportunities more congenial to his health, Fergus sold his shares in the paper mill and made plans for a business tour of the East Coast.[25]

His departure in July 1853 left Pamelia on her own in Moline, and his early letters from the East indicate that he was highly conscious of this fact. "I want you to write to me at least every week and let me know how you get along. . . . But above all see to the children," he wrote her from New York. "You pay so little attention to what I say to you that my mind will be troubled about them all the time . . . do not go from home and leave the children alone."[26] Perhaps taking into account her husband's distracted state, Pamelia made no effort to refute his accusations, but instead reiterated the obvious: "I shall endever to take all the care of the children I am capable of care for any thing."[27]

The letters of summer 1853 from Pamelia to James are the first written record we have in her own hand. They show her to be a faithful, somewhat dependent wife and a conscientious, even fretful, mother. Though her letters gave him little reason to doubt her ability to cope with matters at home, James continued to send advice from afar, reminding her to pick up their newspapers and magazines at the post office, to "keep [the children] away from the River," and, when Mary Agnes contracted chicken pox, to try the "water cure." If she got lonely, she was to send for her mother, since the stage passed her door every day and Mahala would surely travel the twenty miles from her home in Geneseo if Pamelia sent money for her fare.[28]

Though James's letters show his concern with matters at home, they center upon eloquent descriptions of the fine life he was leading in Chicago, New York, Boston, New Haven, and Washington, D.C. "I wish you were all here," he wrote, "you could see enough of the world to enlarge your ideas and views of things."[29] At home in Moline, surrounded by chicken pox and by children aged two, four, and six who constantly asked for their papa, Pamelia had little hope of enlarging her "ideas and views of things."[30] Eight years into marriage, she found herself more and more isolated from public life. She and James clearly moved in separate spheres, and while his travels in the East were expanding his world, the added confinement imposed by chicken pox was shrinking hers.[31] When her husband's letters flooded her with news of the sights he was enjoying, she found it difficult to imagine why he would ever want to return home: "I rather think you will get in the notion of a big life while you are gone. I am allmost afraid you will not want to own us when you come."[32]

She need not have feared, for upon his return James made it clear he had no intention of remaining in the East without his family. In fact, having made a six-thousand-mile tour of fourteen states over a six-week period, he came home convinced that his future—and that of his family—lay not in the East, but in the West.[33] Opportunities there so far overshadowed those on the East Coast that early in 1854 he convinced his friend George Stephens that they should pack up their families, move to California, and set up business in one of the boom towns of that new state.[34] Pamelia had hardly begun to adjust to the idea of a move to California when James abandoned this plan in favor of another: the Stephens family would stay in Moline, while the Ferguses would move to St. Anthony, Minnesota Territory.

Though we have no record of Pamelia's reaction to her husband's announcement, she probably was not overjoyed at the prospect of the move. Minnesota Territory was a vast and largely unexplored region whose western boundary stretched all the way to the Missouri and White Earth rivers, giving the territory an area nearly twice that of the present-day state. Within those boundaries Indians had lived since late glacial times, some ten thousand or more years before the appearance of European explorers. The Ojibway (Chippewa) and the Dakota (Sioux) had ceded some of their lands east of the Mississippi to the United States government in 1837. But lands west of the river, in the St. Anthony area James favored, had been open to settlement by whites for a scant three years at the time he proposed the move northward. Ojibway, Dakota, and Winnebago Indians were still very much in evidence on reservation lands, and many of them were hostile toward the settlers whose arrival had so drastically altered their way of life.[35]

The home James had chosen was located on the Mississippi River at the Falls of St. Anthony, near the mouth of the Minnesota River—close enough to Fort Snelling to seem relatively safe from Indian attack. But there were other factors to be considered. What sort of life could the children look forward to in this newly established, rapidly growing mill town? Educational opportunities were few, even in St. Paul, the territorial capital, whose newspaper had recently described that city's children as "little untaught brats, swarming along the streets and along the levee . . . like wharf rats."[36] And what sort of life awaited Pamelia herself in such an environment? During her ten years in Moline, she had established close friendships. Her mother and other family members had always been near at hand. The 350-mile move up the Mississippi meant leaving those friends and relatives behind.

These misgivings notwithstanding, there was little enough Pamelia could have done to change James's mind. Since it was his work that supported them, they must go wherever that work might lead. There were limits as to how actively Pamelia could afford to protest a plan her husband obviously intended to carry out, with or without her approval.[37]

Whether or not she opposed the move, James's announcement came at a time when Pamelia's awareness of the limitations of marriage and gender was growing. Early in 1853, she and several friends had subscribed to *The Una,* a paper "devoted to the elevation of women."[38] Within its pages she read words that would have been considered outrageous by many of her more conservative friends, though not necessarily by her husband, who prided himself on being a freethinker and a supporter of radical causes. Certainly James shared the paper's editorial opinion that daughters, as well as sons, should be well educated and prepared to make the most of their lives, and he would have taken great delight in *Una* articles challenging traditional religious beliefs.[39]

Yet however much he might have agreed with some of the ideas expressed in *The Una,* James continued to be the primary decision maker in the Fergus home. And though the seeds of unrest had been planted, Pamelia herself continued to operate much as she always had. While she was reading and discussing articles calling for greater business opportunities for women, especially married women, she continued to work in the home. No matter how intriguing she found news of a "Female Medical College," her medical studies remained limited to the lessons she learned from Mary Colburn, the woman who had delivered the Fergus children and sometimes called upon Pamelia for midwifery assistance.[40] And although the report of the February 1854 Woman's Rights Convention held in Albany, New York, contained the names of women who had traveled many miles to attend that meeting, she stayed at home while James toured the eastern seaboard.[41]

And it was James who made the decision to move to Minnesota. Within a few weeks of that decision, he leased their Moline home to their neighbors the Churchills and moved Pamelia and the children to St. Anthony.[42] Soon thereafter he wrote to his father, "I have adopted the migrating habits of the Americans and moved with my family last August to this place, which is 500 [sic] miles further up the Mississippi River by Steam Boat."[43] Pamelia's household goods had traveled by steamboat. A bill of lading issued August 8, 1854, came to $31.18 and contained a complete listing of the goods conveyed. They included four bedsteads, bedding, three tables, two stands, several boxes and bundles of sundries, a keg of molasses, two chests, three buckets, a bookcase, a box of soap, and a bathing tub.[44]

St. Anthony was only five years old in 1854, yet three thousand people had already made it their home. Six miles to the southeast was St. Paul, a city of four thousand. Across the river from St. Anthony lay Minneapolis, a village of three hundred.[45] James declared the society in Minnesota Territory "excellent — being removed from the influences of Slavery," though he admitted people there were afflicted with the "Luxurious habits in dress and living" and the "love of money" that seemed "common to Americans generally."[46]

James himself, of course, fully intended to make money in his new location. He approached Ramsey County officials with a plan whereby he would rent Hennepin Island at the falls, along with water rights "sufficient for a wheel or wheels . . . measuring one thousand inches."[47] When that proposal failed, he was ready with contingency plans, some of which centered upon sites upriver.

With Calvin A. Tuttle, a St. Anthony millowner, he explored the country to the north. "I have just returned from a trip of 150 miles up the river above this place," he wrote his father. "We went by stage and came back in a birch bark canoe Most of this country is still owned by the Indians but where it is not farms and towns are springing up at all the most convenient points."[48] He described in some detail the virgin pine forests and fertile agricultural lands that lay in the upper reaches of the Mississippi River valley. Deer, squirrel, and rabbits were there in abundance, although trappers had

St. Anthony, Minnesota Territory, 1857

taken most of the beaver that had once populated the area's many rivers and streams. Asters, goldenrod, and sunflowers grew wild on large tracts of natural prairies whose rich soils had not yet been turned by plow or spade. Endless opportunities were open to enterprising men willing to accept the challenge offered by the wilderness.[49]

For all his enthusiasm over the lands he saw upriver, James did feel occasional twinges of guilt over leaving Pamelia alone a scant two months after moving her to St. Anthony. The family was living in a house in serious need of repair, and he feared for the safety of the children. In a letter written from Fort Ripley, some 110 miles upriver, he promised to be home in eight to ten days—in time to fix up the house for the winter.[50]

He was as good as his word, but neither James nor Pamelia felt the comforts of home in that house in St. Anthony. They had, after all, made the move to Minnesota Territory with the understanding that they would return to Moline if the right opportunities did not present themselves. By now, however, Pamelia knew that James did not wait for opportunities, he made them. Her hopes of returning to Illinois faded with every trip he made upriver, searching for the perfect site for a dam that could power a city.

2

Early Little Falls

JAMES FERGUS was hardly alone in his search. Up and down the river, enterprising individuals were securing title to the most promising lands, then drawing up attractive maps and lithographing copies.[1] During an 1852 visit to St. Paul, a correspondent from the Pittsburgh *Token* reported, "My ears at every turn are saluted with everlasting din. Land! Land! Money! Speculation! Saw mills! Town lots! etc., etc." Pronouncing everything "artificial, floating," the reporter predicted that, though "the excitement of trade, speculation, and expectation is now running high, and will perhaps for a year or so, . . . it must have a reaction."[2]

Untroubled by such warnings, James Fergus persisted in his speculative ventures, continuing his search for the perfect townsite. By the end of 1854, he had begun to focus on the Little Falls of the Mississippi River, some one hundred miles to the north, in approximately the geographic center of present-day Minnesota. Zebulon Pike had explored the region in 1805, remarking on "the beauty and convenience of the spot for building huts, the fine pine trees for peroques, and the quantity of game," all of which contributed to the suitability of the place for his winter encampment.[3]

Though James Fergus was equally impressed by the beauty of the area and the abundant pine, maple, and white oak forests, it was the waterpower potential apparent in the only natural falls in the upper reaches of the Mississippi that drew him to the place. The river fell eleven feet in a quarter mile at this site, and a crude dam was already in place, providing the power for a small sawmill and a gristmill, both currently operated by William Sturgis.[4] The sawmill's first owner had been James Green, who had taken an 1848 squatter's claim on the east bank of the Mississippi and obtained waterpower by building a wing dam to the island above, providing a head of about three feet. Upon Green's death, his partners, five investors from the surrounding area, had completed work on the mill, then sold mill, site, and waterpower to Sturgis sometime in 1850.[5]

By the time James Fergus and Calvin Tuttle arrived in October

Central Minnesota, 1860

The Little Falls of the Mississippi River, shown here in 1889. By the time this photograph was taken, the town by the falls was beginning to experience the industrial boom of which James Fergus had dreamed thirty years earlier.

1854, the Sturgis mill had already earned the honor of sawing the first lumber north of St. Anthony, and there was every reason to believe the operation could be greatly expanded by constructing a larger dam, one that would span the river and provide enough waterpower to support a town that would rival any other on the Mississippi.[6] Fergus was convinced that the rich timberlands and rolling prairies that stretched along the river at this location could support the broad-based economy necessary for rapid town growth.

Tuttle, whose financial support was essential, concurred with his judgment, and the two men approached William Sturgis with their plan to form a company for the purpose of "making lumber, grinding grain, farming, cutting logs, making a town, selling goods, and doing any other thing or things conducive to the benefit of said company." With his holdings heavily mortgaged, Sturgis was ready enough to accept their proposal. Retaining one-third interest, he sold five-twelfths to Fergus and three-twelfths to Tuttle, and the Little Falls Company became a reality.[7]

The partners in that company were a study in nineteenth-century entrepreneurship. William Sturgis, who had pioneered in Iowa before moving north to Little Falls, was described by contemporary historian Nathan Richardson as "a man of great perseverance and energy" who was "acknowledged to be able to carry on more business with a small capital than any other man in . . . Minnesota."[8] Calvin Tuttle, who had helped build the first sawmill at the village of St. Anthony and then served as territorial treasurer for six years, was well experienced in land and townsite speculation.[9] Fergus himself, as primary investor, would manage the scheme, acting as go-between for Tuttle, who would remain in St. Anthony, and Sturgis, who was to overhaul the dam, finish the flour mill, supply logs, and encourage farming. Fergus would also assume responsibility for keeping the books, managing the milling and lumbering operations, and selling lots carved from the two thousand acres deeded to the company by the United States government.[10]

The plan seemed promising, and Pamelia, having already made the break from Moline and with nothing to hold her in St. Anthony, agreed to the move north. It proved a major concession. If St. Anthony had lacked amenities, Little Falls was primitive. Two houses marked the townsite when James Fergus first saw it.[11] The Sturgis family occupied one of them. Rosanna Steele Sturgis, twenty-one years old and pregnant with her second child, had been a resident of Little Falls since the spring of 1852 when, as an eighteen-year-old bride, she had arrived from Iowa to be introduced to her three stepchildren — seven-year-old Jeanette, five-year-old Sarah Jane (Jennie), and two-year-old John — and to her only neighbors, the children's maternal grandparents, Lydia and John Kidder. From the window of her house, Rosanna could see the grave of her husband's first wife, Dorothy Kidder Sturgis, who had died in 1851 after following her adventuring husband from Black Hawk County, Iowa, to Minnesota Territory. Left with three children, one of them a toddler, William had waited but six months before returning to Iowa to seek a replacement bride.[12] Among Rosanna's first duties as the second Mrs. Sturgis had been the signing of a five-thousand-dollar note that mortgaged all their belongings — including land, lumber, and articles of personal property — to Henry M. Rice, one of the partners from whom William Sturgis had purchased the mill.[13]

With everything mortgaged to Rice — from boots, shoes, and clothes to crockery, groceries, and hardware — the couple had settled into married life. Sometime after the birth of Rosanna's first child, Ann, in November 1853, William had sent his older children to live with relatives in Iowa and Michigan. When Fergus and Tut-

William Sturgis, about 1850

tle arrived on the scene, Ann was the only little one on hand, and
Rosanna was no doubt pleased at the prospect of the company of
other women and children.[14] Shortly after the formation of the Little Falls Company, Samuel M. Putnam arrived to survey the townsite, and the carpenters who followed in his wake began work on
the Fergus home. Over the next few months, sixty men, nineteen
oxen, and eight horses worked long hours to lay out streets and
erect buildings for the company, and Rosanna and little Annie
watched as the town grew up around them.[15]

By spring 1855, the Fergus house was ready and Rosanna Sturgis
welcomed Pamelia, eight-year-old Mary Agnes, six-year-old
Luella, and four-year-old Andrew. Pamelia could hardly have been
prepared for the scene that met her gaze. Along the muddy streets
was a scatter of houses in various stages of completion. The Fergus
home, an eleven-room, two-story structure, was already occupied
by a goodly number of company employees — a pattern that would
persist over the next few years as Pamelia shared quarters with carpenters, masons, farmers, blacksmiths, merchants, land agents, and

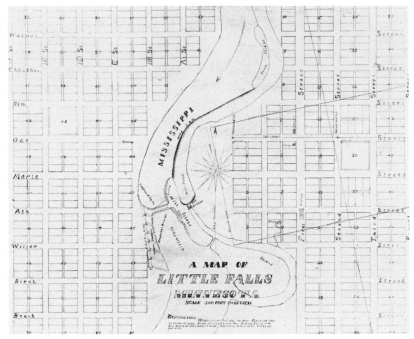

*Plat map of Little Falls, Minnesota Territory, 1856. Like most frontier
towns founded during that era of speculation, Little Falls looked more
impressive on paper than on site.*

others who came and went according to the needs and interests of
her husband's business.[16]

There were no schools, no churches, and no shops, though the
Little Falls Company had almost completed a store. At least there
were neighbors. In addition to the Sturgises and the Kidders,
twenty-one families had settled in the community. Among them
were the Churchills, the Illinois friends who had been renting the
Fergus home in Moline. At James's urging, Orlando Churchill had
come north to manage the company store and live in the quarters
above it. Pamelia welcomed his thirty-year-old wife, Temperance,
and his daughters, six-year-old Alice and three-year-old Flora, as
tangible connections to the world she had left behind.[17]

Pamelia's world was rapidly changing. If luxuries were not yet
to be found in Little Falls, optimism certainly was. The town
quickly drew speculators who had heard that the partners in the Lit-

tle Falls Company had plans for flour and lumber mills powered by a dam that would also serve as the base for a roadway spanning the Mississippi River. On the strength of that promise, many settlers began to move into the area, lured, in part, by the offer of free homesites partitioned off from the company's two thousand acres. By July 1855, the company's store, operating as O. A. Churchill & Co., was serving wholesale and retail customers, offering "Dry Goods, Groceries, Tin Ware, Hard Ware, Queensware, Boots and Shoes, Clothing, Camp fixtures & c. Flower Bacon, Lard, Pork, Farming Utencils, in fact everything usually kept in a country Store."[18] A school was established, run by a teacher recruited from Moline.[19] Joseph Batters built a hotel, the Elk Horn House, and other hotels followed, including the Northern.[20] The editor of the *Sauk Rapids Frontierman* praised the products coming from the company's mill and predicted that "Little Falls will ultimately take rank among the foremost towns of Benton County."[21]

Caught up in the spirit of rapid growth, Pamelia and the other wives shared the dreams of their husbands. They planted apple trees and roses in anticipation of the years that lay ahead.[22] In time, there would be orchards and gardens. And churches. And theaters. Three doctors had already cast their lots with the fledgling town, among them one Timothy Smith, who brought with him his wife Amanda and two young children.[23]

The optimism expressed by Fergus and shared by the new citizens of Little Falls seemed well founded in early 1856, when the town was named the seat of newly designated Morrison County.[24] In the elections that followed, James Fergus was named judge of probate. Family dwellings sprang up on lots that were now selling for one hundred dollars per acre, and by year's end the town boasted eight stores, three hotels, several boardinghouses, a school, and a newspaper.[25]

Demand for lumber was at an all-time high, with orders coming in from towns downriver and from Fort Ripley, located some ten miles north of Little Falls on the west bank of the Mississippi, just below the mouth of the Crow Wing River. The company was doing record business, though most of the money earned at the mill was immediately reinvested in some other aspect of company business. Two of the partners were the picture of optimism, but the third was beginning to fret. Down in St. Anthony, a hundred miles removed from the town his money was helping to build, Calvin Tuttle read

with displeasure letters discussing James Fergus's growing preoc-
cupation with road building and the construction of a "public
house." Out of cash and unhappy about having to mortgage his St.
Anthony properties to support operations in Little Falls, Tuttle felt
his partners had carried matters too far by neglecting the one aspect
of the company's business that was currently supporting their many
ventures. He urged Fergus to postpone his work on the other
projects and to concentrate on enlarging the dam and upgrading the
mill so that they could take full advantage of the lumber market.[26]

Ignoring Tuttle's pleas, James Fergus continued to pour money
into peripheral projects, intent on enhancing the image of the town
and the company. William Sturgis, ever the gambler, followed Fergus's lead, busying himself in other projects and postponing the
repairs on and expansion of the sawmill operations. In a letter written to Fergus during a trip to St. Paul, Sturgis noted that "if we expect to make a town we must have help and there is no time to be
lost this is the time to strike it is conceded by all that this is to be
an important town on the Mississippi."[27]

Despite Tuttle's pessimism, the town seemed destined to fulfill
those predictions. In March 1856, Fergus authorized business
friends in Moline to sell his lots there and use the money to purchase
equipment to be shipped upriver for use in the Little Falls mill.[28] He
informed those friends — and his relatives in Scotland — that without
any advertising to date, Little Falls had "become a fixed face," a
town of forty families, eight stores, the largest hotel above St. Anthony, and more than a hundred young bachelors — but "no girls to
match." To prove his point, James sent out copies of the *Northern
Herald,* "published 'on the far up Mississippi' at our new home in
Minnesota — where we are building another and bigger Moline."
Founded by a Colonel French and quickly purchased by the Little
Falls Company, the paper had been established to advertise for
those things the growing town lacked — notably young women for
the aforementioned one hundred young bachelors — as well as to
"report progress" to friends far and near.[29]

The *Northern Herald* made no mention of the town's social problems, many of which were indicative of its frontier setting. As
Fergus had noted, women were scarce, and many incoming
laborers sought out Indian women as housekeepers and companions, only to abandon them when white wives became available.

When Pamelia discovered that one impoverished Indian woman, Odishquaw Sloan, was living in a shack with her three young children, two of whom had been fathered by John R. "Pewter-Eyed" Sloan, who had since left her for a white wife, she hired the Indian woman as her housekeeper, gave her food for her children, and persuaded James to ask Sloan to provide her with household goods and a living allowance of ten dollars per month. Reproached for having embarrassed Sloan's new bride by hiring his "squaw" as her housekeeper, Pamelia maintained that she had as much right to hire the woman as James had to hire the man, and the Ferguses remained firm in their support of the abandoned family, even in the face of angry letters from the father of Sloan's legal wife.[30]

Racial prejudice was fed by impromptu appearances of warring Indians on the streets of Little Falls. Situated near the boundary line drawn in 1825 to separate territories claimed by the Ojibway and Dakota, the Little Falls area was intermittently traversed by war parties of both tribes. Largely intent on their own rivalries, the Indians generally posed more of an emotional than a physical threat to townspeople.[31]

However, settlers who lived in outlying areas were not always free from danger. In the spring of 1858, a party of Dakota and Winnebago, en route to a battle with the Ojibway, invaded the home of Philo Farnham, located in Round Prairie, some twenty-five miles southwest of Little Falls, carrying off jewelry, clothes, provisions, and two cows worth sixty dollars each. Though Farnham and his family were all at home, they were not harmed. A scant two months later the house was again invaded, this time by a band of Ojibway who did considerable damage to the dwelling but spared its occupants. Unwilling to risk a third attack, the Farnham family moved into Little Falls on the assumption that there was safety in numbers.[32]

Despite such disturbances, Little Falls continued to flourish, and Fergus had no further thoughts of turning back. Clearly, the family's future lay in Minnesota. Then came a major setback. In the spring of 1856, the flooding waters of the Mississippi washed away logs purchased for the sawmill that were valued at forty thousand dollars.[33] In the face of such losses, the partners in the Little Falls Company formed a joint stock corporation thereafter known as the Little Falls Manufacturing Company. Keeping 50 percent of their holdings, they offered the rest to the general public, hoping thereby to gain the cash they needed to remain solvent. Apparently the flood failed to dampen the spirits of would-be investors, for all available shares were quickly sold, bringing fifty thousand dollars in cash to the three partners.[34]

The new stockholders were promptly rewarded for their faith in the company, as stocks quickly appreciated to 250 percent of their original value. Construction was renewed on the dam and on the mills it would power. Property values soared, and speculators continued to buy, certain that prices would go even higher. Territorial immigration was at its peak, and the citizens of Little Falls saw no end to the population boom they were experiencing.[35]

So bright was the town's promise and so great the county's prospects that on November 5, 1856, the Morrison County commissioners authorized William Sturgis to build a courthouse for the sum of $8,000. Having served three terms in the territorial legislature, Sturgis was a trusted, popular figure, and the commissioners required only his personal bond for the completion of the contract.[36] Though signed in earnest, that contract was destined never to be fulfilled. The very month Sturgis accepted the responsibility for the construction of the courthouse, he took on several other major obligations. He paid the Little Falls Manufacturing Company $5,500 for lands along the Little Elk River just north of Little Falls, having the previous summer authorized the surveying and platting of that land for a settlement that came to be called Little Elk.[37] Around that time, in a move that would seem to indicate breach of faith in the company's long-delayed bridge over the Mississippi River, Sturgis established a ferry just north of Little Falls, which he ran for the next three years.[38] In addition, he and his brother Amos opened a store, the Little Falls Emporium.[39]

Meanwhile, the Sturgis family was growing. Rosanna's second child, a boy, had not survived his second year, but in the spring of 1857 she gave birth to another daughter, Catherine. Shortly thereafter, her widowed mother Margaret Steele and teen-aged brother and sister arrived from Iowa City, bringing with them seven-year-old John Sturgis, William's son by his first marriage, who had been living with relatives there.[40]

While the number and nature of his business transactions would seem to indicate that all was going well for William Sturgis, there were signs of impending trouble. As early as January 1857 James Fergus advised storekeeper O. A. Churchill to refuse further credit to Sturgis, who was apparently stocking the Little Falls Emporium through wholesale purchases from O. A. Churchill & Co.[41] By August the Sturgis brothers had abandoned the Emporium, and an announcement in the *Northern Herald* invited citizens to visit "a new store at Little Elk Mills, in the town of Little Elk," where dry goods, groceries, and hardware could be obtained "cheap for cash or in exchange for goods, pine lumber, hay, grain, butter &c."[42] In addition to these business affairs, Sturgis continued his farming activities, and though he appeared to be holding his own in all these dealings, by late summer he owed James Fergus $1,177.66 for five notes signed over as many months.[43] Sensing the increasing precariousness of his financial position, Sturgis sought to protect his property by selling some of it to his mother-in-law, some to his brother Amos, and some to his father in Michigan.[44]

The summer of 1857 brought misfortune not only to the Sturgises but to other Morrison County citizens as well. The warm weather that for the past two seasons had meant record yields for those who tilled the county's virgin fields now contributed to a grasshopper plague that decimated crops. Farmers were hard pressed and townspeople went without. James Fergus, whose own thirty-five acres of farmland had been infested, described the insects as "something like the Locust mentioned in the Bible" and reported that they hatched out in the spring "in immense multitudes . . . [eating] up every thing we planted except here & there a very small patch of corn or potatoes."[45]

So great was the devastation that outside help was needed. In late October 1857, James Fergus was instrumental in forming the Morrison County Aid Society, a group that petitioned the state for provisions in the face of the desperate need. Dr. Timothy Smith was appointed an agent of the aid society and was sent to St. Paul with authorization to buy five hundred pounds of flour or twenty-five thousand pounds of grain on credit.[46]

On the heels of the famine came disaster of another sort as Little Falls suffered the ill effects of the economic depression that swept the frontier and ultimately the nation in the late 1850s. A chain of bank failures on the East Coast caused creditors to call in the loans they had made to speculators in the outlying territories. Left without cash, Minnesota businesses closed, railroads and banks failed, property values plunged, and once-wealthy citizens found themselves in dire straits.[47] The partners in the Little Falls Manufacturing Company were not immune to the disaster, and in early November 1857, Fergus noted that "the difficulty has increased untill it has become a complete panic, a perfect whirlwind destroying and breaking our ablest men, banks and corporations . . . our whole business and merchantile fabric is threatened with destruction."[48]

Over the next few years, St. Paul lost half its population and Little Falls a third.[49] Property in Morrison County depreciated so rapidly that a lot worth a hundred dollars in the spring of 1857 was soon worth less than five. In time, Main Street lots that had sold for one thousand dollars could "hardly be given away."[50] The Little Falls Manufacturing Company faltered in the wake of plummeting real estate values, and ongoing arguments over management practices continued to weaken the Fergus-Sturgis-Tuttle alliance.

That alliance was dealt a further blow when Fergus, who had earlier lost his bid for a seat in the Constitutional Convention held on the eve of Minnesota statehood, announced his candidacy for the state legislature — running on a platform that opposed the taxation assessed for bonds that funded the work Sturgis had done on the courthouse. Though he ostensibly opposed the assessment on the grounds that those bonds had been "issued without the consent of the people, to build a Court house, unneeded, and so far unfinished," Fergus's stand might well have been influenced by the fact that Sturgis had defeated him in the earlier election and had gone on to represent Morrison County at the Constitutional Convention that summer. Though Fergus lost his bid for the legislature as well, his political ambitions were not diminished, and he later served as Morrison County treasurer.[51]

Shortly after the election, William Sturgis declared bankruptcy. Overextended by his land purchases and farm losses and further damaged by the company's financial reversals, he filed the necessary papers in late December 1857; abandoned the courthouse, roofed and enclosed but unfinished; and turned his attention to his newest projects at Little Elk — the sawmill, gristmill, and store. At the same time, the Sturgis family left Little Falls and, moving three miles north, settled into the new house Sturgis had built near the mill site. There Rosanna took up housekeeping for her two children, her

The Northern Hotel, Little Falls, about 1870

stepson, her mother, brother, and sister, and seven laborers involved in William's enterprises.[52]

Sturgis was not the only one with financial troubles in 1857. With construction activities almost at a standstill, John and Margaretha Ault were having difficulty meeting payments on their hotel and other properties. One of the earliest establishments in Little Falls, the Northern had been the scene of many town and county meetings and provided the first chambers for the federal district court.[53] Shortly after it was built, the Northern had come into the hands of the Aults, Canadian immigrants in their mid-thirties.[54] An 1857 notice in the *Northern Herald* called the hotel the largest establishment north of St. Anthony and described its facilities in some detail:

> A large and comodius dinningroom, extensive ballroom, private parlors, and comfortable bedrooms . . . excellent bar . . . well supplied with the choicist liquors. Attached to the establishment there is an excellent warm stable well supplied with hay and grain.

The table of this house will always be supplied with the best the market offers.[55]

Despite its purported luxuries, the hotel did not bring prosperity to its owners, and some three months after running the above notice, they were $2,376 in arrears on their mortgage and in danger of fore-closure.[56]

Equally beset by problems was Orlando Churchill, the Moline friend whom Fergus had invited into partnership in the company's store. Almost from the first, there had been friction between Fergus and Churchill, perhaps due in part to Churchill's drinking problem. When Fergus asserted that he had heard complaints about Chur-chill's treatment of customers, the shopkeeper maintained that in most cases he had only been following Fergus's orders. Angered by reports that Fergus himself has "said more against us than any one [else] in Little Falls," Churchill offered to sell out his part of the store, and in early May his partnership with the company was dis-solved.[57] Fergus bought Sturgis's and Tuttle's shares in the store outright and took over Churchill's shares on credit at what he was later to call an exorbitant rate.[58] Ironically, aside from giving the es-tablishment a new name, Fergus & Company, the buyout accom-plished little, for Fergus hired the Churchills to run the store and they continued to live in the quarters overhead.[59]

As 1857 drew to a close, there were changes that touched Pamelia Fergus in a more personal way. Three days after Christmas, she gave birth to her fourth child, a daughter named Lillie. Good-natured by all reports, the baby afforded some relief from the wor-ries that accompanied the changing Fergus fortunes. The new year started well, with James directing work on the nearly completed bridge while overseeing improvements on the dam. In the spring of 1858 the dam spanned the east channel of the river, running from the east bank to the head of the island, then upstream a thousand feet or more. A sawmill, still owned by the Little Falls Manufacturing Company but now leased to a St. Anthony firm, also extended across the east channel, just below the dam. A large flume running from the east end of the dam downstream along the east shore for about one hundred feet furnished waterpower for a chair factory owned by Reuben Pond and for a large sash and door company and planing mill owned and operated by Z. H. and Harlo Morse. Fergus had spanned the river by constructing a roadway along the dam, between the east shore and the island, then adding a Howe truss bridge from the island to the west shore. By early spring the bridge was in service, though it had minimal use because there were virtually no improvements on the west side of the river, save a few claim shanties and a large farmhouse owned by John Workman.[60]

In May 1858, having been assured that the dam would be sufficiently improved to provide the additional waterpower needed for a flour mill, William Fletcher left a profitable operation in St. Anthony and moved his wife, Emma, and their five children to Little Falls. The Fletchers had only begun the building of the mill when another act of nature brought destruction and discouragement to the townspeople.

On June 4 a heavy storm caused a four-foot rise in the river in the course of a few hours. The raging waters destroyed the dam William Sturgis had built on the Little Elk, sending his nearly completed sawmill and a large boom of white pine logs surging downriver. The loss was keenly felt, for laborers had been making final adjustments on the saw in preparation for the mill's first cutting the very morning the wall of water swept down the Little Elk and into the Mississippi River.[61]

Miraculously, the logs and debris rushing downstream from the Sturgis mill site shot through the open channel at Little Falls, rather than slamming into the dam. Though likely weakened by the flooding waters, the dam showed no external evidence of damage. The sawmill remained in operation, and William Fletcher carried on with the building of his flour mill, about the only construction work in progress that summer. Dismayed but undaunted, William Sturgis also began the task of rebuilding his mill on the Little Elk.[62]

Even as Fletcher and Sturgis worked, new troubles were brewing. Little Falls had always had its share of "rough and unprincipled characters," but that summer of 1858 the deteriorating economic conditions turned drifters into thieves. No teamster dared leave his load overnight, and Indian agents delivering government annuities were ever wary. Highwaymen broke into the barn of John Ault's Northern Hotel and robbed a peddler's cart, then broke into O. J. Simmon's store and took their pick of his stock. They tore down the shanty of R. L. Barnham, the aging justice of the peace who had dared to hand down sentences against some of their number, then snatched the old man out of bed and dragged him down the street in his nightclothes. Townspeople grew increasingly concerned as the agencies of the law seemed incapable of handling the situation. Sheriff Jonathan Pugh himself was rumored to be one of the "rowdies."[63]

After the attack on the justice of the peace, citizens took matters into their own hands, forming a vigilante group to fight what was afterward known as the Little Falls War. Farmers were called in from around the countryside to assist in guarding and protecting houses and shops. For almost a month in the fall of 1858, the vigilantes engaged in search-and-destroy missions against a band of about twenty desperadoes who made camp in the woods outside of town. Eventually the acknowledged leaders of the band negotiated for safe conduct to other points of the compass. The vigilantes accepted the proposal, the rowdies disbanded, and peace returned to Little Falls.[64]

By the end of the Little Falls War, William Fletcher had completed his mill, only to find that there was still no water to turn the wheel. Seeing that Fergus had all but ceased work on the dam, Fletcher realized his efforts had been wasted and resolved to move his mill elsewhere. Over the winter months he took out his millstones and other fixtures, and when spring came he and his son rafted the lighter equipment from their flour mill downriver to Sauk Rapids, then hauled the millstones and castings by wagon. There he entered into partnership with Samuel L. Hays, who had put up a mill but lacked the equipment to begin his operation.[65]

Fletcher could hardly have been blamed for leaving. Weakened by internal bickering, the Little Falls Manufacturing Company, upon whose fortunes the town was vitally dependent, seemed unlikely to recover from its previous losses. Conscious of a need for restructuring, James Fergus traveled to Minneapolis in January 1859 to meet with Calvin Tuttle and the company's board of directors. A review of accounts and a discussion of company debts and obligations disintegrated into a name-calling session in which, by James's own report, he "spent a good part of one day giving them *Hell* about their charges against [him]." William Babbitt, president of the company since its incorporation in 1857, and Calvin Tuttle, known for his fierce temper, raged at each other, a sight that disgusted Fergus, who prided himself on his ability to remain calm in the face of adversity.[66]

That meeting brought matters to a head for Fergus. Immediately upon his return home he resigned as company director, noting that he had no other choice, since the board of directors refused to recall charges they had made against his character. In his letter of resignation he claimed that the board members pronounced themselves "fully satisfied" with his honesty and integrity, yet continued to attack him. "I acknowledge my errors and short-comings," he wrote, "but the greatest of these has been a too strong devotion to the interest and well-fare of Little Falls. I have sacrificed my own property and the property of the Little Falls Co. for its advance and now my property is gone and I have not even the thanks of the Directors (whom I elected) for my pains."[67] In the series of charges and countercharges that followed, Fergus pointed out the company's laxity in keeping its promise to construct a new and larger dam by 1857, noting that he and Tuttle had been forced to spend their own money on this project, then were blamed when they were unable to carry through on it.[68] In turn, the board accused Fergus and Tuttle of overcharging the company for the services they performed and of general mismanagement of company affairs.[69] Tuttle grew paranoid during this time, convinced as he was that the company was trying to swindle him out of the bridge that he had financed by mortgaging his properties in St. Anthony. He was also convinced that Fergus could very well have offered more financial assistance by mortgaging some of his own properties.[70]

There was at least some truth in Tuttle's accusation, for while Fergus publicly claimed to have been financially destroyed by the effects of the flood, grasshopper plague, and panic, he had, in fact, prudently transferred much of his property to Pamelia's name when business had begun to falter, and he had chosen not to mortgage that property to help in the work on the bridge and dam.[71] Disgruntled and mistrusting, Fergus and Tuttle seemed to have but one point of agreement left—they both disliked company president William Babbitt and felt that his attitude had undermined their efforts to build a viable business enterprise.[72]

In the midst of their bickering came still another disaster. In June 1859, major storms again caused flooding on the Mississippi, this time washing out large sections of the dam owned by the Little Falls Manufacturing Company and calling into question once and for all the expertise of its builders. According to town historian Nathan

Richardson, the partners were foolhardy engineers. The bed of the Mississippi at Little Falls was rough and uneven, and the builders, assuming that "it would be much better to construct a dam on a nice smooth sand bed . . . accordingly hauled in [sand] to level up for a good foundation. Any man who can read his Bible could give the result of that kind of dam building. . . . I give their method of dam building as a specimen of the manner in which they did their work generally."[73]

Even as the flood's destruction of the company dam vindicated his move to Sauk Rapids, William Fletcher was completing work on his mill at the mouth of the Sauk River, and by early October the Fletcher-Hays mill, now the only flouring mill above St. Anthony, was in full operation.[74] Little Falls farmers who managed to harvest wheat and corn that season faced the prospect of hauling their grain thirty miles south to Fletcher's mill—when that very mill would have been in full operation at Little Falls, had the partners in the Little Falls Manufacturing Company made good their promises.

Another victim of the company's broken promises fought to stay afloat. Orlando Churchill, who was spending more and more time drinking liquor and less and less time keeping shop, had his inventory seized for nonpayment of debts. This was the last straw for Fergus, who severed all business ties with the shopkeeper. Withdrawing his name from the firm, Fergus commended his share of the remaining stock into the keeping of merchants William Butler and Francis X. Gravel.[75] Maintaining his residence above the half-empty shop, Churchill continued to serve his few remaining customers. Temperance helped out as best she could, eventually taking in boarders, holding fast to the hope that the economy would take an upward turn.[76]

As 1859 drew to a close, such hopes seemed ill founded. The Little Falls economy appeared well set in its downward spiral, and even James Fergus was forced to face harsh realities. If things did not look up soon, he would try his fortune elsewhere. This was, after all, not the only Minnesota town in which he had an interest. Two years earlier he and several other enterprising men had laid out a series of towns in nearby counties. Appropriately enough, the only one that had flourished bore the name Fergus Falls. A reconnaissance trip to the area in November 1859 convinced him that a new start could be made there, even without the capital that had been lost in his Little Falls investments.[77] Eagerly he wrote to George Stephens, his friend in Moline, urging him to come north to the Red River country and join him in developing lumber mills around the Fergus Falls area. Alarmed, Stephens declined, warning his friend against "takeing your little children into the wilderness where they must be deprived of Civil Society and [endure] many disadvantages that you do not think of now."[78]

Perhaps swayed by Stephens's advice, Fergus ultimately decided against the move to the Red River country and redoubled his efforts to save his investments in Little Falls. Without waiting for the approval of the stockholders, he poured most of the company's remaining funds into repairing the ill-fated dam. Still confident of ultimate success, he persuaded friends and relatives to invest in the town by buying up lots while they could be had at a good price. William Fergus of Scotland, James's half-brother, and George Stephens and D. B. Sears of Moline were among those who made investments, inspired by James's abiding faith in the future of Little Falls.[79]

By this time, not even Calvin Tuttle shared that faith. In Tuttle's view, James's resignation had hardly relieved him of his responsibility to account for his actions during his tenure as director of the Little Falls Manufacturing Company. "I have sent a great deal of money to Little Falls and to your charge," he wrote James in December 1859, "and it is but just that I should receive a reasonable answer to inquiries."[80] While expressing dismay at his partner's lack of trust, James continued to ignore his entreaties to see the books or to have full explanations concerning the handling of affairs in Little Falls.

While Fergus's stubborn refusal to open the books to his partner would seem to indicate that there may have been some irregularities in his bookkeeping, there were likely other factors at work. Well known for his need to maintain absolute control in all situations, Fergus would have found it exceedingly difficult to give in to Tuttle's demands, especially in view of the fact that to do so would have raised questions concerning his use of company funds for several projects not specifically authorized by the stockholders.[81] If he was to keep the company books, then he would keep them his way. And he would not waste his valuable time explaining himself to the businessmen of St. Anthony. He had a dam to repair and a mill to get running.

Though as ignorant of the intricacies of the company books as Calvin Tuttle himself, Pamelia Fergus was not ignorant of the growing tension between the partners of the Little Falls Manufacturing Company. Tuttle was increasingly hostile and Sturgis had maintained a low profile since the day two years earlier when he and Rosanna had loaded up their household goods and children and moved to Little Elk. While the Sturgis bankruptcy was not a matter to be taken lightly, at least it had marked an end to that family's involvement in increasingly unpleasant company affairs. Pamelia remained in the midst of the furor, ever mindful of harsh public opinion of company enterprises and unable to escape the gossip that circulated concerning her husband's role in company affairs.

By early 1860 she sensed an urgency in the situation, a worsening of affairs that dampened even James's accustomed optimism. Thwarted at every turn, he seemed to be losing all hope of ever building the city he had once envisioned. Little Falls was dying, and there seemed to be nothing he could do about it. Recovery depended upon capital, and capital would have to be found elsewhere. But where? The nation itself had faltered. The pages of the *New York Tribune,* the *St. Paul Daily Pioneer,* and the *St. Cloud Democrat* were filled with news of depreciating stocks, failed towns, and financial disasters. But on those same pages James Fergus was reading of the discovery of gold in Kansas Territory, present-day Colorado. Expressing the hopes of thousands, the cry "Pikes Peak or Bust!" stirred new hope in Fergus and inspired a new plan.[82] James would leave his family in Little Falls, go out to Pikes Peak and stake his claim. By winter he would be back with the capital he needed to right things in Little Falls. And he would manage this without uprooting his family and carting them off into unknown country.[83]

For Pamelia, the news was hardly welcome. Gold nuggets in mountain streams were a fine fantasy, but little more. How would she and the children manage if James left them behind? She knew nothing about the business, and she had paid little attention to the management of the family farm. Taxes would soon be due on house and other properties. Assessments were periodically levied on company stock. Where would the cash come from? She hardly felt strong enough for the tasks James proposed. She was approaching her thirty-sixth birthday, and her health was poor. An abscessed breast refused to heal, and Dr. Smith, the last of the town's physicians, had already said good-bye to Amanda and the children and set off in hopes of making his way west. Where would Pamelia find medical care if she or one of the children needed it?[84]

The questions were endless. And the answers were not forthcoming from James, for he was lost in his plan and oblivious to her worries. In March 1860 he made a temporary settlement with the board of directors of the Little Falls Manufacturing Company and patched up company affairs as best he could before immersing himself in a new partnership, the Pikes Peak Company of Little Falls, a company consisting of James himself, Pamelia's brother James Dillin, and two sometime company employees, O. J. Rockwell and Daniel Bosworth.[85]

The origins of the Pikes Peak Company remain obscure. The enterprise could not have been long in the planning, since Fergus made no mention of mining as an option as late as December 1859 when he considered moving to Fergus Falls. The company's composition was likely determined largely by propensity, though the skills of each member must have been taken into consideration as well. Twenty-three-year-old James Dillin had lived in the Fergus home intermittently since boyhood.[86] A carpenter with several years of experience, Dillin was a logical-enough choice for the partnership. Twenty-five-year-old Orson J. Rockwell, one of a goodly number of laborers living in the Fergus household as of 1857, was a farmer and a native of Maine. He had most likely worked for Fergus since his arrival in Little Falls, and the two men were to remain partners in the mining business for some years to come. His experience as a teamster made him a good choice for the long journey west.[87]

Thirty-four-year-old Daniel Bosworth, the fourth partner in the venture, was a lumberman. Born in Maine, he had worked in the pine forests of Michigan and Wisconsin before arriving in Morrison County sometime before 1857. There he met and married Caroline Farnham, and he was among those living in the Farnham home in the country near Round Prairie in 1858 when successive Indian raids caused that family to seek shelter in Little Falls. From that time, Bosworth was likely involved in cutting and hauling lumber for the Little Falls Manufacturing Company. At any rate, from his earliest dealings in Minnesota Territory he had been seen as a hard worker and an excellent teamster, both qualities that would have appealed to James Fergus.[88] Bosworth's decision to go west meant leaving behind his nineteen-year-old wife Caroline and their two-year-old son George. But since the couple lived next door to Sarah and Philo Farnham, Caroline would at least have the support of her parents.[89]

That kind of support was not available to Pamelia Fergus. Yet far from worrying about his wife's security during his proposed absence, James Fergus expressed confidence that she would easily be able to take care of herself. A letter penned to his brother William shows no anxiety on her behalf: "I have concluded to leave my family here for the summer where we have a good house and plenty to eat and wear and start for the new Gold mines lately discovered at Pikes Peak in the Rocky mountains about 1200 miles South west from here where there is a large emigration of miners and other adventurers going this spring. . . . the next letter you will receive from me will Either be from the Rocky Mountains or from here next winter after I get home." Despite the casualness with which he introduced the subject of his impending departure, he was obviously not unaware of what his Scottish relatives might think of the plan, for he added, "You might consider this a foolish move for me but I am doing little or nothing here for my self. There I will see the country, probably lay the foundation for a future business, and if nothing else, I may be able with my own hands to dig the gold to pay you for the money you sent me."[90]

In a lengthy memorandum to Pamelia, written in late March, James set forth their private holdings, as well as their remaining company interests. That memorandum ended any hope Pamelia might have had that James's fascination with Colorado gold would pass. Obviously, he meant to go through with this scheme, and he did not intend to take the family with him. They would have to weather the hard times as best they could, he told her, for he could do more for them in the goldfields than on the streets of Little Falls. He would be back by fall with the money they needed to set things right; when he came home she would have far fewer worries than she had now.[91]

Despite her misgivings, Pamelia had no choice but to ready herself as best she could to operate in his absence, for he was now moving rapidly ahead with his plans for departure. By the time he wrote

First page of a six-page letter of instructions written to "Mrs Fergus" by James on March 28, 1860

the memorandum, he had already seen Bosworth, Dillin, and Rockwell off to Omaha to purchase oxen, wagon, and provisions for the trip west, promising to join them in Omaha in early April. For the next two weeks he sat at his desk, sorting through his papers and adding pages to the detailed memorandum he was preparing for Pamelia. "You will find yourself as the head of a family with more responsibilities and very differently situated from what you ever was before," he wrote, adding, "I hope you will meet [the responsibilities] as they should be met."[92] To help her do so, James spelled out in great detail how she was to handle the company business, their land and livestock, even the children.

In dealing with company matters, her prime concern would be to stall creditors and to keep the books away from Tuttle. In case James's vote was needed, he had arranged for her to act on his behalf. All other company business would be seen to by thirty-year-old Charles Freeman, a land agent who had come to Little Falls as a bachelor and had begun his sojourn there as a boarder in the Fergus household. In the interim, he and Fergus had become partners in a real estate business and he had married. Now he and his nineteen-year-old wife, Abby, and their infant son, Fred, lived next door to the Ferguses. Recently appointed county auditor, Freeman was knowledgeable and trustworthy, and James admonished Pamelia to "keep in as good friendship with Mr Freeman as you can, as we are very much dependent on him in our company business."[93]

"Our own individual business is all in your own hands," James continued. "Freeman has nothing to do with it whatever, except to give you advise if you want it." In case of difficulties she could not handle, she was to call upon lawyer James Hall, but she was to consult him as little as she could, since he wanted "big pay" for his advice.[94] Fergus had left her with power of attorney so that she could handle taxes, assessments, and other legal matters, and she had also been given power of substitution to act on behalf of his relatives in Scotland and their friends in Moline who had bought property in Little Falls.[95]

The two hired men, Ben Nickerson, forty years old, and John Currie, twenty-five, would stay on in James's absence, but Pamelia was to give them explicit directions for managing livestock and garden, since they could not be depended upon to handle matters on their own. "I would get the men to kill the largest hog, get a pork barrel from one of the stores, salt it carefully and it will do for your summer pork," he wrote. "The little boar can be cut early in the fall and fatted for next winter. The young sows will have pigs before long. You had better eat them as soon as they are big enough." He advised her not to plant the garden before May 15, not to keep the two calves, and "if the white faced cow jumps fences sell her."[96]

Careful management of such matters was essential, since she would be totally dependent upon the farm for vegetables and meat. She need not worry about flour, since she could obtain what she needed at no cost from the mill at Sauk Rapids, which was now being operated by the newly widowed Emma Fletcher. For her other needs, Pamelia was to rely on her credit with various firms in town.[97]

With business matters attended to, James's advice stretched into more personal matters:

> Last but not least you must take care of your own health, and the health of the children for none of you are overly healthy. If you have any more of those spells send the children for some of the neighbors at once. It might be well if your mother was to come . . . [or for you] to keep one of the children [home] from school, keep them all dressed warm, be careful about letting the girls wear low necked dresses when I go away, as they have not been used to them and will very readily catch cold. Keep Andrew out of and away from the water as much as you can, don't get angry with the children but reason with them, be firm but mild. . . . You must give them all good advice . . . you are pretty well provided for and if your mother comes up you should enjoy yourself.[98]

Knowing that a good many business transactions would need to be discussed in letters from Pikes Peak, James advised Pamelia to "preserve all my letters carfull on file . . . put them up in a paper holder if you can find a spare one as I want to see those that are on business when I come back."[99]

By late March 1860, his preparations for the trip completed, his memorandum written, and Pamelia's objections muted if not answered, James Fergus gathered his wife and children about him to hear a poem he had either composed for the occasion or clipped from a contemporary periodical, copied in his own hand, and altered to express sentiments dear to his heart:

The Pike's Peaker's Farewell to His Wife and Children

Farewell, dear wife, to distant lands
Where Kansas streams bear golden sands
I wend my way through wet and cold
to dig for you, the hidden gold.

Farewell, farewell, my children dear,
Tis for your sakes I leave you here,
to buy for you with toils and pains
The golden dust on Kansas plains.

To buy for you no idle bread
[To] place no finry on your head,
Tis to store your minds with useful lore
That I leave you whom I adore.

Thus children dear, when I'm away
Let not your youthful steps go stray
Obey your mother; the [truth] tell.
Dear Wife and children fare you well.[100]

While there is no reason to doubt James's sincerity in proffering this bit of verse to his family, his words offered scant comfort to the wife he left behind. James Fergus was forty-six years old, his health had been a constant concern of Pamelia's, and there was no way of knowing whether he would even survive the trip across the plains. And what if he did manage to return in six months? A good deal could happen to them in the meantime. After all, he was leaving her in full charge of four children, a house and lots, properties held in trust for others, and a failed business about which she knew virtually nothing. Furthermore, he was taking with him $330—almost all of the family's cash.[101] None of these matters seemed to trouble James as he packed for his journey. By his own report, he had done all he could for them. The rest would be up to Pamelia.

3

Colorado Quest

ON MARCH 29, 1860, James Fergus left Little Falls for St. Anthony, the first stop on his long journey to the goldfields. He stayed that night at the Stone Hotel, writing Pamelia that he had sent twenty dollars to her mother in Geneseo, Illinois, asking her to use the money to visit Little Falls during his absence and suggesting that she bring Pamelia's youngest sister, sixteen-year-old Jane, with her.[1] He also advised Pamelia to take all she could get of the provisions left in the care of Butler and Gravel and belonging to the defunct Little Falls Company store. She might well need them. He noted that he had met with Tuttle and settled some company affairs and had enjoyed a chance meeting with Dr. Timothy Smith, who was at that moment seated at a nearby table.[2]

It is not known how long the doctor had been in St. Paul or what provision he had made for the wife and two children he had left behind in Little Falls. Both natives of New York, Amanda and Timothy Smith had lived for some time in Ohio, where he served in the United States Army. Isaac and Nellie had both been born there. Appearing in Little Falls within a year or so of the arrival of the Fergus family, Smith was welcomed as one of the first physicians in the area.[3] But he was a gambler and an alcoholic, and he soon fell out of favor. Mounting debts finally caused him to look elsewhere for employment, but when he left Little Falls, he traveled alone, promising Amanda that he would send for her and the children as soon as he got himself established.[4] By the time Fergus bumped into him in late March of 1860 in the dining room of the Stone Hotel, Smith had caught a case of gold fever and was already planning to go west. He and Fergus agreed to meet the next week in McGregor, Iowa.[5]

From St. Anthony, James Fergus traveled by stage to St. Paul, where he caught a steamboat down the Mississippi River, delaying a day in McGregor, where Doc Smith failed to show. Two days later he found Smith waiting in Galena, Illinois, and the two men traveled together as far as Moline, where Fergus made business calls while Smith went into Davenport, having expressed hopes that their paths might cross again in the West.[6] Back on the river, James continued to think of matters at home, and on April 8 at Hannibal, Missouri, he mailed still another letter of instruction to Pamelia.[7] Shortly thereafter, he caught a train to Omaha, arriving there some two weeks after his departure from Little Falls.[8]

There he found Rockwell, Dillin, and Bosworth ready with wagon and provisions: "We have three yoke of cattle, and a load of over 4500 lbs. on our waggon, being 9 Blls of flour, 350 lb of side bacon, 100 lb of dried beef, beans, sugar, tea, tools, clothing, bedding and cooking utensils."[9] The four men left Omaha in the company of a wagon train at noon on April 13, 1860, covering twelve miles before making camp for the night. In a letter written that evening, Fergus described hard rains, with winds so strong that their tent had blown over. His partners were repairing it even as he wrote. He had lost his trunk and carpetbag in a fire the week before, along with the books and clothing they had contained, but his trip had been otherwise uneventful. Thus far, life on the trail was tolerable; they had had a fine supper of bread, potatoes, eggs, and bacon.[10]

Two weeks later the train had progressed some three hundred miles along the Platte River, and they were halfway to Denver City, having walked most of the way to spare the animals the extra load. Grass had been uniformly sparse, and they had fed hay and meal to the oxen. "We are ahead of the great bulk of the Emigration," James observed, "probably not more than 1000 teams being ahead of us, but they are coming very fast often from 15 to 30 being in sight at a time." Most of the other wagons on the trail were pulled by mules or horses and made much better time than did the ox-drawn wagon of the Pikes Peak Company. James had opted for oxen on the assumption that roads would be bad, but he pronounced the roads so far "first rate — better on an average than the roads from St. Anthony to Little Falls and nearly a perfect level."[11]

Keeping a promise to Andrew, he reported on the buffalo. "We have been travelling for the last week through the Buffalo country but have seen none, as they are still south of this and don't come here so early in the season, but the whole platte valley is covered with there bones." Since there were no post offices on the route beyond this point, James indicated that he would not write again until he reached Denver. The mining camps were located another fifty to

Denver City, Kansas Territory, 1859. From a woodcut in Frank Leslie's
Illustrated Newspaper.

one hundred miles beyond Denver, and he estimated "it will take
us from 20 to 30 days yet to reach our destination." His estimate was
fairly accurate, but only because, as always, he took matters into his
own hand. When the road-weary oxen proved to be slower than he
had anticipated, he and Rockwell left Bosworth and Dillin outside
Denver to bring in the wagon and struck out for the city on foot,
arriving there around May 25.[12]

Meantime, life in Little Falls was brightened by letters from
James Fergus. "I am so happy and proud to here from you so often,"
Pamelia wrote a few weeks after his departure. "I have just received
two letters and hasten [to] answer them knowing you are so anxious to hear from us."[13] This was likely the last time she was to mar-
vel at the frequency with which she received her husband's letters,
for once James reached his destination and began moving from
camp to camp, letters would be few and far between. Though he
continued to write, several letters would be lost in transit, and those
that did make it would arrive weeks, sometimes months, after they
were posted.

Like other miners in the boom area, James got his mail through
Denver, and he estimated that twelve thousand letters per week
came into that city.[14] Little wonder that many were misdirected, especially considering the rapidity with which mining camps sprang
up, then died out. And there was a high cost to retrieving mail.

"Waiting for Letters," Denver, 1860. From a woodcut by Frank Beard in Albert D. Richardson, Beyond the Mississippi: From the Great River to the Great Ocean *(1867).*

Upon receiving his first letters from the States, James explained to Pamelia that he was paying a twenty-five-cent surcharge per letter when he picked up his mail. Consequently she should write longer letters and put several in a single envelope.[15] Pamelia complied with his request, adding notes from Luella and Mary Agnes to her own paragraphs and sometimes enclosing her letters in those sent by William Butler and Charles Freeman. She kept the promise she had made before James's departure, writing to him every Monday, and sometimes more frequently, even when she had had no word from him for weeks.[16]

She passed along news received from friends and relatives in Illinois and from James's family in Scotland. She considered forwarding a letter and picture from his brother William but decided against it, imagining James's displeasure should they be lost en route. Instead, she conveyed the gist of William's news and added, "You think me very carless some times me think I here you say take good care of . . . [the letters] till I come yes I have put them away in a nice letter box they are not going to be taken [out] or handld till you come."[17]

Her reluctance to risk forwarding the packet from William is understandable. Photographs were rare and precious in 1860. James had only that spring managed to have his picture "struck," thereby keeping a seven-year-old promise to his Scottish relatives.[18] He had sent the pose to his father, along with a daguerreotype of Andrew, aged nine, Luella, aged eleven, and Mary Agnes, aged thirteen. Having taken a copy of that picture with him, he looked at it often during his months in the West.[19]

Lonely for the sights and sounds of home, he welcomed letters bearing news of household affairs: Lillie "was singing one day papa gone to Pikes Peak . . . and her dols name is papa," Pamelia wrote to him. A note from Mary Agnes described a fireside scene: "Luella is popping corn Andrew is melting some le[a]d Mother is going down to see the little chickens Mother hugs and kisses Lillie for her and you both I will let Lillie write some in my letter." Lillie's scribbles followed, then a final comment from Mary Agnes: "Lillie sais . . . I write Papa if anybody asks her whare her father is she sais pikes peek."[20]

Andrew and Mary Agnes were attending school regularly, but Luella was staying at home to help with Lillie and household affairs, since Pamelia had not been well enough to handle her duties alone. "I have had another Abses on the same breast," she explained, "but it was not as painful as the other it is now dischargening at both places."[21]

She had sought medical advice from Mary Colburn, formerly of Moline but now of Champaign. The woman had given specific directions for bathing the breast: She was to "dress [the abscesses] . . . with cloths wet in moderately warm water, that will act as a poultice and becken the humors." Beyond that, she was to "do nothing to heal those abscesses at present, they are a sort of vent to let off the impurities of the blood." Knowing well the tension Pa-

Andrew, Luella, and Mary Agnes Fergus in a photograph taken just before their father's 1860 departure for Pikes Peak

melia was experiencing in James's absence, Mrs. Colburn advised her to be careful about her diet, enjoy all the fresh air she could, avoid overwork, and "keep off the *blues*."[22]

At times, Pamelia could keep off the blues only by losing herself in the problems of others. Those of Amanda Smith offered ample opportunity. Depressed since her husband's departure, Amanda had heard from the doctor only once since he had set out. Her only subsequent knowledge of his whereabouts having come from James's letters, she made frequent trips to Pamelia's doorstep, hoping for still further news. But on a morning two weeks after James had left Smith in Davenport, it was Amanda herself who had the news. Degrading as it was, she shared it with Pamelia: "Docttor Smith was [reported to be] in St. Pall jail." Having just heard the rumor herself, Amanda "looked as if she had cryed a long time." Ironically, for the past few days she had seemed to be pulling out of her depression, appearing "uncommon[ly] happy for her." Now she was once again sunk in the well of despair. Unwilling to send her friend home in such a state, Pamelia urged her to stay, and the two women spent

46

the afternoon together on the banks of the Mississippi River, "a fishing with [their] little boys."[23]

Pamelia had scant time for such pleasures, caught up as she was in carrying out the tasks outlined in James's lengthy memorandum. She reported that John Currie had come up and swept out the chimney and that she had paid the insurance.[24] However, she confessed her failure in another matter — she had let Tuttle have a look at the books: "Mr Tuttle came up here the next week after you went away and seamed to be in a rage or angry at something all the time and he and Charley [Freeman] looked over the books he said he could not see why the books did not ballance as well as they did last year." Her report shows the extent of Tuttle's anger:

> He told Charley that you was a scoundrel and rascal that you had gone of with eleven Thousand dollars of his money in your pocket he told him it was no such a thing and told that you had about forty five dollars he would not believe it he stayed about a week and i guess evry body was glad when he was gone. [He] talked with every body that would listen to him about your dishonesty. Charley has sent a letter to St Joseph for you concerning it Tuttle wanted the notes and books Charley told him that he could not have them.[25]

Freeman's letter echoed Pamelia's own as he noted, "ye Gods what a time we had, part of the time I was mad at other times I could not help but laugh at the damn fool to see him perform."[26]

Pamelia's anxiety over business affairs did not allow her to see any humor in such scenes. And though she assured Tuttle that his attacks on James's character "would not make any differance in my mind," they took their emotional toll. The strain was starkly apparent to Mahala Dillin, who arrived on the scene in mid-April: "Mother and sister got here today. Mother looks at me and wishes she could see Pamelia she says I don't seem a bit like Pamelia." Though shocked by her daughter's worn appearance, Mahala was heartened by the enthusiastic welcome she received from her grandchildren. According to Mary Agnes, Andrew came running home from school with his hat in his hand, having heard that "Grandma Dillin and Aunt Jane had come."[27]

Though Pamelia's spirits were lifted by the arrival of her mother and sister, she continued to fret over business matters she did not understand. With no letters from James to guide her, she was forced to make decisions concerning assessments. The board of the Little Falls Manufacturing Company, seeking to raise the money neces-

Mahala Bellows Dillin, about 1874

sary for the repair of the dam and bridge, had called for a vote to assess the stockholders according to their holdings. She had written to James for advice, but when weeks passed with no answer, she had been obliged to act on her own. Swayed by Hall and William Babbitt, she had voted for the assessments. Faced now with the task of paying the money assessed or losing James's shares, she began to question the wisdom of her decision: "I really wish I could see you to night if it was onely a few moments I feel very unseasy or afraid I have done wrong am very anxious to heare from you in answer to my first letter."[28]

Before she received the hoped-for reply, the predictable spring floods did their worst. "This week has been the longest week seemingly I ever spent," she wrote James, "for you and your efforts have not been out of my mind an hour since last sunday morning when I was awaken[ed] by the breaking away of the bulkhead of the dam. . . . it cracked like a cannon." In a matter of minutes "the corner of the mill was gone" and the cabinet shop lifted from its foundations.[29] Devastating as the event was to enterprises connected with the dam, business uptown went on as usual. William Butler and Francis Gravel were holding their own, but merchandise was moving slowly, and there was no reason to think things would get better. Support for the school was waning, and shorter sessions were planned for the upcoming year: "We have school about six weeks then I here we will probly have no more untill winter."[30]

Keenly aware of her own relatively poor schooling, Pamelia was determined that "our little children must get all the learning that is posible."[31] Andrew was young yet and seemed not to take to schooling well anyway, but Mary Agnes and Luella were bright and deserved the best education she could find for them. Perhaps she and James should consider sending them to school in Moline. They could stay with the Stephens family and earn part of their board by doing housework. Or they could stay with Mahala in Geneseo and go into Moline only during school sessions. It would be hard to let them go, yet she would find a way to manage without them.[32]

She was already finding ways to manage without the advice she had hoped to receive through letters from her husband. The system was clearly not working as they had planned. James declared that "a month is a good while betwixt letters when one is so far away from home," and after receiving three of Pamelia's letters at once—nearly seven weeks after the last of the three had been postmarked—he finally concluded: "You can see by this irregularity in my receiving your letters why you have not got answers to some of the business matters you asked me about, or if answers at all, not in time to do you any good."[33] Ultimately he conceded that, though he was writing home at least every two weeks, she must no longer expect to rely upon his advice on pressing matters, because "it is so long before I get your letter and you get mine."[34]

If the vagaries of the postal system annoyed James Fergus, they were a major problem for another member of the Pikes Peak Company. After nearly five months in the West, Daniel Bosworth had still not heard from his family. "Mr Bosworth . . . says tell his wife for God *sake* to send him a letter," James wrote Pamelia.[35] Married just over three years, Bosworth had never been so many miles away from his young wife, and his anxiety increased with every passing day.

Caroline had, in fact, been writing, though apparently not as often as Pamelia. Sarah Farnham had been seriously ill that spring, and Caroline's attentions had been divided between the needs of her mother and those of her little boy.[36] By midsummer she was also in the process of moving, having decided to go with her parents to Long Prairie, north of the homestead the family had left after the Indian attacks two years earlier.[37] Since the Farnhams traveled the twenty or so miles into town at least once a week, Caroline's move did not end her contact with Pamelia and other Little Falls friends. In a letter that summer, Freeman asked James Fergus to "Tell Dan I saw his wife and Boy in town this morning."[38]

The Indian unrest that had driven the Farnhams off their Round Prairie homestead in 1858 was a continuing factor in Little Falls life. In late spring of 1860 the Dakota and Ojibway were fighting each other once again, and Pamelia noted that a party of victorious Ojibway had passed through town, "hooting Holloring making great nois just at dusk. . . . it was no wonder that Mother was frighten."[39] Hired hand Ben Nickerson was a near casualty of a stray bullet fired by the celebrating Ojibway. He reported that the Ojibway had celebrated their victory over the Dakota by visiting "Pewter-Eyed" Sloan's former companion, Odishquaw, the Indian woman Pamelia had befriended. Inviting her into the street, the warriors danced around her in a circle, waving Dakota scalps and ears.[40]

Despite such excitements, life in Morrison County was relatively dull, and the citizens of Little Falls were eager to hear how their argonauts were faring. "Quite a number here are waiting to hear from you what the prospects are in the land of gold," Pamelia wrote. "If favorable they will go." Among those most anxious to hear she listed Stewart Seely, Johnny Johnson, O. A. Churchill, John Ault—and herself. "I will have everything in readiness to leave at any time you wish," she promised, but hastened to add, "If it does not pay then come back and we will make [other] arrangements."[41]

James was not thinking of coming back, having settled in at Breckenridge Diggings, a site some seventy miles southwest of

Denver on the Blue River, a branch of the Colorado. Awed by the beauty of his surroundings, he wrote, "In the distance in every direction are snow covered mountains lower down are immense forests of pine and spruce while on the river bottom are small spaces and patches of glade, prairie meadow covered with wild sage flowers." Eager for some more tangible means of sharing the sights, he sent Pamelia and the children some petals from those flowers, though he feared they would "all be ground to powder before they get there."[42]

Their camp was high, "probably near two miles above the level of the sea which accounts for the snow and frost although it is a good deal South of Minnesota." The elevation had "a very great effect" on their lungs, and he described the air as "so light that it makes one puff and blow while going up the steep mountains like a race horse."[43] Their appetites were good, but rations were scarce: "We are now reduced to bread, bacon, and beef, varied by corn cake, beans, rice, etc. We would like a few potatoes, some pudding and milk, pies cake so forth, but they are not in our bill of fare. So we content ourselves by cooking what we do have, better than the women do, and make the rest up in keen appetites."[44]

Summer lodging posed no problems: "Men live comfortable here in little bowers or houses made of the branches or Saplings of the spruce and pine, which are scattered all over the country, the builders often only occupying them for a single night, when they are taken possession of by the next comer."[45] The weather was cool to cold. He wore flannels and would likely do so all summer. But the cold kept away mosquitoes and flies. "I have seen very few misquitoes," he reported, "but they didn't appear to know anything about biting." All in all, he concluded, their days were pleasant and "the weather the best for labor that I ever saw."[46] That labor was arduous: "All mining is hard work and particularly mining for gold in the gulches in the rocky mountains. Standing all day in spring, or snow water from the mountains with rain overhead about half of the time."[47]

By early June he reported that the Pikes Peak Company of Little Falls had bought a couple of mining claims, he and his partners were building a house, and they soon would "be at work among the Boulders gravel and water trying to get our share of the precious dust we have come so far to find."[48] The house was one and one-half stories high and twenty by twenty-four feet, admittedly larger than the four men needed. However, since high water had kept them from mining, they had used their time profitably in building a structure they could later sell as a store to William Butler, Charles Freeman, or anyone else of their acquaintance who might follow them. Obviously the area was booming, and there would be many shopkeepers moving in over the next few years.[49]

Barely a month after his arrival, Fergus analyzed the situation in which he found himself:

> I like the mines as well as I Expected although the looks of the country is different and gold not quite so abundant as we expected to find it. there have been a few Excellent locations found where gold is abundant, and a few men are making fortunes but the great majority are not quite realizing their anticipations. there was far too great an Emigration this spring from the states and a great many turned back from Denver before even coming into the mines. I may be disappointed, but I came here to make money and I mean to do it before I go back if possible. It will only require time, patience and some energy.[50]

The views of another argonaut were not as well tempered. Only two months after having been reported to be resting in the St. Paul jail, Timothy Smith turned up in Colorado. In a letter postmarked Gregory Diggings, a camp some seventy miles from Fergus's cabin in Breckenridge, Smith expressed his disappointment in the gold country, noting, "[The] Rocky Mountains are filled up full with people who are not making their salt on an average and I pronounce the whole thing a *humbug*." Though he predicted that there would be a general stampede for the States in August, he colorfully, if crudely, expressed his own enthusiasm for mountain life: "Great *God* Fergus don't it make your touch hole stick out to climb these mountains?" And he added, "I wish you *God* speed in your search for *Gold* and if you and I feal to meet again on Earth (as you said when we parted last) I hope we may in *Heaven*." Smith attached a telling postscript to that letter: "Fergus—I don't drink any whiskey."[51]

Though the doctor had written to his friend, he had not, apparently, written to his wife, for in a July 4 letter, Pamelia told James, "It is said that Mrs Dr Smith has not had but one letter from him since he went away she feels very bad Doc sent her about fifty dollars worth of cloths . . . she would rather have one letter from

Gregory Gold Diggings, Colorado, 1859. From a woodcut by George G. White in Richardson's Beyond the Mississippi.

him than all the fine clothes she felt very fine when he went away unless her looks deceive her she feels bad now."[52]

Smith's letter to Fergus also carried news of another Minnesotan at Gregory Diggings. "Judge Stone is here and well," the doctor reported.[53] A naturalized citizen, Lewis Stone had immigrated to Minnesota Territory from New Brunswick sometime prior to 1850.[54] Age and position had not made him immune to the gold fever that struck younger men. Sixty-four when he set out for Pikes Peak in late spring of 1860, Stone had left his sixty-three-year-old wife Elizabeth at home in Platte River, a small settlement some twelve miles downriver from Little Falls, just above the mouth of the Platte. Living with her were Ezekiel, a son in his mid-twenties, and two young grandchildren. Living next door were her brother- and sister-in-law George and Mahala Stone, who already shouldered most of the responsibilities for the family-owned hotel. A "land lady" with real property valued at four thousand dollars in the 1860 census, Elizabeth Stone was relatively free of the financial worries that plagued Pamelia Fergus.[55]

The little cash James had left Pamelia was soon expended, and she was forced to earn more on her own, noting, "so you see if I had not of sold butter I would of done without a great many things."[56] Her work went on, though she reported, "my health is very poor neve[r] has been as poor my breast is not any thing like well." After months of self-treatment, she had finally gone to Fort Ripley to a doctor who had recommended medicine "to purify the blood." There was one bright spot—he had said the lesions were "not cansores."[57]

Money remained a constant worry, and in early August Pamelia followed a bit of advice from James's memorandum and asked Hall for the money he owed them. She succeeded in collecting only "sixteen dolars of company paper," a fact that nettled her soon thereafter when she discovered that Clara Hall had bought a new carpet and taken on a hired girl. Pamelia wrote James that she had mentioned to the lawyer's wife that she would like a new carpet too and that the only hired girls she could afford were her own daughters. But she hastened to assure James that all of this was said "in good humor."[58]

It was hard to stay in good humor, weary as she was of managing without her husband, but she held on, knowing that, with or without James's help and with or without money from his mining ventures, she must maintain the family home in the manner to which he was accustomed. This entailed overseeing of the planting and harvesting operations; care, feeding, and slaughter of cattle and hogs; preservation and preparation of beef and pork; care of chickens and sale of eggs; care, feeding, and milking of cows; making and sale of butter and cheese; cooking and serving of meals; sewing of clothes, quilts, curtains, and linens; supervision of the children's education, discipline, health, and moral development; maintenance of family ties with James's relatives as well as her own; and regular correspondence with James himself.[59]

In addition, she was now expected to manage whatever business affairs required her attention or signature, though James had previously given her little or no voice in matters concerning the Little Falls Manufacturing Company and had had neither the time nor the inclination to educate her in the proper handling of company affairs. Her situation was difficult, and it was essentially thankless. For running the home and tending the children, she could expect no praise, since she was merely carrying out her expected role as wife and mother. And for tending to James's business affairs she could expect mixed praise at best, since she had no hope of handling matters to his satisfaction.

Far from seeing her new duties as a means of gaining independence and furthering her own position in life, she saw them for what they were—more work to be done on top of her own. No matter how well she managed to carry out the new tasks, she had no delusions of becoming a businesswoman or rising in status by virtue of her work on her husband's behalf. Her intervention in what were considered male affairs would be tolerated by a society not unused to dealing with women whose husbands were temporarily absent.[60]

Her term as head of household was, then, something to be endured, not relished. As a dutiful wife she had had, after all, no choice but to accept the charge with which she had been left and to do the best she could to hold on to whatever was left of the life that had been theirs in Little Falls. Even as she held on, she longed to hear that better things awaited them elsewhere, writing, "I hope you will do well and pick us a home some where where our children can get an education and where properety will not be as risky as it has been at Little Falls."[61]

Unbeknownst to Pamelia, things out in Colorado were looking as risky as they had ever looked in Minnesota. James had taken stock of his position and realized that he would not make his fortune and be home in six months as he had planned. "It is going to take some time before we can make any thing here in mining," he admitted, for "the water is too high and it takes a good while to get a commencement so that the fall months will be the most profitable It is very uncertain whether I shall come home this winter at all . . . unless compelled to by business."[62]

Justifying his decision to leave Pamelia and the children alone for longer than he had intended, he explained that there was "but very little chance for a person to make much the first season, but by sticking to it for two or three years with care and descrition I think they will do well." Though there were no guarantees and the odds were against him, his optimism rivaled the optimism he had felt in the early years of Little Falls, and he wrote, "I came here to make something for my family and I will do it before I leave the mountains entirely."[63]

The men of the Pikes Peak Company of Little Falls were now in separate camps. James Dillin and O. J. Rockwell were working on claims some eight miles distant from Breckenridge, and Jonathan Pugh was with them.[64] The former sheriff of Little Falls, suspected of collusion with the road agents who had plagued the town during the Little Falls War, had reached Colorado ahead of the others. James's attitude toward him had softened with the years and with distance. Pugh had quit drinking since his arrival in the goldfields, and James reported: "[He] looks like a shadow but is as tough as a knot, works hard from morning till night, pays no attention to wet feet, or heavy rains but says he came here to make something, and he is bound to do it if he can. I hope he will such energy deserves success."[65]

Fergus was all too aware that most of those who came west would go home with nothing to show for their efforts. He wrote Pamelia to tell his friends at home that

> there is gold in the mountains, but it is not in such quantities as it was first found in California, that some are doing well and will make fortunes, but that by far the largest portion will not do near as well as if they had remained in the States. . . . I advise all who are doing well in Minnesota to remain there and those whose cases are desparate, and are willing to live among the pines and spruces that grow on the sides or in the ravines of snow covered mountains . . . to come on and [try] it.[66]

Shopkeeper William Butler was among those who read news from the West with eagerness. "Your letter had to go all round the neighbors," he wrote to James. "Every body wanted to read it and it took just a week to go the round every[body] was very much interested with it."[67]

Before James's letters made the rounds to the would-be miners of Little Falls, they were read and reread by Pamelia, who shared them in turn with Caroline Bosworth and Amanda Smith. Frequently, James's letters carried news addressed directly to the wives of the men he was with in the goldfields: "Tell Mrs. Bosworth that Danl is well and will write as soon as he receives a letter."[68] And, on another occasion, "Doct [Smith] like many others don't find gold easily obtained as he expected and is evidently disapointed."[69]

James himself admitted to some discouragement, noting that gold mining was rather like a lottery in which there were a very "few prises of different sizes" as compared "to a great many blanks."[70] And his replies to Pamelia's oft-expressed wish to have him find a place for her and the children were cautious. "You must content yourselves where you are at the present," he admonished, "as I would not like to bring a family into these mountains now."[71] He did not, however, rule out altogether the possibility of her eventually joining him, noting, "If it were not for the high price of provisions, the want of schools, and the absence of proper society I would like to have the children here with me in the mountains to enjoy the scenery."[72]

James understood Pamelia's eagerness to leave Little Falls behind her, for he was not unaware of the psychological impact that town gossip concerning his bad debts might have upon his family. Despite Freeman's insistence that there was no one in Little Falls "that pays any attention to [Tuttle] or believes what he does [or] say[s]," James was uneasy about the accusations being made and cautioned Pamelia to do all she could to avoid confrontations with his former partner and to "make as little excitement about your busness with the Co. or my being off to Pikes Peak as you can," since he was afraid of "the mischief" Tuttle might cause "when he takes his crazy spells."[73]

Even without such advice from her husband, Pamelia was hardly capable of stirring up excitement of any sort. "My health has ben so poor I could hardly get to our own garden," she wrote, adding that her breast was "getting better very slow." Despite her mother's company, she was nearly immobilized by her depression, confessing, "Fergus I cannot half write and it seems as though evry thing goes backwards," adding, "I hope you will live to come home."[74]

Her frustration stemmed, in part, from hearing that the assessments she had voted for would cost nearly twice the amount she had originally been told. And, desperate as she was for cash and despite the fact that he was the one who had advised her to vote for the assessments, Hall had once again refused to pay her the rest of the money he owed James, stalling for time by telling her that he would need a formal order from her husband. At wit's end, she exclaimed, "you see how I get along with business matters."[75]

Pamelia's resolve must have been more apparent than her despair, for a letter from Charles Freeman to James, written at about the same time, noted that Pamelia had "sold a great deal of Butter and milk" and was managing things at home "first rate."[76] As if in affirmation of Freeman's opinion, Pamelia took hold again. Alluding to the troublesome assessments, she ventured to assert that "next time I should use my own judgment" when making business decisions.[77]

James hardly seemed to allow her the privilege. His every letter contained still more advice concerning the handling of day-to-day affairs. She was to keep his tool chest locked and to lock the red barn. She was to see to the corn and potatoes. He had instructed her to sell the colt if she needed money, and when the animal died before she could do so, he was quick to assign the blame: "It was wrong to give the colt cows milk if nature had intended colts to have cows milk a cow would go with every mare."[78]

While she did her best to follow most of James's instructions, Pamelia soon began to rely on her own judgment. When he advised her to butcher the old milk cow, she replied: "I do not think it best to have [her] . . . beefed for we can do with very little met if we have milk and butter." He had advised killing the white-faced cow as well, fearing she would jump fences and cause more trouble than she was worth, but Pamelia reported that since she did not "aper to be unruly" she, too, would be kept. "I can sell butter and milk in the spring early besides having it ourselves," she explained.[79] However, as summer drew to a close, she informed him that she had changed her mind about the white-faced cow. Though she did not jump fences, neither did she give enough milk to warrant feeding her through the winter. When cold weather came, they would have her killed, along with the little pigs.[80]

During the first summer of James's absence, vegetables as well as meats were relatively abundant. Pamelia's garden did well, and Butler provided goods on credit from his store whenever she was in need.[81] All in all, Pamelia felt fairly secure, noting that her "faten hogs look well" and the family had "plenty of butter and cheese." In addition, she had twenty pounds of maple sugar from Freeman, who had told her that he also had money to spare and was willing to let her have some if she needed it.[82]

Glad as she was to be able to feed the family at home, Pamelia worried about James. "Now tell me in your next have you enough to eat this winter," she entreated.[83] In answer to her question, he sent a lengthy description of typical miner's fare:

> The principle living here in the mountains is bread and bacon, or bread, and beef. Those who live in the thickly settled part of the mines or in the towns can get plenty of beef at a low price, from 8

to 24 cts, but those who live on the frontier, or are prospecting, have to depend principly on bread and bacon. Sometimes a few dried apples stewed. occasionally we get some corn meal and make mush, and fry it again when cold. Sometimes we have beef soup, and again bean soup, and those living in Denver or the Gregory Diggings get all the vegetables they want now. They were raised on the Platte Valley last season and are quite plenty and of good quality.[84]

Haunted by his descriptions of a monotonous diet that made him prone to attacks of scurvy, Pamelia found it difficult to enjoy meals at home, noting, "we have set down to the table of vegistables and other good thing[s] we often wish and wondered whare and what you got for your dinner."[85] She urged, "You need [not] give yourself any uneasyness abut us for we are in a land of plenty and nothing to anoy us compared to your troubles if you wer[e] comfortable and happy and where we could get letters from eachother we should have nothing to complain of."[86]

There were indeed fewer problems at home by the end of James's first summer in the mountains. Pamelia's health had improved, and she noted, "It is a great blessing to feel well I am better now than I have been a good share of the time since you have been gone although my breast troubles me some yet."[87] Improved though her situation was, she felt compelled to take issue with James's most recent admonition: "You advise me not to be making up foolish things now Ive leisure I do not seam to have much leisure as yet," she pointed out, "seven of us all the time and most of the time eight that is quite a family and four of them children to make wash and mend for it all takes time."[88]

She found it hard to get the hired men to do farm chores. She had given Ben Nickerson plenty of seed early in the spring and had instructed him to plant their eight lots in vegetables. Too ill to go down to the lots and check on him, she had assumed the job had been done — only to find out that he had put in potatoes, rutabagas, and carrots and left the rest of the acreage to grow up in Hungarian grass. At least there would be five to six tons of hay.[89]

John Currie, whom Pamelia declared "the poorest fellow to set himself to work that I ever saw," was even less dependable than Nickerson. James had leased him a hauling team and wagon in return for his help with planting, harvesting, and making household repairs. John seemed to resent the arrangement, complaining that he

Portion of a letter written by Pamelia Fergus to James, August 28, 1860 could have made more money elsewhere, had he not been bound to stay in the Little Falls area because of his agreement with Fergus.[90] Grudgingly he dug the potatoes, brought in the hay, and slaughtered the pigs and cow, but his resentment of Pamelia called for diplomacy on her part. "He wants some one to set him to work," Pamelia reminded James, "but of all things to have a woman tell him how to manage I have to be vry carful to have things go smooth."[91]

James made it clear that he, too, found it difficult to "have things go smooth" while working "where you have to scale the summits of the highest [mountains] . . . with bead board and mining tools on your back, be out in all weathers."[92] There were no guarantees in the mining business. "Some will make their fortunes, a great many more will only pay expenses, while the great mass will go home poorer than when they left," he predicted. "Still they will have seen the 'Elephant' besides the Rocky Mountains and the pains and the pleasures of a camp life are all worth something to greenhorns Especially."[93]

Those pains and pleasures were starkly evident in his description of an eleven-day trip in which he had walked along the ridgeline, across "the snowy ranges," in search of quartz lodes. He had put off the "laborious and . . . perilous trip" for a few days, since he was "anxious to hear from my family before I undertook it, as I did not know but we might be murdered by the Utes in the valleys, eaten by the grisly bears on the mountain slopes, dashed to peises by a misstep on a treacherous rock over a precipice, or buried among the eternal snows on the summits."[94]

Such letters, of course, heightened Pamelia's concern for her husband: "Don't expose yourself so much a young man might endure such hardships but when a man gets to be of your age such climbing and rambling is to hard . . . now dont undertake any more such Perlous trips among wilds bests and Indians."[95]

Far from ready to take her advice, he confessed that he was becoming enamored of the life he led. He and Daniel Bosworth had celebrated the Fourth of July by climbing to the top of one of the highest mountains in the area, and he concluded that despite all the hardships, "This rambling around among the mountain scenery with me is like drinking with the drunkard or gambling with the gambler. It grows on me, the habit becomes a second nature."[96]

In that same letter of late July, James talked of another habit, one he hated to break. "I have been going west all my life time," he wrote, yet prudence demanded that he try his luck on the east side of the divide. "My duty compels me to go . . . for there is less snow and warmer weather during winter so that mining operations can be more successfully carried on, but I do hate to go back East of the mountains."[97]

Though it went against his grain, Fergus and the entire Pikes Peak Company of Little Falls did in fact cross back over the divide that August, working claims at Fall River, then Clear Lake near Mountain City, some thirty miles west of Denver. That move meant still another change of address, and Pamelia's letters were slower than ever in catching up with him.[98]

She was growing increasingly impatient with his repeated changes of plans. When he observed that he felt justified in staying on because he just might make a fortune in the mines, she replied: "Why you *might* make a fortune in a few years almost any where."[99] Anywhere but Little Falls, she conceded, for "Little Fall is ded ded people are going of[f] on[e] by one."[100] The *Northern Herald* had long since folded, and, according to Freeman, the company's board of directors had sold the printing press to someone "who has started a paper . . . that advocates the interests of 'Honest Old Abe.'"[101] The mill was deserted, and Pamelia reported that "it looks lonesome. . . . it does not look like a once flourshing town." With the dam breached, there was "no runing watter nor never will be again unless the [mill] race is filed up and that prably never will be."[102]

Most of the citizens of Little Falls shared Pamelia's pessimistic view of the town's future, and with no economic relief in sight on the home front, they were "very anxious" to hear from Fergus. "[As] soon as I get a letter," Pamelia noted, "evry body seemes to know it and come to here the prospect . . . all seem to have faith in Mr Fergus that he will do well if any one does."[103] When no letters came, Pamelia was glad to get any scrap of news concerning James's activities. She scoured the St. Cloud and St. Paul papers for his fairly frequent letters to the editor, and when a miner who passed through Morrison County en route home said he had seen James, Pamelia noted that she was "glad to hear of you if it was but one word as all of us widows are."[104]

This was Pamelia's first use of the term "widows" to describe the group of women in the Little Falls area who had been left behind that year by gold-seeking husbands. Over the months since the exodus had begun in the spring, the group had come to rely upon one another for support, drawing together frequently to discuss their hopes and frustrations, as well as to exchange news from their men.

Pamelia was the central figure in the group of Pikes Peak widows, primarily because James was the most faithful correspondent among the displaced husbands and his letters were the most frequent and reliable source of news. Sensing the dependence of the other widows, Pamelia addressed their worries as well as her own:

> Mrs Stone has not had but one letter from Mr S I saw Mrs Russell they look very destitute ther neighbours say they do not know what she will do this winter although they have raised enough wheat for there bread only, they have seven children and she looking for the eight. . . . The neighbors have given a good deal. . . . Mrs. Bosworth . . . complans bitterly Bosworth dont write strange I get so many letters and the rest dont get any Mrs Smith was here last evening all most mad becas she did not get one she has had two she happend to get one of them when I had not had any from you three weeks then she crowed you had better beleve I was glad for her she does not hear from Doctor very often.[105]

Secure in her financial position, Elizabeth Stone was evidently faring well enough at home in her husband's absence, despite her lack of letters from him. The same could not be said for two other Platte River women whose husbands had gone west with Judge Stone. Stone's neighbors, but hardly his equals, Alexander Paul and Robert Russell were subsistence farmers who had been eager enough to trade their plows for miner's picks, leaving their wives to handle families and farms in their absence.

Born in Belgium of French parents, Alexander Paul was a farmer and fur trader. By 1850 he and his wife Mary were in Minnesota Territory with five children, aged one to eight.[106] Over the next decade they lost two children and had five more, so that at the time thirty-six-year-old Mary was left in charge of the couple's mortgaged farm, she was also responsible for the care of six youngsters, aged six months to eleven years.[107] During Alexander's absence, she relied upon the help of two married daughters, eighteen-year-old Harriet Adams, who was living at home in 1860, and seventeen-year-old Mary Stone, who had married Henry Stone, the judge's nephew, and lived nearby in Platte River.[108]

When Robert Russell joined Lewis Stone and Alexander Paul on the trip west, he left his wife, Agnes, behind. It was not the first time Agnes had been left under such circumstances. A native of Rutherglen, Scotland, she had been pregnant with their third child when Robert set out for America in 1848, leaving her in Glasgow. Three years passed before he was able to save enough money to send for Agnes and the children. In July 1851, with seven-year-old Robert, five-year-old Jennie, and two-year-old Agnes at her side, Agnes Russell crossed the Atlantic Ocean, then went by way of the Erie Canal to Chicago, where Robert welcomed them to America. After a winter in St. Louis, the family settled in Sauk Rapids until the birth of Janet in September 1852.[109]

In the summer of 1853 Robert moved the family to a homestead near the mouth of the Platte River. The small log cabin in which they spent their first year leaked so badly that the children took refuge under the table when it rained. A city girl, Agnes had never made her own bread, and most of her recipes called for oats and seafood, items indigenous to her native Scotland but not available on the frontier. Adjustment was difficult, unaccustomed as she was to the sounds of thunderstorms, wolves, owls, and whippoorwills and to the numbing cold of Minnesota winters. Six years and three new babies later, she had finally begun to adjust to her new life when she found it suddenly changing.

After nearly a decade of farming, Robert Russell was more than ready to try his luck in the goldfields of the West. Once again a pregnant Agnes Russell was called upon to take charge of family and business affairs, only this time she was forty years old and far from the relatives who had been her mainstay during the three years she had been left alone in Scotland. This time the children who were her primary responsibility were also her chief support, and that summer of 1860 sixteen-year-old Robert not only worked the family farm but also hired out to other farmers to bring some cash into the home.[110] The money was hardly enough, and without the help of neighbors the growing children would have gone without proper clothing. Assessing Agnes Russell's situation, Pamelia Fergus considered herself fortunate, noting, "when I see them I think we are well of[f]."[111]

Caroline Bosworth and Amanda Smith were the widows with whom Pamelia was in closest touch during James's Pikes Peak sojourn. Caroline had apparently ceased making weekly trips into

Robert and Agnes Russell, about 1851

town shortly after her move to Long Prairie, for in September, Pamelia noted, "I have not seen Mrs Bosworth for two months but see Mrs Farnham evry week nearly Mrs Bosworth is coming up this week."[112] Having kept up with Caroline's activities through contact with her mother, Sarah Farnham, Pamelia felt free to take her friend's part in the ongoing argument over which of the Bosworths was the better correspondent. Charles Freeman also defended Caroline to James, noting, "Mrs Bosworth has written a good many letters to Dan but it seems he does not get them. I mention this that he may know that she does write to him."[113]

One of Caroline's letters that did reach Daniel described a gathering of the widows at the home of Betsy Gould:

> If you could [have] looked into Betz's last neight you would [have] laughfed to see the Pike Peeke widdowed all together Mrs. Furges Mrs. Smith and myself Mrs. Feurges had got a letter from him and came up to let mee and Mrs. Smith hear it. And I had just got one from you Wee had a good time.[114]

It was evident that a spirit of camaraderie had developed over the months since the departure of the men:

> Tell [Mr. Fergus] I hope hee will make lotts of money and when you come home wee will all have a good time. I would advise you

65

the first one that comes home if hee comes without all the rest [would do better] to stay behind untill they can all come for it would bee a bad thing to [have the] Pike Peak widdow[s] get [their] hand[s on] one that had run away and left the rest behind so beware one and all to not come one unless the rest come.[115]

The playfulness of Caroline's letter masked the hardships the women faced, particularly the hardships faced by Amanda Smith. Even the men of Little Falls had begun to criticize the doctor's treatment of Amanda and the children. Charles Freeman had written Fergus that he should advise "Doct Smith that he ought to [be] rode on a rail for not writing home. Mrs S has not rec'd a letter from him as yet."[116] Discouraged at Timothy's continued silence and afraid she might be using an incorrect address, Amanda tried sending her letters through James, who asked Pamelia to "Tell Mrs Smith I will mail her note in a letter to Doctor to Denver he will get his letters forwarded from there."[117] When Smith finally did write home, Pamelia sent the news to James: "Mrs Smith was here . . . she got a letter yesterday . . . which . . . says that Docter is forty five miles from Denver at Nevada City he say their he can get all the gold he wants and will be back in two months but no one believes that."[118]

Pamelia's concern for Amanda and the other widows only increased her need to hear from James more frequently. Once when two months had passed with no word, she confessed, "I have had the blues awfully. . . . Before [this] we had letters so often we had allways got your letter in twenty day untill the last one." Lack of mail affected the children, too. "We was very disapointed in not getting a letter from you," Mary Agnes wrote. "Mother said if she could not get a letter she would read the old ones and so she did read some old ones."[119]

Pamelia's frustration was doubled by the knowledge that James was not getting her letters either. "Where my letters go it is a wonder to me," she wrote. "I have always directted to Denver. . . . I have written you five or six letters since I have [gotten] any [from you]. . . . I feel my lonely situation very keenly sometimes."[120] At such moments, she was doubly grateful for the company of her children, and she shared with James stories of all their activities.[121]

The letters the girls wrote to their father reveal their own particular interests. Luella, not quite twelve, showed an astute awareness of politics, reporting on a Fourth of July celebration in which the

Republican flag had outshone the "Douglas flag" of the Democrats.[122] Now fourteen and acutely aware of social events, Mary Agnes wrote of such affairs as the festive ball they had all attended at Margaretha and John Ault's Northern Hotel.[123] And she wrote of domestic crafts as well, telling her father that "mother has made a bed quilt and made us lots of new clothes."[124]

Although their letters frequently allude to their father's homecoming, the girls, as well as their mother, faced disappointment, for by late summer James Fergus had decided to winter over. Rockwell and Dillin would stay on as well, along with Lewis Stone, Robert Russell, and Alexander Paul. But Daniel Bosworth had set his sights on home. Homesick and discouraged, he had decided to leave the mountains in mid-October and be home by early December, though he planned to return to the West in the spring, perhaps with Caroline at his side.[125]

Timothy Smith had made similar plans, and by late September James reported that the good doctor had already left for the States.[126] He had the word from Smith in person, having seen him for the first time since the two men arrived in Colorado: "I saw him . . . last week he had on a Red shirt common light colored overalls Bob Russells old white hat [he] was all covered with dust and weighs only about 130# he weighed 190 when he left—he goes to Little Falls but is coming back."[127] As broke as ever, Smith had been trying to raise money for the trip home and James had given him twenty dollars.[128]

At summer's end, Pamelia noted that "Grand Mother likes Minesota first rate" and that she had decided to stay through the winter if the girls went to Moline to attend school.[129] That decision had not yet been made, but it was imminent, since Pamelia had finally received James's reply to the letter in which she had suggested sending them away. He was amenable to their going, he wrote, so long as they boarded with the Stephens family rather than with Mahala Dillin, since he feared their grandmother "would let them have there own way to much."[130] Besides, if the girls did go away, Mahala would be needed there in Little Falls, since Pamelia had "neuralgia of the stomach" and "should not be alone."[131] Firm in his decision, James had written to George Stephens in mid-August, requesting that the girls be allowed to live with him and sketching out the route they would travel from Little Falls to Moline.[132] By early September both he and Pamelia had received letters from George Stephens, who promised to "do the best we can or are capable of doing with your children while with us they will be cared for and governed the Same as our own. We have a No. 1 School which will be opened on the 15 . . . I have advised Mrs. Fergus to have them here by that time." Noting that he did not think there would be any tuition fees charged, since "My tax is pretty Large," Stephens promised to be reasonable "about their care and Board," adding, "yourself and my self can settle that matter *easy*."[133]

Even though pressed for money, Pamelia found that finances were not her greatest concern as she readied the girls for their trip to Moline. She was having second thoughts about sending them so far away, and soon after she received Stephens's letter of invitation, she wrote to James, "I do not know what to say abut the little girls going some times I think I canot spare them we shall be so lone some."[134] Despite her misgivings, Pamelia carried on with her preparations. Though all the children had been ill with "hooping cough," she managed to sew clothes for Mary Agnes and Luella, to purchase new shoes for them, and to set aside five dollars each for their spending money in Moline.[135]

By the first week in October the girls were gone, and Pamelia described their departure: "They felt as well as could be expected their mother controled her feelings as much as posable after they had started."[136] Traveling by stage, boat, and train as far as Chicago with Francis Gravel, who was going there on business, the girls then took "the cars" alone from Chicago to Moline.[137]

Though the total cost of settling Mary Agnes and Luella into the Stephens home—twenty-eight dollars—represented a fairly large percentage of the cash Pamelia had on hand for the coming winter, she considered the money well spent.[138] The girls would be able to get the education they needed in order to better themselves. Whatever the cost to her—in money or loneliness—she was determined they should have that opportunity.

Though the girls were gone, Pamelia still had the company of her mother. With Mahala's help, she would carry on. "Grandma is well," she reported in early November, "she is [one of] the best old mothers that ever lived she is so good and kind to me when I am sick [and if] . . . one needs a friend . . . she fills up [that need]."[139]

In the absence of his sisters, Andrew's responsibilities increased. "Andrew is fixing the pig pen this morning," Pamelia wrote, "he has done good many chores he says he dont think that he can *stand* it all this . . . winter he says if Father was her[e] he would not have to do it he does pretty well." There were advantages to keeping the boy busy: "It [is] a good deal better to have him think he has got something to do if he was not employed doing something he would want to be in the streets." She had found the secret to gaining her son's cooperation: "It [is] all a habit," she explained. "[If] I keep him at home [and at work] two or three days he does well if I let him go two or three days without doing any thing and do it myself then it is a greate task to [get him to] do any thing."[140]

In the weeks after the girls' departure, Pamelia took comfort in writing to James: "I have written nearly every week Mother says she wonders what I can find to write about I tell her I don't suppose it mounts to much it certainly does not cost much and when I am done so much time [is] gone."[141]

Much of what Pamelia found to write about concerned the activities of the other widows, particularly Amanda Smith. Though Doc Smith was not yet home, his wife expected him soon and her spirits were up. Pamelia had shared a bit of gossip with her—she had seen "Mrs Bosworth going to Mr Goulds." Amanda was "almost tickled to death" at the news, and Pamelia reported that "she brought out her wine bottle and we had a drink."[142] That afternoon was somewhat shadowed, however, by new trouble facing Amanda. Before Timothy's departure, the couple had taken out a lease on the house she was now living in. That lease was up, the house had been sold, and Gravel, the new owner, was understandably anxious to have her vacate the premises. Unable to afford a move and sure that her husband would send for them any day, Amanda continued to stall.[143]

Not long afterward, things came to a head:

> [Gravel] is having some trouble with Mrs Smith about that house she lived in when you went away he bought the house was to have it at the expiration of six months then his time was out that she rented it for she expects the docttor every moment Gravel has waited six weeks over her time. She promised to [get] out before wittinesses at a certain time they waited three days they got tired he then took the sheriff who is Pecot put her things out put in theirs they have had a big time.[144]

Though her household goods were in the street and though the "neighbors tryed to prevail on her not to stay," Amanda "throughed herself on her own responsibility" and refused to be moved: "report says Mrs S stood in the doore with a women wepon the broomstick and told [the sheriff] not to come in and Ike had the hatchet Henriett More had an iron poker and little Nell run at him struck him told him he was a bad man. . . . [She] still stays their both family are their now. . . . So they all have there troubles."[145]

All of the widows had their troubles, but Amanda Smith seemed to have far more than her share. Two weeks after her standoff with the sheriff, Amanda left the Gravel home and, ever hopeful of the doctor's imminent arrival, she and the children took up residence with Elizabeth Stone in Platte River.[146] A month or so later she finally received a letter from her husband. He had gotten as far east as Omaha by early November, but he needed more cash in order to get home.[147] Somehow Amanda managed to come up the money, enclosing it in a letter that carried the news of her eviction.

Whether or not the receipt of cash inspired Timothy Smith to send a letter of thanks to Amanda, receipt of her eviction news provoked a letter of indignation to James Fergus: "I received a letter from my wife yesterday and she says that without any notice Mr. F Gravel had the sheriff set her things out into the street — now if you hear that same French (son of a bitch) has had the *shit* kicked out of him you need not wonder." In the same letter, Smith told Fergus that he intended to "start for home tomorrow," though he noted, "my health has been very poor since I left the mountains."[148] At home all of Little Falls took up the vigil for Doc Smith, though few of the townspeople believed his health had anything to do with his continued delay.[149]

Concerned as she was about Amanda's plight, Pamelia had problems of her own to solve. With winter coming on, there were many preparations to be made. She set John Currie and Ben Nickerson to cutting wood from the Fergus lots across the river and assigned to Andrew the task of splitting logs and chopping kindling. The first cold wave had already hit.

James, too, was thinking of the winter ahead. Well aware that there were cracks in the walls, especially in the kitchen, he urged Pamelia to have John plaster the kitchen and bank the house with mounds of dirt. She followed his advice and by late November was able to report: "we have got the little plastering done the house partly banked and I think John is doing it well." In answer to James's warning that the vegetables in the root cellar under the house could freeze in a hard winter, Pamelia described the precautions she had taken: "we have got [down] a good carpet with plenty of straw under it . . . in the setting room and it all helps to keep the cellar warm and I do not think it will freeze this winter."[150]

In answer to still more letters expressing concern over her preparations for winter, she assured him, "We are comfortable our house is warm the sullr [cellar] good." She set his mind at ease as to the food situation as well, reporting, "Our largest hog weighed over two hundred pounds the last springs pigs weighed upwards of seventy they were very nice pork." The white-faced cow had been killed: "The beef [weighed] about four hundred and fifty so we have meet a great plenty . . . flour enough to last five or six months or more our [root] culler is [full]."[151]

Her report of Ben Nickerson's careless planting of the eight lots drew a reprimand from James: "There is no use saying anything about it, but you ought to have had an immense quantity of potatoes, turnips, etc the way the season has been if John & Ben had managed right, they both want somebody to tell them what to do, and how to do it."[152] Pamelia knew well the truth of that statement, for it had taken her months to learn how to manage the two men effectively.

She had worked hard at other managerial skills as well, continuing to dun Little Falls citizens who owed money to her husband or to the company, though she found this task as unpleasant as it was difficult. As Charles Freeman had reported to James, "Tuttle has taken away nearly all the notes that were good for anything," leaving Pamelia to collect from people who were as destitute as she.[153] Nonetheless, she worked away at the task, lamenting, "No one has paid me any thing yet I have doned till I am ashamed almost but then I think I need not [be] if they are not."[154]

Having met with many skillful dodges, she had learned new approaches. If the debtors had no cash, let them pay in turnips, livestock — or furniture. She had taken two bureaus for the girls in settlement of one debt.[155] Better to gain something of value than to consider the notes totally worthless. She kept her ears open for news of any income that came to those who owed her and made sure she was among the first to present a bill to the newly solvent debtor. Her persistence sometimes paid off in cash, and she reported those small triumphs to James. John Long had finally given her the ten dollars he owed, "so I have sixty five dolors now in my posesion."[156]

By late October she had managed to handle all the assessment troubles, explaining to James that she had paid in full those levied in June, but when a second group came due in October, she had opted to pay only those assessments levied on stock belonging to Mr. Stephens, to her relatives in Illinois, and to James's relatives in Scotland. Why pay those due on James's own shares, since he had left orders to offer those shares to any creditors who tried to collect in his absence? If the stock was to be given away, "why keep it to trouble one self about"? Why not let the new owners make the payments?[157] It was a bold move, and one that Freeman was quick to praise: "Mrs. Fergus has arranged the balance all satisfactory and has some money left she manages things first rate."[158]

James was not unaware of his wife's growing abilities and self-confidence. At first he had tried only to reassure her. "Don't fret and keep yourself in bad health about such things," he had written her in the midst of her worries about paying the assessments, "only do the best you can & I will be satisfied."[159] A brief while later he took a different tack, accentuating the positive side of his prolonged absence: "My going away has [been] and will be a great benefit to you, by throwing you on your own resources and learning you to do business for yourself."[160]

By the time she read that letter, Pamelia must have sensed the truth of her husband's assertions. While she had never asked to be thrown on her own resources, she had certainly grown more competent during James's absence. Having begun her term as surrogate head of household in the expectation that her husband's letters would be her guide in all things, she had finally let go of that assumption and had begun to manage things on her own.[161] This was no easy task. On the one hand, she was still living out Victorian expectations of the pious, submissive wife who took no action without first asking her husband's advice. On the other, she was becoming an increasingly skilled businesswoman, a role she played with sufficient subtlety to avoid offending any of the men James had left in charge of his affairs.

Her position in dealing with Charles Freeman was particularly awkward. She had known him since the days of his bachelorhood when he had boarded in the Fergus household, and he and his wife Abby were now her next-door neighbors and close friends.[162] Even so, she could no longer afford to ignore the lackadaisical manner in which he was handling the collection of notes owed to James. Since the bills awaiting collection had remained in her keeping, she was well aware of how infrequently they were taken out of their box. "Charley says he has not colectted any thing but is going to," she wrote, hastening to add, "He seems very kind often asked if I have things to use to eat and so on we are on the best of terms."[163] Over the years she had found no reason to doubt his honesty, though she was bothered by his lack of openness: "He took several [notes] yestrday said they had got to do some thing he had waited long enough he has [collected] . . . some I know . . . [but] kept a secret the terms."[164]

Being in the dark about such matters added greatly to her frustration. "I see a little how the matter looks and here [hear] a little and guess a little," she wrote.[165] She wanted to know more. If she was expected to keep the family going in James's absence, then she needed to know more about his business dealings. Summoning her courage, she made her position plain: "Now then [I want to know] how Charley collect[s] for you on what terms how much percentage I want to know some thing about that." Still, she hastened to assure James that she was not broadcasting her doubts concerning Freeman's competence — "It is all snugled right up in this little breast of mine."[166]

When James himself proved negligent on a business matter, Pamelia called him to task: "And another thing I have been looking for a regular order [such] as Hall talks of. . . . I have written [you] before about it but think you have forgotten it he [Hall] avoids me although I never ask him since about three months ago he said he must have a *regular* order I want you to send it not so much that I need the money but I would like to tell him what I thought of him." Chiding James for his negligence, she even dared an ultimatum — "Now in six weeks I shall look for answer." And she seemed to be actually looking forward to a confrontation with the formidable Mr. Hall.[167]

Though James did not provide the requested order, he reiterated his trust in her abilities: "Use your own judgment, then if necessary consult your friends [but] dont let every body know your business."[168] She assured him she had heeded his advice about "keeping my troubles to my self about business and such matters," noting, "I have done it generly only consulting Mr Freeman and Mr Gravel some times."[169]

She had spoken to Francis Gravel recently in regard to his buying one or more horses from the team John Currie had been running. Currie's lease on the team and wagon ran out at year's end, and if James was thinking "of staying two or three years," she preferred to get rid of the horses and any other stock that required her to keep hired hands about the place. She and Andrew could take care of the cows by themselves, and Andrew could keep the new colt, but otherwise she intended to lighten her load, thereby moving the family closer to self-sufficiency.[170]

Self-sufficiency was highly prized in Little Falls as the winter of 1860 came on. Throughout the first year of Fergus's absence, Freeman had kept him apprised of the status of several Little Falls merchants, including Orlando Churchill. "Churchill is drunk nearly every day so that he staggers about the streets he has discharged all his clerks and his wife has to attend store while he is in Bar alley rolling on [his] pins [legs] and drinking whiskey."[171] Doubting he could hold onto the store much longer, Freeman had predicted, "he must go under before long."[172]

Largely through the efforts of Temperance Churchill, the store survived, though Freeman reported in early December that Orlando was "going to the Devil as fast as he can go." Having overextended his credit in Chicago, Churchill was now buying "a load at a time in St. Paul to keep along. . . . A short time ago went to Saint Paul and came home with a black Eye that he got in a whore house row while down there and now there is scarcely a day passes but what he is so drunk as to be unfit for business."[173]

Margaretha Ault's situation was pathetically akin to Temperance Churchill's. The Aults continued to struggle to hold onto the Northern Hotel, with Margaretha supplementing their income with her midwifery practice.[174] Ault himself, according to Freeman, was still "as fat and good natured as ever, [though] his day of probation expires this month if he does not make some arrangement about his mort[gage]."[175] When Freeman's prediction came true and

Little Falls, 1878, looking north on First Street. The two-story building on the right is the store once operated by Temperance and Orlando Churchill. The veranda of the Northern Hotel is visible at the far left.

the Aults lost the hotel, John Ault's talk about going west grew more and more serious. By year's end, Johnny Johnson and his wife, Ellen, were running the Northern, and Pamelia reported that John Ault was "some wher neare the Fort [Ripley]," involved with "whiskey and some fancy ladys," while his wife was "washing and making a livin for her self."[176]

In the midst of her fretting over the welfare of Temperance Churchill and Margaretha Ault, Pamelia took comfort in the news from Moline. The girls were well settled, though Mary Agnes was "a little home sick" and Pamelia avoided writing "much about home to her." Luella, on the other hand, seemed "very contented," and Pamelia felt they would both be contented, once Mary Agnes got "acquainted." The girls were impatient for the arrival of the Christmas holidays when they would go to Geneseo to visit their Aunt Mary, Pamelia's sister Mary McHose.[177] In a letter to her father, Mary Agnes spoke of their enrolling in dancing lessons and attending a "panerama of Docter Kanes last voige to the Arctic regions," a presentation she declared "worth the money."[178]

Pamelia was teaching ten-year-old Andrew at home as best she could, though he seemed to prefer anything—even doing chores—

to studying. He had helped get in the hay and dig the potatoes, and Pamelia reported that "he is a good boy to wait on me and is happy in doing his chors."[179] Charles Freeman spoke well of Andrew, too. In September he wrote that the boy had "traded Richard Steele 'out of a gun' and [was] making sad havoc among the small Birds and occassionally brings down a pidgeon." He seemed to be "a very good boy in the main — but once in a while has a set-to with some of the other Boys and sometimes is heard to swear a very little but he is improving every day."[180] Freeman had no way of knowing the impact his words would have on a father so far from home. Fergus had not wanted his son to have a gun during his absence, and he was opposed to swearing by anyone. He let his displeasure be known to Pamelia, Andrew, and Freeman in short order.[181]

He was also concerned to think that Andrew's hunting ventures might lead him too far from home: "I forgot to tell Andrew . . . not to go gunning when it snowed nor to go so far away from town that he could not find his way home, grown persons get lost verry easy either east or west from Little Falls consequently it is unsafe for boys to be out alone I hope you will tell him about this and see he don't go away unless some grown person is with him."[182] He was worried, too, about the boy's being out on the frozen river: "Tell him he must be careful about skating on the ice below the spring on the slough. There is so much spring water coming out of the bank all the way down that it makes the ice very rotten and dangerous, better keep off from it altogether."[183]

By early December, either of his own volition or at Pamelia's urging, Freeman had sent news of Andrew's improved behavior: "Andrew is altogether a diferent Boy from what he was when you left is as quiet as any Boy in Town stays at home and does up the chores in good shape reads and writes every day and is a first rate Boy has got over his swearing and fighting propensities entirely."[184]

Freeman also kept James abreast of the growth of the youngest Fergus child, Lillie, a mischievous little girl whom Grandmother Mahala called "an awful baby."[185] "Lillie grows like a weed and swears like a pirate when she gets mad," Freeman wrote. "[She] is the smartest child you have got makes more fun than all the rest of the Town."[186]

Freeman's fondness for Lillie was surpassed only by his pride in his own little Freddie. "You ought to see our Boy," he wrote when the baby was around four months of age. "He knocks the socks off any thing in this country."[187] As the Freemans' neighbor, Pamelia was very much aware of, and sometimes amused by, their parental pride, noting, "They have a baby and it would be funny if any bodyels had [one] half so pretty."[188] Nineteen and far removed from her own mother, Abby frequently sought Pamelia's advice on matters concerning her firstborn, and the Fergus children spent many hours in the Freeman home. Thus Pamelia and the children shared the couple's devastation that November when eight-month-old Freddie died.[189]

Charles Freeman could hardly bring himself to tell James of the death. He filled seven pages with news of the Fergus family and Little Falls affairs before pouring out his grief in a single closing paragraph:

> We lost our little boy last month and oh what a blow it was for us it seemed as tho we could not give him up but it was "natures stern decree" and we must abide by it. Every boddy that saw him would remark "what a sweet interesting child." It seems as though I can't be reconsiled to it. Fergus you don't know what it is to loose an only child.[190]

Francis Gravel also mentioned the tragedy to Fergus, but he added a brighter note: "Freeman folks have lost their boy a few weeks ago But rather think by appearance of things they have made a new provision."[191] Though no surviving letters give Pamelia's account of the child's death, she "was ther a good deal before their baby died," and in later years Abby wrote, "I shall never forget the day I passed with you when I see those tears shed like a mothers . . . God bless them."[192] The Ferguses spent Christmas day with the Freemans a month after they lost the baby. Abby cooked a big dinner and invited Pamelia, Andrew, Lillie, Mahala, Jane, and "some of her neighbours" to come over and share it. Ever preoccupied with thoughts of her father, Lillie, who was just a few days shy of her third birthday, scribbled a note to him and wrapped it around a piece of Christmas candy. Pamelia shared her sentiments: "I tell you Papa we want to see you it dont seem as if we could wait so long."[193]

Mary Agnes and Luella were also missed at home that Christmas. From Moline they sent holiday greetings, and Luella expressed her delight over the recent election news, scrawling in large letters, "HURRAH FOR LINCOLN." To her father, she wrote of their plans to come west: "Would you like to have me come out and cook for you Mr Stephens is talking to Agnes about what a nice time we will have a catching and killing wild animals. . . . I talk some of coming out there in the spring with [him]."[194]

It is hard to see how there could have been money to send the girls west in the spring when there was hardly enough to get the family through the winter. In November James had written to suggest that Pamelia sell some of their property to obtain the money she would need for them to live on in the coming year. He could send her nothing, for he was making only enough to sustain himself. Still he maintained his belief in the future, sure that he could make more in Colorado than in Minnesota.[195] Ironically, the very day before he penned that letter, Pamelia had sent him her honest opinion of the Pikes Peak venture: "I tell you I am sorry you went but if you are well I am contented I am not sorry on my own acount or the familys but your own but you done what you thout for the best and it is right to me." This expression of loyalty was followed by a strong qualifier: "But you must never send for us and you must not make any calculations to stay longer than next fall." And she urged him to come home and "see how things are going," rather than continue his fruitless search for gold.[196]

Heedless of her advice, James was now talking of a new business venture. He had bought a one-third interest in a quartz-crushing mill at Mountain City, using money advanced by George Stephens. The mill had a sawmill attached, to provide uninterrupted work for the crew whenever the quartz mill was down or the influx of ore was slow. There was still no money to send home, but Stephens was due out in the spring, and between them they could surely make a profit.[197]

Buoyed by the news, Pamelia looked toward the dawning of a new year and reassessed her situation, concluding, "in reality we had not ought to complane other husbands go away and leave their family destitute and not even write once in three or four months that is worse than my trouble we have a plenty at present and . . . a good warm house and plenty of wood."[198]

Pamelia was especially concerned to hear of James's poor health. He complained of a hernia, and she advised him to "get some nut gaul and grate it into some fresh lard or suet oil" and to "be careful about lifting heavy lifts."[199] He replied that he was taking care of himself and that "Docters are plenty, probably 3 to 1 from any other business. I think I am acquainted with as many as twenty." Few, however, were earning their way as physicians. "Some are connected with quartz mills, some working lodes, and some working by the day," he reported.[200] Describing her own health as "pretty good now," Pamelia wished that her mother, Mahala, who had taken such good care of her, could tend James as well: "I wish you had her to nurse you a little while then I think you would get well do try and nurse yourself."[201]

Grandmother Dillin herself was not feeling well and said that if she could just have a good visit with James Dillin and James Fergus then she would be ready to pack up and go home to Illinois. Tinsmith Robert Hamilton had come calling, "I supose to see Jennie [Jane Dillin] though he did not make any event."[202] The likable bachelor had been much in evidence in the months since James's departure, mending kettles, tin cups, and other household items and passing time with Pamelia and the children — and with Pamelia's sister Jane.[203]

And Daniel Bosworth was home from the goldfields, though his homecoming was hardly the one he had planned. Charles Freeman described the scene: "Dan Bosworth arrived here on yesterday [stage] well and hearty and in good spirits [but] his wife had just left with the old folks for Long Prairie. They say Dan swore some and I guess he did. He told me he was never so mad in his life. You can imagine his 'phelinks.' "[204] While Caroline Bosworth had not met her husband's stage, Amanda Smith most likely had. Ever since sending the doctor the money he had requested for his fare home, Amanda had faithfully awaited his arrival. Disappointed once again, she at least gained knowledge of his latest plans. On a brief visit with the Doc in Omaha, Dan Bosworth had been given to understand that Smith was setting out for Little Falls the very next day. Dan was, in fact, surprised to find out that the doctor had not gotten home ahead of him.[205]

Pamelia's chance to visit with Daniel came during his first trip to Little Falls after having finally caught up with Caroline and settled in at home in Long Prairie. They may or may not have discussed the rumor Daniel was hearing at home — that James Fergus was "a spreeing in the mountains."[206] Such rumors must have caused Pamelia much anxiety, for though James rarely drank and had little patience with those who did, distance and changed circumstances had been known to affect the habits of more than one wandering man.[207] Even if her faith in her husband's continued sobriety allowed her to ignore or dismiss tales of his drinking, she was left with the problem of helping the children deal with these rumors in addition to the old favorites concerning their father as a man who skipped town to get out of paying his debts.

Anger, not anxiety, was Daniel Bosworth's reaction to the rumors, as he wrote to O. J. Rockwell:

> The first Christian man I met in Little Falls asked me if James Fergus was a spreeing in the mountains. It rialed mee wen hee asked mee sutch a question, and I said to him. The man who said James Ferges was a Drinking was a God Dam Liur.[208]

Bosworth's righteous indignation concerning rumors of mountain "spreeing" might have stemmed, in part, from a wish to offset any rumors that might have been flying concerning his own activities at Pikes Peak. Known for an occasional spree at home, he was a logical target for local gossip of this sort.[209] In Pamelia's presence, he emphasized his hard work in the mines and the arduous nature of his long journey home. He had driven an ox-drawn wagon from Denver to Iowa, where he had left his team in the care of friends — on the chance he would return to the mines in the spring — and had made his way to St. Anthony on horseback. From there he had caught the stage to Little Falls, arriving home some seven weeks after saying good-bye to James Fergus in the goldfields.[210] And he had come home broke, without "a cent of money." In fact, he had borrowed money in St. Anthony to cover the stage fare home.[211] But Daniel Bosworth soon concluded that he could do little better in Little Falls than he had at Breckenridge. He sent a report to Fergus: Money was "verry schearch," and "Little Falls is one of the most God forsaken place in the world."[212]

Though things were bad in Little Falls that December of 1860, they were looking up in Little Elk. Against the odds, William and Rosanna Sturgis were faring better than they had since their earliest days in Minnesota. Francis Gravel reported to Fergus that "Wm Sturgis has done very well this fall . . . making first rate flour getting out logs this winter."[213] Even so, Sturgis was restless and hardly satisfied with his situation. The new year had barely begun when Fergus had a letter from him, begging for news from the mines and asserting that Little Falls was "cripled broak down worn and *Dead* as *Hell*." He saw no prospects for himself in Minnesota except "to stay against my inclination and judgement to attend the *funeral* [of Little Falls] which I think will be in almost another year." Depressed as he was about his own lot, he envisioned the bright prospects that Fergus had in the West, "which is every day being more and more developed at the stroke of a pick."[214]

Pamelia hardly shared William Sturgis's romantic view of James's situation. The loneliness she had felt over the Christmas holidays tinged her New Year's greetings with sadness. "We are all scattered and we cannot help but think [of the old days]," she wrote to James. "I use to go down to the barn and look aroun[d] and see our little animals and you seemed so happ[y] . . . my prayr is that we shall see thos days again but O how I shall know to apreciate them."[215]

Throughout James's absence, Pamelia's letters indicate that she had made every effort to keep his memory alive. Every game, every meal, every walk by the river occasioned a comment about James, and those comments were not lost on the little girl who awaited her father's return. "Lillie is playing visits," Pamelia wrote, "she sometimes sings could I but climb wher[e] Moses stood and see my Papa."[216] Since she had no photograph to send James, she promised to "cut of[f] one of her curls for papa," and she assured him, "Lillie often talks of papa and is anxious [to see you]. . . . She remembrs you as well as any of us."[217] And "Lillie sends a kiss to Pa" was a frequent refrain in Pamelia's letters.[218]

In an uncharacteristically soft moment, James revealed the extent to which his youngest child had charmed him: "Papa got your letters in the middle of mothers and although Pa don't understand your writing yet, he was just as well pleased with it as though he did." And James tried to help her understand the reasons for his absence: "Papa must go to work . . . so that Lillie shall have something to eat and wear, and have a good education when she grows bigger."[219]

Though Lillie's joyous response to hearing such passages was reassuring, Pamelia was curious as to whether the child had retained a physical image of her father: "A few evenings ago I asked her if she remembred papa she [said] yes Papa had long beard down here putting her hand around her chin and black on here putting her hand on top of her head I suppos she meant white." It was an accurate enough description of the bald-headed, long-bearded argonaut.[220]

Determined that Mary Agnes and Luella should also maintain contact with their father, Pamelia admonished them to write to him often, even if that meant they had no time to write to her. They were faithful to the task. Mary Agnes reported to her father on their growth; she was now five feet four inches tall and Luella four feet eleven inches, and their relatives had declared them "fleshier than we was when we came hear."[221] They had spent the Christmas holidays in Geneseo with their Aunt Mary, and Luella raved over the delicious apples that had abounded in her uncle's orchard, adding, "O how I wish that I could send you some but there is no use of wishing when I can't is there Papa?" She described her Christmas gifts: a hoop skirt, "a new round comb," and a ball of soap, as well as "an India Rubber ball," and "a little book named Plato."[222] Though there was no direct reference to gifts from their father, he had apparently promised them golden rings, for Mary Agnes noted, "we will send the measure of ower finger."[223]

George Stephens also kept Pamelia and James apprised of their daughters' activities. "The girls are going to school and are getting along very well. Luella has many friends while Agnes is not so fortunate in makeing friends."[224] Both girls were learning to knit and sew, and both liked to skate, though the ice was poor.[225] Both were "improving finely in their studies," with Luella the better scholar, according to Stephens: "Luella if properly educated will be *more* than a common woman—she gets her lessons easy while it requires strong efforts in others to do so."[226]

From his newest diggings at Gold Dirt, Colorado Territory, James reported that he had received six letters all at once, including two from Pamelia and one from the girls. He complimented Pamelia on her letters, though his praise was double edged: "As for your letter all I have to say if you keep on improving you will soon be a *good* letter writer."[227]

Bent on becoming a good bill collector as well, Pamelia had shown Hall the "regular" order she had finally received from James, but to no avail. Convinced that her attempts were hopeless, she let the matter rest, but not without venting her frustration: "Hall is working at his old traid cheating the widows," she told James.[228] It was not the first time Pamelia had charged the attorney with taking advantage of her inexperience and that of her friends. The previous fall she had credited Hall's defeat in a bid for the legislature to the fact that the town had little use for a man who would take advantage of a woman left on her own:

> Arthur [Garden] asked me the truth of it [said] that he had heard so and so and [that] it was hurten Hall very much he was up for representative and people wer[e] making a hob[b]y [horse] of it. . . . I told him I was sorry if I had been the means of his not getting the representative he laugh[ed] and said a man must have a cariacttar [character] and . . . it was a mean action . . . to do such a thing to a lone woman when her husband was gone.[229]

While Hall continued to be a bother, Pamelia was at last free of her troubles with John Currie, whom she had earlier noted was "acting very foolish drinks very hard and Gambles when he can get any money."[230] Having worked out the debt he had incurred when he leased James's horses, Currie was no longer in Pamelia's employ.[231] "I was glad to get read [rid] of John you may be sure," she noted, adding, "We have got old Ben [Nickerson] back to our hous agane." Having received no instructions on what to do with the team Currie had used, she had sent Freeman down to St. Anthony to try to sell the pair.[232]

She herself had found Little Falls buyers for the heifer and some pigs.[233] She had planned to allow Andrew to have the newest colt, but that one, too, had died, and though she was sorry to lose it, she assumed no responsibility for the animal's death and put the matter in perspective: "I dont supos their is any use crying for spillt milk, if we all live to get together once more and enjoy our little children."[234]

Thoughts of the separated family weighed heavily on Pamelia during the early months of 1861. "I have nothing new to write this morning," she noted in February, "but like to call to mind the plesent scenes of former days when we had our children around us and the future looked bright before *us*."[235] With the promised reunion so far distant, she wondered how she could survive: "I shall [wait] very anxiously for the next eight months to pass and try to make the time as short as posible."[236]

To brighten the dark winter days, she opened her home to

others: "we had a suppris party her[e] last night they danced till one
O clock all seemed happy the young men got oisters had a soup and
a crowd." The Freemans, who were indeed looking forward to the
arrival of a new baby, had stayed to help afterward.[237]

Such evenings seemed pleasant to James, especially in light of his
own lack of good company. "You speak of sometimes being lonely,
now I tell you, if you was shut up in these mountains among the
snow, half clad and half fed, working day and night except when
asleep or eating, no acquaintances, few newspapers, and the
prospects gloomy ahead, then there would be some chance of feeling lonesome and having the blues."[238] The letter had its effect.
"Half clad and half fed rings in my ears day and night," Pamelia
responded, then offered the apology which his words seemed to demand: "You speak of my saying I am lonely I do not mean to complain or whine or plague you for I am aware you have all you can
bear."[239] In regard to his doing without, she admonished, "Now
Fergus get you some warm cloths if they are to be had dont be so
eager to save evry dime for us your health is evry thing to us."[240]

In the interest of her own health, Pamelia had left Grandmother
Dillin in charge of Andrew and Lillie and traveled down to St.
Cloud to have her teeth fixed. Talk there had centered on the upcoming inauguration, and she indulged herself in rare commentary
on the world outside Little Falls: "The war is the topic of the day
now tomorrow will be a great day at Washington . . . the 4th of
March when Lincoln takes his seat in that big chair. . . . The flag
of the stars and stripes is waving big in Little Falls this morning the
read white and blue that makes Tyreny *tremble*."[241]

With the thawing of the river, Mahala and Jane had begun to talk
again of going home to Illinois, though Pamelia wrote, "I don't
know how I can spair them."[242] Her need for Mahala's continued
assistance increased when Luella wrote her father that she and Mary
Agnes would like to stay on in Moline until the end of the school
term.[243] When she heard of the plan, Pamelia gave her reluctant approval, noting to James:

> They are just the age to learn [and] here [there] is no one to take
> any intrest in a good school. . . . You must make arangement for
> them Childrens, do you think . . . [the Stephens] are tired of them
> if they are I think we can get them another place. . . . I tell you I
> see the ned of education and . . . feel the need of our childrens im-
> provemet. . . . [We must] give them a chance to know for them-

selves and [to] have confidence in themselves I feel as though if I onley had half the mathematic[s] that Jane has I would be very glad.[244]

Having settled into their new environment, the girls had written "not one word about home," so Pamelia judged them to be well contented. She was careful not to let her own loneliness show in her letters, though at the thought of waiting still longer to see them, she admitted, "it seems sometimes as though I must call them some pet name and if I could [I] would smother them with kisses."[245]

She was lonely for her husband as well as her daughters. By mid-April, the six-month absence James had predicted had stretched into a full year, and Pamelia felt a need to make her priorities clear: "I know we like to count dollars and cents but what are they compared to a little enjoyment the short time we stay here on earth You are working hard and faring hard I am aware when we think of the past present and future and the ups and downs you have had in life it allmost makes me shuder and give up."[246]

The negative side of mining was very much in evidence. "Let the times be ever so bad," James admitted, "a living can be got from the soil, but it is a very risky business getting it from the bowels of the Earth in the Rocky Mountains." He attributed his own lack of success to inexperience—"mining and running quartz mills is a trade, and has got to be learned like any others."[247] Still, he remained undaunted: "I hope soon to report better things. . . . the prospects ahead are far better than any time since I came to the mountains."[248]

James's continued optimism was beginning to wear, and Pamelia took a stand: "You must come home next fall and make a home for us in Illinois or Iowa . . . we never can spare you to [go] back to their again. . . . You say you still hope to make your pile. . . . You are very energetic and dont seem to think [about the fact that] our time is short her[e] at best Now I want to enjoy you and our little children riches I do not want enough to be comfortable is all I ask."[249]

Even as she wrote of her own husband's overdue homecoming, Pamelia was still looking for the long-awaited arrival of Dr. Smith. Back in November, having lost patience with Amanda, she had declared her friend "a foolish woman" for sending money to the doctor in Omaha.[250] "I think she sent him nearly all she had," she reported later, "[but] she has since sold her poney now she is flush again."[251] Her attitude toward Amanda had softened with time: "I tell you the woman is all most crazy other women here from their husbands and she does not . . . if you see or here or have an ocation to write to Doct say somthing for her if he doesnot [do something soon] he will not have a wife long so say Freeman and all the rest of the neighbours."[252]

Amanda's family in the East had continued to write her, urging her to give up and come home, and not having received a single line from Timothy since his letter asking for money, she had begun to take that option more seriously. "She says she will go soon if she does not here from the Doctor," Pamelia wrote. "She would start now if she had money she has written often to Omaha to the postmaster and others one of the Goodhue boys has got back heard of him in Omaha."[253]

Pamelia passed on to James one bit of news she did not share with Amanda: "The comon report [here is] that he has another wife Mrs S has not heard that I do not think [She] has not heard in five month now she says her only hope is that you will hear some of him and write."[254] But James was in no position to be of much help. "I have heard nothing further of Dr Smith . . . if I knew where to write to I would write him, but I hope he has got home before this time." While he had no idea of Smith's whereabouts, James was fairly certain of one thing: "I don't think he will come back to the mountains as I don't know any thing he has to come back for."[255]

James was able to supply more information, if not more help, to Mary Paul, who had also written him in early January looking for news from her husband. Losing ground in her struggle to provide for herself and her six children, she appealed to James's feelings as a father:

Being placed as you are away from home and loved ones you will simpathise with me in my great afliction I do not know what has become of my husband I have not heard from him since last september then he told me he would start to come home the first of october I am in a sufering condition without any thing to keep myself with my children are sick and destitute and as you [know] how I must feel I hope you will lend me your aid in trying to find whare he is I am afraid he is dead but if he is in the land of the living I should be very glad to know it . . . I hope you will write to me soon as you get this I saw your wife with her sister 3 days ago they were well I hope you will excuse my poor writing and the liberties I have taken in writing to you.[256]

Pamelia echoed the woman's plea, calling the family "very destitute," and soon thereafter James addressed the matter in letters to both women: He had heard from Robert Russell that Paul had not only written his wife, but had also sent her money — twenty-five dollars on October 15 and fifty dollars on November 15.[257] Though Mary Paul might have taken some comfort in the fact that her husband was indeed "in the land of the living" and had at least attempted to send her money, the knowledge did little to alleviate her financial worries and Pamelia reported that the "Pall family['s] neighbours have helped or [they] would have suffered."[258]

That was in February. In April, when Pamelia dropped in on the Pauls during a visit to Platte River, she found the situation little improved. Mary had still not heard from her husband, but she showed Pamelia the letter James had written in response to her plea and she was "very thankful" for his efforts. Desperately in need of a job, she was contemplating a move into St. Cloud, fifteen miles south of Platte River.[259]

While in Platte River, Pamelia also called on Agnes Russell, where she found a more pleasant situation. Agnes's nearest neighbor and closest friend, Mrs. John Higgins, had visited Little Falls earlier that winter, reporting that "Mrs R she had got a little money from him was able to send all the children to school . . . [Mrs. Higgins] spoke in prais of her managing."[260] Pamelia's visit confirmed the good news: "They seemed comfortable and happy herself with eight very pretty Chldren sat eating to the table and evey thing looked nice and clean." The new baby was now five months old and doing well, though still unnamed, since Agnes was waiting for Robert's final word on the matter. She was receiving money from him periodically, though his most recent letter had noted that his financial prospects looked "discourgeing."[261]

Discouraged as he was, Robert Russell was nonetheless in close touch with his family, and he shared some hometown news with James when the two men met in Gambol Gulch that spring. "Having received 28 papers from his wife lately at diferent times," Russell gave James Fergus all the news from Platte River, Sauk Rapids, and St. Cloud.[262] A few weeks after that visit, Russell was back in

James's camp at Gambol Gulch, having accepted his invitation to take up a claim with him.

Known as a man "of convivial habits" who "frequently drank to excess," Robert Russell had apparently reformed, for Fergus reported that he "neither drinks nor swears now since he has been in the mountains." James judged him to be "a strong advocate of religion," since he "asked where meeting was held the first thing when he came over here." Remembering his friend's behavior back at Platte River and weighing things in light of his own agnosticism, Fergus was more amused than impressed by the transformation: "Poor Robert to think of him asking *whare* the kirk was tickled me."[263]

Russell settled down to work on James's claim at once, but within days of his arrival, he sustained a crippling injury. He was working underground when an ore bucket fell some eighty feet to the bottom of the shaft, striking his shoulder and fracturing a bone. Since the shoulder would not likely mend "before the first of May," James carried Russell's blankets and other possessions back to his cabin in Mountain City, where he had chosen to recuperate.[264] News of the mishap heightened Pamelia's anxiety: "I was sorry to hear of that acident of Mr Russell it is uslless to say do be careful for I have flattered myself that you wer very causious."[265]

Even as she worried about James's safety, Pamelia had other problems on her mind. With hindsight, she had begun to regret some of her earlier decisions. Having sold the heifer in order to pay the hated assessments, she now had less butter to sell and lamented, "if you had been here yould have done differat and their would not have been any assesments to have paid."[266] On other fronts she felt more competent. Though winter was clearly over, she saw no point in clearing away the dirt they had banked against the house and dared ask, "What do you think of letting the banking remain around the house it has now settld down to the wall or if we only rake it away on the front . . . end towards the road."[267] When he protested that leaving the dirt banked would make the yard appear uncared for, she assured him, "I have got the yard and lain all raked up clean and nice."[268]

In early April Pamelia had noted that work on the dam had resumed and was progressing nicely: "Grandmother and I have just got back from a walk to the damn they are filling on rock now."[269]

Within a week the picture changed: "With a heavy heart and sad feelings I sit down to inform you in my weak way of still [more] misfortune of Little Falls the watter is very high in the missipy the new damn and mill are expected to go all the time the floor on the other side of the mill is gone the watter is poring through with . . . fury."[270]

By late April the mill—Pamelia's one visible link with a time when her family had been intact—was still standing, though the new wing of the dam had been washed away.[271] But in early May she reported, "Last night the Sout[h] east corner of the mill . . . sailend down stream with a crash. . . . Some say it all will go and Sturgis said to day their was not much of it left and he thought that much would not be [here for] long."[272]

That prediction was voiced on a day Pamelia had spent with the Sturgises. She and her sister Jane had received an invitation to join William and Rosanna on an outing to gather wintergreen and see the countryside, and Pamelia had accepted with eagerness. Although the Sturgis children still came into Little Falls to school, she had not seen much of the family since their move to Little Elk. Two more babies had arrived—Henrietta, already nearly two, and Nellie Jane, a babe in arms—bringing the total number of Sturgis children to seven. Only six were at home, for Jennie, Rosanna's fourteen-year-old stepdaughter, was spending the spring with her grandparents in Michigan.[273]

Traveling by ox-drawn wagon, Pamelia, Jane, and all the Sturgises had driven up a high knoll from which they could see Little Falls—and the rising Mississippi River. After supper William had driven Pamelia and Jane back home, all the while complaining of how dead Little Falls was. Despite Sturgis's negative comments, Pamelia noted in her next letter that he had thirteen men working at his mill and planned to keep them working right through the summer.[274]

Though William Sturgis was faring well enough, Daniel Bosworth was not. Ever since his arrival in Little Falls he had talked of little else but his return to the goldfields, though the report was "that he will not take his wife with him becaus he has not the money."[275] He could hardly afford to go himself, but he kept Caroline on edge by setting off in February, only to turn back within a few days of his departure. He left again in March, but by mid-April

Pamelia reported that he had returned to Long Prairie — "his home if he has any" — having discovered that the oxen he had left in Iowa had "all died but three."[276] Unwilling to give up on his plan, Daniel continued to look for a way back to the mines, and Pamelia declared, "I do not know what he will do nor he either."[277] Through all this fretting, Pamelia's concern lay with Caroline. Pregnant within a month of her husband's return, she had been unwell for some time and was, by late spring, "very delicate indeed must be waited on."[278] The condition of his oxen and of his wife finally made the decision for Bosworth. For the present, at least, he resigned himself to lumbering and working as a teamster in and around Long Prairie.

Orlando Churchill was also still living in Little Falls — though there was every reason to believe that he might not be for long. His frequent trips to St. Paul had led to an affair with Augusta Byers, a German servant girl who had once lived in Ault's hotel. He talked of little else and carried with him "the likenes of gusty and a little boy shows it when he is drunk 'their is the boy it bairs my name to' tells Mrs C to tell the little girls they have a little brother and a nice little fellow to."[279] Though the town buzzed with such gossip, Temperance had continued to ignore the affair, even after the arrival of the child left her little room to doubt the extent of her husband's involvement with Byers. Finally, events in early May proved too much for her:

> Mr Churchill started last wednesday for St Paul report says that he is not coming back at least I hear that Mrs C told him he need not he has received letters from Gusty Biers all winter by Andrew the stage driver so they did not come in the mail last weak while he was gone in St Paul once came to the ofice I think I have told you that Gust had a *baby* in this letter she asked for 25 dolars and told him to be good to his wife long as he stayed with them that they would soon share each others love and so on.[280]

Within a month Churchill was gone–"for good they say." And yet Temperance, who had "lost the use of one of her eyes" from "nerviousness," was "misirable in both body and mind" without him and had hopes that he would reform and return to his family. Her sister, Eliza Holmes, was now living with her and was helping to manage the store.[281] For Temperance, Alice, and Flora Churchill, life in Little Falls had never been worse.

But there was one bright spot for the Churchill girls. The school situation had greatly improved, due to the work of a Mr. P. H. Taylor. Twenty-five boys and fifteen girls attended his classes that spring of 1861, and even Andrew Fergus, ever the reluctant scholar, had shown enough interest in his studies that he "spoke a piece on Washington's grave at Mount Vernon." Pamelia was lavish in her praise of Taylor: "The people think that he is the best teacher that ever has been here he had a little examnation the last term a great number of the towns people went in to here their resitations. . . . Mr. Taylor wrote a dialog for Janett Sturgis and Jenne [Jane] Dillin on secession, and several speches wer[e] made on the subject as that is all the excitement now."[282]

The subject of secession did indeed stir excitement. The election of Lincoln had spurred unrest in the South, and by the time he took office in early March, seven states had withdrawn from the Union. When war actually broke out, Little Falls, situated just below Fort Ripley, felt the impact at once. Pamelia reported, "Our greates excitment is war The mesenger went past her[e] last night to warn the troops at Fort riply to move we shall see them on the march this week report says and one hundred volenters at St Cloud will take posession of this Fort."[283]

The unrest was felt in the Fergus household. After having spent nearly a year in Little Falls, Mahala Dillin was talking of going home to Illinois since "war and Indians disturbe her much."[284] And the onset of war meant the end of school for Little Falls children. Taylor announced his resignation and joined the Union Army.[285] In the wake of heated disputes between the "secesh" and Unionists, Pamelia reported that some of the strongest Southern sympathizers were leaving, "so our comunity is getting less and less."[286]

The town that had once boasted one hundred eligible bachelors had long since lost its surplus of men. The failing economy had forced out many small businessmen and farmers. A number of them had followed the example of James Fergus and gone west to seek their fortunes. Other than Taylor, the town had relatively few young, healthy men to answer their country's call. Some of those who enlisted did so for other than patriotic reasons: "[Chessman] Gould has enlisted . . . his family will be supported while he is gone some say he has only enlisted . . . [because] he is hard up."[287] Pamelia's former hired man, John Currie, who had always longed for faraway places, had cast his lot with Uncle Sam.[288] Over the next few months still others joined the army — Metcalf, Peacot, Morse, the Camp boys — leading Pamelia to speculate, "There will not be many men left if all go that expect to."[289]

In Moline the patriotic spirit of the Fergus girls was high. "Hurah for liberty . . . three cheers for the union the constitution and the laws," Mary Agnes wrote her father.[290] Pamelia shared her daughter's sentiments, yet when troops began moving from Fort Ripley to points southward, she cringed at the realities of war: "When we see a hundred men armed with guns and glittring s[t]eel it allmost makes us shuder."[291] At home in Illinois, her brothers were eager for combat. Rumor had it that William Thomas Dillin had enlisted already, and Hiram was "crazy to go." She and her mother wondered whether James Dillin, away in the goldfields, also felt inclined to enlist.[292] Ultimately she reported, "Hiram has enlisted expect[s] to go soon."[293]

"Our newspapers are filled with war war and sad scenes," she reported in mid-June, "yesterday the vollenters that was sent to Fort Ripley was ordered to go South." There would be no more than twenty men left at the fort to keep peace with the Indians. Among those who had gone south with the Fort Ripley volunteers were Taylor and Currie. When Currie stopped to bid the Fergus household farewell, Pamelia observed that he and the others "seemed to feel very gloomy knowing the fate they would be likely to meet."[294] Despite her sorrow over the young men whose lives would be lost in the war, Pamelia remained adamant in her support of the Union cause, noting, "I see by the paper that Jeff Davis would like to come to terms but I hope they will take his head first."[295]

One of her letters concerning the Civil War drew rare praise from James: "You improve very much in letter writing. This is the best you ever wrote me and contained the most interesting news." Yet he added, "be a little more particular about your spelling and putting in all the words."[296] Her spelling so dismayed him that at one point he composed an entire letter pointing out her most common errors: "you spell Stade for Stayed, Keepped for Kept, . . . herd for heard." His list contained forty-one paired words, and his letter concluded with the following advice:

Write your letter first out on your slate, rub out alter and correct untill you think the spelling is all right, and [the letter] is as good . . . as you can get it. Then write it on paper with a pencil, correcting any further errors you may see, then copy it in ink, and your letters will certainly look better than they do now.[297]

In light of Pamelia's insecurities concerning her lack of education, such comments might well be considered brutal, though James no doubt considered it his duty to help his wife better herself. After all, if she aspired to a finer life, then she must prepare herself for it. Though Pamelia seems to have taken his comments in stride, it is not hard to imagine the emotional toll such criticism took on a woman who found time to scribble out the lengthy, news-filled epistles she sent him "every Monday morning."[298]

Meanwhile, other matters occupied Pamelia's thoughts. It was planting season again, but Ben Nickerson was drinking heavily and could not be depended upon. She first considered renting out their farmland "on thirds," but ultimately decided to tend it herself. Having sold the team, she arranged to have someone else cultivate the field and got Ben to plant cabbages, peas, potatoes, and other vegetables needed for the household, then plant the rest in corn.[299] She was aware that James would likely question her decision to grow corn and conceded, "probly some other crop would do better but that [is what] I can see to the easiest."[300] It was good that she chose the easier crop, for later that spring she let her one remaining hired man go, reporting to James that Ben was "crazy drunk all the time nearly." She had manure hauled in and wheat planted on the land Ben had been using in return for his labors.[301]

The summer of 1861 boded well for crops. In early June Pamelia wrote, "My corn and potatoes look well for the time they have been planted," but "the worms have troubled my small seeds." Her use of the pronoun "my" to describe the garden characterized her letters of this period, reflecting her evolving sense of ownership in the family enterprises. "I have hoed some in my garden," she reported in another letter, adding, "[I] have a good one. . . . My corn [is] the best in town and all my garden I am told is the best one." She and Andrew had worked hard to keep the weeds down and the plants flourishing, but she reported a major setback: "I went down to the eight lots last night and their [Robert] Hamilton['s] little pigs had been in and rooted and spoilt a great many of my potatoes and cabage that I had worked so hard among when he was idleing in the barroom and other places."[302] Nonetheless, her next letter indicated that she had salvaged her vegetables and continued to be pleased with the growth of her corn and wheat, so that she was able to report, "I think we will have all the flour and vegitibles we shall need."[303]

News of livestock was equally good — the old cow had a new calf and the young one gave a "large mess of milk."[304] Pamelia made good use of the milk, reporting, "this morning I have put a cheese in the press it will [go] twelve or fourteen pounds." She had some nice young pigs, and they were doing well.[305] News from the girls was heartening as well. They had completed their examinations without missing a single question, and Mr. Stephens had agreed to send them to a private school during the months when the public school was not open.[306] Mary Agnes wrote that she and Luella were studying five subjects, "Geography Arithmects, . . . composition Reading and spelling" and concluded, "we like the [new] school very much."[307] These letters contain no mention of their earlier plans to join their father in the spring, though Stephens himself did depart for Colorado early in May.[308]

Upon his arrival in Mountain City, Stephens discovered a despondent James Fergus. James had just written Pamelia that he was contemplating selling out his interest in the quartz mill "on the best terms I can," but he was not optimistic about those terms:

> I cannot expect much, and may loose the $1000 I put in from Stephens altogether, besides my winters work which has been a very hard one. I never worked so hard in my life nor lived so poor and I will not do it any longer if I never make any thing. I have not complained of what people usually call *bad luck* but some times I think my cup of misery and misfortune is full . . . if some of our friends could see how we have to work and live here and see how we look sometimes they would not be so fast for coming out.

Characteristically, he saw his dismal plight as reason for optimism: "Not being able to get any lower, every change I make must be for the better, which makes me hope on."[309]

He had indeed had a run of bad luck. In late April, within a month of Robert Russell's accident, James himself had nearly been killed while being lifted out of a shaft by rope. The loop in which his foot had been resting broke, leaving him dangling by his hold on the rope, twenty-six feet from the surface and eighty feet from the bottom of the shaft. Though shaken, he was proud of his survival, boasting, "I had no idea of having my brains knocked out by a fall of 80 feet on to the rocks at the bottom of a mine in the Rocky Mountains."[310]

He had been with Russell, "whose arm is getting well," to see Alexander Paul, whom he described as a hardworking man who was "doing his best," but "put too much of his labor into claims for a man that had so large a family to support."[311] Though Paul had been "unfortunate in the way of getting or sending money to his family," James's unbounded optimism shone on the prospects of others as well as on his own, and he predicted that by fall Paul would "do well."[312] Unable to wait any longer for the promised change in fortune, Mary Paul had made the contemplated move to St. Cloud to look for work. When Pamelia wrote the news to James, she did not mention whether Mary had taken the six children with her or had left them at home.[313]

The Russells were faring well enough and had received a long letter from Robert. He was "glad that the people there [at home] are for the Union. It is a noble thing and may God save . . . the American Republic, for it is the haven to all nations and the pride of the world. I hope to get back and see the Stars and Stripes still waving over this our land of adoption." After assuring his wife that he had "not so bad an opinion of my old queen as she thinks," he thanked her for the cherished picture of his new son and told her she could "name the boy [her]self."[314]

His letter was divided into separate sections directed to each of his three eldest children. He asked sixteen-year-old Robert to plant some corn and enough cabbage "to make at least one barrel of crout," a delicacy he sorely missed in the mountains. He complimented twelve-year-old Agnes on her writing, comparing it favorably with his own, and he advised fourteen-year-old Jeannie to bathe her sprained wrist "with salt and sweet milk."[315]

Russell's own injuries had mended and he was back at work: "We are down 125 feet and it is all dry and comfortable only we get pretty black — black as coal diggers. . . . I work week about, nights and days. I have $3.50 a shift. This week I will have seven shifts making $24.50. This is about as high as they are paying for good blasters." He closed on a somber note: "Last week there was a man killed and another badly hurt. The shaft broke in on them. The man that got killed had a wife and two children [here with him]. They are going to raise money to send them home."[316]

Those miners "still among the living" had been hampered by late snows, and James Fergus talked of extending his stay in the West until the quartz mill was well established, delaying his return to Little Falls until at least late autumn.[317] Alarmed at such hints that he might stay even longer, Pamelia urged, "You must come . . . and see [to] your buissness here."[318]

The business most on her mind was payment of taxes. Frustrated by Freeman's lack of attention to them, she had fretted: "Charly seems very kind but not enough interest nor energy to suit me people say so I here why dont she have Charly do this and that he has done a good many things and is willing but the most of my little afairs I prefer to do my self."[319] Even so, she was reluctant to tackle something so far beyond her ken as the taxes: "I know nothing about those things onley they have to be payed if they are advertised at cost I go [about] but little [and] h[ear] but little of mans bussiness but I saw something in the paper that called my attention to it I did not know what to do Mother says go and see to it yourself then you will know." Heeding Mahala's advice, she had gone down to check on the taxes herself, reporting, "I only had to regret I had not went before."[320]

Having found out exactly what they owed, she had passed that information on to Freeman and had received his assurance that he would collect enough old notes to make the payment. She had heard no more from him and the deadline was fast approaching. "Now the first day of June is near at hand and I suppose thirty or forty dolars has got to be had for taxes I have written you before about it. . . . Probley if I new more about such things they would not trouble me as much."[321]

Though she feared their property would be sold to the highest bidder, they were spared that disaster. "Our taxes are not payed yet," she reported nine days after the deadline, "but as good luck would have it Mr Elwell did not send the list in time to be advertised in that paper so now they will have to lay over till fall Charley did not make any effort to pay them. I spoke to him as much as I dast to but the appointed time come [and he did nothing]."[322]

She was hardly in a position to pay the taxes herself, for she could not sell butter "at any price" and so had no income to speak of. Still, she maintained, "if it was not for the trouble of our properity or the fix thing[s] are in I should feel first rate tending to my little duties but if I feel satisfide with them the thought will come what does it all amount to sure enough."[323] Weeks later James wrote, "I am sorry that times is so hard and that you find so much trouble about the property . . . now my advice to you is this. . . . Do the best you can and let trouble and hard times go."[324]

As frequently as Pamelia read "[just] do the best you can" in James's letters, his advice was difficult to follow. In the midst of her tax worries, she heard rumors that the company was about to levy another round of assessments. She had also just weathered another visit from Tuttle, who had come into town, "blowed as usul [and] got great sympthy from some." The unpleasant scene heightened her determination to leave Little Falls:

> Yes Fergus go any where to get out of the sound of little falls. . . . I heard from the Children last week they seem contented I hate to have them ever come back to Little Falls I want to bid farwell to it We may as well be in the debths of the forest as here.[325]

Realizing she had perhaps complained too much about her lot, she closed with "good by next time I will feel better may be."

Caught up as he was with troubles in Mountain City, Fergus dismissed business problems at home. "I am sorry the dam is going or has gone out," he wrote, "but it cannot be helped. They have not got Fergus now to blame for all their mishaps."[326] Though free of blame for the latest failure of the dam at Little Falls, Fergus had new worries. In the eight months he had been in the area, Mountain City had grown to include ten stores, two hotels, a theater, a Masonic hall, and six quartz mills. Yet those mills, including his own, were now idle and the workers penniless. Once more he had failed to provide work for men who had depended upon his business for a livelihood.[327]

In a letter written months later to his brother William, James explained his activities following the acknowledged failure of the quartz mill in a single sentence: "After losing all I had . . . in this milling and mining operation I went off west some two hundred miles to the Snake Mountains."[328] Cut off from civilization and depressed over his failures, James wrote very few letters home that summer of 1861, leaving Pamelia at a loss as to his health and well-being, as well as his financial situation. Sensing James's despair, yet unaware of its extent, Pamelia wrote urging him "to settel all up their and come back and pick up the titles you have here I don't see why we cannot live on the crumes as well as eanybody."[329]

Her urging him to come home did not mean that she was any less eager to leave Little Falls. Her first choice was to return to Illinois. According to her sister Mary McHose, the orchards there were "white with fruit blosomes," and Luella had written that "the gardens wer full of flowers [so] you se[e] that is the country [for us]." Anticipating James's reaction to her suggestion, she added, "I know you hate to put your hand to the plow and look back but I dont see any thing here to live for not even a school."[330]

There had, indeed, been no school since Taylor joined the Union Army. And there had been little church, either, though Pamelia knew that fact would hardly alarm her agnostic husband. There was talk of bringing in a Congregationalist minister, but Pamelia conceded, "We have not had any preaching this long time [and] I do not know but we are just as good." Her situation in general was comfortable enough, though she fretted over those things over which she had no control, noting, "I can live on very little and alone not trouble a bit if it is nesary but I do hate to see others make sport of your hard earnings."[331]

Her loneliness was often acute, and she wrote that she "nedles to say droped now and then a tear. I know it is babyish but I canot help it and just as often as I sit down to drop a few lines to you [the tears] will come right along." The tears fell even when matters at home went well: "Every thing looks pleasent and how little we enjoy it [It] is hard for us to enjoy any thing if I do half forget myself in glea or joy suden as [it is] thought it is chect by some thing seems to say whare is he then the thought of all your hardships and why need I try for comfort."[332] As still more time passed with no word from James, she grew more despondent: "Four weeks is a long time to look for a letter but hope keeps . . . the heart whole."[333] And she continued to write: "I was again disipointed yesterday in not getting a letter from you but you say keep writing and so I will although [there is] nothing new that I can write."[334] "My Dear Husband," she wrote on the last day of June, "I am once more seated at your old desk just where you have sit many long tedious hours thoug[h] the time seems long since then and very long when we are looking for a letter from you as we have these last four weeks and all in vain."[335]

Not having heard from James since late spring, Pamelia was

growing more desperate with each passing day. "O how anxious we are looking for a letter from you Dear *Husband*," she wrote in mid-July. "This is the fifth or six letter I have written since having any from you." She was well aware that George Stephens was now in Colorado, and she could only hope he would find James and send news. She half-expected that news would be a report of James's journey home: "If you are in the land of the living I think and hope that you are on your way home and it may be posible you will drop in suddingly when I am not lookin for you." Even though she half believed that wish and thought he might be out of reach of her letters, she continued to write them: "You told me to keep writing and so I will."[336]

Ironically, as Pamelia waited out the summer with no word from James, Amanda Smith was hearing from her husband with uncharacteristic frequency — receiving two letters within weeks of each other. One came in mid-May: "Mrs Smith has a letter from the Doctor from Omaha he is going to Fort Kerney [Fort Kearney, Nebraska]." The other in early June: "Mrs Smith has heard from the Docter he was then on his way to Fort Kerney she expects him to send for her."[337] That news was confirmed by a letter from the doctor himself to Fergus. Late in August, Smith wrote that he had spent some time with Lewis Stone at Fort Kearney. Judge Stone was on his way home with instructions to Amanda that she and the children were to travel to St. Joseph, where the doctor would meet them and take them to Kearney City for the winter. In the spring they would set out together for the mountains of Colorado Territory. There was also the possibility that they might stay on in Kearney City, where Timothy was considering buying part interest in a store. Anyplace in the West offered brighter prospects than anyplace in Minnesota. By Amanda's own report, Little Falls was "played out." A better life beckoned from afar.[338]

Enthusiastic as he was about his family's move west, Smith was typically silent on such details as the exact time and place of the proposed meeting in St. Joseph. But at least his plans clearly included her and the children, and the ever-trusting Amanda could talk of nothing but the promised reunion. Timothy's failure to return to Little Falls on schedule was forgiven if not forgotten. After all, she had the doctor's own report to Judge Stone: Too sick to travel, he had wintered over in Omaha and had been in Kearney City since May.

The doctor's report of his activities was contradicted by rumors circulating in the gold camps. Alexander Paul sent word to James Fergus that he had talked with a man who had seen Smith in St. Joseph during the winter. The fellow reported that the "Dr. was flat broke and was not doing any thing that he knew of, unless gambling when he could get anything to gamble with." This news arrived in the one letter Pamelia received in the summer of 1861, and it was accompanied by a disclaimer: "I give it just as I heard it, and you had better not repeat it further than telling Charly Freeman and let him tell Mrs Smith what he thinks best about it" and by an added comment that probably held as much truth for James himself at that moment as for the good doctor: "I think myself that the Dr is hard up somewhere, cant get home and don't like to write to his wife."[339]

That wife was soon in readiness for the trip, though her possessions were, by now, meager, consisting only of "what she has not sold [and] she has been selling the last six months not to get money that is unexpected but [to get what she needs] to live on." Pamelia had her doubts that the long-awaited journey would ever take place: "I hardly think she has money to take her home but she is going to start I expect her here tonight she will stay among her friends a day or two."[340]

If Amanda and the children did indeed leave Little Falls in September 1861, they left with even less than they had planned to take. At news of her impending departure, Hall had her possessions attached, citing a debt the doctor owed him. When "Uncle Lewis Stone" wrote him the news, Timothy Smith was irate: "That I owe debts in Minnesota and elsewhere I acknowledge and my friends know that as soon as I can I will pay but that I owe Hall one cent no body who knows me and my relations to Hall will believe."[341] Assuming that by now Fergus was most likely heading east, Smith wrote a letter asking him to intercede once he reached Little Falls: "I wish you would look after [the matter] and see that Hall's folks dont get Nellie's Doll and Ikes saddle. I will send you money to redeem such things as my family had become attached to."[342]

Pamelia was far less sure than Doc Smith that James Fergus would be coming home to his family. Through the long period in which she had received no letters, she had feared the worst. Thus when James's letter of July 10 finally arrived in early September, it was more than welcome, despite its dismal contents. Scurvy had plagued him all summer, keeping his gums and teeth sore and his skin broken out in an angry rash. And he had at last come to realize that he could not continue long at this sort of work, writing, "I want to do something, get into some shape to make money . . . in an easier way than I have been trying in these mountains or I won't last very long . . . the longer I stay here the poorer I get I believe there are more broken men in these mountains than in Minnesota, at least three out of every four mills are laying idle."[343] Pamelia's spirits were buoyed; though he was broke, ill, and discouraged, at least James was alive.

When George Stephens saw the hopeless situation surrounding the quartz mill, he offered to pay all Fergus's expenses if he would pack up and go home. "He sees . . . that there is [no] certainty of my makeing money at present," James wrote, "and that if I was at home I might collect some thing on old debts and prepare either to go into some business in Minnesota or come out here next spring with my family." But James was not yet willing to give up and go back to Minnesota with nothing to show for his labors: "Although flat broke like thousands of others here I thought it my duty to decline all those friendly offers, and go home later in the season."[344] A day later, he followed that hint of his homecoming with the words Pamelia had waited so long to hear: "I will be home this fall or may be sooner and either bring the children with me, if they are not home before that time, or send for them soon after."[345]

At about the time she learned the proposed dates of James's return, Pamelia received word that Mary Agnes and Luella were getting homesick.[346] "I think if the children are discontented at Georges they better go to Sister Marys [in Geneseo]," Pamelia suggested to James, unwilling that they should come home to the education that Little Falls would offer. Even so, she noted, "[Their mother] would be very happy indeed to see [them] . . . and have them near her [so] that she could put her arm[s] all around them at night and say these are mine."[347]

She was doubly lonely, for after more than a year in Little Falls, Mahala had finally returned home to Geneseo. She had begun to make plans for departure in late April when she received news that there were problems developing between her sons concerning the family farm, but she had delayed for two months while Jane Dillin looked in vain for a teaching job in the Little Falls area. Indians had again caused Mahala great worry, for she had heard that in the absence of the regular army, the Dakota were planning raids in the area. Better to travel while she could than be trapped in Little Falls during any agitation. Though reluctant to leave her daughter and grandchildren in such a perilous situation, she had been increasingly anxious to get home.[348]

Upon Mahala's departure in midsummer, Pamelia told James, "Probley you will feel bad when you here that I am alone but you need not I shall try and get a girl to come and go to school which I think I can or get a couple of boarders."[349] She was comforted at the thought that Grandmother Dillin would now be close to Mary Agnes and Luella, but she added, "they are *my children*. It is a great trial to have them away, but I counted the cost before they went."[350]

Reaching home, Mahala reported that the girls were quite ready to return to their mother. Mrs. Stephens had even made traveling dresses for them, but had said they were welcome to stay, since it would be hard to get them home, due to the war and the lack of available escorts. While it was true that the girls were very homesick, Pamelia hoped that Mahala's return might make them more willing to stay on.[351]

Schooling opportunities in Little Falls were worse than ever. Though Andrew was attending classes taught by a Mr. Morse, the man could not maintain control of the children and Pamelia planned to take the boy out of school entirely if matters did not improve. Ironically, Jane Dillin would have been a welcome addition to the school in Little Falls, according to Pamelia, who reported: "She would have taught cheaper and I think better than [any teacher] we have had for a long time."[352] But Jane had gone with Mahala to Illinois, having been unable to find employment there or in any of the surrounding school districts, since "in all the districkets some frind [of the board members] was chosen."[353]

Upon reading of Pamelia's intention to get a girl to board with her, James advised, "Don't take boarders unless for company *It won't pay*. Live by yourself and take your comfort. I have good courage and although unfortunate here I don't mean always to be poor. It will be our turn by and by."[354] He upbraided her for losing heart:

Your letter of August 5th was received by last mail by which I see that you are somewhat discouraged and have the blues. This is occasioned more than anything else by your being newly alone but keep up good spirits amuse yourself as well as you can. . . . Recollect there are often a great many ups and downs in this world and we have got to take them as they come our duty is simply to do the best we can and then be contented.[355]

James reiterated his earlier promise: "I will be home sometime this fall and see to things." As for coming sooner, he argued, "If the times are really as hard as you think they are I can do little or nothing there, and that very fact makes me the more anxious to try and find something for a future business here where there is some money." When she was tempted to feel sorry for herself, he wrote: "Just think how much hard work i have done since I have been here and how much I have endured and have not made one cent. Still I have hopes."[356] She replied, "You say you think I had the blues I dont think so . . . [as for] amusement I need none out side of my own doorstep I am buisy all the time the neighbours complain of my staying at home as much as ever and I am hapyer in so doing than I can be in visiting . . . [though] of cours their are exceptions."[357]

Despite her attempts to keep up good spirits, Pamelia's blues persisted. She was concerned about her brother Hiram, who was serving in the Union Army. "Our Minnesota folks here are very much pleased with the conduct of the Minnesota Regiment at the battle of Mannassus," she had reported earlier, but she ached at the prospect of her brother's involvement in the conflict.[358] Further, the company had moved to collect the assessments she had chosen not to pay the previous fall, and James's shares had been bid off for lack of payment.[359] In all Pamelia's darkness, Lillie provided the one bright spot. She was fascinated with the Freeman's new baby girl—"She says she is going over to Freeman['s] to see the baby"—and she was sensitive to her mother's moods and determined to cheer her up: "Lillie says dont cry Mam[a] papa will [be home] to morrow and . . . [fetch you a horse] and me [a horse] . . . no use of crying and so who could cry with such advice."[360]

At least James was homeward bound. His letters of late August continued to assure her that he and O. J. Rockwell were attempting to tie up business matters in the mountains so that they could start the long journey home.[361] James Dillin would not be coming with them. He had joined Colorado's First Regiment and was at Camp Weld.[362] Other friends in the mines, notably Robert Russell and Alexander Paul, were undecided. However, by the time Pamelia received James's letter, Judge Stone was already enjoying the comforts of home in Platte River, though, as James had predicted, "the old man" had come home "flat broke."[363]

Stone's financial condition did not differ that radically from Fergus's, though Fergus had a subtle way of shifting some of the blame for his failure to make his fortune: "I could do something . . . if I was to stay here this winter, but I promised you I would come home and I will." He would spend two weeks working as a millwright to earn the money he needed for the journey, then he and Rockwell would set out on September 15, going first to Moline so that he could pick up the girls.[364]

Since his homecoming would mean his availability to creditors, he advised Pamelia:

> You had better not say anything about my coming home if I leave at the time I expect to I will be home about the 25th of October if I don't stop to long at Moline Geneseo, etc—you need not direct any more letters to me here unless I write you again to do so but you may enclose one *inside* of one to one of the girls at Moline . . . about the last of this month—I don't want it directed to me because the Co. owe some there and they might bother me. You need not tell any body when I am coming home.[365]

At home, Pamelia had taken in a single boarder—tinsmith Robert Hamilton, a twenty-four-year-old native of Ireland who had been in Little Falls a couple of years and who had become a frequent visitor in the Fergus home during Jane Dillin's long sojourn there. "I had Robrt come here becaus I was liable to be sick in the night," Pamelia wrote James, "then it was lonesome to be all entirely alone and it was almost imposible [to] awake Andrew. . . . I have not had but one sick spell since grandma went away nor any since Robrt came but before [he moved in] I was unwell [for] two or three weeks the neighbors was very kind [to] come and stayed with me and I was advised to get some one [and] he [Hamilton] had spoken to me a long time ago."[366]

Hamilton had been close by, even before his move into the Fergus home, for he had had his little house moved down by their lot in early May. The house had "the Post ofice in front and tinshop in back," and Robert was prospering, despite the poor economy.[367]

Still, he was lonely and wanted someone to cook and wash for him. Moving in with Pamelia and the children seemed an ideal solution to his problem and hers.[368]

But by the time this letter arrived, James had left the mountains. There is no record of how he traveled or of exactly when he reached Moline, but it is quite likely he followed the route George Stephens had taken a few weeks earlier — traveling by wagon or coach to Denver, then joining a train from Denver to Omaha and on to Moline.[369] Stopping in Moline to pick up his daughters, James pushed on north, and by early November 1861, the Fergus family of Little Falls was reunited, though James Fergus was even then planning a future in which Little Falls played no part.[370]

4

The Interim

SOME IDEA of James Fergus's reaction to his homecoming can be gleaned from a letter he wrote to his brother William in Scotland. After explaining that Mary Agnes and Luella had been going to school in Moline since September 1860, he added, "I came that way and brought them home with me. So you may suppose there was a happy meeting when I came home." That letter makes clear his pride in Pamelia's accomplishments: "My wife had been living pretty much alone during the last summer. Her mother had been with her the year before but was obliged to go home to Illinois where she lives last spring. My wife had only our little son 10 years old and youngest daughter 3 at home with her in a very large house. She had not seen the girls for over a year, and they were 500 miles from home I had been gone nearly twenty months and was about 1200 miles from the girls."[1]

Though there is no written record of Pamelia's reaction to her long-delayed reunion with James, the tone of her letters over the nineteen months of his absence would suggest that she was pleased and relieved to have her husband home again, grizzled and worn as he was. She had been lonely and concerned about his health. Now she had his company and could see that he was well. And his homecoming also meant reunion with her daughters. It had been over a year since she had seen them, and in their absence Mary Agnes had turned fifteen, Luella thirteen. Having said good-bye to two little girls, she welcomed home two young women.

James's return also meant an end to Pamelia's responsibilities as surrogate head of household. For one and one-half years she had held her own on unfamiliar ground. If company affairs were still hanging heavy, at least she had managed to save the land and livestock they would need to survive. And Fergus still had his tools and his reputation as millwright. Now that the family was reunited, they could eke out a living there in Little Falls or return to Illinois or Iowa, where Fergus had succeeded before and could succeed again.

But Pamelia had not taken seriously enough lines James had penned in the midst of his homecoming preparations:

> I have made up my mind that unless business is better in Minnesota than I think it is, or . . . I can get something there that I can make something at I will try to get back here next season either with or without my family and go into some steady business with some of my friends or if I can't do that to go in to mill wrighting.[2]

Certainly the situation James found on his return to Little Falls was, if anything, worse than it had been in 1860. While some of the larger industrial cities of the North were recovering from the economic depression that had pushed Fergus toward bankruptcy, frontier settlements like Little Falls remained "ded ded." Hearing rumors that James was home, creditors rushed in with reminders of unpaid bills and accumulating interest. A proud man, Fergus found it painful to admit that he had come home poorer than he left, though that admission was all he could offer those who circled about, waiting for their share of the gold he had vowed would be his.

Others waited for James to fulfill promises of another sort. Though Amanda had already left Little Falls, the Smith family still needed Fergus's help. The doctor's letter asking him "to make sure that Hall's folks don't get Nellie's Doll and Ike's saddle" was waiting for him when he got home.[3] And having decided against coming home himself, Robert Russell asked James's help in a letter whose phonetic spellings suggest the author's Scottish origins:

> I was glad to hear from you that you got home safe and wall i do think that if i was home all whould bee right but i will not bee home this winter nor do i now whan or whan i will have the means. . . . I shall bee glad to have you cuall and see my wife and if the[y] nead any thing that you can do for tham you will do me a grait faivar and i will bee glaid to return the complament if in my pour [power] writte to me and i will be glad to writte to you and i do think that this country will bee all right yet give my best respicks to Louas Stone and all inquring frands and my love to my wife and famaly.[4]

Lewis Stone had arrived home that fall, some few months before Fergus, and he was already making plans to return to the mines — his lack of success on the first trip notwithstanding. This time the judge intended to take his wife with him.[5] There was some question as to whether the Russells would accompany the Stones. Though Robert Russell had hoped to persuade Agnes to bring the family west with the judge, since "being along with one that had crost the plains would be a grait help [to them]," she had so far refused to consider the plan.[6] Never having completely regained her strength since the birth of her last child, Agnes protested that she had neither the physical nor financial resources she needed to prepare the family for the journey.

Mary Paul was not struggling with such decisions. Alexander Paul, like James Fergus and Judge Stone, had come home from the mines, but unlike them, he had no desire and no plans to return. Rather, he had given up the homestead at Platte River, Mary had quit her job at St. Cloud, and the family had moved to Little Falls, where Paul had taken up the plow he had once laid aside. In the coming spring he would be farming lots he rented from Fergus.

In the first round of visits, James Fergus also called on Dan Bosworth, whom he had not seen since Bosworth departed Colorado in mid-October 1860. The Bosworths had a new baby boy to show him—born in the fall of 1861. And Daniel had new work. Having finally begun to readjust to life in Minnesota, he had taken a job the previous summer, hauling timber along the Red River Road to markets in the north for fifteen dollars per month— an income that did little to temper his fascination with the West.[7]

Other men shared that fascination. Despite the fact that James Fergus had come home without the promised riches, some of his friends still hoped to seize the chance for themselves. From the first, John Ault had been especially eager for news from James's letters, and he queried Fergus closely upon his return. Having lost the Northern Hotel at the end of 1860, he and Margaretha had spent the last year running the officers' mess at Fort Ripley, but the prospects of life in Minnesota were not nearly so inviting to John Ault as those in the West.[8]

William Sturgis was of the same mind. Though his mills at Little Elk were doing well, the lure of the frontier still had a hold on him. He had left Michigan to found towns in Iowa and he had left Iowa to found towns in Minnesota. Moored too long in one spot while others moved on with their dreams, Sturgis pressed Fergus for more information on business prospects in the mining towns of Colorado Territory.

While Fergus knew that Sturgis and Ault had long maintained their interest in going west, he had assumed that Charles Freeman had given up on the idea. Yet it was Freeman who now seemed most likely to make the move. He was thinking of taking Abby and the baby to her parents' place in Iowa and leaving them there while he and his brothers-in-law explored the West. Fergus probably encouraged the plan; it would have been uncharacteristic of him to dissuade anyone from following a dream.

One who did not seek Fergus's counsel, but who was nevertheless also making plans to go west, was James Hall. Though he was not sharing the news with Fergus, he was talking to a reporter from a St. Cloud newspaper. As Morrison County was "advancing backward pretty fast," Hall told the reporter, he thought he would "get away while he had something to get away with." Fergus, reading Hall's comments in the paper, responded with a letter to the editor: The attorney had no call to speak so ill of Little Falls, since "it is well known that the [lawyer] brought little or nothing here with him . . . [yet] few families in the state have lived better or easier than his since." It was also well known that "Friend Hall had the peculiar faculty of getting 'big pay' for . . . a little fishing . . . a social game of cards, much social chat, and very little work." In closing, Fergus pointed out that the attorney had left many matters unsettled in Little Falls, and his fellow citizens hoped he would find somewhere else to live.[9]

In late February 1862, James received a somber letter from his brother William: "I have the mournful intelligence to tell you our Father is no more he departed this life on Thursday evening at half past seven o'clock that is the 23rd of January 1862 at the advanced age of 81 years." The old battle had at last ended. There would be no more opportunities for James Fergus to prove his worth to a father whose strict standards he had never quite measured up to. The man he had fled Scotland to avoid posed no further threats. And, despite earlier threats to the contrary, his father had indeed left something for the wayward son who had forsaken hearth and home, crossed an ocean, and committed himself to the American way of life — he had left him twenty pounds sterling, or about one hundred dollars.[10]

James responded to his brother with a note of condolence and instruction: "Give my love and sympathy to your mother [James's stepmother] who has so long been his companion and who has borne so patiently the peculiarities of his temper and who so nobly

and faithfully performed the duties of a mother to *all* his children."
His brother was to apply the twenty pounds sterling to the debt
James owed him from the failed Little Falls project. He felt that ob-
ligation keenly and saw little hope of any other means of repayment
in the near future, for "the war has ruined a country already pros-
trated by speculation."[11]

Though he saw the war as an obstacle to recovery in Little Falls,
James was convinced that it was a righteous conflict that must be
won by the Union:

> By the time this reaches you, you will have learned that the United
> States are very likely to crush the proslavery rebellion now waging
> against its government and with it I hope Slavery forever but this is
> not a matter so Easily accomplished as talked about over four mil-
> lions of slaves valued at an average of over a hundred pounds a
> piece, are not to be torn from those who think the[y] own them
> without a struggle. There is one thing certain however Slavery will
> never have the influence in governing the United States that it has
> had, and in most of the border states it will be done away with al-
> together.[12]

As the war continued, Fergus and others not directly involved in
the conflict waged battles of their own. Fighting to salvage what he
could of his business in Little Falls, James bartered and sold as much
property as he could, including land Pamelia had obtained from her
two brothers in exchange for her interest in her father's estate in Illinois.[13]

Through that winter and spring of 1862, Fergus was in touch
with the friends he had left behind in the mines. He heard several
times from Robert Russell, who had enticing news: Things were
"not so vary duall" there that winter. There were no fewer than
eleven mines going in Nevada City and all were doing well.
Though most of the lodes were paying off, Russell's own claim had
yet to turn a profit. Already seventy feet down, he would have to
go still deeper, and the venture had already drained him of every
dollar.[14] Two weeks later Russell had not yet struck "the black," but
he hoped "for the bast nothing like try try a gain thar has been a
good manay . . . thought i ought to stope but . . . i will not
stope for awhail . . . i have grait confadince in it yet." Russell was
committed not only to his claim, but to the West. "As faur as i can
see this is the place yes for a man and the place that's good for a man
is good for his famaly." He was sorry to hear that Fergus was "flat

brouch," but if he would "try and cum out" Russell would do as much for him as he possibly could.[15]

Later in the spring, Russell was ninety-five feet down in his shaft and still had not struck gold. He was "poore as a church mouse" but enjoying good health, and he was waiting for a letter from his wife advising him of her plans.[16] Robert knew that Elizabeth Stone "was making hir salf rathar bisie with regard to hir [Agnes's] afairs," and he was incensed: "Now she neid not give hir salf any bouthar about my wife or Childrens rags i belive that the[y] nevar cost hir eany thing."[17]

But Russell held his temper; he needed to remain in Stone's good graces, for he had written the judge asking him to trade Agnes's "old cattal" for a yoke of young oxen. With her two good cows and one yoke of oxen, he thought, his family would be able to make the journey safely. "My children have nevar seen mutch of the world nor traveled eany. . . . my wifs hilth is poore . . . [but] i think that the tripe would hilpe hir . . . the Doctr says she might stand it if she got fair wathar and you know that on the plains the wather is plasent." Robert was quite anxious to have his family join him. If Agnes did not make the trip with Judge Stone, she must come later, for Robert "nevar intand[ed]" to go back to Minnesota. Perhaps if Agnes did not come out with the Stones, she could make the trip whenever Fergus was ready to start west. But even as her husband continued to fashion her travel plans, Agnes made a firm decision: She was no longer thinking of coming out because the children were all in need of clothing and she had no money to outfit them. She would wait until Robert was able to send her the necessary funds.[18]

In no mood himself for waiting, Fergus remained firm in his resolve to seek his fortune in the West. But where? George Stephens was convinced that there was no money to be made in the Pikes Peak region, unless James would consider taking up freighting rather than mining.[19] His judgment was echoed by Pamelia's brother, James Dillin, who reported that prospecting in Colorado remained "a poor busyness."[20] Even as Fergus debated the wisdom of returning to Colorado, news of a rich new discovery in what was soon to become Idaho Territory suggested his destination. Getting to the new strike would be relatively simple. Congress had recently appropriated fifty thousand dollars to help ensure "the protection of overland emigrants to California, Oregon, and Washington Territory," and Captain James L. Fisk had been appointed to lead an expedition that would open a northern route to the Salmon River goldfields.[21] Late in the spring of 1862 James Fergus made up his mind: He would join the Fisk expedition and try his luck once more.

5

Montana Gold

THE SIRENS still sang for James Fergus. The disappointments of Pikes Peak were behind him. The goldfields of the Salmon River country now beckoned, and the Fisk expedition would lead him there. Commissioned as a hedge against increasing Indian hostility and named for its commander, Captain James Fisk, the Fisk expedition of 1862 — and others that would follow in later years — was intended to encourage overland emigration via a northern route as a means of tying Minnesota's destiny to the development of the Pacific Northwest. Loosely organized as a military maneuver and rendezvousing at forts along the way, the expedition was to follow the Stevens route, which had been laid out some ten years previously as the railway link to the Pacific. Like the Holmes train of 1862, which preceded it by a matter of weeks, the Fisk train was made up largely of Minnesotans. Two-thirds of the 130 members of the expedition were from the St. Anthony, Minneapolis, and St. Paul area; nine were from the Little Falls area.[1]

They were a varied lot. John Ault, who had left Margaretha to run the boardinghouse at Fort Ripley with the promise that he would send for her when he was established in the West, was making the trip in the company of two Fort Ripley acquaintances, Robert Ells, a lumberman from Maine, and C. H. Klein, a laborer known as Dutch Henry.[2] By the time Fergus had readied himself for the trip, Ault, Ells, and Klein had already driven their wagon down to St. Cloud to join the expedition while it was camped there over the third weekend in June, en route to Fort Abercrombie, the official assembly point.[3] David Bentley, formerly a carpenter in Little Falls but currently residing in Otter Tail County, and William Wright, a Little Falls blacksmith, were also joining the train.

William Sturgis had been ambivalent about his plans. First intending to take his family with him, he had later, inexplicably, decided that it was "too late in the season" for them to make the journey and had asked O. J. Rockwell to look after them and the mills in his absence. Rockwell had agreed, but then, at Fergus's urg-

The wagons of the 1866 Fisk expedition to Montana encamped in evening formation. Andrew J. Fisk, Captain Fisk's brother, is standing in the foreground.

ing, had decided to join the expedition himself, a last-minute move that left Sturgis thinking he had no choice but to stay in Minnesota. Rosanna was twenty-eight years old, she had no business experience, and she had six children at home. He hesitated to leave her in sole charge of affairs.[4]

James Fergus seems to have had no such compunctions. Pamelia would once again take over the household in his absence, and this time she would be managing without the help of Charles Freeman, who had bid farewell to the Ferguses in late spring. Freeman had originally planned to go west alone and leave Abby and year-old Kate with relatives in Iowa while he went on to the Salmon River mines. Ultimately he decided to keep the family together and continue along the Oregon Trail with an eye toward establishing a business in Walla Walla, Washington Territory, or in Portland, Oregon. As James made preparations for his own journey, the Freemans were already a month into their long trip across the plains.[5]

Freeman would not be around to offer advice, and the company records were in Pamelia's care: "I give you the notes and the most important books to take care of let nobody have them but Gravel and Butler and not them if Tuttle is about. . . . If Tuttle comes up keep the books I give you out of his way and don't let him have the notes but tell him that I offered all my property to our creditors while I was back except our homestead and they can have it yet and that is all I can do."[6]

James penned those instructions in a June 22, 1862, memorandum he left for Pamelia, a document much like the one he had left her two years earlier. "Mrs. Fergus," he opened, "I expect to be back next winter, but in case I should stay longer than I intend I leave the following memorandum for your assistance." This time he assured her there was little in the way of company business for her to tend to—nothing that could not wait for his return. However, she still had the control of all lots in his brother William's name, as she had had during his previous absence, as well as "control of certain lots belonging to George Stephens" through the same power of attorney.[7]

He noted that she had twenty-five dollars in cash and reminded her of her other sources of funds or credit. Butler would let her have up to fifty dollars in goods from the store. She had a small note against a John Shea, and Benjamin Daggett would pay her "something for the use of the barn." She had "plenty of vegetables growing . . . two cows and some hogs"; she had a note from a Mr. Rice that she could apply toward more meat for the family, and James was sure that Alexander Paul, who owed him money on a note, would let her have potatoes and turnips. Because he was taking all the flour the family had, James instructed Pamelia to order more from the mill at Sauk Rapids; Emma Fletcher still owed him payments on her husband's old debt. Since selling an occasional sack of flour could be another source of income, he advised Pamelia to get as much as she could from Mrs. Fletcher and keep a few extra sacks on hand.[8]

After admonishing her to "keep Andrew from the water and from going any distance from home to hunt as he may easily get lost," James gave her instructions that revealed his ultimate plan: "Be preparing to go away next spring by selling every spare article you have. . . . sell one or both of your watches, the Red Barn, the eight lots, your land over the river or anything else you can sell." She was to write him in five days, addressing that letter to Fort Abercrombie, in twelve days to Pembina, in one month to Fort Benton, and after that to the Salmon River gold mines.[9]

The note to Pamelia completed, his plans for the family's move to the West fairly well formulated, James Fergus left Little Falls once more, this time traveling west to Long Prairie, then south to

Round Prairie and Sauk Centre and through the Alexandria woods to Fort Abercrombie, where the Fisk expedition was gathering for the trip across the plains. On their way to the fort, he and O. J. Rockwell stopped in Long Prairie, where they ate a meal with Philo and Sarah Farnham. They saw Caroline Bosworth with her two little boys, and later that evening they encountered Daniel Bosworth hauling logs along the Red River Road, and stopped a while with him.[10]

On July 4, Fergus camped two miles from Fort Abercrombie, choosing to stay clear of the holiday festivities in full swing at the fort and spend his time repairing his wagon tongue, broken when a badger startled his steers. Soon after his arrival in the area, he was "very much surprised" to receive "a letter from Sturgis that he was on the way." Having made hurried arrangements for his mill foreman, Edward Grady, to act as his agent for operations at the mills, William had left Rosanna in charge of all his other affairs and was on his way belatedly to Fort Abercrombie. Though Sturgis was forty miles from Fort Abercrombie at the time he wrote, James predicted, "As we will only go about six miles the first day . . . , [Sturgis] will easily catch up with us."[11]

Though some of the emigrants urged Captain Fisk to follow the example set by the Holmes train and take a 250-mile detour that would skirt Dakota territory, Fisk remained firm in his decision to follow the Stevens route as originally planned. His one concession to the dissenters was the acquisition of one of Fort Abercrombie's twelve-pound howitzers as insurance against Indian attack.[12] The captain's decision to take the direct route meant that there would be no scheduled mail service until the expedition reached Fort Benton around the first week in September. Since mail from that fort took weeks to make its way to the States, Pamelia could not expect to hear from James until at least October. That would mean three months without letters. It was more than either of them had anticipated, yet it was just one more inconvenience to be endured. Once James was settled in the mining camps, they could hope for better communication.[13]

For now, he was intent on firing a final barrage of advice: "I hope you will keep your temper and recollect that you have considerable responsibility resting on you now. I hope also that the children will agree well with each other and do all they can to help their mother and that Andrew will recollect [that since] . . . Pa is gone he must do what he can to fill Pa's place stay at home help about the crops etc." Pamelia was to see that her crops were well secured, her cellar wall fixed, and her woodshed filled with dry wood by fall.[14] "I Expect to find a place where we can move to next season," James reminded her. "Sell off any spare furniture you have got as we can have little or none over this road if we go this way. You must keep this business of moving next season in mind and shape your business accordingly. If we go we will probably take 3 waggon 3 yoke of oxen and 3 yoke of cows."[15]

A few days later he reported that the expedition had moved only twenty miles the first three days, delayed by the need to build several bridges.[16] Sturgis had caught up with them easily, as had John Ault, who had been plagued by bad luck since his departure from Fort Ripley.[17] By Fergus's own estimate, there were 50 wagons, 150 men, and a number of families on the expedition, but only one with small children. The sight of the women and children made him lonely, and he noted, "I wish you were all along but I hope to take you over the same road next year."[18]

At home in Little Falls, Pamelia was attempting to follow her husband's list of instructions. On June 30, five days after his departure, she dutifully sent a letter to Fort Abercrombie. "The children are all [being] very good," she wrote, "I was afraid I should have trouble with Andrew but he does very well." There had been illness: "Luella is almost blind with sore eyes Mary had the rheumatism quite bad and Lillie has . . . had sick spells all are better now." Having had some experience in seeing Papa off, the family had settled into a routine. "After you went away," Pamelia reported, "[Lillie] set down and wrote grandma and Jenne [Jane] a leter that you had gone and they must come ageine as if it was a natural consquence."[19]

They had killed a little pig and were going to have green peas, beans, and roast pig for the Fourth of July. "How I wish you had some," she wrote, "but you will be a great ways from home."[20] At the thought of the miles that stretched between them, her old apprehensions returned: "You did not look very well when you left," she admonished, "make you [a] good bed in your wagon now don't sleep on the ground if it [is] for nothing else than to keep out of the way of snakes." She begged him to "write every chance."[21]

With the weather threatening rain, she had asked William Sturgis to buy James "an oil cloth coat" on his way to Fort Abercrombie, but she could not be sure he had found one.[22] Even as she made that last effort to ensure her husband's health and comfort, Pamelia must have realized the futility of her actions. Months, perhaps years, would pass before she saw him again. His well-being was no longer in her hands.

Though he had been told that he could send no letters between Fort Abercrombie and Fort Benton, James was able to post one at Fort Union, sending it by a guide returning to Minnesota. The Fisk train arrived at the fort on August 11, having seen no other emigrants, but many Indians, during their month on the trail. None of the Indians had attacked, though they had made several attempts to steal horses under cover of darkness. Thousands of buffalo roamed the northern plains across which they had traveled, and the expedition had killed "several hundred besides some antelope and a grisly bear, so we have had plenty of fresh meat of the best kind." A buffalo shot the night before was lying "a few rods from where I write with only some of the best meat cut out."[23]

Wood was scarce, and most of their cooking was done over fires of buffalo dung. Aside from the fresh meat, food was poor, and the one spring they had found "came off a coal mine." In general they drank from seeps and ponds whose water was brackish and foul, though fairly abundant. James blamed the water for the fact that he had been sick for most of the journey, though he had felt well enough to drive his own team. He had dropped a wagon tongue on his instep and was lame for several days, but was now better. They had largely blazed their own trail until a few days back, when they had fallen into the tracks of the Holmes expedition where it had joined the Stevens route. They were now 376 miles from Fort Benton, with plans to depart the next day.[24]

As was his custom, James included in his letter news of other Little Falls citizens who were also bound for the Salmon River country: "Our party consists of Sturgis, Rockwell, Mr Wright, David Bently, a half breed [Peter Cardinell] and myself. Ault and Robert Ells cook at the same fire and sleep in our tent. Sturgis and Bently have a tent of their own."[25] He included as well a hint at a change of plans, directing Pamelia to write him "say once a month to Florence City Salmon River Gold Mines and one or two to 'Deer Camp' Bitter Root Valley, Washington Territory." In the midst of his travels, James had obviously heard of new gold strikes in the southwestern portion of present-day Montana and was keeping his options open. After reporting one wedding and one birth on the trail, the wanderer closed with "Secure for yourself a husbands and a father's blessing."[26]

Although Fergus was regularly picking up news from the mines, he had obviously not yet heard of an event that had recently occurred in Nevada City, Colorado Territory. There, on July 28, 1862, Robert Russell was caught in a mine cave-in. Fatally injured, he lived only five hours after being pulled from the rubble. At his request he was buried with Masonic honors by the Gregory Mines lodge of which he had been a member. In his report to the Russell family, the lodge master described it as "the largest funeral ever seen in the mountains, as befitted a loved and respected brother." Nothing was realized from his estate, and Agnes and his eight children were left in poverty. The eldest child was eighteen at that time and the youngest, whom Robert had never seen, was not yet two.[27]

Unaware of his friend's death, James Fergus continued on his way. The journey, though relatively uneventful, took its toll. "I have wished many times since I left home that I had you all along," James wrote, "[so] that I would not need to go back to Minnesota or travel this long road again, for it is a long journey when travelled with ox teams."[28]

"We can only send our wishes after you," Pamelia wrote in late July. "It seemes a long time to look ahead for you to come or even [to] here from you." Just how long, neither she nor James could have imagined. It was January 1863 before James received and read that letter, and the news it carried was by then nearly six months old. The children were doing well, though they all missed their father and their "Mother canot keep the tears back but then I know it foolish." Andrew had shot two ducks, and "if you ever saw one tickled boy he was one." He had also killed a piglet that morning. Since this one weighed twenty pounds, while the one they had killed for the Fourth of July celebration had weighed but ten, "you see they have grown some."[29]

Though her pride in her garden was still strong, she had been unable to get outside help in tending it:

We get a long with our hoeing as well as could be expected its im-possible to get any one to do . . . any thing we have done all so far [ourselves] our turnips look nice but we had a hard time of weeding them our corn is cleaner than [any other corn] I have seen . . . I am not ashamed of that and some of our potatos we have hoed twice their is a few under the hill that [we] hoed only once but . . . we must neglect something we have the two men yet boarding so you see we all do what we are able to.[30]

One of the two men boarding with Pamelia was twenty-five-year-old Robert Hamilton, the tinsmith who had moved into the Fergus home shortly before James's return from Pikes Peak. Now a prime prospect for the military draft, Robert was involved in much of the joking around town about cutting off toes and fingers to avoid induction.[31]

Avoiding induction might well have been in the minds of a few of the men who traveled west on the first Fisk expedition, though draft dodgers were not among the types James Fergus noted when, in later years, he characterized the entourage as a generally despicable band: "I have often thought that Minnesota got rid of more hard cases the trip I came through in than I ever saw together, broken down lumbermen that would pay nothing, broken down merchants, and scalawags of all sorts."[32] But that derogatory comment was made in retrospect. In 1862 Fergus saw himself and his fellow argonauts in much the same light as did the *St. Paul Press*—a "victorious army . . . sent forth by Minnesota to clear the path of emigration and commerce to the Pacific."[33]

When he and the other members of that army arrived in Fort Benton in early September, James heard enough rumors concerning the overpopulation of the Salmon River diggings to strengthen his earlier feelings that he would do well to try newer sites. "If we hear of any thing good as we go along [that is] within reach, or if we fall in with any good paying diggings ourselves I may stay [in this area] if not I will probably sell out [my team]. Keep on to Oregon. Select some place to settle or come home as soon and as well as I can."[34]

Knowing Pamelia's anxiety concerning the Plains Indians, James reported that encounters on the trail had all been friendly:

The first two weeks [after leaving Fort Union] we were surrounded by friendly Indians of the Crow and Gros Ventres tribes (the last name is French and is pronounced Gro Vaunt—in English big-belly—) They travelled with us camped near us, and traded with us

FORT BENTON;—HEAD OF STEAM NAVIGATION ON THE MISSOURI RIVER.

Fort Benton, 1862. From a lithograph by Gustavus Sohon in John Mullan, Report on the Construction of a Military Road from Fort Walla-Walla to Fort Benton *(1863).*

giving horses, buffalo robes and dressed skins in Exchange for blankets sugar tobacco etc. We are now in blackfeet country but have seen none of them yet although the[y] are [said to be] friendly. Several thousand of them left this post a few days ago. The traders say there is quite an excitement among the Indians themselves at the present time and the country is full of war parties. An Emigrant train is reported masacred south west of this [post] by the Snake Indians. Every thing however is quiet on our route and as we are pretty strong we do not consider ourselves in danger.[35]

At Fort Benton the Fisk expedition split up, with some members going on to the Salmon River region; others stopping at Prickly Pear, site of present-day Helena and about 120 miles southwest of the fort; and still others trying their luck at Deer Lodge, some sixty miles beyond Prickly Pear. Within three weeks James was writing Pamelia that he had cast his lot with the last group, and he made it clear that since it was too late to take oxen and cattle on to Salmon River, he planned to winter in the area, as did O. J. Rockwell, John Ault, William Sturgis, and David Bentley.[36]

The letter from Deer Lodge shows a concern for matters at home not evident in any of James's earlier writings, perhaps because he was keenly aware that he had no way of hearing from Pamelia any-

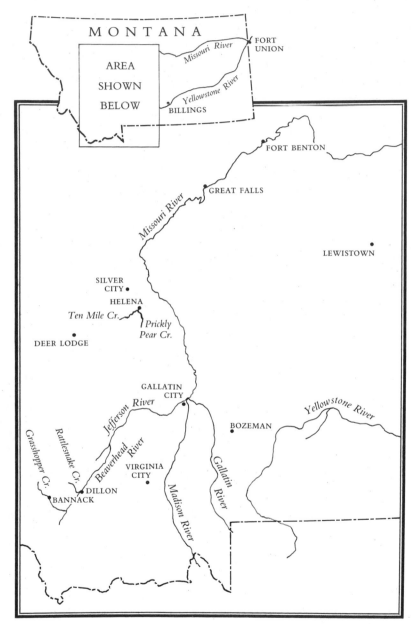

The Montana of James and Pamelia Fergus, showing places of importance to the Little Falls immigrants between 1862 and the 1880s

time soon: "I want to hear from you. To know that my family is at home alone without money, causes me a good deal of anxiety if I can get any United States bills I will send you some this winter, if I don't come home. I wish I was at home now to help you in with your crop."[37]

Ironically, even as he penned those words, Pamelia was bringing in her crops under the most fearful of circumstances. For, though the members of the Fisk expedition had experienced no hostile confrontations with Indians in the West, the families they had left behind found their lives threatened by Minnesota tribes. Within six weeks of the day Captain Fisk had borrowed the twelve-pound howitzer from Fort Abercrombie, the commander at that fort had reason to wish he had never let the gun go. Though caught off guard, he should by rights have anticipated the trouble. Minnesota's Indians were starving. The harvest of the preceding fall had been meager, and the United States government had fallen behind on its annuity payments — so that the Indians had not received either their allotted provisions or the money with which to buy those provisions.[38] The situation was further aggravated by the ineptitude — and corruption — of Indian agents, and there was every indication that things would get worse, not better. Ironically, at the height of the conflict, the forts that had once provided protection from Indian hostility were woefully understaffed, with the heart of the Union forces engaged against Confederate troops to the south.

Then on August 17, 1862, four Dakota killed five whites at a trading post near Acton. The incident sparked six weeks of battles in which at least 450 — perhaps as many as 800 — white citizens and soldiers and an undetermined number of Indians were killed.[39] Many more settlers had their homes raided and burned, and the rest lived in terror of attack. On August 27, a vanguard under the command of Colonel Henry H. Sibley lifted a week-long siege at Fort Ridgely. Surveying the situation, Governor Alexander Ramsey asked President Lincoln for federal assistance. Reinforcements eventually arrived, and the Battle of Wood Lake on September 23 effectively ended the war, though there were occasional raids in the months thereafter.[40] News of the fighting spread quickly to Little Falls, and though the Dakota did not usually venture that far north unless in pursuit of their longstanding enemies, the Ojibway, the citizens feared for their lives. Even as Sibley moved in to quell the

Dakota attacks to the southwest, Hole-in-the-Day the Younger, the Ojibway leader, was mounting an offensive at Crow Wing, a scant twenty miles to the north of Little Falls. Ojibway warriors from areas still farther north responded to his call, but by mid-September other tribal leaders had denounced Hole-in-the-Day in favor of a truce offered by the United States government.[41]

Even so, the people of Little Falls feared the worst. Though Fort Ripley lay between the town and the Ojibway forces, the garrison, undermanned and ill-equipped, scarcely inspired confidence. The town fathers hastily fortified the courthouse that William Sturgis had never completed, offering it as a nighttime refuge to townspeople and to families from outlying areas. Thus it was that Pamelia Fergus and her children spent each night for several weeks that September of 1862 sequestered with their neighbors in the barricaded courthouse. It was hardly a suitable refuge, for, according to a contemporary observer, the embattled citizens had only enough provisions to last forty-eight hours and "the supply of water was short."[42] Nonetheless, the citizens of Morrison County poured into town each evening, taking what comfort they could in the fact that they were not, at least, alone in their fear of the Indians.

Rosanna Sturgis brought her six children down from Little Elk.[43] The Bosworths and the Farnhams came in from Long Prairie.[44] And Agnes Russell brought seven of her children up from Platte River. Robert, her eighth and oldest, was away from the homestead haying at the beginning of the outbreak and returned to find the Russell house empty — to find, in fact, all of Platte River deserted.[45] During the daylight hours families returned to their homes and tried to restore some semblance of routine to their lives, but the harvest was slow and business suffered even more than usual, as everyone was preoccupied with thoughts of Indian raids.[46]

Sometime in September, Pamelia wrote James a detailed account of the Indian conflict at home, but since she followed his original instructions and directed that letter to Florence City, Salmon River Diggings, a site Fergus never reached, he never received her full account of the war.[47] Camped first at Deer Lodge and soon thereafter at the Beaverhead gold mines some one hundred miles to the south, he lived in such isolation from the outside world that he did not report reading newspaper accounts of the fighting in Minnesota until November 2, weeks after the fact:[48]

Fort Ripley, 1862

At Deer Lodge [sometime before the middle of October] we heard that the Sioux had been committing degradation on the Minnesota River, and yesterday we heard again that the Sioux had killed 500 whites on the Minnesota River, that Hole in the Day had stated to the whites at Crowwing, Little Falls, etc. that his Indians to the number of 500 to 700 were . . . joining the Sioux on a crusade against the whites, that he could not control them any longer, and that the whites must take care of themselves, that Gov Ramsey had called out every able bodied man in the State to defend it against the Indians . . . [and] that the Indians had cleaned the whites out of the Mississippi River down to St Cloud including Little Falls.[49]

James's immediate reaction was "that I had better go home at once," but rational thinking prevailed, and he decided "on reflection I thought that I would be too . . . late to lend any help but now I don't know what to do."[50] Ultimately, an article in a San Francisco paper that seemed to indicate that Little Falls was not in danger after all swayed his decision: "I hope Little Falls and vicinity is safe. It would be too late for me to do any good now and unless I hear worse news from Salt Lake . . . I will not come home at present. . . . I will leave for home the first bad news I hear which I will be very sorry [to have to do] . . . as I am now in a fair way of do-ing well."[51]

In a letter dated December 13, Fergus expanded on his knowledge: "We have received papers and telegraph dispatches giving us more definite accounts of the Indian massacres in Minnesota. I am satisfied for now that the Indians did not go as high as Little Falls and that you are all safe—and I hope well, but I have received no letters from you yet and don't expect any until the Express returns again."[52] Thus did James reassure himself that he had decided rightly not to return to Minnesota.

Eventually he and the other miners gained further information through letters from friends and relatives in Little Falls. "Ault and others got long letters telling them who was killed by the Indians among our acquaintances etc quite a number of newspapers came in," James reported, "but the[y] were all bought up in a few minutes at $1 each before I could get any."[53] Storekeeper William Butler had written, admitting, "Although there was no body hurt here . . . the most of us were awfully scared. I do not wish to ever . . . [go] through such [a] scene again."[54]

Butler reported that some of the women had been less cowardly than the men, and Pamelia's account of her confrontation with Reverend W. B. Dada, the Congregationalist minister, relayed nearly a year after the fact, bears out that observation. "I thought I would go among the neighbors and see if it was really so that the Indians wer[e] upon us," she recalled. "I met Mr Dada at the gate with two satchels and a bandbox said I why Mr dada what is the matter where are you going [you are] not going to leave [are you] he looked as though he had been crying said I Mr Dada I came to get consolation at this hour of trial and our preacher is the first one to leave. He wiped his eyes and went on."[55]

Other men, including Pamelia's boarder, Robert Hamilton, had stood their ground. "I fer one was prepaired for them and I was bound to die hard," Hamilton wrote. "Andrew and I loded all the guns in the . . . house and we were prepered for them all the time we ar expecting . . . more trouble in the Spring with the misrebal read skins the[y] will be afraid to do any thing more to the whites as long as we have so many companys of men in the State." According to Hamilton, the government had put three hundred Indians in jail, "getting them fat at *Uncle Sam's* expense." He predicted, "the[y] will keep them a while and let them go in time to fight us in the Spring."[56]

Another report of the scene in Morrison County came from the hand of Rosanna Sturgis, who gave a full, if exaggerated, account of those days in a letter to William that was not received until the next June, some eight months after it had been written.[57] "We are not safe at Little Elk and not much safer at Little Falls," Rosanna wrote.

> There is such excitement here about the Indians that I felt much troubled about your safety. . . . They have massacred 6 or 8 hundred men women & children. . . . Old man Mcdonald is supposed to be killed . . . Ed Russel and Charlie Batters and Andrew Austin and a Duckman that lived with Russel are all killed they were horribly mutillated. They say Charlie Batters was split open and his insides pulled out and strung along through the road. And Russel was choped up. They have a hundred & fifty prisoners now (women and children).
>
> It would make your blood run cold to read the acccount of the way they have butchered the whites. I read of one case where they hamstringed a woman and dragged her along by the feet until she died. Another where they cut a woman open and took her child from her and throwed it in her face. General Pope has been sent up among them to wipe them off the face of the earth, but I am afraid it will be like the Southern war it will be easier talked of than done.
>
> The Chipiways broke out at the same time that the Sioux did. It is generaly believed that it is a premeditated move, that the three tribes were to rise at the same time and try to clean the whites out of the whole of Minnisota. All that kept the Chipiwas back was the want of ammunition. . . .
>
> Everyone [in] the country moved . . . into Little Falls, and staid until it was settled. We were among the number. They had the court house fortified and we all slept there nights and went out to the houses day times. It is feared the Chipiways will rise again when it comes time for their payment. If they do I am sure I don't know what we will do. . . . Ed [Grady] says if there is another outbreak he will send us to St. Paul and set up to housekeeping and he will come back and fight it out but I hope we will not come to that.[58]

Rosanna added a postscript to her letter: "Don't borrow any trouble about us we will take care of ourselves if there is any trouble. But I am in hopes there will not be."[59] There was no more trouble, and Rosanna, in typical fashion, settled back into harness and got on with the business at hand.

Pamelia, too, was soon attending to routine matters. Assuming James had gotten the letter in which she had detailed the trauma they experienced during the Indian war, she later dismissed the matter out of hand: "But it is settled now I am told and we are here as well as could be expected though many of our neighbours have left the country." She commented on the larger implications of the conflict, noting that General Pope had been sent to St. Paul, six hundred soldiers had been assigned to Mille Lacs, and three hundred more had been sent to Fort Ripley. These were men sorely needed in the Civil War, since "our Southern genrals . . . manag[e] to prolong this war and soon their will be no more United States those six hundred solders is all useless and what an expence to government."[60]

News from that war had brought sadness to the citizens of Little Falls, especially to schoolchildren who recalled with fondness the teacher who had led them in recitations concerning the secessionists. "Mr Edward Taylor is killed," Luella wrote in a note to her father, "he lived at Bell Prarrie his wife has gone to the Fort [Ripley] with her two little children to wash for a living."[61]

Though there was hope of opening a session by mid-November, there had been no school in Little Falls for some months.[62] But the children had plenty of other things to keep them occupied. According to Luella, they had done their share to prepare the household for winter: "Agnes, Andrew, and my self have brought in the shed most full of wood it is full to the door Agnes and my hands are as rough as brick bats and so stiff I can hardly hold the pen to write."[63]

Winter was already in the air. Pamelia reported that "The wether is quite cold and every thing looks gloomy and lonesum," and Luella noted their first snow: "The other day it snowed a little and I called Lillie to the door and she jumped up and down and clapped her hands and said Goody Goody Papa is coming in the winter when the snow comes and she kept running to the door to see if you were coming she was very much disappointed to think you did not come." Lillie was now almost five, and her play often consisted of pretending to do the chores she saw her mother and siblings doing: "She is now ironing on the table and joggles so I can hardly write."[64] Later that day, as Luella sat down to add a note to her mother's letter, Lillie joined her and added a message of her own. When asked to translate her childish scribbles, she "read" them aloud: "Mrs Seers baby is dead and they took it out to the graveyard and put it in the ground."[65]

Despite the deaths of babies and the war with Indians, farm and

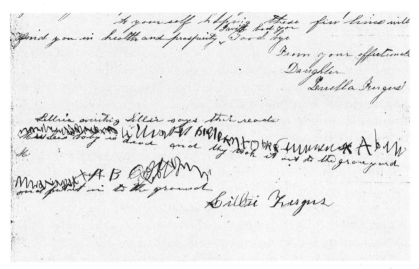

*Last page of a family letter to James on October 9, 1862, showing writing by
Luella and Lillie Fergus*

household affairs were on schedule. "We are doing as well as could
be expected," Pamelia reported. "We have all our crop in and the
celler nearly banked and our corn husked we had about forty
bushels in the ear. . . . I shall not have to ask many favours of any
body."[66] She had followed James's instructions and prevailed upon
Alexander Paul for her share of the turnips grown on the Fergus
lots, but reported, "Mr Paul as usual put all his turnips that he raised
on that land in his own celler. . . . I will keep watch of him and
get the pay for the turnips if I can so you see what is a mans
promise."[67]

Though she and the children seemed ready for a safe and comfortable winter, Pamelia could hardly bear to think of the unknown
conditions under which her husband would spend the season. The
last word she had received had been posted from Fort Benton in
September, and she had no clear idea of his whereabouts: "O Papa
[how] often we wish [for you] and talk of you and [wonder] how
we can live this long cold winter but that's not all when we wonder
whar Father is and then think away among the Indians . . . people
here have such fear of them that never can [we] think of them only
with dread."[68] Writing letters that she doubted he would ever receive provided so little comfort that Pamelia left many things un-

said. "I have a great deal to say and will be very patient till you come."[69]

James was equally uncertain of the mail, so uncertain that at times he wrote duplicate letters, sending one copy via the Salmon River route and on to Oregon and one via Fort Benton and the Missouri, hoping that at least one of them would arrive safely and within a reasonable length of time.[70] In mid-October Pamelia finally received a letter sent "by way of Oregon." They "had been anxiously hoping to hear [for] many days but hardly dared to hope for fear [they] should be disipointed."[71] James was to wait even longer. He did not receive his first letter from home until January 27 of the new year. Dated July 28, 1862, that letter came via Oregon and Walla Walla to Deer Lodge and thence to the gold mines in the Beaverhead area, costing him two dollars in the passage.[72]

During the six months in which James had received no direct word from his family, what little news he had been able to obtain about Minnesota had centered upon the Indian war there. Caught up as he was in his work at Beaverhead Diggings, he remained true to his earlier decision and gave no further thought to returning home. Located in and around present-day Dillon, the diggings lay between Rattlesnake Creek and Grasshopper Creek, both tributaries of the Beaverhead River. Though not as rich as those in the Salmon River area, the diggings were better than those at Pikes Peak. Miners working on their own were making five, ten, and fifteen dollars a day, while those working for wages averaged four dollars a day. James was optimistic:

> There is no doubt but we are in an Extensive gold country . . . but this whole mining country belongs to the Snake Indians who are hostile and miners have to work in large parties. Next season there will be so many people here that they can spread out and work other diggings. There are about 450 men and a few women to winter here. I don't know yet what we shall do as we have only been in three days.[73]

By early November, having made up his mind that this strike was rich enough to support him for a while, he asked Pamelia to pass the good news on to the citizens of Little Falls: "While at Pike's Peak I never advised any body to go there, neither do I advise people in general to come here, but I think prospects are far better for a poor man here than at Pikes Peak, and I say to you friend if you have nothing to do at home, if you cannot help to defend your country in this her hour of distress, better come here and do something than spend your time there in *idleness*." He asked her to "tell Butler that I expect him next season . . . we will build a store this winter for him if he don't come we will sell it."[74]

He was by now living some twenty miles west of Dillon in Bannack, a rapidly growing settlement that had developed in an unusual pattern that reflected the political divisions of the day:[75]

> On account of the Indian [danger] we have all built together on vallies. . . . the Secesh whiskey rowdies [are] on one side of . . . [Grasshopper] creek and the civil quite Union men on the other we have regular streets and several families I saw some little shavers playing hide and seek in prospect holes today and can hear them playing out of doors nearly every day. . . . There has been a new discovery made today not more than half a mile from our cabin. Rockwell has just come in from making claims on it Speaking of our cabin let me describe it it is 17 x 19 ft inside [with a] door and [a] plase for a window in the side next the street, fireplace in one end beds in the other with room for our flour and provisions under them. The back side is calculated for a work bench this winter as Bentley has his tool chest with him and I have some [tools].[76]

William Sturgis and John Ault were also in Bannack, though neither was mining. Both had found better, more remunerative uses for their skills. Almost immediately upon arriving in the area, Sturgis saw the urgent need for a sawmill. Miners were breaking up their wagons and using the boards to build their sluice boxes. But the need for lumber went beyond that. With winter coming on, more substantial housing than tents would be needed. Hearing rumors that remnants of an abandoned mill were available at St. Mary's, an Indian mission some 150 miles to the northwest, Sturgis made the trip through the mountains in early winter and returned with a rusted saw blade and scrap iron, which he incorporated into the first sawmill to be built at Bannack.[77]

Just as quickly, John Ault saw another need to be filled. The former proprietor of the Northern Hotel sketched the plans for a "public house," and from Sturgis's mill he got the lumber to build his saloon. When James sent Pamelia a crude drawing of Bannack just weeks after he had arrived in the camp, he noted that "Ault's House or Hall is at the extreme left at the top of the sketch it is much

*Bannack, Montana Territory, looking north across Grasshopper Creek, winter 1862–
63. This sketch by Englishman Robert Halliday was enclosed in a letter that James
Fergus sent to his family in January 1863. Fergus and O. J. Rockwell lived in the cabin
at the far right in the foreground. Fergus noted that the drawing failed to show that his
dwelling was two stories high and had a chimney in the center. John Ault's tavern can
be seen across the creek on the far left, and Indian lodges appear in the foreground.*

bigger than it looks as only the front of the main building is seen.
It is nearly in the centre of the town up and down the stream."[78]

Though Ault had been one of the first miners to hear from home
after the Indian conflict, Margaretha was not hearing from her husband in turn. She learned only secondhand, through Pamelia, that
Ault had finished the saloon in time to usher in the new year of 1863
with a "big ball" that enlivened the Montana winter scene.[79] More
reassuring to her was the news that her husband had confided to
Fergus that he was now well ensconced and determined to have "his
wife here next summer."[80]

As reassuring as the news was, there were other things to be considered in planning a move west, and Pamelia's anxieties were easily
fed by other passages in James's letters:

> On our way from Deer Lodge . . . we met two men coming from
> Beaver head who reported that the Snake Indians had come in to the
> mines told the miners they must leave, were helping themselves to

provisions etc and they expected that by that time the miners were all murdered, and advised us to turn back but we had started after gold and was bound to have it if possible, Indian or no Indian. So we concluded to camp a day or two and wait the course of events. In two days two other men came along who stated that the miners had made an arrangement with the Indians (about 1500) buying the privilege of mining by giving them three oxen, some beans, flour, sugar, tobacco, pipes, etc So we drove on and here we are.[81]

Pamelia's reaction to this passage was firm: "Now Fergus do not stay their among them Indians what does it profit a man if he gain the hole world and loose his own soul I had rather trust my luck of get along [here in Little Falls] with the children than to have your weight in gold and be deprived of you or think you never can come back."[82] And though her earlier letters concerning Indian dangers were, for the most part, free of the blatant racism encountered in the letters of many frontier women, from this time onward her attitude showed a decided change: "I forgot to tell you that 29 soux Indians wer[e] to be eridicate[d] last friday at Fort Snelling," she wrote, "I have not seen the papers since but I must tell you the people are very indignat that government does not hang them all at once." She reported with anger that, while three hundred Indians had been brought to trial, only twenty-nine had been convicted. (The actual number of Indians condemned to die was thirty-nine.) Outraged locals had attempted to take the law into their own hands. Anson Northup had rounded up a mob and made a rush to take the prisoners and "masicree them as they deserve but some good traitor informed the captain of the fort" and the Indians were saved. "I wish we had some more Northrops," she concluded.[83]

Besides altering Pamelia's attitude toward Indians, the 1862 disturbances brought other changes: "Times are quite lively here [with] so many soldiers Minnesota seventh eight and ninth regiments are retained at home on the Indians acount they have built largely at the Fort [Ripley] and at the Agency [Crow Wing]."[84] Despite the influx of soldiers, the girls were still bored, and Mary Agnes wrote, "I wish that I was there with you It is very lonesum here nearly all of the people have moved away since the Indian trouble."[85]

The "Indian trouble" had still further repercussions. Pamelia reported "evry thing [is] very high so much has been waisted and destroyed by the Indians and [on] their acount."[86] She had had to kill a good milk cow because the animal had gone dry "in the time of the Indian excitement [when] I did not milk her very regular . . . if it was the least dusk we dust not be out nearly every ladys cows went dry."[87]

The butchered cow provided income as well as beef for the family, since Pamelia had "sold ten dolars worth of her." Having managed her meager resources well over the last six months, she was fairly optimistic about her situation, reporting, "I have not had one doller from anybody but Robert [Hamilton, her boarder]," though she had gotten "three or four pair[s of] shoes from Butler['s store] but we have plenty not exactly plenty but manage very well with what we have."[88]

She was managing quite well, at least as well as she had managed when she had had Charles Freeman next door for support. Yet she missed the Freemans, and they her. They were well settled in Portland now, and Freeman had written that he and Abby would be perfectly satisfied "if [only] Fergus and his family were in this valley."[89] Abby's nostalgia was unrestrained: "Mrs Fergus I often think of the good old times you and I used to have—it almost makes me homesick when I reflect on those days passed and gone. . . . May I live to see you all once more. . . . If I ever have the money to spend I shall visit [my friends] & that dear little spot where Freddie is sleeping."[90]

The Freemans were gone. Pamelia's mother and sister were back in Geneseo, and there were no plans for them to come up to Little Falls. The group of widows was smaller now, and more scattered. Caroline Bosworth, living with Daniel in Long Prairie, came to town only infrequently. Amanda Smith was gone, and Pamelia had no idea where she was, though James was still hearing from Timothy Smith's creditors, who thought that Fergus could put them in touch with the doctor.[91] Though Mary Paul was living in Little Falls, she and Pamelia had never been particularly close and the incident over the turnips grown on the Fergus lots had left matters strained. Elizabeth Stone had gone to Denver with the judge that previous spring, and Agnes Russell, the one true widow among them, remained in Platte River.

At one time after Robert's death, Agnes had considered taking the family home to Scotland, but she had ultimately decided that she should remain in America for the sake of the children. It was for their future that she and Robert had emigrated, and it was for them that she endured. Her oldest son continued to oversee their farming operations, worked on other farms when possible, and logged in winters. Jennie, her oldest daughter, sixteen at the time of her father's death, took a teaching job. Income from such sources helped Agnes hold onto the homestead and provide for the family.[92]

Margaretha Ault and Rosanna Sturgis seemed to be doing well, considering their inexperience. But they both lived some miles north of Little Falls now, and Pamelia saw them less frequently than she had in years past. "Mrs Sturgis has just sent a note to Robrt [Hamilton] to bring me to her house this afternoon with his horse and bugy," Pamelia wrote, but she had little hope of going, since she expected Robert "will be to[o] buisy."[93] Since she disliked asking favors of anyone and had no means of transporting herself to Little Elk or Fort Ripley, Pamelia primarily relied on receiving Rosanna and Margaretha at home since both made periodic trips to Little Falls, at times en route to St. Cloud to purchase supplies: "Mrs. Sturgis was here yesterday we were talking about going to St Cloud some time the coming week I told her that if she went in a double sleigh I would like to go along." But the next morning Pamelia was disappointed to see Rosanna pass "strait by" her house en route south in a two-horse sleigh. She lodged her complaint with James: "I suppose she never though[t] of me but I think I shall survive the shock."[94]

As of late January 1863, Margaretha Ault was "doing well," since the influx of soldiers had given her "from 25 to 30 boarders."[95] However, though she knew that John expected her to make the trip west that summer, Margaretha made it clear that "she dare not go for she was afraid of the Indians here and more to go their."[96]

In stark contrast, Rosanna Sturgis, who lived in the most isolated of circumstances in the dense forests surrounding Little Elk, professed little fear for herself or her family.[97] Instead she concentrated her energies on business affairs. In a long letter to William, she conveyed news of the mills. It had been some time since Ed Grady had taken a raft of lumber from the sawmill down to St. Paul: "It was in the middle of the [Indian] excitement and he could not sell it for anything. . . . He was obliged to sell it to old White for little or nothing for we was about out of provisions."[98] Still she had not yet gone into debt for anything and would

try to make a living out of the concern this winter. If we can that is all we expect to do. . . . Ed has got a contract to furnish lumber for a barn at the Fort [Ripley] large enough to hold 300 horses. That will bring us something. . . . We have had no grinding to do since you went away to speak of until yesterday. It began to come in. I think we will have plenty now. There has been several thrashing machines burned and laid to the Sioux.[99]

The effects of the Indian war continued to hang over Little Falls as the new year rolled around. Prices had been driven up and "every thing is very hgt [high]," Pamelia reported to James late in 1862: "oats .50 cts, flower $5 dolars a barrel butter 25 coffee 30 cts per pound . . . calico 25 cts yd."[100] With resources stretched to the limit, debts were harder than ever to collect. "I have asked Gravel to come over and look at some of those notes and see if he could get anything on them," she reported in late January 1863. "He told me very politely that he had plenty of such notes on the same men." When she could not get cash she bartered, getting bushels of wheat for an otherwise worthless note and selling a stove "for eight dollars five in money three in coffee at 30 cts a pound."[101]

Though James had admonished her to "get all the flour you can from Mrs Fletcher," following his instructions had been a problem.[102] Emma Fletcher's property had been garnisheed and she had been told not to pay any of her old debts — in cash or flour — without first going through her lawyer. Pamelia at first withheld, then shared with James the news concerning Mrs. Fletcher's refusal to provide the promised flour, noting, "I have thought sometimes that I would not say any thing about it to you for it would trouble you then I would think I had ought to."[103] Communication by letter seemed strained, and she longed for a face-to-face exchange: "Some times it seems as if I could not wait till you come home I want to talk with you about so many things."[104]

At least she was not alone in her dilemma. The other widows of Little Falls felt many of the same anxieties, and Pamelia still took comfort in her meetings with them. Conspicuously absent from these meetings was Clara Hall, the wife of the town attorney who was in Colorado Territory, at times in the Mountain City area and at times in Denver.[105] Wherever he was, rumors of good fortune followed him, and James ordered Pamelia to send the note Hall owed her to a friend at Pikes Peak who would see that the lawyer paid it.[106] James was sure Hall had money enough to do so, for friends in the Pikes Peak area had told him that "Hall has preempted 160 acres of land adjoining Denver and is rich."[107] Clara Hall had, from the first, been an outsider, and news of her husband's success in Denver did nothing to improve her status with the other widows.

With news from the West even more scarce than it had been when the men were in the Pikes Peak area, the widows and others were particularly eager to share Pamelia's letters from James: "Mrs Ault nor Mrs Sturgis does not here from their husbands and come here to see if their are mentioned in my letters."[108] Once when she received a "long and interesting letter" from her husband, Pamelia reported "a great many has been here to see your letter."[109] A great many also came to see the letters Pamelia sent to James. A proud man, James wanted those letters to be worth seeing, and at one point he informed Pamelia that the two letters he had just received had not contained very much news, a fact that bothered him greatly, since "Sturgis got no letters, but came to me to Enquire what news I had."[110]

Much of the news from Pamelia's hand concerned family affairs that would hardly have been of interest to others: "Agnes Andrew and Lillie are in bed and asleep Robert has just gone to bed and . . . I [am] here writing alone at the old desk."[111] Other letters centered on the children's health and schooling: "Luela and Andrew go to school I should have sent Lilie but they got the measles in school and I did not like to have her have them this winter. . . . Mary's health is poor she has been [to school] but a very little yet I do not know what ails her . . . I think it more nervousness than any thing. . . . [Andrew] is a very good boy he feeds the cow regular and brings in the wood."[112]

School sessions were so sporadic and the teacher so poor that by early March Pamelia reported that "Luela is teaching our own [at home] and seven or eight has come in Mr Elwell came here wanted her to teach his little boys." Home school was scheduled to end when the district school opened within the next two months — with the promise of a new teacher. Even under the best of circumstances, Pamelia feared Andrew would not do well in the classroom: "I can tell you Andrew he cant learn but the girls do their best he seemes to try but he canot he has not been well for two or three weeks and is as cross as his skin can hold."[113] James's solution to the school situation was simple enough: "If there is no school and you have not enough to do for the girls let them read good useful books, and store their minds with good useful knowledge, far better than to read novels that draw the mind from the ordinary realities of life, and have a tendency to make young people dissatisfied with there lot."[114] Though he hoped the children would heed his advice, he realized that his absence gave him relatively little control over their lives:

> I ought as a duty to send much good advice to the children but hard labor every day leaves but little time for thought or reflection. They must therefore pay the more attention to what Mother gives them, and for the remainder depend upon their own judgment and good books. Borrow what [books] you can and take good care of them, and buy a few. Money is never wasted on books that give good advice or instruction to the young. Even good history helps to enlarge the mind.[115]

Of his own business James had much to say. While maintaining that there was gold to be found in the mines at Bannack, he reported that his income and that of several other men from Little Falls came, at least in part, from trades they had practiced back in the States. Sturgis had his sawmill, Ault his tavern, and James himself, along with David Bentley and William Wright, had fallen back on carpentry skills.[116] In a journal entry shared years later in an article he wrote for *Rocky Mountain Magazine*, Fergus described his activities of January 21, 1863: "Morning bright and pleasant; another coffin to make—three in a few days. The first man died of apoplexy, induced by drinking too long and too freely of his own bad whiskey; the second was shot in cold blood in mid-day, and the murderer [Henry Plummer, a highwayman of some repute] is still at large, untried, unpunished, and no one molests him; the third, a young man in the prime of life, lately married, died of fever."[117]

Violence was a way of life in Bannack, and James reported an incident in which two "drunken rowdies had a difficulty with some Indians about a squaw, in a lodge within a few rods of our cabin, and during the fuss [the two white men] shot two Indians and two Indian children dead." In response to this slaughter, the "squaws and children set up the most dreadful howling I ever heard." This brought in other Indians and several whites, one of whom acted as interpreter and tried to convince the Indians that the whites did not intend to massacre them. But in the midst of their talk, "the same two friends" and one additional man "returned in the dark . . . and poured another volley of 18 shots into the lodge amongst white men and Indians killing one white man who was interpreting, and wounding three more."[118]

A posse was sent out, among them O. J. Rockwell, and the drunken men were brought back into town where the miners "decided to give them a jury trial." Only two of the lawyers in town would take part in the trial, and both of them were engaged by the prisoners. Justice on the frontier had its own peculiarities: "Strange to say not a man of them was hung, only banished, on the ground that it was not murder to kill Indians, and the white men were killed accidently." The verdict did not sit well with the majority of the miners, for they believed "that a great wrong has been done to the Indians and to ourselves, an atrocious massacre has been committed and nobody punished." Their interest in the case was not entirely altruistic, for James reported that "hundreds of naked mounted savages are ready to revenge the murder of their kindred, and pick off every straggler that comes in their way." Some believed the retaliatory attack was imminent; others thought the Indians would wait until spring, satisfying themselves in the meantime by stealing cattle and horses. While there were some men in camp who, like James, felt that the Indians had every right to plan retaliation, there were many miners who "would shoot an Indian whenever they see them if it were not for there own safety."[119]

Such passages strengthened Pamelia's growing conviction that she and the children were better off in Little Falls than they would be in Bannack—at least for the time being—though James had already made his wishes clear to her in a lengthy letter written in mid-December 1862. He noted that though some of his friends had "thought the country too new and too much in the wilderness to bring a family to," he had "thought differently then and do now." Others obviously agreed with him, for he reported, "There must be from twenty to thirty families here and they all appear to be healthy and contented." And he reminded her of the 1,200 soldiers stationed at the garrison in Salt Lake City some 350 miles to the south. The Indians would not risk a major conflict with so large a force.[120]

He did concede that living expenses would be high, "but goods are coming in very fast, flour will be brought in abundance from Salt Lake, beef is plenty of the very best quality, so that next season I think a family can live for about one half [of what] it costs now, and womens labor pays as well if not better than mens, and you are all workers. At washing mending cooking etc a woman can earn from $20 to $25 a week." As for educational opportunities, he predicted, "There will be children enough here next season for a good school."[121]

On that optimistic note, he launched into his final pitch:

Now then I have told you something about the country the prospects, the Indians etc Are you willing to come, and if so, how. There are . . . several ways. By Steam Boat up the Missourri river by St Paul & St Louis to Fort Benton will cost about $650, for yourselves and baggage, and about $350 from there here, that is $1000. There may be some difficulty on this route from the Souix Indians if the Government does not completely conquer them this winter. Then there is the way overland that we came. John Whitford promised to bring you out if I did not come back, or I can go after you myself. To come with Whitford you would require two wagons and four yok[e] of good cattle from five to eight years old which would cost about $400. Your outfit would cost about $200 more, which is $600 you might be able to trade your house or something else for oxen and waggons, or [have] John Whitford raise a team for you and I could pay him here . . . you can get a driver for his board, so you have your load brought here for nothing. You could sell your bedsteads, chairs and all your heavy things the balance of the money for your outfit and what you owe I will have to send you but I would send you all the money I could any way to buy supplies to use here Now the next and most certain plan is for me to come after you by myself I would start home about the 10th of March get home in two months Stay there to get ready one month Start for here 10th June and get here in 3 months 6 months in all it would cost me . . . $300 I could earn while gone $700 making $1000 . . . you had better try this winter whether you cannot trade the Red barn or our house for oxen waggons etc The Red Barn was worth about $200 when I left the house and lot would be cheap at $500. Trade off the barn if you can. You have a power of attorney to deed it.[122]

Well aware that conditions in Little Falls made it highly unlikely that she could get a fair trade for her property there and terrified at the thought of taking her family through Indian territory after the experiences they had been through the previous fall, Pamelia was firm in her reply:

We are all anxious to com to you but we canot come the coming spring on the acount of the Indans I do not think that their will be any train going through next summer I was talking with Gravel and

Butler to day they think that it would be very dangerous crossing
the country even if their was as large a party and as well equiped as
when you went I think if you can stay their and do any thing and
not be in danger of your life you had better stay I am sure if you
come home and see and know what we do you would not go back
for all their is their . . . we will wait [until a year from this coming season.] It is a long time to look ahead for us I will asure you,
but before this you have probly got Butler's letter he says he told
you he did not think it prudent to undertake the journey.[123]

Even as Pamelia wrote those words, James was having second
thoughts about his chances in Bannack. His claims had produced
only moderate yields, while adjoining claims had made rich men of
their owners. Disgruntled with his partners, Rockwell and Bentley,
he noted that one claim Rockwell had refused to help him buy for
five hundred dollars the summer before was now worth one hundred thousand dollars. Clearly, they had come into the area too late
to acquire a share in the richest ore. Hoping to do better elsewhere,
James had made a long trip north to the Prickly Pear diggings, but
he returned convinced that he might as well stay on in Bannack.[124]

No longer certain his fortune lay in mining, he wrote, "I have not
made up my mind what to do yet when you come on. . . . I have
thought some of selling goods with somebody. Also of bringing a
hundred or two of cows from Oregon and raising stock in this
country."[125] In a later letter, he discussed still another possibility. "If
I don't go to mining I think I will go to building Quartz mills after
a while in company with Mr. [Ard] Godfrey of Minnehaha below
Minneapolis who came out with us."[126]

The possibility of a westward journey was a frequently discussed
topic around Little Falls, one that engaged young and old alike.
Nine-year-old Ann Sturgis garbled news she overheard from adults
and wrote her father that "Mrs Fergus [was] going through next
spring" and so was Ed Grady, but she made no mention of any plans
her own mother might be making.[127] Indeed, Rosanna Sturgis was
giving no thought to going west, since she was managing quite well
on her own and expected her husband home that summer.[128] William was discouraged with affairs in Bannack. Though lumber was
selling well there, the miners were "a parsol of howns," and only a
very few mines would ever prove profitable.[129] In contrast, the
mills at Little Elk were proving quite profitable in his absence: "Mrs
Sturgis was here two days ago they get along nicely . . . [the fam-

ily] is said to live better than ever."[130] Rosanna's apparent satisfaction with life at Little Elk gave rise to gossip: "I think that Grada [Grady] gets along with the family well and the neighbors whisper better than old Bill him self."[131]

Margaretha Ault was doing relatively well, too. She had carried some thirty boarders through the winter and had become more receptive to the idea of making the crossing: "We expect Mrs Ault her[e] to day she expects Ault to send for her and if he think[s] she had better come she is ready . . . if no[t] she will wait [and] come next summer."[132]

The widows were not the only ones debating the prospects of going west. William Butler had long been weighing the merits of the move. But the thirty-two-year-old bachelor had another factor to consider in his plans now—he was getting married. For three years he had courted Temperance Churchill's sister, Eliza Holmes, a schoolteacher who had lived with the family since her arrival in the late 1850s. In the spring of 1863, about the same time he married Eliza, Butler expanded his business. He and Francis Gravel bought out Orlando Churchill's store, and the new bride and groom assumed occupancy of Churchill's former quarters above the shop.[133]

Though Butler was ready to give up his dream of going west, his business partner was not. Francis and Hermine Gravel continued to discuss the trip, even though they had three children, the oldest four and the youngest a newborn, and even though they had just invested six hundred dollars in buying out Churchill's store. If James Fisk were to mount another expedition, the Gravels would seriously consider joining it. In the meantime, Gravel was keeping an eye on affairs at home for the man who had preceded him west: "Your family are getting along well and with great economy. I have repeatedly told Mrs. Fergus to not suffer for anything wanted in her family and hope she does not . . . so long as we can help her in any way what ever, but she is very careful and reserved."[134]

Careful and reserved—and proud. Having more than once assured James, "We will get along some way we have no idear of suffering," she was furious to hear of a rumor to the contrary: "Some one told . . . that we were entirely destitute and without provisions . . . this is very agravating but I hope we shall not always live here in the face and eyes of such trials." In the midst of pressing problems it was not always easy to maintain her dignified public demeanor. "A great deal of land in the county sold for taxes," she wrote James, reminding him that she herself had no means of paying their own taxes and was expecting him to send the money he had promised.[135]

Keenly aware of the dangers of losing their property for nonpayment of taxes, James was equally aware that sending home the money Pamelia needed would be no easy task. The mail was not to be trusted, since any letter sent from Bannack was quite likely to contain enough money or gold dust to make robbery an attractive prospect. He had sent her thirty dollars in treasury notes via letter and a hundred dollars in gold dust by a Charles Miles of St. Anthony—none of which she had as yet received. And while he could suggest that she use that money, when it came, to pay taxes on the house, the eight farm lots, and her land across the river, he could not assume she would ever receive it.[136]

Nonetheless, he had no choice but to try to send more money. At first he planned to rely on his trusted friend, "an honest, honorable, and reliable man," Ard Godfrey. Having given up on the idea of the quartz mill that he and Fergus had briefly considered buying, Godfrey now planned to return to Minnesota. "I have $175 ready to send home by him," James reported, "but the road to Fort Benton is infested by robbers."[137] When Godfrey delayed his journey home, Fergus had a change of heart: "I rather think I will not send you money by Mr. Godfrey but will send you a little at a time by letter."[138]

By the time that letter reached Pamelia, she was preoccupied with larger issues:

> The sad news from home fill[s] me with sorrow and grief—our Dear sister Mary [McHose] has gone from this world she died March 22nd and left eight little Motherless children to mourn her loss it seems as I never new a Mother so much needed to care for her little ones she died of congestive chill and only sick one week she was composed and reconciled to go and bid them all farewell and talked to the children that they must be good . . . and I feel as though if I got some money from you that I ought to go and see those little Motherless children and sisters [Jane and Eliza] and Mother . . . but I will content myself to do as you think best, but if I go Andrew must go with me I could not leave him at home but the girls could take care of Lillie as well as I.[139]

Luella's letter of the same day offers a more specific reason for Pamelia's trip to Illinois: "Mother think if she goes down this spring

Mary Dillin McHose, about 1860

and Mr McHose is willing and you are willing she will take Josie [a little boy about two years old] and take care of him." Even little Lillie was party to the plan: "Lillie cried today," Luella told her father, "and said Mama must write to Papa and tell him he must buy Josie nothing could pacify her till we told her we would write you."[140]

The death of Mary McHose filled Pamelia's letters for months thereafter.[141] At one point, intent on making her position clear to James, she used the form of address she reserved for moments of firm resolution: "Now Fergus I want to go home if you can spare me the money I want to get one of Marys little children if McHose will let me have one of the youngest." She then asked his preference: "a little girl now four months old, or a little boy two years old if I take any which had you ruther we would have."[142] By mid-June, she had nearly settled upon the baby, for the infant was currently with Mahala, "and that is to[o] much of a charge for her to be a wake nights I want to go and get it myself I thin[k] Mchose will let me have it although he did not want [sister] Eliza to have it I think [her husband] Levi drinks very hard."[143]

James's reaction to the news of Mary's death was kind enough: "I am sorry to hear of Marys Death her little Children will miss her very much her family and friends will miss her and Even I will miss her sensible letters that she used to write you. Few women possessed more good commonsense." While he did not veto Pamelia's proposal that they take in one of her sister's children, his initial reaction was less than enthusiastic: "About the little boy, I have no objections to your taking him if Mr McHose is willing, but it will cost you considerable to go after him particularly if you have to take Andrew with you. If you go I hope Andrew can be a good boy & stay at home."[144] While James did not suggest that she pay for the trip to Illinois with the money he had sent earlier and designated for taxes, neither did he forbid her doing so. He left that decision to her.

In late June, nearly two months after James had sent that money east, Pamelia had still not received it, and his accounts of mail robberies worried her: "I hope you will not send any more by letter . . . I have written you that I wanted to go home very much but [I would] rather wait than have you send me money at a risk." The exchange rate was also a factor to be considered: "Your gold dust will be worth [more than] the money."[145]

But as the weeks wore on, Pamelia vacillated: "I do not know what to say or think about going home but if I get the mony you have sent of which I think ther is little hope, and the river should rise by the midl of August I think I had better go."[146] A day after she wrote those words, James penned lines on the same topic. "I think it is doubtful whether Mr McHose will be willing to let you take his child out here," he warned her, "and you must come here any way next season. . . . I am afraid too if you go below [to get the boy] Lillie might get sick or some of the other children."[147]

His concern was valid. Luella had written her father of "a great deal" of sickness in Little Falls, and, predictably, infants were among the most vulnerable: "There has been eight little babies die here this Spring and there are three more not expected to live."[148] Pamelia herself had written him that the entire Wheeler family had smallpox and she was thinking of having the children vaccinated.[149] Nevertheless, since they were basically healthy, she felt justified in leaving them and made her intentions clear: "I may star[t] to see my Mother if I do I [s]hall leave Lillie and all the children they seem perfectly well they will all go to school for the next six months Miss Camp will teach I calculate to get her to stay with the girls."[150]

The girls supported Pamelia's plan, for both had fond memories of their Aunt Mary, with whom they spent the holidays during their year-long sojourn in Moline. Luella, in particular, was adamant that her mother go to Illinois to help the McHose family: "Grand Mother is not very well and wants Mother to come down there. . . . I hope she will get her money so she can go."[151]

But in September, five months after first hearing of her sister's death, Pamelia faced reality: "I canot go home neather will I have money not enough to buy what we need and pay any taxes for we lived prety close last winter every thing is so high though nothing compared to your prices."[152] And a letter from Mr. McHose soon thereafter closed the issue: "I got a letter from McHose today in regard to his baby he say he would like me to have it if I lived near but poor Mary did not want the children seperated."[153]

More or less reconciled to that news, Pamelia resumed her chronicle of day-to-day affairs. School sessions in Little Falls had resumed under Miss Camp, the woman in whose care Pamelia had thought to leave the children during her trip to Illinois. Seventeen-year-old Mary Agnes described her new teacher as a "mere girl (for she is only twenty)" and reported that she had sixty-three pupils in her charge.[154] One of them was the ever-reluctant scholar, Andrew, whose mother observed, "I must say Andrew lag[g]ed and I am afraid he always will he does not care whether he goes to school and I have tryed my best."[155]

Her expectations were much higher for Lillie, who was now nearly six and was proving to be as eager a student as her two older sisters: "Lillie was up early this morning with her slate and book teasing Mother is it schooltime."[156] Although the little girl had "just comencest to read little words," Pamelia noted that she "writes a great many letters to papa for instance when mama does something she does not exactly like." That very morning with the girls away at Sabbath school and Andrew out and about, Pamelia had left Lillie alone for a while: "I told her she must keep house [because] I must go and see Mrs Fullers baby it was very sick [I told her] she should write her papa and so she did on her slate all complaints about keeping house and if you had of heard her spell and tell what she wrote you would laugh hearty."[157]

According to Pamelia, "Luella [does] well . . . other[s] say she will pass an examination of comon school and Mary will pass on domestic affairs."[158] Indeed, Luella could likely obtain a teacher's certificate at once "if she needed one," Pamelia reported, "but she is to[o] young to teach."[159] Luella herself had written months earlier that she might like to teach "when we go to Salmon River next Spring," adding, "Teaching school is all the talk among young ladies if they can do sums to fractions they can teach a school."[160] Jeanette Sturgis, now eighteen, was one of those who was talking of teaching school—but she was "very shy about it" as she did not want "her father to know."[161]

James was as ambivalent as Sturgis about his daughter's plans to teach, though he eventually wrote his approval of Luella's taking the teachers' examination—provided she did not "Keep School anywhere in that country." His reasons were sound enough: "The children about Little Falls are too well acquainted with her and she is not old enough to go off among strangers to teach."[162] And Luella acquiesced for the time being: "You spoke of not wanting Agnes or I to teach any where around Little Falls Mr and Mrs Elwell spoke to me about taking a Belle Prairie School I told them I was to young and did not want to teach they thought I was sixteen instead of fourteen."[163]

James apparently had no other qualms about his daughters preparing themselves for employment, for he urged Pamelia to let Luella and Mary Agnes

> learn all they can and when they come here I will try and get them goods of some kind to sell or a school to teach or may be a post office. A small stock of Lady or rather women and childrens goods would probably sell well as there are a good many women here now and more coming. Let them make themselves qualifyed for such business and I can get them plenty to do. Besides there will probably be some cooking to do.[164]

The girls were becoming well qualified for all manner of housework and cooking jobs. Mary Agnes reported that "Monday is washing day," noting that she handled the washing and Luella the housework, while Pamelia and Andrew spent the day hoeing in the garden.[165]

The unexpected frequently broke into the everyday routine. "Now I must tell you [that a] littl acident hapened [to] Luela," Pamelia wrote:

> She was wading across the slough cut her foot badly though it be well in a week or to I think there was an arter cut we had quite a

hard time to stop the blood I hapen to bee their [Though I] had not been their five minutes If the girls had of been alone I think she might have bleed to death but if ever any thing of the kind ever hapens [again] they will remembr this The read [red] blood spurted we corded her leg sewed it up we stayed to Mrs Dows last night I did not like to move her for fear it might bleed again . . . if Robrt [Hamilton] can get his horse he will bring her home in the morning she now feels well got all over her trouble only schoo[l] keeps five days longer [and she] feels bad becaus she can not go.[166]

Luella added a note to her mother's letter: "I came home this morning from Mrs Dow's I am sitting here by the desk with my foot upon a stool it is my right foot (the same one that I sprained down to the river I believe I told you about that) it is cut right on the heel and side it does not pain me as much as it did I can put my knee on a chair and carry the chair and walk on one foot."[167]

Concerns over such accidents were added to other worries. The drought that had plagued the area that summer of 1863 meant a lean harvest and extra work: "[We] have to bring all our wattrs from the barn well this one is dry I think filled up if it was possible I would have it dug deeper [but] we can get no one [to help us]."[168] Two weeks later, the situation had worsened: "If it should rain now the potatoes would grow but any of the wheat fields or oats would burn like tinder if their was a match tuched to them and we shall have no hay for our cows and the future looks dark to get any thing to eat another year."[169]

While dry weather threatened disaster for the farmers in Minnesota, sunny days made life easier for James and his partners in Bannack:

We live where we are at work three miles below our cabin and have only a very little spare time when we come home on Sundays to write, for instance we have travelled three miles home since breakfast took our picks to the Blacksmith shop, read our letters and papers. I have washed two over shirts two undershirts two pair of drawer[s] washed my head etc have to write another letter besides this, take them to the office and get home with a load of flour on my back before supper, to be ready to commence another weeks hard work.[170]

The demanding schedule eventually took its toll, and James collapsed with an ailment of "liver and bowels."[171] Disabled and discouraged, he reported that "the expenses of a few weeks sickness here would buy a farm in Minnesota."[172]

Then, on the evening of June 1, 1863, as James Fergus lay ill in his cabin in Bannack, he received the news that would alter his fortunes. He had just finished his dinner and stretched out on his cot when

> our butcher came along with his meat on horseback, and told us that there was a big excitement up town about some new diggings found by a party that went out last Febry I knew that Henry Edgar who used to be with Joseph Whitford was one of that party, and I thought I would try and go up to town and see him. So I went up sent Rockwell in search of him. He came to our cabin in the evening, and Rockwell went off with him this morning. I think they have found good diggings about 5 days travel from here but there are so many going that it is doubtful whether the[y] all get claims. Several hundred went. . . . If Rockwell gets a good claim I will go down there.[173]

The strike Rockwell went to explore had been made less than a week before by six weary men en route home from three fruitless months of prospecting. While camped in a gulch some fifty miles east of Grasshopper Creek, Henry Edgar and his companions had decided to do a little prospecting in a sandbar in hopes of getting enough gold to buy some tobacco when they got home to Bannack. Within a few minutes they had panned enough gold to warrant staking out extensive claims along a one-hundred-foot stretch of the creek bank. After naming the bars for each other and the gulch for the thick stand of alders growing along the creek, they headed into Bannack with stories of the richness of their find. On June 1, the night James Fergus lay sick in his cabin, they agreed to lead a party to the gulch — provided the claims they had staked were honored. The crowd agreed to the terms and about two hundred men, among them O. J. Rockwell, followed Henry Edgar and the others back to Alder Gulch.[174]

Within a day or so, James had recovered enough to join Rockwell and examine his new claim. He was promptly elected deputy recorder for the new site and reported to Pamelia that a group of miners had claimed 320 acres for a townsite and named it Varina. Two weeks later he noted that "some 20 stores and grog shops (in tents and bowers)" had been erected to serve "some 1800 people, most of whom however are out looking for more diggings." Optimism was high. "As more gold country is found miners become more excited and all are feeling well thinking that they are now in gold country and that they may possibly make their pile."[175] And with good reason. So rich were the diggings that, when James tried to enclose a small nugget in a letter to Pamelia, he gave up, concluding, "The nugget is too heavy, I can't put it in the letter. I will keep a few nice ones and bring them home." His own prospects were excellent, for he had a share in the claim Rockwell had staked during the first influx of miners, and he was thinking of buying another.[176]

Competition was keen. Within weeks more than ten thousand miners filled a seventeen-mile stretch of the gulch, most of them scrapping for a claim along Alder Creek, a stream James described as a bit smaller than the Little Elk north of Little Falls. Some early settlers estimated that at one time as many as thirty-five thousand people lived within a ten-mile radius of the original townsite, which had been renamed Virginia City, since a perceptive judge with Union sympathies had recognized the name Varina as that of the wife of Confederate President Jefferson Davis.[177] Many who came into the area, including Lewis Randall of Little Falls, had formerly worked claims at Pikes Peak. Others ended up there after meeting disappointment in the goldfields of the Salmon River country.

They came with their dreams and their bedrolls, dotting the creek bank like flies. Within days they had scarred the landscape, not only with their picks and shovels, but also with their careless use of fire. When Fergus arrived on the scene the gulch had been a burst of color, with the bright new green of the alders set against the white of cherry trees in full bloom. In the middle of June, however, a fire raced along the banks of the stream, destroying the trees and blackening the gulch.[178]

Even so, the scene retained its beauty for James Fergus and others like him who had given years of their lives to the pursuit of gold. For this time the strike was rich, and he and his partners had gotten there early enough to get their share of the bounty. "These new diggings are proving to be very rich," he reported, "better than anything found within the boundaries of the United States since the California discovery. Many men will make there fortunes here."[179]

He now firmly believed that he would be one of those men, though he warned Pamelia against spreading the news around: "I

have about $1000 in cash by me now and [am] making from $25 to
$50 a day, but I want you to keep that to yourselves as our creditors
will be more likely to try to collect something from me when I come
home if they think or know I have money."[180] In another letter he
mused, "I could sell out and have $3000 in gold, but I can do better.
I have two years work ahead in our claim . . . you need not tell
anybody how well I am doing or when I am coming home."[181]

Though James now had money to send to Pamelia, getting it to
her safely still posed problems. He inquired as to "whether the
money I sent you went safe, so I can send you some more. I first
sent you $30 in Treasury Notes by letter, then $100 in gold dust by
Miles, then $25 in Treasury Notes by letter."[182] Four months had
passed since he had sent the first installment, but Pamelia had not
yet received any of the money. "If I [do] get it," she wrote James,
"I will pay the taxes I have mentioned for the interest now is heavy
they are now drawing 24 per cint."[183] Though her own money had
apparently been lost, she was relieved to find out that at least George
Stephens had received the money James had sent him as partial payment for the girls' expenses during their stay in Moline.[184]

Meantime, Fergus was fuming over what he called Pamelia's
"misdirected" letters, urging her to "take more time and more pains
in writing and directing your letters."[185] Under the best of circumstances, letters were taking six weeks to travel each way, so that
three months usually passed before Pamelia or James could hope to
receive an answer to a written question. James deemed misdirected
letters inexcusable. "Be particular about your address," he admonished her. "Sometimes you write Washington, sometimes
Dacota, and now Nebraska Territory. We are now in Idaho."[186]
Since the boundaries of present-day Montana were in a constant
state of flux during the years James was mining there, Pamelia's
confusion is understandable.[187] Beyond the general confusion,
James noted, "There is another Bannack City in Idaho on the west
side of the mountains in the Boise mines. *Be sure* and put Beaver
Head on your letters."[188] Pamelia's own explanation for her incon-
sistencies of address was logical enough: "The reason we directed
so many ways was in hopes you would get some [of them]." And
she added the spirited comment, "Maybe James Fergus did not
know where he was."[189]

The letters he did receive contained her worried comments about the danger he faced from Indians — "Now Fergus keep a good look out for the hateful things."[190] He assured her, belatedly, that the Snakes and the Bannocks, the two tribes most often seen near the mines, had made a treaty with the government, "so our Indian troubles will probably be at an end for the present." As to her worries over paying off taxes in order to save their property at home, he answered, "I think but very little of Little Falls property anyway, if my family, and what little property I have left there was out of it and what little my friends own I would not care if the rest of it was in hell (if there is such a place)."[191]

His attitude toward Little Falls and toward his creditors there and elsewhere had changed markedly. Before this time, he had seemed determined to pay up all he owed. Now he outlined a new plan to Pamelia: "As a matter of course I don't want you to be telling my plans and calculations abroad because I am owing old debts which might bother me when I come home after you. I am not afraid of them here." Apparently many of his creditors had taken company stock in lieu of cash and were now regretting that decision: "Most of our creditors took large securities which the[y] allowed to depreciate in value and now I can't help it. . . . They must be content with what they have got, as [for] the future I intend to look out for my self."[192] Despite this apparent flippancy toward his creditors, Fergus did respect some of his debts, for he continued to send drafts to George Stephens in payment "for girls board, expenses etc and an old debt."[193]

At Little Falls, "where there is nothing doing and where you can make nothing," James had despaired of ever getting far enough ahead to get out of debt. Now he was his old optimistic self, for at Virginia City there was "plenty to do and plenty of money for doing it."[194] As the population of Alder Gulch grew, so did James's estimates of what could be earned there:

> These new diggings are proving to be both richer and more extensive than the Bannack Diggings and easier worked, although we have only one claim we expect to take out $2000 a piece out of it during the summer, although that much is no fortune it is enough to pay all our expenses in moving out here, buy all we need to come out with, and have something left to start with after we get here, but I may do better. We have bought another claim which may prove good, and hope to buy more.[195]

From his first week on the Alder Gulch site, James had known that Pamelia and the family must join him there. "Within another year I think there will be a large population in this country," he wrote. "There are a great many families now at Bannack mostly from Colorado, and there must be at least a score of women here [in Virginia City] and quite a number of children. . . . I often wish you were all here Luella or Agnes could do the Recording and you could earn from $20 to $30 a week by doing our cooking and keeping a few boarders."[196] She could, he insisted, "make $1000 a year" doing little more than she was doing at home in Little Falls.[197]

It was an inviting enough prospect, but there was another side to the story of James's proposed new life in Virginia City. Its rough and rugged environment was hardly a place in which to raise children:

> One day last week three gamblers and Robbers took a man out of a tent into the street and shot him dead. The miners held a meeting tried and condemned two of them to be hung, the gallows was built their graves dug, and the men ready to be taken out to be hung. A letter was read that one of them had written to his mother. He was blubbering and crying, a few women present commenced blubbering. Some of the men became tender hearted. Some one moved that the prisoners be banished which was carried and they mounted their horses and left. The gallows is still standing and the graves still open. These men belonged to a group of highway men and it was a crime to let them go.[198]

Such events did little to dampen James's enthusiasm, however, for the Fergus family had seen and survived the days of lawlessness and vigilante justice in Little Falls. He began to dwell more and more often on the topic uppermost in his mind: "I am satisfyed to stay *here*, glad I came *here*, and I wish my family were *here*." Though ruffians were currently in the majority, he assured Pamelia that "there will be plenty of people including women and children to make a very good society before I can get you here."[199] And there was far more to recommend the area than mining: "It is a pleasant place to live. There is good farming land on the Beaver Head and Jefferson Rivers. The grazing is fair summer and winter most Everywhere where there is not too much snow." Favorable living conditions aside, there was plenty of gold, and that was, he reminded her, "the main thing we are all after."[200] Reluctant to leave such rich diggings, he asked her advice. "If you can think of any way that I could get you out here this fall or even next spring without my coming after you," he wrote, "let me know."[201]

This was certainly no time for James to think of making the long journey home. Life at Virginia City was hectic and productive, unlike life in Little Falls, which Luella had described as so dull that "Every day is alike and Every day like Sunday." James played upon the contrast: "Not so here. All excitement. Every body expecting to get rich or at least expecting to get a good claim. . . . there is very little time here for walking or play. All is . . . energy. Excitement and work."[202] Even Sundays at Virginia City were busy days, since "there is always something to do where men do all their own work. . . . There is cooking to do, washing, mending, trading, settling, fixing up tools, sluices, etc and if there is any time to spare a little work on prospecting."[203]

Luella was quick to respond: "I hope you will hurry and come after us, for we want to get out of this place."[204] Pamelia and the children read and reread his letters with great interest, and Pamelia noted that "Luela has been comparing your letter to the map."[205] Pamelia herself was less enthusiastic, writing:

> I will endever to answer all your questions but . . . the most interesting one to me I do not know how [to answer] that is [the one about] my feeling . . . in regard to coming their of course if you come after us we will go and think it for the best but you are doing *I* think pretty well and [though] it would be very pleasent for us all to be their . . . We could not sell our house here for anything now nor even next spring nor the barn . . . and it is unsafe Even if we could [make arrangements to leave here and] get their now or even next spring I should be timid on the acount of the Indians.[206]

Nothing James wrote could allay Pamelia's fears concerning the dangers of the long journey that lay ahead of her. "You spoke of Capt Fisk train he has went through [already]," she wrote. "It is said that he was not going where the Indans were and many of us would like to larn that rout[e]."[207]

If her enthusiasm was muted, it was with good cause. She was depressed: "I have been very g[l]oomy and sad for some time I hardly know the reason unless it is becaus[e] I have got no money yet."[208] Because the money James sent had not come through, she had not been able to pay the taxes and lived in constant fear that their property would be sold at public auction: "It is allready a wonder some one has not bid it off it is only because no one has thought of it."[209] In the midst of her worries, the stockholders of the Little Falls Manufacturing Company had called a meeting and sent her a notice. Surmising their intentions, she had "sent them word to go to the Devil I would have nothing to do with them the[y] figure around me to try and get the old assessments out of me but they can't."[210]

Constant worries over taxes and assessments would have been sufficient enough cause for Pamelia's depression, but there were physical reasons as well. Her teeth were bad: "I have [had] the tooth ache for about two weeks So people have to suffer when they get strayed out of civilization their is plenty of Docttors ther you say though I think I shall have all mine puled out before I start."[211] And she was still bothered by "sick spells": "You must excuse all blunders for I feel very bad at present I can hardly colect my thoughts enough to make one sentence."[212]

Through all of her problems, Pamelia's boarder, Robert Hamilton, had been "very kind." Her mainstay during the Indian conflict, he had also done odd jobs around the house and farm and provided her with a means of transportation. In addition, his presence in the household had meant increased financial security: "We get two dollars and half of Robrt for his board we have done 20 dolars worth of washing for him since you left."[213] And Hamilton seemed to be contented with the arrangement: "I am still making my hom[e] at your house and I must say the[y] are verry kind to me only onse and a while the[y] give me a scolding but that is nothing new for the[y] would do the same to you if you was home."[214]

Hamilton himself had managed quite well, despite the hard times. "I still keep making tin ware," he wrote James, "I have sold it as fast as I could make it so you see Business is good with me."[215] As postmaster, he was visited by many people on a fairly regular basis, and he had taken full advantage of that fact by setting up a small store in the front room of the building that served as tinsmith's shop and post office. Though Pamelia had thought there "would not be many buyers," she reported that Hamilton's early-day convenience store "seems to do the most business," selling "t[w]o barrels of sugar to butlers one." Though his stock was relatively small, she conjectured (while cautioning James, "never repeat this"): "If he had a [complete] stock of goods [he] would have nearly all the trade." Gravel and Butler were also well aware of that possibility, and

Pamelia noted that "it makes Butler look cross to see three or four teams stand before Roberts doore."[216]

During James's second absence Hamilton had, in effect, become so much a part of the family that when Pamelia began to talk of going west she saw him as a factor in the trip, though she could hardly have known what his exact role would be. From the first he had sought James's opinion as to the advisability of his making the move west, though his fear of Indians made him cautious in his planning. "You want your family to come out to you in the Spring," he wrote, "but let me tell you as a freind it is not Safe for them to go at present for every paper that we get states that we are going to have an Indian War in the Spring and your family is all right at home and you need not be afraid the[y] shall not want for any thing."[217] By early September 1863, having become more open to the idea of a spring crossing, he wrote Fergus to ask whether he should bring along his heavy "Tinner's Tools" and assured James that if he did not want to make the long trip home, Pamelia and the children were more than welcome to travel in his company, as he and Francis Gravel were definitely planning to make the crossing.[218]

Pamelia seems to have become amenable to making the trip without her husband. She agreed that since James was finally making money, he should not plan to come home for them: "Now then Mr Fergus," she wrote, "if you can dispose of our house in any way without coming home I think if the Indians are not troublesome next summer we can come to you in company with some one [for] if the Indians are not troublesome [t]here will be quite a number coming to that country . . . if Robert and Gravell come they would be better coumpany for us than to go with a train."[219]

There was one potential obstacle—Robert was in danger of being drafted into Morrison County's Civil War unit, the Fifth Minnesota Regiment. Around the first of the year volunteers had been called for, and the hundred-dollar bounty had helped persuade seventeen men to join. Since this number exceeded by two Morrison County's quota for the period, there had been no draft yet that year and many, including Pamelia, had assumed that the war would be over before there would be time for another draft. But in July she wrote, "I was going to say when Vicksburgh was taken the rebelion would be knocked on the head with the Lord's hamer but I see they are still fighting and are a going to keep doing so."[220]

Consequently, by early August 1863 the draft situation had changed. "I am told the draft will comence in this state tomorrow," Pamelia wrote, adding that "here in Little Falls exist the same spirit as did in New York and other places."[221] Some two weeks later Robert Hamilton asked James, "Are you going to have a draft out [there]? . . . We Expect to have one next week I think I shall be drafted along with the rest of the boys," adding that he was one of the few men left in town who were sound and fit for duty.[222] In early September Pamelia reported: "The 14th of next month the draft comes off Robert thinks certain he will be drafted so of course then he will go if his country calls for his *blood* he will *go* if this war canot be *ended* without him hes ready Yes he is ready to walk rite up the *colettors office [and] pay his three hundred dolars* [and buy his way out of the draft]."[223]

Hamilton was not the only man who was worried about the draft: "Our friends are somewhat scart of the draft Butler in particlar he say[s] he want[s] to pay his three hundred dolars and so does Robrt but I think he will [go] I will hate to have him leave us we should fee[l] more lonely truly."[224] She had read that John Currie had been "wo[u]nded at gethesburgh in the shoulder."[225]

Her own brother's experience had taught her what war did to young men: "I had a letter from poor Hiram last week in which he sent his likeness he looks sad and care worn and sick and we have had James [Dillin's picture] lately [he] looks healthy and well their is a great contrast in the two brothers but I hope this war is on its last legs [That] seems to be the popular opinion."[226]

While Pamelia remained hopeful about the end of the war, hostilities flared again on another front. The Indian situation at home remained unsettled; Luella had reported earlier that "the President has made a treaty with the Chippewa and I guess there will not be any trouble with [them]," but the Dakota had once again been active during the summer of 1863. "They have begun their bloody work again," Pamelia wrote. "A family of eight have been murdered within six miles of Minneapolis. . . . The government have made provisions to scour the big woods twenty five dolars offered for every soux scalp their has been two taken."[227]

While such conditions renewed her doubts about the wisdom of their attempting the trip to Virginia City, Pamelia was equally afraid of having James make the trip home: "Dear husband dont start [home in] those Indian times." Though the second Fisk expedition had made the crossing safely that summer, a group of miners returning home from the West had been waylaid, and local newspapers had carried accounts of the attacks: "You will probly here of those miners being murdered on the Missouri before [you read] this before I heard the particulars my blood chilled of cours some ones poor heart aches and Fergus I feel for them."[228] The fears were felt very close to home: "Mrs. Ault and Mrs. Sturgis hasn't heard from their husbands for a long time. Ed Grady was in here this afternoon to see if we heard anything from you. We was glad to tell him for Mrs Sturgis was very anxious for we heard that Mr Ault and Sturgis were not masscreeded in that band of miners that wer killed in the Missouri it is generally believed here that the Indians will aim at the returning men from the gold country."[229]

The Indian hostilities made those at home in Minnesota as watchful as those returning home on the Missouri River. "We was at Mrs Sturgis yesterday and we talked of our widowhood and looked now and then to see if some Indan's face was not pressed against the window I should hate to live where Mrs Sturgis lives but she says she is not afraid."[230]

Uncomfortable as she was with the Indian situation, Rosanna had no intentions of leaving Little Elk. William, however, was apparently unaware of that fact. During the summer he had reportedly spoken of bringing his family out west. In fact, James had written that Sturgis, who was now shipping lumber to Virginia City from his mill in Bannack, intended to have his brother Amos accompany Rosanna and the children out "by the Platte River route."[231] In Little Falls, Pamelia had heard "whispered around" that "Amos Sturgis is expected here to move Sturgis family to that country by the way of Missouri river and Fort Benton they are allways working at some thing sorta sly."[232] While rumors of a pending trip west circulated freely, Rosanna herself was saying nothing about her plans, doing nothing to ready herself for the trip, and acting as if she still half expected William to show up at home.

Margaretha Ault, equally out of touch with her husband, was vacillating: "Mrs Ault was here two days ago she wants to go and is sorry she did not go with Captain Fisk she has money enough but would prefer to go by land."[233] Margaretha's impatience increased with her worry. Not having heard from John in three months, she sent a message through Pamelia: "Mrs Ault wanted us to tell you next time we wrote to be so kind as to write to her and tell her where Mr Ault is and what he is doing she has not heard from him for three months she writes regular once every two weeks."[234] Since Fergus and Rockwell had moved over to Virginia City, they had seen little of John Ault. Though he still had the tavern in Bannack, he also had the wanderlust. He had claimed 160 acres in Gallatin County, some eighty miles to the northeast. There, as a member of the Gallatin Claim Club, he had helped plat a town at the junction of the three forks of the Missouri, investing this time not in a mining venture but in the future development of a fertile valley.[235]

While John Ault carried on with his far-flung activities in the West, Margaretha continued to support herself with her boarding-house at Fort Ripley, doing "fairly well" in Pamelia's opinion. On her way home from a shopping trip to St. Cloud, Margaretha stopped to visit at the Fergus home for a few days. She had "just got a sewing mechion cost 69 . . . and good clothes [makes a] good living I wish I could say as much for my self," Pamelia noted.[236] Pamelia's small spate of jealousy easily dissolved in the good spirits of the ensuing visit. "We have had a good visit us widows," Pamelia wrote James and once again added a message from Margaretha to John: "Mrs Ault says tell Ault she has not heard from him in three months and she will stay to the Fort this winter but no longer."[237]

It was by then early November and Pamelia was as resigned as Margaretha to spending at least one more winter in Minnesota. She would be lonely: "How I wish I could see you. . . . It would seem very long indeed to us to wait another year." But she would manage: "I think with two hundred dolars we could live our wood would be the worst trouble."[238] She had tried to follow James's advice and have wood cut from their land across the river, but she had found it "very hard to get anyone to do anything then beg and big pay dont satisfy them."[239] With an early winter coming on, her cellar stock, as well as her woodpile, was low. The parched fields had yielded a poor harvest, and "what few potatoes we had were very poor and are worth a dolar a bushel we did not raise anything but the few potatoes."[240] And her purse was empty. There was no cash on hand for even the simplest things: "The weather is quite cold and it will cost a little to get us warm shoes and stockings."[241]

Even as Pamelia was settling in for the long winter, James was making plans for the spring. The means by which his family should journey west was still very much on his mind. "If Gravel and Butler come and Robert and them were used to the road and to such travelling," he wrote, "I would not come after you but let you come with them." However, he noted that "from their inexperience in such travelling, I will either have to come [home] myself or get some experienced man to bring you out."[242]

His first choice would be Daniel Bosworth, for "He is the most capable man I know of in that country if it was not for his getting on a spree once and a while."[243] Daniel was "well posted about teams and traveling, is energetic, and right every way but the drinking. I think I will write him about it." By Pamelia's report, Bosworth would be a good candidate; he was as enamored of the West as ever. But Caroline, who was carrying their third child, hardly shared his enthusiasm. Dan was still hauling timber and, according to his father-in-law, would "like to come if he could rais enough to come with his wife [but she] wont consent to let him go without her and he can hardly rais enough to come with her."[244]

With Bosworth's role doubtful, James remained ambivalent. He might decide to come home himself, stopping in at Moline to follow up on a quartz mill offer made earlier by George Stephens, in which case, he wrote, "I will try and be there by the last of February and will consequently be home but about 10 or 15 days." By whatever means, Pamelia would soon be heading west: "You may commence now to make your calculations for that time will soon roll around."[245] As soon as the crop was gathered, she should have the garden fence posts pulled up and hauled to the house. They would make good firewood, and she would have no need of them in the spring, for she would be packed up and ready to cross the plains long before planting time.[246]

Since goods would likely be hard to sell in such slow times, she should start now to sell "everything you don't need, all your furniture, including bureaus and every thing of the kind; if we need them here we can buy them in Salt Lake, or new at Omaha. The blue chest upstairs and some trunks will hold all our clothes. Use up all useless and half worn clothing and bedding such things wont pay the freight."[247] Besides, he assured her, "Every body finds their own bedding in a mining country, and it generally consists of blankets and Buffalo Robes. If we need more than you have, we can get Buf-

falo Robes at Fort Benton about 275 miles from here for from $4 to
$6 each."[248]

Oblivious to the value a quilt had for the woman who had made
it or had received it from her mother's or grandmother's hands, he
wrote, "Quilts don't answer very well on the road. They get torn
too easy."[249] This was no time to think of favorite items whose sen-
timental value did not justify transporting them across the plains.
"[Sell] all your spare dishes if you can get a good price for them,"
he urged, "we can buy new in Omaha, light things that are useful
of course you can carry . . . your stoves and furniture you will
need until we go away and may have to sell at auction but any thing
you can spare sell when ever you get a fair price for it and a fair price
now in Minnesota is not much."[250] Lest she fret over the loss of her
stove, he promised, "If we come by the Platte route I will buy a
good new cooking stove on the Missouri River." They would not
need the heating stoves either, for "Chimney fire places are mostly
used for warming." He added a reassuring note: "The winters are
not as cold as in Minnesota."[251]

He was making money steadily now, so that even the bad weeks
were good when compared with his work at Pikes Peak and Bannack: "Week before last was the poorest weeks work we done since
we commenced about the first of July, we cleared only about eighty
dollars a piece above expenses, and the last week was the best, we
cleared over five hundred dollars a piece in gold dust as good as
$600 in treasury notes, it would take me a long while in Minnesota
to clear that much." And he was optimistic that he would continue
to make good money. "I don't expect to clear less than from 50 to
$100 a week all winter," he wrote. "I could leave here with nearly
$4000, besides what I have sent you, but I want you to keep these
things to yourselves."[252]

Though he had plenty of money on hand, getting it home to
Pamelia still posed problems. According to his calculations, he had,
by late September, sent home a total of $715, including $60 in treasury notes sent by a D. D. Hackett who was to mail the notes when
he reached his home in Troy, Minnesota, and two $250 drafts on a
St. Paul bank.[253] While James's careful accounting of the money he
had sent arrived in good time, the money itself did not. In early October Pamelia wrote, "Your letter of August 27th sent by D D
Hacket is just at hand but no money in it the envelop was cut open

the money taken out and mailed at Salt Lake he did not bring it to Troy Winona County but mailed it at Salt Lake September 14. The letter was open [and] underscored on the end The eges [were] turned inside the [envelope] so that it held the letter safe." Having studied the envelope carefully, she raised doubts about Hackett's honesty: "Their [is] no doubt in us but it was [taken] out by him or at Salt Lake [for] the envelop is worn on the edges that is [t]urned in the same as [it's worn on] the other edges." Her dismay was evident: "I do feel bad now their is ninty dolars throud away and we need it I can tell you but it is gone now we have to do the next best thing [and] not try to send any more not run any riske in coming home."[254]

One of the $250 drafts sent from Virginia City had arrived, but not the other. "It seemes that some one is watching my name as it comes through the post office," Pamelia noted. Not only was the draft missing, but so was the letter she assumed "contains a good deal of information in regard to coming out their and fixing the house and a thousand things." In particular, she had wanted his opinion as to whether she should "see to having those houses taken down over the other side of the river and have them rafted to St Cloud" to be sold for lumber. According to Robert, "They will pay and be worth one hundred an[d] fifty or more [if rafted and if we] . . . leave them they will be throughed away."[255]

Though Pamelia never got that particular letter, she received instructions enough from the West — most of them suggesting ways to spend the money she was not receiving: "There are a good many things to do with it, besides paying what I owed Gravel and Butler what you owe them and others There is the taxes on the house and lot on the eight lots on your land across the River this last has to be paid in St. Cloud on the Red Barn lot and on the 4 lots up by Mrs. Steele's . . . the rest of the taxes you will leave untill I come home or advise further about them."[256]

Whatever money was not needed to pay the taxes should go toward outfitting the family for the trip west:

It will naturally suggest itself to you that we need some good comfortable clothing made up and particularly for the children before we move out here and this winter is the time to make it when you have not much to do. If goods were low I would advise a large supply but as goods are very high and will be much lower as soon as the war is over, a full supply for a year or two years at most will be enough, and that should be of the most durable kind—for service more than looks. I spoke in a former letter of buying you a sewing machine It might be well for you, to buy one now if you could get a good substantial one of the kind [you want] in St. Paul or elsewhere at a fair price.[257]

Finally, there were a few luxury items to be included. "I want you to keep taking the New York Tribune, the St. Paul Press, the Boston Investigator and any other papers you want."[258]

What Pamelia wanted most was the sewing machine. "In your former letter you spoke of a sewing machine," she wrote. "Such a one as I want will cost 50 or 55 dolars Wheler and Wilsons best finished cost 65 at the doore Mrs Ault has just got one [for] 65 dolars, but it [is] nice well finished."[259] Though she had not yet received enough money to warrant making her purchase, Pamelia was unusually optimistic because "quite a long article appered in the [St. Paul] press today by Capt Fisk it told what a great many wer doing that went out with him in 1862 all doing well Ault of Fort Ripley was building James Fergus and OJ Rockwell was each averaging $100 dolars a day clear this was the best of all." As might be expected, this rosy report had given the men of Little Falls "the gold fever bad Robert [Hamilton] could not eat any dinner." Ever mindful of James's admonition against telling anyone of his improved fortunes, she added, "I told them [all] that O J Rockwell JF [story] was only newspaper trash but I wished it was so."[260] This same notice also prompted Philo Farnham to write Fergus: "There is verry flattering letters in print concerning your locality written by Capt Fisk, it has set our whole town in an uproar for the mountains nothing talked more except the draft."[261]

In general, the family was doing well. "We have had no snow yet," Pamelia reported, "but the weather is very cold but we have a nice warm fire those railes [from the garden fence] make a nice fire." In the absence of other help, she had been busy with home repairs: "I fixe[d] the windows and doores myself I tried to get Fuller to do some such work [but] he is all buisy but we get along very well our celler is warm and we have our share of comforts."[262] Andrew had played the huntsman. While skating on the river he had found a deer with a broken leg, killed it, dragged it home, and dressed it out for the table. They planned to make moccasins from the skin.[263]

The concerns of Mary Agnes and Luella were those of their

peers. Both had recently been "down in the mouth" over a twenty-dollar cloak Jeanette Sturgis had bought that fall.[264] Luella was saving toward a subscription to *Portrait Monthly*, a publication featuring the principal officers in the Union Army.[265] And seventeen-year-old Mary Agnes reported that a friend "asked me if Robert [Hamilton] and I would stand up with her [at her wedding] I told her yes I say that she was joking but mother says not."[266]

In early December 1863 Pamelia was in high spirits, and her letters reflect that fact: "Good morning husband it is a lovely morning the children ar[e] gone to school Andrew took Lillie on the sled and she was as happy [as could be] she had her dinner in a little basket and a large red aple in it."[267] But toward month's end she sank into despair. She had been ill for about six weeks, having first complained of weakness, a rash, and a fever.[268] Two days after Christmas, too weak to write for herself, she asked Luella to write to James. That letter opened on a thankful note: "We received your letter dated November 9th containing the draft of four hundred and thirty dollars Thursday. It came in time for Mother a nice Christmas present."[269]

By the next morning Pamelia was able to add a few lines: "I am very thankful that I am able to write you this morning last night I felt very bad I have been sick now six weeks I have Docterd myself as well as I could and taken Jaynes medisons had a bad night last night thought I was about done for this wourld have changed my mind this morning and think I will get rite along." Despite having been ill for so long, Pamelia reported, "I have begun to get ready [for the trip west] and sewed some for the next year and so has Mrs Gravell we can get [a] Wheler an[d] Wilson sewing or Singer or Horns in St Cloud as soon as I get able I will go and see them I think now since we got the draft we can have wone."[270]

Even as Pamelia slowly struggled to regain her strength and get on with the myriad tasks that had to be accomplished before they went west in the spring, a crucial letter was making its circuitous way toward Little Falls.

6

The Crossing

BY MID-NOVEMBER 1863 James Fergus had finally formulated his plan for the family's trip to Virginia City. His hurried letter of November 15 outlined that plan for Pamelia. O. J. Rockwell was going home over the winter to visit relatives in New York. On his way back to the mines, he would stop in Minnesota to pick up the Fergus family and Margaretha Ault and accompany them across the plains. Fergus was providing him with four hundred dollars in gold dust to cover family expenses and one hundred in payment for his trouble. The proposed schedule was somewhat tentative: "[Rockwell] will probably be their in February, will leave Minnesota in March and Omaha in April and will get here about the last of July." If she preferred, Pamelia might leave Little Falls ahead of her household goods and "go to Illinois to see your folks and meet the wagons at Fort Des Moines."[1]

The letter contained an enclosure: "Mrs Fergus Please forward the enclosed letter to Mrs Ault, it is from her husband."[2] John Ault's letter to Margaretha ostensibly contained the same instructions as those James was forwarding to Pamelia, but almost from the beginning the Aults' plans began to go awry. Even before the decisive letter arrived, Pamelia realized that her friend's health was going to be a factor in any plans. Margaretha had just spent a week visiting friends in Little Falls, and, Pamelia noted, "Mrs Ault is ready to come through with the rest [though] she looks pretty well fag[g]ed out if Ault is thier tell him she feels as though she was neglected she has not heard from him in five months she wonders what he is doing."[3] Luella, who with Alice Churchill had spent some time that fall at Fort Ripley visiting Mrs. Ault, had heard of a different plan. "Mrs. Ault has been quite sick and is not able to go with us," she wrote her father. "She expects to go with Fiske she has written to Ault for means and expects to get them before she starts."[4] There was no news forthcoming from Little Elk. Rosanna Sturgis was either not involved with any travel plans or was not revealing them.

Yet Pamelia Fergus and Margaretha Ault were not the only gold rush widows who were scheduled to make the crossing with Rock-well. Belle McGuire, wife of James McGuire, a mining partner with Fergus and Rockwell, would be joining the train at Grinnell on March 20.[5] Daniel Bosworth was "bending his forces to come," de-spite Caroline's opposition, and Pamelia predicted, "I think he can [go in] good shape."[6]

William Butler was no longer talking of crossing the plains, but Francis Gravel had become increasingly interested in the venture. His only doubts concerned who would go and how. "I have not yet determined whether [to take] my family along or not," he wrote Fergus. "[I] rather think it pretty hard trip for a family of small children."[7] And at this point he, like Margaretha Ault, was more inclined to join next summer's Fisk expedition if the captain mounted another train, seeing more security in traveling in a government convoy than in crossing the plains without that protection. Pamelia did not have that choice; her destiny lay in a trip across the plains with O. J. Rockwell.[8]

James admitted it was not the ideal plan: "This arrangement with Rockwell is not quite as good as if I went home myself but it is the next best, he is well posted about teams, the road, travelling, etc and it costs me much less than if I went home. He is not able to work and goes cheap. He will bring teams of his own from Omaha with supplies."[9] Knowing Pamelia would need still more money in order to provide herself with the needed wagons and staples, James ex-plained what he had worked out. "I will send some money by him [Rockwell] — all I can get him to take and will send the balance in drafts. . . . I will send you instructions in future letters what to do with the property there and a bill of what things I want brought out." His next words were true enough: "Now by the time you get this you will have but little time to get ready in."[10]

Pamelia received and read those prophetic lines around the end of December, at a time when she "could only set up a couple of hours in the day." Her first reaction was despair. "I must tell you I had a good cry when we got the few lines that Rockwell was on his way to this country and expected to be hear so soon," she wrote on January 10, 1864. "I told the girls it was no use," she wrote, "and [I] was sorry he was coming [and] that I would not be able [to get ready]." But since that time she had been "taking Doctr D. James Albertive" and was "getting real well." Though not yet well enough to go out and buy the long-anticipated sewing machine, she had "done the girls and I consederable sewing." She had not managed to sew the buffalo overcoating he requested because she had no way to obtain the skins, but she promised to make coats for them all in Virginia City if James provided the hides.[11]

Pamelia was not the only member of the Fergus household shocked to receive word of Rockwell's imminent arrival. The news threw Robert Hamilton and Mary Agnes into a panic. For some months they had been subtly preparing Pamelia for the possibility that Robert might accompany the family west—not as a boarder, but as a son-in-law. Whatever knowledge Pamelia may have gleaned from their hints she had not yet passed on to James, for on January 5, realizing that time was of the essence, the young lovers themselves sent the news to the goldfields. Hamilton wrote first, noting that he had delayed putting his intentions into writing because he had been certain James was on his way home:

> But as your famely got a letter from you last week Steating that you had sent for them and that you was not comming home I thought I would make known to you that I have be[e]n keeping company with your daughter Mary and have her consent to be my wife. I write with her consent to know if you will give yours, all that is wanting is your consent to make us happy. I hope you will agree with us and remember that you was onse young your self and can amagin how we feel in this matter.[12]

Mary Agnes's letter was equally persuasive: "I agree with Robert in thinking that all that is wanted is your consent to make us happy, I have long loved Robert, I liked him first because he shun[ned] bad company but I found about six months ago that I could not leave him very well so with your consent he says that he will come out whare you are and bring me as his wife what do you say Father." Anticipating her father's argument, she noted, "Perhaps you think I am to young I am almost eighteen [and] as Robert says you was once young yourself and may know with what feelings we write Mother will write tomorrow she is not very well but is geting ready as fast as she can to come out their."[13]

If Mary Agnes expected her mother to plead her case, she was to be disappointed, for though Pamelia did write to James some five days later, she made no mention of the letters written by the young people but dwelt on her own health and her preparations for the trip west, reporting, "I have sold some of my furniture and am told I can get five hundred dolers for the house." Mrs. Fletcher still had no cash with which to pay her husband's old debt, but Pamelia noted that "she had a pony and if it is a good one we can get it and [sell it to raise money to] help buy our oxen if we do so we will get some flour and close up that debt."[14]

In the midst of her preparations and her worry over Mary Agnes's wedding plans, Pamelia entertained a visitor, Margaretha Ault, whose health was still too poor for the pending journey. In the course of the visit the two women discussed rumors of another Fisk expedition, and Pamelia reported to James that Fisk "will come through some way he is writing and making speeches and [t]here is a great many all around the country talking of coming some as early as we do." She hinted that there were other reasons Margaretha Ault would not be coming west: "Mrs Ault did not hardly like it when Ault did not send her money she says if she was ever so able to come with Rockwell she would not, it would cost so much."[15]

"I have been looking for a letter to tell us just what to do," Pamelia continued. "I think we will get it this week." She needed the promised letter, for in addition to getting the family goods ready and handling their personal business affairs, she had to deal with the remaining company business: "I hope you will not forget to tell me what to do with the company books and papers you know that their is almost a trunk full."[16]

Soon after she wrote those words, she received a letter James had written on November 21 and 22 and sent with Rockwell, who had mailed it to her when he crossed into the States. That letter answered her questions concerning company as well as family business. She was to pack all the company books into one of their old trunks and leave them with Gravel and Butler, unless one or both storekeepers decided to make the trip west themselves. She was also to leave in their care the notes still owed to Fergus and to the company, in hopes that they might be able to collect some money when the economy improved. She was to ascertain what Fergus owed the company and what the company owed him and bring those figures with her. She was to bring out his own business papers and books and the best of the books in his library. She should give away the worn-out books and all the pamphlets, then buy a few more good books in Omaha. In addition, she was to "pay for one year of the Weekly New York Tribune to be directed to Virginia City. . . .

also the Boston Investigator and Scientific American," though he did add, "If you are busy I can send for them all from here."[17]

The November 21 letter contained, as well, a three-page memorandum listing items she was to bring on her journey, "exclusive of what things you will bring from home that I dont think of, leaving you and Rockwell at liberty to vary it according to circumstances such as scarcity of money, high prices, etc." James was keeping a copy of the memorandums so that he could update his list occasionally and send the updates to her.[18] His directions as to how she was to maintain her list were explicit:

> Copy it into a memorandum book . . . leaving a space between the different headings so you can put down any thing you think of and in the same book you may put down what articles you want to bring from home and as you pack them up at home, or buy them at Omaha or elsewhere, mark it with a pencil, so you may know it is packed or purchased and . . . use the green chest up stairs my tool chest (what of it is not needed for a mess chest) and some of the old trunks up stairs for packing and buy three or four good trunks with locks for yourselves to keep your clothing etc in.[19]

Then came an underlined section: "Have the sides of your wagons boarded high up with thin boards (siding) to keep things from falling out. Have a step put on to the tongue of the waggon you ride in, and never let one of the children go out or in the waggon under any circumstance without stopping it, as many get killed . . . by the waggon running over them." Lest she feel overwhelmed by all that had to be done, he assured her, "Rockwell will help you about everything."[20]

The heading on James's long list read "Outfit Memorandum," and the list was divided into sections bearing such titles as "Teams," "Provisions," "Clothing," "Stationary," and "Extras for Use on Road." Since he intended for her to sell all she could of their extraneous household items in private sales and to auction off the rest during her final days in Little Falls, he envisioned her packing all the items she would take from home in a single covered wagon, drawn by three yoke of oxen. Rockwell would drive that wagon, and she and the children would go by stage, train, and boat to Illinois to visit her family. In Iowa, Rockwell would buy two additional covered wagons, six more yoke of oxen, and a good milk cow.

He would buy their provisions as well, including six hundred

Outfit Memorandum

Teams &c | **Clothing**

3 good covered waggons / One Suit of good clothes for
1 from Little Falls Balance / Myself—including hat & boots
from Iowa, / 1 Every day coat
9 Yoke of good cattle / 2 pr Do pants
3 from Little Falls Balance / 2 pr good Shoes from Little
from Iowa, / Falls Same as I bought with me
1 Cow / 1 pr good boots
7 Tent / 1 Doz pr good socks
                / 1 pr good under shirts
                / 1 pr good woolen over shirts

Provisions / 2 pr good drawers
600 ℔ flour / 2 pr woolen Mittens
300 – Meal / 12 pr good Every day shoes for
50 – Beans / yourself and girls
100 – Rice / 1 pr good boots for Each
2 Bbls crackers / 4 pr Shoes for Andrew
300 – Bacon / 2 pr Boots for do
200 – Hams / Shoes for Lillie
50 – dry beef / Stockings for yourself and Girls
50 – Cheese / Do for Andrew
50 – Butter / Do for Lillie
400 – Sugar / Woolen Shirts for family
20 Gallon Syrup / Do Drawers Do
50 – Black Tea / Dresses or Dress Stuffs
100 – Coffee / Clothing or cloth ___ for
400 – Dry apples / Andrew
400 – Do peaches
20 – Salt
40 – Dessicated Vegatables
    Raesins
    Saleratus
    Pepper Spices
    Vinegar to use on the road
    Codfish

*First page of an outfit memorandum that James Fergus sent to his family on
November 21, 1863*

pounds of flour, three hundred of meal, fifty of beans, one hundred of rice, fifty of cheese, fifty of butter, and four hundred of sugar; two barrels of crackers; twenty gallons of syrup; and specified amounts of black tea, coffee, salt, bacon, ham, dried beef, codfish, and dried fruits and vegetables. Cooking on the trail would require a camp stove, camp kettles, and a tin reflector, as well as frying pans. For use in Virginia City she would need to buy a large cookstove, a bread pan, milk pans, water buckets, sausage cutter, table dishes, matches, and a half-dozen good brooms.

Her "washing apperatus" was limited to a washtub, washboard, two flatirons, starch, soap, and concentrated lye for making soap at her new home. As he had promised, she was to bring along "one good strong sewing machine" with an assortment of needles, threads, and yarn, as well as a heavy-duty needle for sewing buckskin. She was to pack up their feather beds into the smallest possible bundles and wrap them in two "Indian Rubber Spreads" that would be placed on the ground inside their tent each night before the feather beds were rolled out.

His clothing list opened with an entry indicative of his vision of the James Fergus of the future: "one suit of good clothes for myself including hat & boots." His own wardrobe was to be rounded out with one everyday coat, two pair of everyday pants, two pair of "good shoes from Little Falls same as I brought with me," one pair of good boots, a dozen pair of good socks, two good undershirts, two good woolen overshirts, two pair of good "drawers," and two pair of woolen mittens. Pamelia, Mary Agnes, and Luella would each need four pair of everyday shoes and one pair of good boots, while Andrew would need four pair of everyday shoes and two pair of boots. Shoes for Lillie and stockings for Pamelia and all the children would be needed, along with assorted woolen shirts, drawers, dresses, pants, or materials with which to make them.

The "stationary" items he recommended included two reams of good white letter paper, one ream of foolscap, a half-dozen memorandum books, one book of legal forms, two of "bill" paper, and five dollars' worth of stamped envelopes. Writing utensils included two gold pens for the girls, one box of steel pens and holders, two large bottles of ink, and two dozen lead pencils. The children would need schoolbooks and slates, one or two good maps, and reading books. For lighting Pamelia would need a box of candles, candle molds and wicking, two lamps with durable chimneys, and some extra chimneys.

Along the trail they might make good use of oxshoe nails, tongue bolts, wagon grease, tar, spirits of turpentine, oxbows, and an extra yoke and chain, as well as a supply of whiskey for dosing cattle poisoned by bad water and for making vinegar once they arrived in Virginia City. James needed extra gold pans, a pair of gold scales, a pair of spectacles, some padlocks, two half-boxes of window glaze, two kegs of assorted nails, a few papers of assorted screws, and a package of "miners shoe tacks." Pamelia was to bring along his tool chest and tools, packing his tools separately and using the chest as her "mess chest" on the road. A shovel, pick, and hoe were needed, plus a half-dozen handsaw files, one flat file, and one bucksaw. She was not to weight down the wagon with wood, but could cut what she needed along the way or use buffalo chips for her campfires. He would need additional ammunition—five boxes of cartridges "for my pistol," shot, powder, and caps. Miscellaneous items included a looking glass, garden seeds, flower seeds, and a sidesaddle.

Sensing that the list might look formidable to Pamelia, he added a comforting note that ended in familiar advice: "If some of these articles should be forgotten it will not matter a great deal because they can all be purchased here only at higher prices. Don't fret yourself about anything. Do your best and let the rest go."[21] Knowing she would need a considerable amount of cash with which to make her purchases, he sent four hundred in gold dust to her in a packet he mailed the day after posting the memorandum. He explained that the dust would bring five hundred in treasury notes, adding that he had already sent five hundred more by Rockwell.

"In selling what things you have on hand, [deciding] what things you ought to bring out, what things you ought to buy and the quantity," he wrote, "much must depend on and be left to your own judgement." If the railroad seemed likely to come through Little Falls in the near future, then it might be wise to hold onto the property for a while and hope that its value would increase. On the other hand, if it seemed likely that the railroad would be routed to St. Cloud instead, then she would do well to get rid of all the property she could before leaving town. Taxes were overdue on the property they owned, as well as on property owned by George Stephens,

William Fergus, and others whose affairs had been left in Pamelia's hands. She was to consider what was owed on each property, then decide whether that property had enough value to warrant paying the taxes. And she was to bring him a careful accounting of the taxes she decided not to pay. Such decisions would not be easy, and she could ask Rockwell's advice as needed. However, James warned her that Rockwell might "be late in getting there, have too much to do, and hurry things through to fast, that will be his worst fault, he will want to start too early."[22]

He offered a few more lines concerning the pending trip. She was to get rid of most of the furniture, even his old desk, since he did not think it would pay to haul it across country. Besides, he added, "people dont use much furniture here anyway, and we may not stop in this country long." Weight was a major consideration, since James estimated that three wagons could carry about 8,500 pounds in addition to Pamelia and the children. She was to weigh the goods carefully before packing up and was to put 3,000 pounds in two of the wagons and only 2,500 in the wagon in which the family would be traveling. She was to give careful thought to the meals she would prepare during the crossing: "Use plenty of potatoes, meat, dried apples etc on the road, and use as little grease and salt as possible. Leaving off vegetables and living on fine flour, bacon etc is bad for the blood and very liable to produce scurvey."[23]

They had once considered hiring Pamelia's brother William Thomas Dillin to drive her wagon across the plains, but Rockwell's presence now made asking Thomas to join her an optional matter. If Pamelia wanted Thomas along and he chose to join them, then James would pay his board and other expenses. In that event, Pamelia was to make sure he drove the wagon in which she and the children rode.[24]

On January 30, 1864, having regained her strength and carried out most of James's instructions, Pamelia finally addressed the issue she had avoided in her last letter: "I suppose before this you have a letter from your Daughter Mary in regard to her maring Robert this is new to me although he has lived in the family so long he is tired [of waiting] and so is she One can find no fault with his habits I have not talked with them in regard to their geting maried he would like to have me give an answer and as things are we have got to take them."[25]

Faced with the need to make the decision on her own, she hastened to assure James, "If you was here of cours I should leave it to you, but I have no one to consult and it would not be policy to speak of it I do not know exactly how you will regard it she is a good girl and will be near us." If there was to be a wedding, then there were certain practical considerations: "Now I do not [k]now your circumstances but judge from reports their [they are] good . . . and if you can send more money to Omaha send it I would like to get her a few things." Having finally put into words the news that she had so long withheld, she ended the letter with a telling line: "I have a great deal to say but can't write so good by."[26]

The following day — the last day of January 1864 — she again sat at the desk and wrote to James, making no mention of the letter she had written concerning Mary Agnes's plans. Thanking him for writing "so plain in regard to our good[s] and oxen," she noted that she had been glad to see on the list "so many thing[s] that I expected to do without in that country . . . [for instance] a good suit of clothes [for you]." Though the generous list had been a pleasant surprise, she soon found that the money he had sent would not cover the items she was to buy. He would definitely have to send her more in Omaha. She had worked to sell what property she could and was not paying the taxes on what she could not get rid of, since Gravel had told her he felt sure the railroad would bypass Little Falls and cross the river at St. Cloud or Sauk Rapids, making their property worth even less in the years ahead.[27] By renting out the eight lots they had used for their crops, she had raised the $504 she needed to pay the back taxes on their home and the four lots on which it was located.[28]

She had finally made up her mind on the sewing machine and had ordered a Wheeler and Wilson model: "It does a good business I do not expet I can sew as well now as I can one month from now." The disappointing news was that, though she looked forward to a visit with Margaretha Ault in the coming week, her friend would definitely not be making the trip west with her: "Mrs. Ault is quite sick yet [and will] not be able to come with us."[29] With neither woman feeling well and the one harried with preparations for a trip the other could not take, the visit must surely have been strained.

Shortly after her visit with Margaretha, Pamelia received another letter from James, who, still oblivious to Mary Agnes's plans to marry Robert Hamilton, was more concerned about another aspect of their pending trip: "Now about Rockwell. He is lively quick active generally has good judgement but is *very careless*, fidgity and peevish the last two pecularities are aggravated by ill health." In view of Rockwell's careless nature, James noted, "you must see that nothing is lost or wasted on the road pick up all your dishes knives forks etc after camping and look all about the camp after the teams start to see that nothing is left."[30]

Having heard many horror stories of accidents on the trail, he enlarged upon an earlier suggestion: "It would be a good plan to have the waggon you ride in fixed so you could go out and in at the hind end in place of the front there would be no danger of being *run over* and you could go in and out when you please. Rockwell may object to it as he is always in a hurry but it can be easily done and may be the means of saving some of your lives." He had still more advice concerning the family's diet: "Use as little *bacon* on the road as possible and as little *salt* buy potatoes and other vegatables whenever you can and fresh meat. It is only by such precautions that you can keep in good *health* on such a trip."[31]

And he offered one further suggestion — a bit of handiwork for the trail. Flour sacks were bringing an excellent price in his area, for grain was being shipped from the fertile, but sparsely settled, Gallatin Valley south to Salt Lake. She might consider buying two bolts of cloth and making them into flour sacks as she traveled across the plains.[32]

At about the same time that letter arrived in Little Falls, so did the Wheeler and Wilson. Luella sent her father the news: "Mother has bought a good sewing machine and can sew very well with it." That news aside, Luella's letter dwelt primarily on Rockwell's arrival and their pending departure: "Rockwell is here he got here the 2nd day of Feb and we were very much surprised as we [had] not expected him for at least two weeks. He has been down to St Cloud and has just got back this evening with four yoke of cattle and one waggon two yoke [are for our wagon and the other two] are for Gravel and Robert. Gravel is going to take his family."[33] The decision had been made. The Gravels — Francis, Hermine, Frankie, Clara, baby Emilie, and a nursemaid — would be traveling with them. But Margaretha Ault would definitely not be going. "Mrs

The Wheeler and Wilson sewing machine that Pamelia bought before her journey to Montana Territory in 1864. Inset: Detail of the table.

Ault was here to day looks very feable. She will not be able to stand a journey so soon but thinks that she will come with Captain Fisk Company."[34] She had written to Ault "for means" and planned to go to Canada until he sent her the money she needed to make the trip west.[35]

Though Rockwell did not plan to leave Little Falls until around the first of March, Pamelia had decided to follow James's suggestion and leave early, taking advantage of the opportunity for a final visit with her family in Illinois. Luella reported, "We are going to start the 24th or 25th of this month for Illinois we will go as far as St Paul in a waggon to save paying stage fare Mrs Gravel is going with us to Illinois and is going to stop at a hotel in Geneseo while we visit and Mr Gravel is gone to Chicago to buy goods."[36]

Though preoccupied with plans for their pending journey west, the Fergus family remained acutely aware of the war in the East. The Minnesota First Regiment was expected to arrive in St. Paul that very day, and Luella noted, "I presume we shall see John Currie before we leave." Other Little Falls soldiers had recently come home as well, but since the president had called for more soldiers from Minnesota, and Little Falls was expected to furnish five of the required number, "most all of the old soldiers are going to reenlist for $402 bounty."[37]

Though they could not have known it at the time, a former resident of Little Falls had enlisted in the Union Army and was at that point serving at Fort Lyon, Colorado Territory. During the month of Pamelia's departure for Moline, her brother James Dillin wrote to James Fergus in Virginia City: "Your Old Friend Doc Smith is here in Charge of Our Hospital He looks well." But the news was not all good: "I think [he] punishes about as much whiskey as ever. His family is at Fort Laramie." He was surely as beguiling as ever: "[He] wanted to see your letter first thing says he is going to write you a long letter."[38] If the doctor passed along any news of his family, Dillin did not repeat it. Whatever her circumstances at Fort Laramie, Amanda Smith was once again an abandoned woman.

Meanwhile the time for Pamelia to leave Little Falls was fast approaching. "I am sorry that we neglect writing you when Mr Rockwell arived here we wer very buisy and did . . . not think how very anxious you would be to hear from him," she wrote James. "We are now making ready to start [and] are packing our things."

She had managed to follow his instructions concerning paying off a Chicago creditor with lots deeded to James by a Little Falls debtor, a complex transaction that she was glad to be done with. In lieu of the $150 Mrs. Fletcher still owed them, Pamelia was bartering for "a good yoke of oxen" and a supply of flour for their journey.[39]

She had sold all the "household stuf" for which she could find a buyer, though in some cases she had accepted blankets and cloth in lieu of cash. She had arranged for the care of their property, reporting that "mr Workman will see to our houses and land over the river." She had raised the money she needed to pay taxes on their home and the surrounding lots by renting the eight garden lots to Mr. Elwell, but she had paid no more taxes after Rockwell's arrival, since "every body is talking of leaving" and property values were at an all-time low.

Because William Butler had decided to forgo the trip west, Pamelia counted on him to close up those affairs she herself had been unable to complete: "Mr Butler will see to our house and the red barn I told him not to rent them He said at any time if they could be disposed of he would write us."[40] She finished packing all her things for Rockwell to load and asked William Butler to board up the doors and windows of her house.[41] She had done the best she could. On February 22, 1864, having made her good-byes to the widows and other friends, Pamelia ushered her four children to the wagon where Hermine Gravel and children were waiting to depart Little Falls. From St. Anthony the two families traveled to Illinois by stage, arriving in Geneseo a week later.[42]

Pamelia's first letter of the crossing was written from Moline early in March: "We are all [arrived] safe at Mothers one week ago the children are their now I will probley go back in three or four days. I am here to have some dental work done could not get it done in Geneseo."[43] She was, in fact, having her remaining teeth pulled and a pair of false teeth fitted, a plan devised the previous fall.[44] There were "a good many cases of small pox in town," and she noted, "I have been vaxinated this morning I am glad I did not bring Lillie with me now when I go home I will vaxcenate [the children] before starting my journey."[45]

Though George Stephens had that day received a letter from James with one enclosed for Francis Gravel, Pamelia did not forward Gravel's letter because Rockwell, Hamilton, Gravel, and

Johnny Johnson were all scheduled to leave Little Falls that very day and were to meet the Fergus family at Grinnell, Iowa, later in the month. Pamelia's brother, Thomas Dillin, had agreed to make the trip, and she was relieved, since they were having difficulty getting teamsters to drive the other wagons: "Rockwell got teamsters . . . but they backed out before we left Since we came here we heard that more backed out Thomas says people here have offered forty Dolars a month to drive a train through quite a number are going around here."[46]

She was now worried about the high cost of oxen—at least one hundred dollars per yoke in Iowa. Overwhelmed with the responsibilities she faced, she wrote, "I will [be] glad when we get started and . . . glad when we get to the end of it," closing her letter with a promise to tell James "all about a hundred things I supose I have forgotten [to write] of here."[47]

Then, on March 26, from her mother's home in Geneseo she wrote the news she had hesitated to convey: "I hasten to communicate to you though with somewhat reluctance our daughter Mary was married to R. S. Hamilton day before yesterday. I hardly know how to advise you or what to say or what is necessary to say he is here at present. . . . Mary was maried at her grandmothers by the Justice their at Oakly our family my two sisters [Eliza and Jane] and Mr McHose [sister Mary's widower] were present and after the mariage we had a comfortable dinner." With the wedding behind her, Pamelia offered James but a single further line concerning the ceremony and the couple's plans: "I wish I could answer a thousand questions that I know that you want to ask."[48]

Had Pamelia chosen not to mention the marriage until the family arrived in Virginia City, James would have received the news from at least three other correspondents. In an undated letter written from his army post in Denver City, Colorado, James Dillin wrote to his brother-in-law: "I had a letter from Sister Eliza saying that . . . Agness and Hamilton was married which was surprising to me."[49] On April 8 a friend from Muscatine, Iowa, conveyed the news in a single sentence: "Some two weeks ago Miss Agnes was married to Mr Hamilton of Little Falls of which you no doubt are advised."[50]

And on April 20 Margaretha Ault noted that she had heard that "Robert Hamilton went down to Rock Island & he & Mary were married." She added a cautionary afterthought: "Well Mr Fergus as you got married . . . you must expect your children to do so." Margaretha's loneliness in the wake of Pamelia's departure was apparent: "I was at the Falls a few days ago and saw your house & it seemed as though I must go in I could scarcely realise that your family had gone."[51]

Within days of the wedding, Robert Hamilton had left his bride with her mother and set out for Chicago where he was to meet Rockwell and Gravel, who had gone there to buy goods and oxen at prices rumored to be lower than those in Omaha.[52] Though "anxious to get started," Pamelia enjoyed the rare leisure of the next few days. "We are having a nice visit and in a nice country," she wrote. "Mr. McHose has taken me out considerable in the bugy," she reported, and all she had seen on those outings with her brother-in-law had reminded her of all she had given up since leaving Illinois and all she would be giving up by moving west: "He has a very inviting situation here he has about 15 hundred fruit trees set out here and a nice cotatage house and full of everything if we had our house here in this country I should want to stay I have lived a mong the Indians and the frountears long enough and lik[e] improvments and good society."[53]

Pamelia had, indeed, spent most of her life "among the Indians and the frounters," staying in one place just long enough for the effects of civilization to begin to be felt, then moving on to a more primitive environment. Born into the frontier society of upstate New York in 1824, she had emigrated as a teen-ager to rural Henry County on the raw western edge of Illinois. While her subsequent move into Moline had temporarily given her the benefits of a more cultured society, she had lost all of those benefits when she followed James to Minnesota Territory. There, moving backward in time, she had assumed once more the burdensome domestic tasks she had learned as a child of the frontier.[54] And there she had accepted the pressing social obligations of establishing the schools and churches deemed essential to the intellectual and moral development of her children.[55] However liberating and invigorating James Fergus may have found his pioneering experiences thus far, for Pamelia moving west had always meant greater confinement and heavier obligations.[56] The move to Virginia City promised to be the most drastic of all, since she would be moving to still further "frountears," traveling so far back in time and so deep into wilderness that the refinements of civilization would likely never catch up with her.

If "improvments and good society" were not to be hers in the Far West, at least she would enjoy them to the fullest extent during her few remaining days in Illinois. Impressed by luxuries she had been without for the past ten years, she described the McHose home as "interesting hung with maps and pictures and good books," and she speculated that "living in a country where improvements are it seems they can enjoy [themselves] and life." Then, realizing the impropriety of her words, she hastened to assure James, "but I will have some nice books for you when we come." She had faithfully kept up his newspaper and magazine subscriptions, and she had ordered the books he had requested. He had asked for maps as well, and she reported that "Mr. McHose has a nice map He has sent for one like his for me."[57]

Even as she worked to carry out James's requests, she continued to ready the children for the trip. She made arrangements to "get their likeness" taken so that those left behind would at least have pictures by which to remember them. At the thought of the pending journey, she wrote her dearest wish: "O how I wish you could have come home but you thought it was for the best."[58]

In early April they were under way. Pamelia and the children traveled to Muscatine, Iowa, where Simon Stein, an early business acquaintance of James's, entertained them overnight. Stein wrote to Fergus: "Your Family — the company — consisting of Mrs. Fergus = Agnes = Luella = Lillie = Andrew = & Thomas Dillen = have all started from here this morning for 'Idahoe' They are all in good Health & Spirits — & as they might not have any convenience for writing to you for some days to come I thot proper to inform you of their progress thus far." He had seen them off to Grinnell himself, via "the cars." In Wilton, Hamilton was to join them and accompany them to Grinnell, the western terminus of the railroad. There they would join Rockwell and his crew, John Johnson and Lawyer Moore, the Gravels, and Belle McGuire on the wagon train that was to depart for Virginia City on April 9.[59]

Also among those waiting with Rockwell in Grinnell was Daniel Bosworth. He traveled without Caroline and the children, for he had hired on as a teamster at the last minute and would be returning to Minnesota rather than staying on in Virginia City. With

Bosworth was Farnham D. Seelye, a forty-one-year-old native of New Brunswick who had been involved in lumbering at Little Falls and was also in Rockwell's hire. In addition to the Little Falls contingent, Pamelia estimated that there were at least thirteen other wagons, with twenty men, ten women, and at least a half-dozen children aboard.

From the moment of their arrival in Grinnell, Pamelia was caught up in preparation for the crossing. The bundles and boxes brought from Moline had to be stored in whatever nooks and crannies were left in the Fergus and Hamilton wagons. Bedding, cooking items, and other essentials had to be double-checked. And tasks for the coming journey had to be assigned and accepted. Knowing James had planned all along for Thomas Dillin to drive the wagon in which she and the children rode, Pamelia reminded Rockwell of that fact early on: "When we got to grenall I told . . . [Rockwell] or talked with him rather that I wanted the teams turned over to me and I would have brother Thomas drive them." Rockwell ostensibly agreed, but the next morning Farn Seelye, whom Pamelia termed "a very medlesom man," was put in charge of the Fergus wagon. He was also assigned to share their meals, though he would sleep in Rockwell's tent with the other drivers. Having no need for the man's services and no desire for his company, Pamelia asked Rockwell why he had not kept his word and made Thomas her driver. He replied "that he did not know as he should" and stood his ground. Thus it was Farn Seelye, rather than Thomas Dillin, who drove the Fergus wagon out of Grinnell and onto the road that would take them west.[60]

Those first days of travel were anxious ones for other reasons. Ten miles west of Grinnell they bogged down in the spring mud surrounding the Skunk River bottom. Robert Hamilton's wagon, laden with his tinsmith's metals and tools, sank to the depths, and from that point on his heavy load was repeatedly blamed for slowing the progress of the train. At Des Moines the train crossed the Raccoon River on a rickety bridge, one team and wagon at a time, then camped in the river bottom, the site of the present-day city, for at least a week.[61]

The trail was so heavily used that there was almost no grass for the oxen, and what hay and corn were available in Des Moines sold for such exorbitant prices that Pamelia lamented it was "costing a fortune" to make the crossing and they were all "nearly dis-couraged" by the expenses they were incurring and the hardships they saw before them.[62]

When they at last left Des Moines, Farn Seelye remained Pamelia's driver, though by that time he had already demonstrated a fond-ness for the bottle. They followed the Raccoon River bottom west to Guthrie Center, arriving there on April 23, seventeen days after leaving Grinnell. Having covered only 105 miles in those seventeen days, Pamelia was discouraged enough to write: "I can tell you nothing only that were here and its strange I wish we had never started I had a great notion to go back when I got to grenell now I wish I had It seems impossible to get their."[63]

"I tell you," she continued, "camp life has no charm for me but the children think it fun they want to eat all the time." Their meals were adequate, if not bountiful. She had been baking "light bread" and reported that the "little cow from home" was giving "a nice lot of milk."[64] Eggs were high, for farmers along the route had raised the price from seven cents to fifteen cents per dozen at the beginning of the emigration season.[65] Andrew was enjoying the pony, and though they had barely begun their journey, Lillie was already ask-ing, "How much farther till we see papa?"[66]

Though Hermine Gravel had a baby, a two-year-old, and a five-year-old to look after, she had a nursemaid to help her, and Francis Gravel himself was doing some of the cooking. Pamelia and the girls were taking care of their own housekeeping, and she reported, "we wash and keep house in a tent that cost 34 dolars it [is] four widths of ducking long [and] three wide." The nine-by-twelve-foot canvas created a home for seven: "Thomas and Hamilton sleeps inside with us." Though Hamilton had first expected that he and Mary Agnes would "be independent," high prices had forced him to give up the idea of a nuptial tent.[67]

The trail was as crowded as the Fergus tent. "The ro[a]ds are full of teams," Pamelia reported, "we hardly camp one night without two or three camp fires in sight and at Missouri river tickets are for five days a head for crossing so it [is] no use to be their [early]."[68] On May 6, almost a month after leaving Grinnell, they arrived in Omaha, where Pamelia received a letter James had mailed in early March from Virginia City.[69] Though he had intended to send her $1,000, he had sent only $750, explaining, "Now I have to pay 90 cts in gold dust for a Dollar in green Backs."[70] Belle McGuire had received money from her husband in the same post, and both women were relieved to know they would not run out of funds before the crossing was completed.[71]

When Rockwell told Pamelia he had enough cash to cover her expenses without the $750, she went shopping in Omaha. "I thought that I would get me some good cloths as our two large girls was young [I] gave them the best but knew at the same time you would not like to see me behind my neighbours in regard to a good dress if we was able if we were not you know I was contented so I borrowed forty dolars of Thomas got some trinkets and [ran up] a bill of about a hundred [that] Rock payed."[72] In addition to the aforementioned dresses, the items purchased on that rare shopping spree included cotton, trimming, braid, ribbon, flannel, thirty yards of prints, eighteen skeins of silk, twelve yards of bleached muslin, six papers of pins, five yards of chambray, as well as socks, hose, combs, shoes, shoestrings, and other items that might prove scarce or expensive on the frontier.[73]

After leaving Omaha the train traveled along the Platte River Road. "My Dear Husband," began Pamelia on May 13 as they neared Elkhorn, Nebraska, some twenty miles west of the Missouri River, "We are yet alive but better dead." She reported that "Farn Sealy le[a]ds the van[guard] if any one goes ahead in the morning he is mad but if he get[s] his oxen yoked first he is off [leaving] the rest to come when they get ready. . . . if Farn Sely is drunk and sees fit to camp [we] pitch tents in the road [He] goards the cattle till evry man and woman in camp are enraged Rock stands by says not a word afraid of Sealy I suppose it only for my children that I endure this."[74]

"Both of Robrts men have left him today," she reported, "Sealy [is] at the bottom of it I dont know what he will do." Johnny Johnson and Lawyer Moore had already pulled ahead of them, choosing to maintain a one- to two-day lead rather than put up with Seelye's antics, and she predicted that "Gravell . . . will not stand the dust and girt [grit] of Sealy all summer by a long ways." And, having agreed to the journey because his sister needed a driver, Thomas Dillin was now "vry sorry that he came not that he has any trouble with any one but hates the [company] of a Sealy."[75]

Furious about matters over which she had no control, Pamelia noted, "I feel a good deal like talking but it [is] of no use . . . [but] if I was at home I would be mighty glad to stay [there]." Risking James's anger, she let him know exactly how she felt about the arrangements he had made that put them under Rockwell's care: "[You were] foolish to send for us by a man you know so well he does not regard the truth [but] use[s] your money just as he pleases [with] no regard for your family. . . . next time I cross the planes it will be with my husband or on my own hook this is the awfless mess I ever was in."[76]

"Evry thing is larnt by sad experience her[e]," she noted. "We are without a stick of wood. . . . we have two very heavy loads though [there is a] . . . very good yoke [of oxen] on the provision wagon two mean yoke and one yoke of cows to our load."[77] Nine days later, on May 22, while camped about thirty miles from Columbus, she reported that "Rockwell has bought another team at Fremont and litened our loads Macguires and ours so we come right along." Her emotional load had lightened as well, and she reported that they were "getting along nicely now the grass is good our cattle the men say look well and feel well and we all feel better." They were about seventy miles from Fort Kearney, and James was to "calculate from that when we will be their."[78]

They had settled into a routine in which they were on the road by 5:30 or 6:00 each morning. "We are cooking to day," she reported, "making light bread fryed cakes and stewing aples getting ready for the road early." The weather had been generally good, but they had had a severe storm. "Deliver me from a thunder storm on the plaines," Pamelia wrote, though she admitted she still had not seen the worst: "I thought we had one bad storm but Rock says that was nothing." Mary Agnes was doing the washing and "she says tell Father she did not get the letter that you rote her," a letter conveying James's initial reaction to her request to marry Hamilton. Pamelia urged, "You must write her another she wants to here from you on the subject she rote about."[79]

As Pamelia wrote, Andrew was "runing bulets" for a revolver Thomas Dillin had lent him, and she added, "Our company [is] good for over a hundred shots," meaning they could fire that many times without reloading in the event of an Indian attack. Though they had not been bothered thus far, their ponies had gotten loose one evening and until they were found the following day, everyone was sure they had been stolen by Indians. "Two days back," she reported, "the Indians stole eight yoke of oxen and the poor man [who owned the wagons] was left right in the road I felt bad for them poor folks so far from any one and very likely poor." At the thought of Indians, she closed her letter with a wistful line: "I [would] just like to peep in [your] cabin just now for our lit[tle] tent looks Indiany."[80]

From that point onward the trail often looked "Indiany," and at each fort they visited they heard reports of the latest depredations, though the only Indians they encountered on the plains were friendly enough. One evening, a small band wandered into their camp and, according to Luella, "were looking around in our wagons, seeing what they could see. They were very curious." On impulse, Pamelia, sitting within a few feet of an Indian woman who was staring at her, "drop[ped] her teeth." Never having seen artificial teeth, the woman "ran over to the other Indians, screaming and yelling, and they all took up the yell, leaving our camp in a hurry. A little later, they came back with a larger crowd and look[ed] at mother . . . [thinking] that she was a great prophet or witch. They were afraid and yet they wanted to see if mother would do the same thing again. She would not, however, and it was not long before they all pulled up and left us." The Indians, who were part of a band Luella estimated at "probably one hundred and fifty . . . all told," did not return again.[81]

At Fort Kearney they had intended to cross over to the south side of the Platte River, but they found it much too high for a crossing — so high, in fact, that "Rockwell could not get over to get some letters."[82] Thus they settled into the long journey, taking the northern route along the Platte River across the rolling plains of Nebraska. On June 17 Pamelia again wrote to James. They were about thirty miles east of Fort Laramie, having traveled approximately 380 miles over the past twenty-five days. "We expect to be at Fort Larmy . . . tomorrow," she wrote, "so we are getting along slowly I hardly know which way we will come."[83]

Neither did O. J. Rockwell. In December James had asked Pamelia to "Tell Rockwell that I think a good deal of the travel next season will come in on the Jacobs cutoff," a route later known as the Bozeman Trail. The cutoff left "the Salt Lake road about 150 miles above Fort Laramie and [kept] on the East side of the [Bighorn] mountains altogether striking the Missouri River at Gallatin then up the Jefferson here." The advantage was clear: "The distance would be some 4 or 5 hundred miles nearer than by Salt Lake." That meant about six fewer weeks on the trail.[84] The route was also less heavily traveled and therefore offered more grass and water for livestock and more wild game and firewood for the emigrants. But it also offered far more danger from the Indians.

Knowing the decision loomed closer with every passing day, Pamelia had pressed Rockwell to write at once for James's opinion, but "he decline[d]." The wagon master was in no mood to receive her advice, having just resumed command of the train, which Daniel Bosworth had led ever since Rockwell "had bad luck [and] got kicked by a mule." The accident had "strained his ancle [but] its a little better now [he] can step slitely on it and we are glad."[85]

There had been other mishaps. "Bell McGuire fell out of the wagon," Pamelia reported. "The wagon run over her instep she has not stepet for a long while." The most serious casualty was five-year-old Frank Gravel, who "bar[e]ly escaped with his life this morning it['s] heard to tell how bad he is hurt some say his leg is broke. . . . I do not think it is." She expressed her own diagnosis in laywoman's terms: "The cords are badly drawed up will kneed great care to come out all right."[86]

Both accident victims had fallen beneath the wheels of a moving wagon, the very type of mishap against which James had warned. Though Pamelia wrote him of the injuries, she neglected to mention that she had not provided the rear entrance to the wagon that he had advised. Rather, she emphasized the positive—the Fergus family was safe and sound, though Mary Agnes had been somewhat sick. Keeping close watch on the condition of her livestock, as well as that of her children, Pamelia reported, "The oxen look pretty well the feed is generaly good." The weather had been fair and hot, "but Sunday night we had a storm on the Plat," one that lived up to Rockwell's stories of prairie storms: "I will asure you we had eight cotten stufed comforters wet through and not a dry rag to put on except those in our trunks every thing was wet in the wagon through a thick blanket and cover the storm was terible about twelve O clock at night."[87]

"I hope to get . . . a letter from you at the Fort," she wrote. "Last night I dreamed I saw [you] coming I had been straning my

eyes a great while but before you got to me or I was positive it was
you I awoke alas it was but a dream." Her sleep was disturbed as
often by worry as by dreams. "Now I must tell you . . . we have
thought of the Indans and I guess all are [thinking of them] if the
truth was known." As they approached hostile Indian country they
had been joined by other wagons, so that their party now numbered
around forty-five men. And they had begun to "correll at nights,"
with four men standing guard. "We here of Indan depridations see
but few squaws and old men," Pamelia wrote, though she predicted,
"times a head I am afraid are hard." The new members of the train
were apparently well armed, for she now reported that "our company has about two hundred and fifty shot," including "one gun
[that] shoots sixteen times."[88]

They had "plenty of aminition and all are ordered to sleep with
[their guns] so that they can put their hand on them at once."
Though admitting that they had "had some frights," she concluded
that they might as well press on, since "it looks a[s] dark behind us
as before." That night they camped outside Fort Laramie, as
planned, heading out before daybreak and making a breakfast stop
while Rockwell consulted with officials at the fort, as noted in
Luella's brief postscript to her mother's letter: "We are opposite Fort
Laramie and Mr. Rockwell is going over we have come twelve
miles this morning Ma is getting breakfast and told me to finish this
we shall see you soon if all is well."[89]

After consulting with the officers at Fort Laramie, Rockwell
chose to keep the train on the north side of the Platte and avoid the
long journey down toward Salt Lake. However, tales of Indian attacks had convinced him to forsake the Bozeman Trail, the route
originally recommended by Fergus, in favor of a route being carved
out just ahead of them by mountain-man Jim Bridger, who had
departed Fort Laramie around May 27 to lead a group of wagons
through treacherous terrain along the west side of the Bighorn
Mountains, thereby avoiding the prime Indian hunting grounds
through which John Bozeman had traveled.[90]

Leaving the Oregon Trail at Red Buttes, just south of present-
day Casper, Rockwell headed the train due west toward the Bighorn River and then turned north. With the Wind River Mountains
to their left and the Bighorns to their right, they traveled alongside
creeks with such ominous names as "Poison Spring" and "Bad Wa-

ter," finding poor grass and little wood. Shortly thereafter they entered a dry and desolate stretch of badlands. After traveling for a good many miles without finding water, the oxen became irritable. By the time the wagon train encountered a seep, the emigrants themselves were near panic. Rockwell ordered the men to dig down several feet. When they struck water he rationed the scant supply, allowing only one bucket for each ox until all were watered. A "free-for-all fist fight" broke out when "someone violated this rule by giving his favorite oxen two buckets of water." Soon after the prolonged session at the muddy watering hole, the train arrived at Wind River, "a beautiful mountain stream with more than enough water for all."[91]

For a while the train followed that stream, which becomes the Bighorn River upon emerging from Wind River Canyon. After crossing the Bighorn, they subsequently forded the Grey Bull and Stinking Water rivers before turning west once more toward the Yellowstone.[92] The route was rugged and there was evidence that more than one wagon had been wrecked on the rocky terrain. Hamilton's heavy load of tin proved too much for the wagon and the trail, and a wheel snapped under the strain. Unwilling to delay, lest he be caught again without water for the cattle, Rockwell pushed on, leaving the bride and groom to cut timber, fashion the needed parts, and catch up with the others as best they could.[93]

By July 31, having been rejoined by the Hamiltons, the train was camped fifteen miles west of the Yellowstone River, and Luella noted, "Mother says she is so thankful we are so near she has nothing more to say." They had survived the most dangerous portion of their journey and were in a festive mood, though Luella wrote her father that "Agnes has had the erysiplas & been poisoned & has been sick three weeks." She was getting supper and noted, "we have corn bread, wheat bread trout bacon molases & tea. I went fishing today and caught a large trout. We have quite a large train and are getting along nicely but I must away to finish getting supper & give the man this." Remembering well how often her father's work had preoccupied him, she begged, "you must hurry & get your work done so we can talk when we get there & not interfere with your work," then closed her note with "a kiss for Pa Hoping to see you soon I will bid you good bye."[94]

Reaching the headwaters of the Missouri, they followed the

Madison River south. On August 14, 1864, a little over four months after leaving Moline and almost six months after leaving Little Falls, Pamelia and the children arrived in Virginia City. For the first time in over two years, the Fergus family was once again united. Unfortunately, there are no letters describing the reunion, no written records detailing the relief, joy, and awkwardness of the long-awaited moment that marked the end of their overland journey and the beginning of a new life.[95]

7

The Settling

IN THE ROUGHLY CONSTRUCTED, sod-roofed cabin that James had built for them in Virginia City, Pamelia set up housekeeping, glad to be under a solid roof and out of the canvas tent that had been her only shelter for so many months. But even as she busied herself with the myriad tasks attendant upon turning house into home, she must have had a sense that she had slipped backward in time, surrounded as she was by scenes reminiscent of her early days in Little Falls. Nine years and a thousand miles had brought her full circle — back to a raw frontier environment. Here again were the crude beginnings of a town — though its population was already ten thousand.[1] Here again were champions of vigilante justice.[2] Here again were ill-staffed schools and churches, set up in homes and storefronts.

Yet, contrary to her expectations, Virginia City in 1864, primitive as it was, offered more luxuries than had Little Falls in 1855. A variety of stores already lined the unpaved streets — a bookstore, a stationer's, a confectionary and bakery, lumberyards, a drug emporium, meat markets, "a photographic gallery," a boot shop, a reading room, dry goods stores, and "bathrooms" that featured shaving and hairdressing salons.[3] The premier issue of the *Montana Post,* the territory's first newspaper, off the press August 27, 1864 — two weeks after Pamelia's arrival in Virginia City — invited townspeople to attend a performance by May's Ethiopian Minstrels at the theater building in the post office block. Dramas featuring local actors were also advertised, as well as prizefights and lectures. For a town that was barely a year old, Virginia City was doing well in providing entertainment for its citizens.[4]

Pamelia Fergus settled into her new home and cherished what connections she had to her old. It is quite likely that two letters carrying news from Little Falls had reached Virginia City ahead of her. In mid-April, while Pamelia was on the trail somewhere west of Fort Des Moines, Margaretha Ault sat down to write the Ferguses. Soon after Pamelia's departure, Margaretha had received a letter

Virginia City, Montana Territory, about 1864

containing another invitation from John to join him in the West—but once again no funds to cover the expenses of the trip. On her own, Margaretha "had not the means" for such a journey, noting, "You can not get a decent yoke of cattle for less than eighty or a hundred dollors and waggons from seventy-five to eighty."[5]

Still other considerations weighed in her decision. While she did not blame Pamelia for choosing to follow her husband west, Margaretha reminded her friend that "Mr Rockwell said he would not advise me or any other women to go to that country." And while she "had [her] mind made up all along to go with Capt Fisk," she had just that week read in the papers that Fisk was not taking another train across because "there is going to be a great expedition against the Sioux this Summer."[6] All things considered, Margaretha Ault would stay where she was.

Happy to report that her health was much improved now, she asked Pamelia to tell John that she was "not in the least discouraged" about her situation. She only wished that "Mr Ault would come home next fall The times are very good here now A man can make a good living St Cloud is getting to be a smart place A man could start business there with very small capital."[7] Even as Margaretha wrote those lines, and as Pamelia read them, both women knew that it was highly unlikely that John Ault would return to Minnesota and that it was questionable whether Margaretha would ever be willing or able to cross the plains on her own.

Discouraging news of other friends from Little Falls awaited Pamelia in a letter her husband had recently received from her brother James, still serving in the army at Fort Lyon. He had heard that "Doct Smith has finaly got [out] of the service although it is my opinion the best thing he could have done would have been too stick to it."[8] In the absence of any news of the doctor's wife and children, Pamelia could only conjecture that it was unlikely that Amanda had yet found the good life.

Not that she herself had found it either. But there were promising beginnings. She added the few items of furniture brought from home to those already in the cabin, hung her curtains, set up her sewing machine, and proceeded to carry on as wife and mother in the company of the husband from whom she had so long been separated. Not that she had much of his company. His days in the mine were long and arduous, not unlike the days he had spent in the foundry at Moline and at the mill in Little Falls. And in addition to his work in the mines, he continued in his post as deputy recorder, serving also as president of the Fairweather Mining District, election judge, and county commissioner.[9]

As always, Pamelia found plenty to fill her hours, and her routine soon expanded to include cooking and washing for several Virginia City men who had no wives or daughters at hand to tend to such duties. Robert Hamilton set up his tin shop, selling lead pipes, washbasins, dippers, and teakettles, then broadening into general merchandise and grocery items.[10] He and Mary Agnes were expecting their first child, and they soon moved into a cabin of their own. Luella, Andrew, and Lillie assumed their share of household responsibilities, and Andrew and Lillie attended classes at Rev. Thomas Dimsdale's school, where Luella occasionally served as substitute teacher.[11]

From all outward appearances, the Fergus family would seem to have settled easily into their old routine, but later letters suggest that James and Pamelia did, predictably, have some major adjustments to make. An undated letter from James, most likely written in the fall of 1864, suggests that the couple now found themselves unevenly yoked after pulling in separate harness for so long. Small wonder, since Pamelia was expected to give up entirely the leadership role she had been obliged to play during James's absence and become again the obedient housewife and devoted mother of their early married years. While she had never intended to continue to manage their business affairs, Pamelia now knew far too much about such matters to ignore them completely. Having learned to manage hired hands, deal with tax and real estate agents, cajole debtors, and mollify creditors, she found it hard to return to her old role of acquiescent, unquestioning wife, readily deferring to her husband's judgment in matters outside her sphere. Yet that was essentially what was expected.

And even as James expected Pamelia to step gracefully back into her old sphere, she expected him to allow her to have full charge of that sphere. But this was not to be. In the realm of child care, James had never hesitated to offer his advice, and after nearly four years of acting as a single parent, Pamelia found herself once again subject to his lectures. In the realm of housewifery, having become accustomed to cooking to suit herself and the children, she was suddenly expected to conform to James's latest dicta concerning a healthy diet.

Ironically, though there were clearly deeper issues at stake, it was Pamelia's failure to meet her husband's standards of nutrition that afforded him the perfect opportunity to voice his dissatisfaction with what he saw as disgraceful insubordination. Beginning with a description of a dinner at which James had publicly upbraided Pamelia for oversalting the food and she had defended herself in front of the family and guests, the letter he wrote leaves no doubt about his displeasure with his wife's behavior:

> Mrs. Fergus I have not had an opportunity to give you my private opinion of the disgraceful scene that took place before Mr. Gilpatrick Thomas Dillin and your own family at dinner one day last week in which you made use of such language as never fails to disgrace or at the very least lower a female in the estimation of all respectable people. Profane language is allowable to men by common custom but when used by a woman it is generally allowed that she only has to add drinking and then she is prepared to become a public woman. They are the only women whom everybody expects to hear swear and even some of them have never stooped so low.[12]
>
> I have worked hard for my family for some years at very dirty laborious work have done my own cooking and washing have gone poorly clad that I might send all my earnings to my family notwithstanding my old age and few men of any age have done that or worked so [hard] as I have. I have had few vegetables have been out most of the summer on bread and bacon my blood is in bad order so is that of my family I have kept myself tolerably healthy by using little salt or as little salted food as possible. I have learned from the best physicians and the best medical works that salt is not healthy

without vegatables this is the judgement of the civilised world and before my family came here I lived accordingly I have spoken to you often on this subject and wrote to you about it before you left home. On the day in question I told you that a certain article of food was too salt[y], a good woman would have felt sorry that such was the case, would say that she would try to be more careful in the future and would try [to do] so. In place of that you [chose] to stir up discord or for some other reason said it *was* not too salt[y] and that you could not taste any salt in it. It contained so little Now any person of common sense would know had he tasted the food that what you stated was untrue, positively untrue — but had it been so and I had wished it to have still less salt it was your duty to make it so. I did not pay so much money to bring my family here that I might live worse than I did before. Such scenes only tend to degrade us to a level both in my eyes and in that of all good citizens . . . and more than that it embitters my life in my old age. I have always wished to keep good company to associate with respectable people and have my family do the same [but] to do so they must first behave respectably themselves. A great deal depends on first impressions and first acquaintance. I endeavored before my family came here to open or prepare the way for them and with my old mining clothes I was respected and received into the best society in the place, better than I can go in to now or take my family into.[13]

Here Fergus broke off his long invective to address a related issue — Pamelia's friction with Belle McGuire and O. J. Rockwell on the long journey across the plains: "I was at peace with every body had no enemies no clashing or hard feelings. Now I cannot say so. The jarring between my partners family and you has made a difference."[14]

Then James came, at last, to the heart of the matter, letting Pamelia know in no uncertain terms why there were serious problems between them, problems that threatened their relationship as well as his social standing: "The great trouble is that you pay no attention to the wishes of your husband, even to his positive directions at times." And with that statement he launched into an attack that was a far cry from his earlier advice of "do the best you can and let the rest go":

At Little Falls you did not copy the bills as I directed nor stop at Chicago, nor ask Thomas to fix the waggons nor put your flour in double sacks I would not have written to you to do these things if I had not wanted them done and if my own wife pays no attention to my directions how can I expect Rockwell or any body else to do it but [he] will come far nearer [doing] it than my family for I gave him no directions and he did what he thought was best I gave my wife directions and she did not do them. You say the bills answered all purposes, that was none of your business I wrote you to have it done and that was sufficient. Mrs. Sturgis Mrs. Ault or any other [wife would] . . . not enquire whether it was right or wrong.[15]

Though he did not specifically mention a letter from William Butler that would have been delivered shortly before Pamelia's arrival in Virginia City, that letter might well have been on his mind as he wrote. While Pamelia had followed James's instructions and left everything in Butler's charge, she had failed to give him power of attorney, causing him to miss an opportunity to sell James Dillin's house. And though she had made a bargain with John Elwell to use her lots in exchange for his payment of her taxes, Butler reported that "owing to the prospects of another drought worst if any thing than last years, Mr Elwell says that he will not ocupy the lots, so you will have the taxes to pay."[16]

Drawing his bill of complaint to a close, James gave some indication of the reason he chose to write out his argument, rather than talking the matter over with Pamelia:

I wish you would do a little thinking and find that you have some duties to perform when I talk with you you either remain silent which is a disrespect that no thinking person would ever offer or make use of language that you know is untrue or swear and use abusive language.

You ought to be thankful that you are situated as you are and treated as you are. I would say more but language cannot convey my contempt of such conduct and scenes as the one I first [found] fault with. [I am] certain I would never come near such a person if circumstances did not compel me, I would let you find some lower element in which to practice your contrary nature and your profanity.[17]

Over the four years of their separation, James had never shown such displeasure with his wife's behavior, perhaps because he had always assumed she was doing exactly as he asked. Had he been able to see across the miles and observe the subtle changes that occurred between Pamelia's first acquiescent meeting with the shareholders and her final feisty dismissal of their claims, he might have realized that she had learned to stand up for herself. Only a few months into his Pikes Peak sojourn, sensing her increasing ability to take care of matters in Little Falls, he had predicted, "My going away has [been] and will be of great benefit to you, by throwing you on your own resources and learning you to do business for yourself."[18] Apparently, he had never stopped to consider what such "learning" might mean in terms of their relationship.

Over the past four years, his pompous criticism of her spelling and "putting in all the words" and his admonition to use her "leisure" wisely might have set her fuming, but knowing that the miles between them meant that long months would pass before any damage done by her angry reply could be repaired, she had limited herself to small retorts and kept the anger locked inside. However, once she resumed day-to-day interaction with the man whose caustic remarks increased in proportion to the time they spent together, her tolerance lessened. She, too, had pride, and to have her cooking held up to public ridicule so that James could wax eloquent on one of his favorite issues — the dangers of salt in the diet — was too much. The exact words she used to rebut his public censure cannot be known, but the strain that had arisen between two people who had grown accustomed to living life on their own terms cannot be missed. No matter what her hardships in Little Falls, Pamelia had been the undisputed head of household. No matter how hard his work in the mines or how long his hours, James had been responsible only for himself during his years in the West. Now, forced to meet on common ground, they found themselves unable to decide where to give in, how to live and let live.

It was a difficult time, and the troubles between them might well have contributed to James's decision to take an unforeseen step the following spring. He was making good money from the dozen or so claims he owned in the Bannack-Virginia City area, and he still held twenty-nine claims in Deer Lodge County, many of them in the Silver Bow District that was later to prove among the state's most profitable mining areas. Yet he was restless. The influx of gold seekers was threatening the prosperity of the established miners. Their numbers caused such a drain on supplies that by the spring of 1865 flour that had sold for twenty-seven cents per pound the summer before was selling for a dollar per pound. Wealthy and poor alike were doing without bread, and in late April 480 men were involved in a flour raid, the news of which eclipsed locally the news from Appomattox.[19]

Furthermore, the claims James owned at Virginia City had apparently yielded their best ore and were now playing out. From past experience he had learned the importance of selling out at just the right time to avoid being left with useless holdings. Things looked bright to the north. Gold had been discovered in the Prickly Pear drainage where he had already staked a few claims. In January the *Montana Post* had predicted that "Last Chance [Gulch] will be a lively place next summer."[20] And a mid–April entry sent many men scurrying north to Helena: "The diggings here at 'Last Chance' . . . take the lead of anything in Montana, at the present time, and there are many gulches still to prove. . . . [Most are] probably as good as Alder Gulch."[21] That spring the Last Chance Express began running a semiweekly stage route between Helena and Virginia City.[22]

Weeks before the Last Chance Express went into operation, and barely eight months after Pamelia and the children had arrived, James Fergus was already hard at work on a choice claim in the heart of what would eventually become Montana's capital city. Once again Pamelia was left in charge of affairs at home, and this time there is no evidence that she longed to join her husband in his new location. Even though Virginia City lacked refinements, Pamelia had established a home there and was reluctant to leave her daughter and son-in-law. Furthermore, she was not at all sure she would be happy in Helena: "We had much rather live on the claim [here] I am not very particular but I must be buisy for some purpus and their are so many going their to take boarders that I dont want to try it." She had already built up her boarding clientele in Virginia City: "Mr Gilpatrick payed me for his board since you left," she wrote, "and John partly and Randle for three weeks since you left."[23]

She intended to buy a cow and some chickens so that she could once again count on butter-and-egg money: "I think we can buy some chickines and get some gardenseeds and buy one or two cows you did not say for me to do so and I suppose cows are scarce but chickines are expected in evry day from Salt Lake. . . . now write me and tell me if it is best to buy some cows if I can find them I expect they will be hard to find this time of year." Then, as if to let him know that she would not lightly entertain the thought of following him one more time, she added, "I most hate to leave those seasoned boards I have used for shelves."[24]

Pamelia's letter dwelt on her concerns at home and did not touch on news that shocked the world that April of 1865 and reached Virginia City some two weeks after the fact. It was Luella who wrote that news to her father: "I presume you have heard before this the very sad news of the President's death. . . . I would send you an extra but we could not get one here as they have all been sold." Her lengthy recounting of the assassination was followed by a description of Virginia City's reaction to the news. A few men had made speeches, and "most of the secesh women met at a house in town and rejoiced over it . . . but they were told if they were not careful they might not feel so good. The secesh men were very quite the Union stores were draped in mourning the Union ladies are trimming their bonnets with black to let the secesh see that there are some loyal women out here."[25]

While expressions of Union and secessionist sentiments must have been heard in Helena as well, that fledgling settlement had not yet sufficiently caught up with Virginia City to offer its ladies boardwalks on which to show off their black-trimmed bonnets. The town was primarily inhabited by grizzled miners, for many of whom Last Chance Gulch was the aptly named terminus of a long road that had begun at Pikes Peak, wound down to the Salmon River country, up to Bannack and Virginia City, then north to Helena.[26]

Within a few weeks of his arrival there, James Fergus had found enough promise, if not enough gold, to convince him that his future lay in Helena, not Virginia City. In that belief, he sent word to Pamelia to prepare herself and the children for the move. She was less than enthusiastic, replying, "We are as well off here as their."[27] Yet ten days later, on May 13, 1865, nine months after her arrival in Virginia City, she packed her goods and moved to James's homestead on Last Chance Gulch. Her departure was difficult for Mary Agnes, and Robert Hamilton reported that "Mary forgot that hur mother had gon[e] and went to the House and found the Doar Locked." Though James urged the Hamiltons to follow him to Helena, Robert had no desire to leave his store. And her loneliness for her mother aside, Mary Agnes was equally reluctant to leave Virginia City. She had shown her father's influence and invested

Bridge Street, Helena, Montana Territory, 1865

some of their profits from storekeeping in mining claims, and Hamilton reported that she had "a Severe Attact of quartz on the Brain she has got Four Hundred feet of quartz and wants ten thousand."[28]

Nothing James said could dissuade the couple from holding fast to what they had, not even a slump in prices during which Robert advised James to order all his goods through Virginia City since prices were at rock bottom.[29] The market was resurgent though, supporting Robert's optimism, and by October 1865 he was selling sheet iron so fast he worried about running out before the first of the year. He worried, too, about his father-in-law's dealings with O. J. Rockwell, whom he called "as big a villan as ever lived," adding that "many a better man has stretch[ed] hemp than he." Instead of selling James's Virginia City house when he might have done so at a profit, Rockwell had rented it out at only twelve dollars a month.[30]

Hamilton was soon rid of his nemesis, however. In late autumn of 1865, O. J. Rockwell and James McGuire, sometime mining partners of James Fergus, packed their tools and made the return trip across the plains, Belle McGuire and the children in tow.[31] Hamilton, predictably, applauded their exodus: "Rockwell had a face to do any thing he would steal from you this minet and the next would make you beleve he was your freind."[32]

Late in 1865 the Gravel family was also on its way back east. Though Francis Gravel had come to Virginia City as shopkeeper rather than miner, the business slump of that spring had made him wary of staying on. He may also have been swayed by the long-range effects of the injury his son had sustained on the trail. "I am very sorry that the mines turn out so poor particularly on Gravel's [account]," William Butler had written Fergus earlier, "for he has gone there with his family at a great expense, and invested [a] good deal of money in goods to take there, with the expectation . . . to settle there permanently, and now if he has to sell his goods for less than he pay'd for [them] and come back, it will ruin him, but such is life, and he has no body to blame but himself."[33]

At the time the Gravels set out for Little Falls, Pamelia and James were still living on the 160 acres James had homesteaded that spring near the middle of Last Chance Gulch.[34] Despite early prospects of a bonanza, Fergus had discovered that his claim contained but "a trace of gold and silver" and that his 160 acres was destined to be dug up or built on by other miners, his homestead claim notwithstanding.[35] By late December 1865, he had given up both the mine and the homestead and was casting about for new directions.[36]

Hamilton advised him to give up mining altogether and take up ranching. He himself was now considering a change and might not order any more merchandise for the coming season.[37] Fergus also had offers to return east and go into business with his former partners. Both George Stephens, in Illinois, and O. J. Rockwell, who was now farming in Missouri, urged him to join them in their separate enterprises. But he never seriously considered those offers. His destiny was clearly in the West.[38]

Another old partner still saw it that way too, though, like James, he was now looking in new directions. In the flush of success with his sawmill at Bannack, William Sturgis had built another at Montana, a new mining camp northeast of Bannack, and he was soon shipping lumber by oxteam to Virginia City, Deer Lodge, Helena, and the Salmon River diggings in Idaho Territory.[39] The very nature of his business involved him in road building, and he had ambitious plans for a toll road from the mines of Montana Territory to Salt Lake City. Through the fall and early winter of 1865, before James and Pamelia gave up their homestead in Last Chance Gulch, Sturgis pushed the road down through the Beaverhead Valley, keeping a six- or seven-man crew constantly at work.[40] In addition to building the road, Sturgis was back at his old trade of town building. He established a stage station, a post office, and a Wells Fargo agency on the Red Rock River, some ten miles east of Bannack. He called the place Sturgis and bought up the surrounding ranchland.[41] While William was building his new dream in the West, Rosanna was finally making plans to leave Minnesota. She had the Little Elk property on the market, but prospects were poor.

Prospects were poor in Last Chance Gulch as well, and James Fergus was ready to be done with the place. Early in 1866 James put in a homestead claim on 160 acres of land on the south bank of Ten Mile Creek just outside of Helena, and he and Pamelia, Luella, Andrew, and Lillie moved once more. It was a temporary measure. Shortly thereafter James sold the claim to one of Pamelia's former Virginia City boarders, Stephen Collins Gilpatrick.[42] Since Gilpatrick did not intend to move immediately, the Fergus family stayed on the homestead while James worked at various mining and construction jobs in the area.[43] Once again Pamelia found herself in limbo, ever aware that another move was inevitable and having no idea where that move might take her.

That spring of 1866 Mary Agnes traveled to Helena to have her first child, James Lincoln Hamilton, and Luella returned to Virginia City to help with the baby. In early summer, little James became seriously ill.[44] And though Robert wrote in mid-July that "Baby is getting better slowly," a letter written two months later told a different story: "Mary is taking it awful hard the loosing of our darling Boy I have hur go out as much as I can to keep it off hur mind I can't bere to think my self about him but he is Happy and he has paid a Debt that we all ow[e]."[45]

Luella, who had been in Virginia City during the baby's illness, brought disturbing news when she returned to Helena. There were telltale signs of serious friction in the Hamilton household. Robert showed extreme jealousy when Mary Agnes went anywhere without him or allowed young men to call at their home. He refused to provide his wife with clothes and shoes. And he ridiculed her—and even Luella—in the presence of others. Vindicated in his earlier assumption that the match would never work out, James wrote two lengthy letters of advice to the couple—one to each party. In addition to advising Mary, "Don't talk back so much to Robert. When

Mary Agnes Fergus Hamilton (right), shown here in 1893 with her sister Luella and brother Andrew

he abuses you with his tongue let him go on," he could not resist reminding her of the circumstances under which she had married: "You was imprudent in marrying Robt knowing him as well as you did and your mother was just as much to blame as you."[46] With Hamilton he spared no words: "I never expected you to agree well because you could not agree when single, but I did not expect it to come to throwing sticks of wood to telling her to go home, etc., etc. In my letter in answer to yours asking my consent I discussed with freedom why I thought you ought not to get married [because] your tempers did not suit."[47]

Despite the friction between them, Fergus continued to rely on his son-in-law, and Hamilton continued to offer both advice and, when needed, money. In early May 1866, when James asked his help in buying a ranch, Hamilton advised, "I dont think it pays to move every six months," offering instead to send six hundred dollars toward buying some cattle if James would stay put.[48] But by fall of

Robert Stavely Hamilton, shown here about 1900

1866, when it was obvious that Fergus was firm in his intent, Hamilton relented and sent four hundred dollars in gold to help him buy a ranch in the Prickly Pear Valley, some miles north of the Gilpatrick land.[49]

Pamelia was likely even more reluctant to move this time than she had been to leave Virginia City, for she and James had invested considerable time and money in planting an orchard on the site they had sold to Gilpatrick, and though half the trees had died of winterkill, the other half seemed likely to survive.[50] Sensitive to her loss, James once again ordered fruit trees and, soon after they were settled on the new ranch site, planted an orchard that would, he hoped, one day rival those Pamelia had so admired in Illinois.[51]

As the Ferguses planted the young trees that fall of 1866, they received some unexpected good news from William Butler, their primary Minnesota correspondent. Their Little Falls house had finally sold, and though the town continued in its economic decline, Butler had been able to get six hundred dollars for it.[52] There was other good news: Orlando Churchill had "left off drinking entirely," was living at home in Little Falls with Temperance and the girls, and had been elected auditor of Morrison County.[53]

That letter, dated October 12, 1866, also noted that "Mrs. Ault is here from Canada." Although she had moved to Verona, Ontario, to be with relatives when the end of the Civil War reduced the number of boarders at Fort Ripley, Margaretha Ault continued to visit Little Falls. "She says that she is going to Montana next spring," Butler reported, a prospect he termed doubtful, since he felt she was "pretty poor."[54] While the Ferguses had not heard from Margaretha in some time, they had heard from John. By late 1866 he had moved to Bozeman in the Gallatin Valley some ninety miles south of Last Chance Gulch. Though he was running a sawmill there, he had maintained his interest in mining and asked James to find out how the "Baley Load is geting along . . . an if it is worth any thing . . . I should like to see if there is any chans at a fair prise If it could be got please let me here from you by return of mail." Ault added that he would like to visit the Ferguses, but "it is imposable for me to cum for a while as I have got a good del to do this winter." His letter made no mention at all of Margaretha or of her purported travel plans.[55]

Timothy Smith was also still in the West, though he did not have a "good del to do." James Dillin had run into the doctor once more, this time at Fort Collins, where he was "about played out as he can hardly bum a drink of whiskey any more."[56] Dillin sent no word on Amanda and the children.

At least prospects seemed promising for one of the widows of Little Falls. In the fall of 1866 William Sturgis wrote to the Ferguses from his ranch in the Beaverhead. Enterprising Rosanna had finally "sold the Little Elk property for something." After paying off all their debts, she would likely have enough left to bring the family out in the spring.[57] William Butler soon confirmed the news of Rosanna's success: "Mrs Sturgis has sold her Little Elk property with all her fine pine land—the 1200 acres, to Messrs Wait[e] Clark and Kimball of St Cloud."[58]

Even as Rosanna worked to ready her family for the trip west, Elizabeth Stone was making plans to return home to Minnesota. Five years earlier she had made the trip west with the judge. His death at Fort Collins in January 1867 left her with twelve hundred dollars and little else. At one time she had been a well-to-do influ-

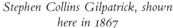

*Stephen Collins Gilpatrick, shown
here in 1867*   *Luella Fergus Gilpatrick in her
middle years*

ential woman, but Lewis Stone's sense of adventure had depleted
her resources and left her a thousand miles from home. With no further reason to remain in the West, Elizabeth set out for Minnesota
to live among her eight children, most of whom still resided in Benton County.[59]

The same month Elizabeth Stone became a widow, Luella Fergus
became a bride. On January 1, 1867, eighteen-year-old Frances
Luella was married to her mother's former boarder, twenty-eight-
year-old Stephen Collins Gilpatrick, who had sold the Helena
ranchland he had purchased from James a year earlier, bought a
home in town, and opened a grocer's shop and stationer's store.[60]
While the Gilpatricks were moving into their new home, Pamelia
and James were still trying to dispose of their old home in Virginia
City. Robert Hamilton had been tending it for them since O. J.
Rockwell's departure for Missouri, and in early January he wrote to
ask James the lowest price he would take for the house, since the
worsening depression in Virginia City meant there was no "regular
price for property in this place when the[y] sell the[y] sell for all
the[y] can."[61]

The depression in Virginia City did not at that moment concern
Rosanna Sturgis. For better or for worse, she was on her way west.

Advertisement for the Missouri River steamer Luella, *1867*

Five years after William had joined the Fisk expedition of 1862 and left his family in Little Elk, Rosanna was finally setting out to follow him. With her were her seventeen-year-old stepson, John, and her four daughters, aged six to fourteen.[62]

The Ferguses read of Rosanna's departure in a letter from Margaretha Ault, who explained, "I expected to go with her but I am afraid my money [from John] was lost on the road for I have not received it as yet . . . this is the third time i have tried to come . . . in two weeks more i shall go to Canada and stay there till Mr Ault comes home." Though more disillusioned than ever, Margaretha was still trying to maintain contact with John: "Enclosed you will find a letter I wish you to mail to Mr Ault for he seems to get them safer when i send them in this manner."[63]

If Margaretha Ault had been frightened in the past at the thought of overland travel, she must have been equally cowed at the prospect of making the trip west as Rosanna Sturgis was making it. With Fisk having decided against another expedition, Rosanna had opted to travel by river steamer—down the Mississippi to St. Louis, then up the Missouri to Fort Benton, Montana Territory.[64] Although river travel was somewhat less expensive than overland travel, it was also less reliable.[65] The upper reaches of the Missouri River were shallow, and gigantic snags concealed beneath the water were capable of piercing the hull of any vessel — even 150-ton steamers. And those upper reaches were also controlled by hostile Indians, who found the slow-moving boats an easy target.[66]

Having lived among Indians ever since moving to Little Elk, Rosanna Sturgis was not one to be deterred by rumored hostilities. The letters she wrote to William while aboard the steamship *Luella* are those of a woman accustomed to crisis and inured to danger. From the vicinity of Sioux City she reported that they were "still alive and all well and moving along slowly but sure." They had lost three days because of winds and had just passed the wreckage of another steamboat, but her spirits remained high as she was enjoying the "very agreeable company of ladies that are going cleare through." There was plenty of traffic on the river: "There was five Boats passed here Sunday bound for the Mountains," and she hoped the *Luella* could overtake them before getting "up into the Indian country." A boat ahead of them had reportedly been attacked by two hundred Indians who had robbed and killed the crew and passengers and burned the boat. But that was likely just another "Indian story" and she did not know "whether there is any truth in it or not." Though seemingly nonplussed, she did have some concern for the family's safety, as evidenced by the last line of her letter: "I will close hoping our lives may be spared to reach our Journeys end."[67]

Their lives were indeed spared; the *Luella* reached Fort Benton safely on July 8, 1867, two and one-half months after leaving St. Louis. But William Sturgis was not there to meet it. Busy at the ranch, he had arranged to have an ox-drawn wagon meet his family. The capable Rosanna loaded children and trunks into the wagon and began the 250-mile trip south to the Beaverhead Valley.[68] For the first few days they followed the Mullan Road, traveling past the Great Falls of the Missouri and into the Prickly Pear Valley — passing through ranchlands owned by James and Pamelia Fergus.

While there is no written record of a visit with Pamelia, Rosanna knew where the Ferguses were living and would most likely have stopped to visit. On the ranch Rosanna would once again have seen Pamelia working to establish herself in a new environment. She would have seen the saplings that were to be her orchard, the first-year garden that was already supplying produce for Stephen Gilpatrick's store in Helena, and the poultry and milk cows that provided her butter-and-egg money. Though Rosanna was still a long way from her new home when she said good-bye to her friend, her glimpse of Pamelia's life in the Prickly Pear would have given her a preview of the life that awaited her on the Beaverhead.

The summer Rosanna arrived in Montana, a former Little Falls resident died there. James Fergus wrote friends back east that Johnny Johnson, who had made the journey out in the same train as the Fergus family three years earlier, had been killed in a shoot-out over a prostitute.[69] Upon receiving James's letter concerning Johnson's death, William Butler replied that he was "very sad" to learn of the tragedy and inquired if Johnson had left any property or money for his two little boys.[70]

From Butler the Ferguses gained news of several other Little Falls friends and acquaintances. James Hall was dead. Immediately upon his return to Minnesota from Pikes Peak, Hall, who had never been one of Little Falls's favorite citizens, had moved his family to St. Cloud and there resumed the practice of law. Late in 1867 un-finished business had called him back to Denver. On his way home, early in 1868, he was taken suddenly and seriously ill, dying in Cheyenne at the age of forty-three. Apparently he had left his family destitute, for Clara Hall had sold her furniture and was living in a rented house, leading Butler to surmise that Hall's "fortune of Denver was like his Fortune he had in Iowa when he first came here, all humbug."[71]

Temperance Churchill was also dead. In October 1867 Butler had written that she was seriously ill and not expected to live, but that Orlando was still at home and still sober. Temperance died some six months later.[72] Butler also reported that Francis Gravel had settled the family in Little Falls and resumed his shopkeeping. Since their return from Virginia City, Hermine had borne two more babies and, according to Butler, "Gravel and his family . . . all seem to be contented here."[73]

James Fergus too seemed to be contented. Ranching brought the satisfactions that mining had not. The ranch on the Prickly Pear was prospering; he and Pamelia were marketing produce, grain, meat, and hay to businesses and friends in the Helena area, as well as to the military posts that now spanned Montana Territory. For a time Andrew had worked alongside his father, but James soon bought an adjoining ranch for his son, and eventually purchased and leased a third ranch in the valley.[74]

In the spring of 1871, twenty-one-year-old Andrew displayed a bit of his father's entrepreneurial spirit by taking out a restaurant license and converting his ranch house into a way station. Located on the Mullan Road near Silver City, the station provided a welcome rest stop for stages, wagons, and military detachments traveling between Fort Benton and Helena. Encouraged by their son's success, James and Pamelia moved to Andrew's ranch the next year, added a few rooms, and expanded the small restaurant.[75] Later they procured a hotel license that allowed them to offer overnight lodging, as well as food, to their guests. For nearly a decade the station did a lively business.[76]

Over that same decade, James was actively involved in the politics of Lewis and Clark County. Always a man of action and community affairs, he had served in Little Falls as judge of probate and had run for a seat in Minnesota's constitutional convention. In Virginia City he had been deputy recorder, president of the Fairweather Mining District, election judge, and a Madison County commissioner. And though he lost a bid in 1866 for a seat in Montana's Territorial Council, he was appointed a commissioner of Lewis and Clark County three years later, an office he held through most of the 1870s.[77]

With James involved in politics as well as ranching, management of the stage station fell, almost by default, to Pamelia. Though she had expressed dismay at being left to handle family finances back in Little Falls during James's sojourn at Pikes Peak, she showed no such reluctance after her arrival in the West, and James himself noted that "Mrs. Fergus always kept the purse after we came to Montana and was more careful about spending money than I was."[78] If the managerial skills she had gained in dealing with Little Falls creditors were put to good use at the stage station, so were her diplomatic skills. When the ranch was invaded by a band of sixteen Crow Indians in search of the Flathead party who had stolen their ponies, Pamelia offered the warriors the food of her kitchen and the warmth of her barn, maintaining her composure throughout a thirty-six-hour siege. The incident was so widely discussed that it took on the aura of legend, and no one was prouder of his wife's behavior than James Fergus himself.[79]

He had other reasons to be proud. In addition to managing the stage station, Pamelia expanded her already thriving butter business. Known for butter that was "always up to standard in quality and in weight," she sold fifty to one hundred pounds per week to restaurants, stores, and private customers in the Helena area.[80] During these years Pamelia and James shared more interests and worked more closely than they ever had before, and James later indicated that her work at the stage station marked a turning point in their marriage. They never really understood one another, he maintained, "until we worked together or had interests in common or rather until she had her own way with the . . . Stage Station."[81]

Certainly at the stage station Pamelia was "buisy for some purpus," yet during those years her children remained an important part of her life. In addition to Andrew, Lillie — now a teen-ager — was still living at home. Luella and her four little boys — George, James, Collins, and Frank — were nearby in Helena, as was Mary Agnes, the Hamiltons having sold their store in Virginia City and established themselves in the town that was soon to be named the territorial capital.[82] In August 1873, a month after their move to Helena, Mary Agnes gave birth to another son, Thomas Moore Hamilton.[83]

Earlier that year the Ferguses had heard again from William Sturgis. Since his family's arrival in Montana some five years before, he had sold most of his other interests and had concentrated his efforts on ranching.[84] Two sons had been born on the Beaverhead Valley ranch — William, Jr., some ten months after Rosanna's arrival, and Arthur, now just one year old. Sturgis's report was succinct — "All well two fine Montana boys" — but cordial, inviting the Ferguses to come see what fine land he had settled on and sending along some black currants, white raspberries, and white gooseberries "without bryers" as proof of its bounty. Rosanna added a line along the margin of the letter: "We will be pleased to hear from you."[85]

Within months of writing that letter, William Sturgis had silver, not gooseberries, on his mind as he and four partners struck a rich vein near Glendale, some twenty miles north of the Sturgis ranch. Almost immediately they accepted an offer of one hundred thousand dollars for the claim from a mining company in Indianapolis. The Hecla Mine was to become a major producer of silver, but

Sturgis did not stay around to see it develop.[86] He was fifty-six years old, his health was failing, and he longed for a less strenuous life-style. He wanted a better education for his children than they could obtain in the beautiful isolation of the ranch. And the death of his father meant that there were new responsibilities and opportunities in Sturgis, Michigan. Once again Rosanna prepared to cross the plains.[87]

Shortly after the Sturgis family's move to Michigan, another Minnesotan-turned-Montanan went home for a visit. Lewis Randall, who with his brother Leonard had first gone west during the Pikes Peak excitement and later followed the gold strikes to Montana, returned to visit Little Falls in 1874. The report he sent back to James Fergus confirmed the wisdom of the move they had made a decade earlier. Little Falls was

> the most desolate looking place I ever saw for a place that . . . [was] as lively as it was in 56. There ain't more than half as many houses now and not the least mark left to show that there ever was a bridge and a mill there. But the people that live there think it will be a hell of a place in a year or two. It may be a place some time but I think we will all be under the sod first.[88]

Another of the original Pikes Peakers was no longer in Little Falls when Randall visited there in 1874, but he was close by. Having finally given up his dream of going west, Daniel Bosworth was living on a farm near Browerville, about ten miles north of Long Prairie, with Caroline and their seven children. He was logging on the Mississippi and was periodically away from home on drives up the Red River of the North to Winnipeg. Lately he had been thinking of establishing a logging camp of his own near Fort Ripley.

Margaretha Ault had long since left Fort Ripley. Her destiny seemed tied now to Ontario rather than Montana. A letter written in 1872 indicated that her patience with John had brought her no rewards: "I must tell you that about a fortnight ago I was talking with a gentleman that had just come from Virginia City to Verona [Ontario] and he knew you well and I assure you that it seemed so much like home to hear from you and he gave me a good deal of information about the country, but he did not know anything about my husband." Margaretha reported that she had "maintained" herself "by going out as midwife just as I did in Little Falls although I find it very hard to be thrown upon my own resources so many years for I have not received the first cent from John Ault since he went away. . . . I think if I was there I could make a far better living than I can here although I have good health and I thank God for it."[89]

She had found that her reputation, as well as her finances, had been damaged by her husband's long absence:

> I must tell you that the part of the world I am in the people likes to talk very much and since Mr Ault does not send for me they talk a great deal about my character and what kind of a woman I must be for him to stay away as he does . . . you knew me in little falls when John kept the Northern Hotel and when I kept the Officers Mess at the Fort and you know how comfortable John and I lived together. . . . I hope the time will come when I see you that I can tell you far more than I can write for I am the same Mrs Ault as I was when you knew me and sustain as good a character. . . . If John don't write that is no reason why I should be blamed for it.[90]

And after keeping her silence for years, she was finally moved to express regret that her pride as well as her illness had kept her from going west in 1864: "If I had known what I know now sick as I was I would have gone with you when Rockwell came for then I had means to go but it is different now." Thus, though the "gentleman" she spoke of in the beginning of her letter was going back to Montana Territory the next month, Margaretha held no hope of going with him, though she promised, "I will send you my likeness."[91]

That was the last time the Fergus family heard from Margaretha. The last news they had of John himself came three years later in 1875—from the man who was handling his estate. John Ault had died in Bozeman, leaving property valued at two hundred dollars. James Fergus wrote home to William Butler about the premature death—Ault was in his early fifties—and his eulogy was characteristically to the point: "Poor John he has made a great deal of money in this country, he ought to have had his wife here and been well off but he has lived fast, been always in debt, spent his money in eating, drinking and with women. I think he thought a great deal of his wife, but with him it was out of sight out of mind."[92]

Butler's response was hardly sympathetic: "He left considerable debts here. He owed me quite a little bill, but of course [I] never expected to get it so I am not disappointed I think such men are better dead than a live. So you see that I am not a mourner of John Ault."[93]

While the 1870s seemingly brought only trouble to Margaretha Ault, the early years of that decade brought relative contentment to

Pamelia and James. The stage station proved to be a profitable enterprise, and their ranching investments did equally well. By the end of the decade James Fergus and Son had several hundred head of top-grade stock cattle, some fifty head of quality brood mares, and six thoroughbred stallions, and James and Pamelia had managed to accomplish one of their foremost mutual goals — ridding themselves of the indebtedness that had so long clouded their lives.[94]

But as financial worries dissipated, the couple faced a personal crisis they could never have anticipated. In 1876 they discovered that their youngest daughter, eighteen-year-old Lillie, was pregnant. No extant letters or journals reveal how long she managed to keep her condition a secret from her parents or describe their reactions, once the truth was known. Nonetheless, James's constant concern with public appearance makes it easy to guess his opinion of the disgrace. As tension built and accusations flew, Pamelia was caught in the middle. To make matters worse, there was no hope for a quick marriage, for by the time Lillie's changing figure had given her secret away, the baby's father, Frank Maury, a twenty-five-year-old Civil War veteran, was in Iowa, having set out in early spring to look for farmland closer to his own family.[95] Lillie remained at the stage station with James and Pamelia until September, when Frank finally returned to claim his bride. By this time she was within weeks of delivery, and the time for a formal wedding was long past.[96] On September 2, 1876, the couple said their vows before a judge and set out at once for Key West, Iowa, a small farming community near Dubuque.[97] Within days of their arrival there, Marion Maurice Maury was born.[98]

The departure for Iowa, which had effectively removed Lillie from the gossip of neighbors at home, had also removed her from her mother. Homesick, she wrote that she "would of been there now but all of you seemed to think it was death to stay there Frank wanted to stay; but I knew until we were out of Montana the folks could not breath natural I would like to see you so much Mother but you know I would not be there 24 hours until they would wish me in Iowa again."[99] When Pamelia's letters betrayed her own loneliness, Lillie fell into the role she had so often played as the toddler in Little Falls, advising, "Mother we must cheer up," yet admitting, "I get a little lonesome sometimes, [too,] for all I have to think about is out home & one can not think of one thing forever & not feel like going there Yes Mother I can tell how you feel, now, I have a child too & can think how I would feel if any thing should happen [to] him & [he] be taken away from me But you don't miss me more than I do you."[100]

As much as she missed her mother, Lillie knew that going home would carry a steep price. James Fergus had chosen not to attend his daughter's wedding, and for some months after her move to Iowa, he and Lillie did not write to each other.[101] However, he did write to Frank Maury, offering to let the couple purchase his Prickly Pear Valley ranchland "on very liberal terms," an offer they refused rather than go so deeply into debt—and perhaps because they doubted the wisdom of moving back to Montana and facing James's constant reminders of the disgrace their "mistake" had brought to the family name.[102]

If support from her father was limited, Lillie at least had that of her sisters, both of whom sent clothes for the baby, and of her brother Andrew, who stopped by to see his new nephew in early October during a trip east to visit the Philadelphia Centennial Exhibition of 1876.[103] At that time Andrew was twenty-six and still unmarried—to the constant concern of his sister Luella. Fearing her brother was still a bachelor only because his standards were too high, she warned him, "You need never expect to get one like mother you won't find one in a hundred or more."[104]

In the relative affluence of her later years at the stage station, Pamelia enjoyed many of the comforts of civilization—from a stereopticon with American and European scenes to a home illuminated by gaslights. There was money enough for luxuries. And money enough to buy and breed racehorses, yet, according to James, not money enough to send Pamelia east to visit her daughter and grandson.[105] He was steadfast in his decision, though every letter from Iowa increased Pamelia's need to go to Lillie and bring an end to their estrangement. Resigned, Lillie herself resolved to describe the baby's every action in her letters, declaring, "You see I am going to tell you every thing so if you can not be here you can imagine how things look."[106] She sent tracings of her son's hand, scraps from the clothes she made him, and locks of his hair, knowing that if only her mother could hold him in her arms, the old hurts would be forgotten: "He is so pretty I think if you could see him you

Frank and Lillie Fergus Maury with their children (left to right) Elsie, Claude, Marion, and Merle, about 1889, when they lived in Dilley, Oregon

would [pencil slash here] O shaw you can not see him now & what is the use of wishing I am getting tired of here wish I was in Montana."[107]

Wishing did not alter the distance that stretched between mother and daughter, and while little Marion cut his first teeth, took his first steps, and spoke his first words, life at the stage station continued much as it had before Lillie's departure for Iowa. Pamelia sold butter, cheese, and eggs and cooked meals for ranch hands and overnight guests.[108] Her life was busy and productive, and she must at the very least have assumed that her days of moving were finally at an end. In that assumption, she was mistaken.

8

Endings

By the late 1870s, civilization was encroaching on the ranchland in the Prickly Pear Valley. No longer able to let his cattle roam freely over open range, James Fergus was forced to confine them to his own pastures and feed them more often than was profitable. The township in which he had located was "all inside railroad limits" and no homestead over eighty acres could be claimed there except by a discharged soldier.[1] The cattle ranch James envisioned could not become a reality within the confines of his present location. Friends had moved farther east, where they reported tall grass, abundant water, and few worries about rules and regulations.[2] James decided that he and Pamelia should rid themselves of the burden of the stage station and move to the vast, open plains of central Montana. All practical reasons aside, James felt the old stirrings, the need for "elbow room" that had first called him west.[3]

For Pamelia, the proposed change was a drastic one. She would be leaving a world in which she had frequent visitors and much to occupy her mind and hands and moving to a desolate area where her nearest neighbor would be at least twenty miles away. She would be leaving behind her daughters and grandchildren and trading weekly trips into a thriving capital city for long months of isolation.

How much her opinion counted in the decision made by James and Andrew is not known, but in the spring of 1880, after finishing the branding, the two men set out with a wagonload of supplies to search for new range. After covering five hundred miles in twenty-four days, they returned to announce the location of their new home—a large spread north of the Judith Mountains on the Armells and Box Elder creeks. About thirty miles northeast of present-day Lewistown, the site was some two hundred miles east of Helena.[4]

Over the next few months James Fergus sold the stage station with its surrounding land, plus most of the household and ranch goods. Though willing enough to part with the six to eight extra bedsteads and the many table settings they had used in running the stage station, Pamelia was once again forced to part with items she

Pamelia Dillin Fergus, aged fifty-six, 1880

might well have preferred to retain, for Fergus insisted upon keeping their load light and buying new items once they were settled on their new land.

Pamelia had almost a year's reprieve before the move was made. During that time she made the long-awaited trip east to visit Lillie, Frank, and little Marion and to spend time with her mother, brothers, and sisters.[5] Upon her return from the Midwest, Pamelia remained in Helena while James and Andrew moved their livestock and equipment eastward and began establishing their new base of operations. Its isolation and its vulnerability to Indian attack were revealed in the purchases James made that fall: two gun belts, three Winchester rifles, fifty .44-caliber cartridges, and an ample supply of powder and shot.[6] He also purchased a pocket compass, an essential tool for moving cattle about on the open range, especially in harsh weather.[7]

Having helped Andrew build the cabins, stables, and corrals that he and the hired men would need to survive the winter, James returned to Helena to wait for spring. At sixty-seven, he had high hopes of establishing a ranch that would stand as a monument to all his previous efforts to "make his pile," but by the time he had completed the move and taken stock of his new situation, he informed Andrew, "Our expenses have been very heavy. It is a good thing we did not buy sheep. It will take all we have before we can make anything there."[8]

That winter of 1880–81 was one of the harshest on record, and as Pamelia and James shivered in Helena, where temperatures dropped to thirty-one degrees below zero, they worried over Andrew out on the plains.[9] In a letter dated December 1880 and wishing them all a "mary Christmass and a happy New Year," Andrew noted, "I could here the Indian drums last nite at 11 O clock I expect they wer haveing a dance their drum sounds plain here 3 miles distance."[10] As the months crawled by, letters concerning clashes with Indians, near disasters in blizzards, and troubles with his hired hands made their way slowly to Helena, usually taking longer in transit than did the letters James was receiving from his relatives in Scotland.[11] Andrew's reply to his mother's question concerning life on the Armells was bluntly honest: "You wanted to [know] what I thought a bout your comming down here I think you would not like it much It would be rather lonesome Thare is nothing atractive here but grass."[12]

Soon after James returned to the Armells ranch that spring of 1881, the full extent of the isolation into which Pamelia would be moving became all too clear to Luella, who expressed her concerns to Andrew: "I don't think it is any place for Mother for you know how she use to be left alone hours at a time down at that old place [on the Prickly Pear] and it was not safe then . . . if it was not for Father and you being there all the gold in Montana would not get her to live there."[13] But James and Andrew *were* there in the wilderness, engaged in the work necessary to the survival of the ranch, and Pamelia was drawn to follow. She remained ambivalent throughout the spring, however, for in a diary entry that April, James noted that he had "got letters from Mother saying Andrew advised her not to come." His reaction was characteristically to the point: "I telegraphed her my regrets and asked if I should return her things." Predictably, Pamelia yielded, and in September James traveled up

The Fergus house on the Armells ranch, 1912

to Helena to fetch her home to the newly completed ranch house on the Armells.[14] It would be the last move she would be asked to make.

It was a move that took her farther into the "frountear" than she had yet been. For three long months after moving into her new home she did not see another woman, or anyone else, save James, Andrew, their work crew, and an occasional customer for milk or butter.[15] At one point that fall she invited a milk customer to bring his wife along the next time he came by, but when he obliged her, she found herself trying to converse with a full-blooded Indian who could speak not a word of English.[16] For a woman who had found pleasure all her life in the close company of friends, such isolation was particularly trying. Yet frustrated as she must have been, Pamelia took some comfort in knowing that, for the first time in their married life, James Fergus seemed utterly contented. He announced plans for still another orchard, and it was clear that this time he planned to harvest the fruit from their trees—season after season after season.

Once again Pamelia worked in harness with her husband, overseeing the planting of produce, the milking of cows, the care of chickens, and the cooking of meals for the men who joined Andrew and James in tending the cattle and, eventually, the sheep they brought onto the land. In May 1883 James reported to a friend that Pamelia "works hard, doing nearly all the work for nine men, makes butter, raises chickens, has flowers and plants indoors and out and is always busy."[17] The woman who did all that work was, at that time, nearly sixty.

A roundup on the Armells ranch, early 1880s

James would later recall those early years at the Armells ranch as among the happiest in his married life, noting that the girls were married and gone and Andrew not often home, so that "we were always together and thought far more of each other than we did when we were young. I think people of good sense generally do, haveing lived so long together they become so used to each others ways become more like each other are more forgiving and one becomes as it were a necessity to the other, I know it was so with us."[18] And if Pamelia's view differed from his, there is no written evidence of that fact.

The ranch prospered, but even as it did, Fergus, seemingly a man who needed a solid debt structure beneath him, once again extended his line of credit to a thin edge.[19] As of 1883 he owned $30,000 in cattle, $5,000 in horses, $1,500 in implements, $2,750 in ranchland and buildings, $1,000 in Box Elder property, $1,000 in grassland, and $5,000 in sheep, against which he counted over $29,000 in debts.[20]

Counting the riches of the Armells holdings in other than livestock and farm implements, Fergus included a survey of his library in his inventory of household and farm goods. The list of his favorites from among 2,500 volumes includes such titles as *Life of*

Pamelia and James Fergus, 1880

Voltaire, Plutarch's *Lives,* and Gibbon's *Rise and Fall of the Roman Empire,* as well as a dictionary of mines, several medical texts, books on cattle and horses, and histories of Scotland and Montana. Though a staunch agnostic, he owned a Bible and a translation of the Koran, as well as several books on religion.[21]

In 1878 James Fergus had been elected to serve as Lewis and Clark County's representative to the Territorial Council. While his move to the Armells ranch distanced him from his old constituency, it did not lessen his interest in politics. He was twice elected to public office as a representative of Meagher County. In 1884 he served in the Constitutional Convention, and the following year he sat in the Territorial Council—as the oldest member of that body.[22]

Pamelia often accompanied him to Helena during legislative sessions, taking full advantage of every opportunity to visit with her daughters, their families, and old friends in the Prickly Pear Valley. In January 1884 James wrote home to Andrew that they had arrived safely and that "Mother and the girls . . . talk so much I can't write."[23] Welcome as such visits were, Pamelia no longer considered Helena home, for despite her occasional grumblings against "the frountear," she was, in her bones, its child. Her ambivalent response to the civilization that surrounded her in the capital city is captured in James's lines to Andrew during the 1884 session: "Mother says tell them she is tired of staying here, wants to go somewhere, would prefer to go home; too much noise, too many houses, too many people, and too many locomotives howling around, would rather hear the coyotes, but stop, she says dont tell them the last."[24] Just a week later he wrote again, "Mother and I have an invitation to a big ball at Mings and Mother is getting a new silk dress made for it."[25]

At the close of that legislative session in mid-February 1884, rather than returning directly to the harshness of winter on the central Montana plains, Pamelia and James boarded a train for Portland to see Charles and Abby Freeman, their old neighbors in Little Falls. Though Pamelia had long anticipated the reunion, she was to be disappointed. The day before the Ferguses arrived in Portland, Abby had crossed the Columbia River to visit a friend. When the river froze over that night, she could not get home. "Mrs Freeman . . . telegraphs for us to wait till she comes," James wrote Andrew, "but as our passage is paid we cant do it." That night they left by steamer for San Francisco, and Pamelia never saw Abby Freeman again. Still, she had enjoyed recalling with Charles the days they had spent together in Little Falls twenty years earlier, the days when she had come of age.[26]

Returning from their trip to the coast, Pamelia settled in once more to the routine of life on the plains of Montana. James himself was preoccupied again with ranching activities — and with accepting the honors that had begun to come his way. In 1885, in recognition of his contributions to the early development of the territory and of his stature among its citizens, the territorial legislature named the county newly carved from Meagher County for its premier resident. James wrote his brother William in Scotland with ill-concealed pride: "A county here in Montana over 100 miles long and 60 wide was named after me last winter by our legislature . . . the only vote opposed to it being my own."[27]

Neither James nor Pamelia was prepared for what came next. In the fall of 1886 Pamelia began to feel "shooting pains in her right side and her right breast swelled." When she finally showed the swollen place to James months later, he consulted all the medical books on

Left: Crazy quilt that Pamelia Fergus was piecing at the time of her death in 1887. Right: Pamelia's embroidery bag, filled with thread used to embellish the quilt.

the ranch and quickly came to the alarming conclusion that his wife had cancer.[28]

Andrew took her to Helena at once, and though James wanted her to go to the States if surgery was necessary, Luella reported that the doctor in Helena had told them that wounds healed more quickly in the high altitude and low humidity of the West than in the East. That advice aside, Luella reported that "Mother did not want to go [east] She decided herself." Thus surgery was performed in Helena on March 20, 1887. Luella immediately wrote to her father that "the cancer had not adhered to the muscles so they had only to remove the whole breast there were no lumps under the arm." Two days later Pamelia was resting comfortably in a bed in Luella's parlor, sipping the wine James had sent to help her regain her strength.[29]

But two months later the discovery of a lump under her arm necessitated further surgery. When the incision had healed sufficiently, Pamelia began to ask to go back to the ranch house on the Armells, writing Andrew, "It seems a long time an[d] I want to . . . see the old home." She worried about her garden: "[I] forgot to tell you about the Gladilos in the little culler pleas pull the tops off and stick them in the groud . . . be careful of my littl rose . . . opsit your window." And in answer to James's questions concerning her pain, she assured him, "I take my wine evry night

Pamelia Fergus, 1884. This photograph,
taken in California, is on display in the
Fergus County Courthouse, Montana.

and I sleep well . . . but I want to be home."[30] Finally, Luella gave in to her mother's pleadings but warned James that he must get a housekeeper so that Pamelia would not overtire and he must learn to use the syringe to inject morphine when her pain became unbearable. Grateful to be home among her flowers and her fruit trees, Pamelia quietly celebrated her sixty-third birthday on June 22.[31]

Toward summer's end she could no longer enjoy walks in the out-of-doors, and soon thereafter she conceded that it was time to return to Helena.[32] In early October James helped her into the buggy, drove the 125 miles to meet the train, then drove himself back to the ranch after promising to follow her to Luella's within a few days.[33] He could not have known how close the end was. On October 4 Dr. Steele wrote James, "Mrs F is rather worse this morn she cannot last very long. It is impossible to do anything but try to palliate & try and make life tolerable as long as it does last I expect Mr G[ilpatrick] will telegraph you before this reaches you."[34] Three days later, on October 6, 1887, with James still at the ranch, Pamelia Fergus died.[35]

When the family gathered in Helena on October 10 for the

funeral, Lillie was with them but Andrew was missing. He had taken a load of cattle to Chicago by train before his mother's departure for Helena and did not learn of her death until days later.[36] Wilbur Fisk Sanders, a fellow pioneer, delivered the funeral oration, an address actually prepared by James himself and reflecting his own ideas about life and death: "While she could not understand how she could live after death, or locate a heaven or a hell, she clearly comprehended the duties appertaining to her station in life and in their performance was an obedient child, a faithful wife, a loving mother, a true friend and an honest woman, performing her full duty in all stations in life, beloved by all, leaving not an enemy behind."[37]

Back on the Armells ranch a few days later, James wrote to his daughters and their friends:

> Everything is as usual but no Mother here. How I would like to tell her about my trip and how she would like to hear it. How I started in a snow storm. How you waited for me to get there. . . . How I was met with kisses formerly so repugnant to me, but tolerated and rendered pleasant by the friendship and warmth with which they were given. . . . [Of] the pleasant burial plot . . . of the delicacy without being hinted at of leaving a space outside of hers for Father . . . as if to protect her if needed in death as in life. . . .
>
> But Mother is beyond all that, she has fulfilled one of natures laws; she and us following the same laws will soon be forgotten. Still while she was but little to the world she was wife and mother to us and will live in our memories while we live. . . . Through a long life I have tried to be a stoic and philosopher, but this has brought me down to humanity, and here alone I can pour out a flood of tears, which of itself will be a tribute of love.[38]

For another fourteen years after Pamelia's death, James Fergus continued to live with Andrew in the isolation of the ranch on the Armells. Visiting his family and friends in Helena only periodically, he stayed close to home, contenting himself with "hard labor, good books, and papers" and becoming, by his own report, "almost a hermit."[39] Though he made a trip by train to the Chicago World's Fair in 1893, he did not enjoy the experience and was so out of sorts that he did not even stop in Moline to visit his old friend George Stephens. Nor did he see anything he recognized as the train passed through Fergus Falls en route to Illinois.[40]

It was the last time Fergus ventured outside Montana, and, except for brief visits to Helena, the last time he was away from the

James Fergus at the Armells ranch, 1897

ranch. In September 1897 he wrote Nathan Richardson of Little Falls that he was "going down hill fast, can't do much but read and write; so I am lonesome and want to hear from old friends who are still in the land of the living." Though he loved the ranch, it was located some thirty miles from Lewistown, the county seat, and without Pamelia's company, he complained that he had no one "but cowboys, sheep-herders and horse-men to talk with."[41]

Less than a month after he wrote that letter, tales of gold strikes in the Klondike stirred old feelings, and, wizened and bent as he was, eighty-four-year-old James Fergus announced his plans to go north—"provided Andrew, whose health is not good, can spare me." To those who protested that a man of his age was in no shape to make such a journey, James replied, "We all have to die sometime.

My friends can bury me under some old pine tree, or better still, underneath the moss where the ground has been frozen for thousands of years and will be for thousands of years to come."[42] Despite such bold assertions, James Fergus never made it to the Klondike.[43] He died at the Armells ranch on June 25, 1902, little more than a year shy of his ninetieth birthday, and was buried beside Pamelia in Helena. After his father's death, Andrew continued to operate the Fergus Livestock and Land Company. In 1910, at age sixty, the confirmed bachelor married Hazel Akeley, a woman some forty years his junior. The couple remained on the Armells ranch, raising three children of their own — Agnes, Pamelia, and Andrew James.[44]

Though the ending to Pamelia's story is known in full, the subsequent histories of the other widows of Little Falls are, for the most part, difficult to establish.[45] Of the lives of Amanda Smith and Elizabeth Stone, nothing more is known. Never completely well after the birth of her last child, Agnes Russell lived another fifteen years after Robert died in the mines. During those years of true widowhood, she managed the meager earnings of the Russell children "with proverbial Scotch thrift," holding the family together until the older members married. At that point she moved in with her oldest son, Robert, and she died in his Benton County home in 1877 at the age of fifty-seven.[46]

Alexander Paul died intestate in 1873, leaving forty-eight-year-old Mary and three minor children at home. The Paul homestead had not been proved up, yet Mary managed to hold onto the land. She survived her husband by sixteen years and, on her death in 1889, was buried next to him on the family farm in Burnhamville, some twenty miles southwest of Little Falls.[47]

By 1870 Caroline and Daniel Bosworth were living in Hartford, a village near Burnhamville. In 1882 Daniel headed the largest log drive ever recorded to that date, taking five million feet of logs over fifteen hundred miles from Otter Tail County and across lakes to the Red River of the North and then to Winnipeg. But he returned from that trip a sick man.[48] The diagnosis was cancer of the stomach, and he died a few weeks later in a St. Paul hospital with Caroline at his side. Forty-one years old and left with seven children, Caroline survived her husband by some years, though the exact time and place of her death are not known.[49]

Margaretha Ault died in Verona, Ontario, on February 2, 1896.

*Hazel Akeley in 1908, two years before her
marriage to Andrew Fergus*

*Mary Agnes Fergus Hamilton, Andrew Fergus, Lillie Fergus Maury, and Luella
Fergus Gilpatrick at the Armells ranch in 1910*

Her obituary, printed in the *Little Falls Weekly Transcript,* did not mention a second marriage, despite rumors to that effect during the 1870s.[50]

After leaving Montana, Rosanna and William Sturgis maintained contact with the Ferguses through sporadic letters from William to James. "We have a little House sufficient to keep us from the poor House but nothing for our children," William wrote his old partner early in 1884. Though the sixty-seven-year-old adventurer admitted he was still thinking of far horizons, he remained in Sturgis, Michigan, confessing that he "dare[d] not make another move for fear of making a bad rustle worse." His letter had a poignant conclusion: "I hope you hold no animosity against me I can assure you I have none against you."[51]

Five years later, in March 1898, eighty-year-old William wrote James that he was feeling fine, but his wife was suffering from dropsy. In the years since his last letter, the couple had lost two of their children, but the others were all doing well.[52] Barely three months later, in May 1898, sixty-four-year-old Rosanna died.[53]

It is quite possible that she died wondering whether her husband was once more bound for the goldfields, for during a visit earlier that year with Nathan Richardson, Sturgis had declared his intention to try his luck in the Klondike, little knowing that his old friend Fergus was simultaneously considering the same plan.[54] Whether because of Rosanna's death or his own ill health and poor financial state, William never made that trip. Indeed, he turned south, not north, spending the next three winters in Florida and dying in New Smyrna in 1901 at age eighty-four. His obituary hailed him as one who had "been upon the advance guard of civilization nearly all his life."[55] Those words describe equally well James Fergus and the other central Minnesotans who had once given in to the lure of gold and adventure and headed west, leaving children, homes, farms, and businesses in the care of the gold rush widows of Little Falls.

Notes

The following abbreviations have been used:

BenCC   Benton County Courthouse Records, Foley, Minnesota
FPMtHS   James Fergus Papers in the Montana Historical Society Archives, Helena
FPUM   James Fergus Papers in the Mansfield Library Archives, University of Montana, Missoula
L&CCC   Lewis and Clark County Courthouse Records, Helena, Montana
MC50   1850 U.S. Manuscript Census Schedules
MC60   1860 U.S. Manuscript Census Schedules
MC70   1870 U.S. Manuscript Census Schedules
MCHS   Morrison County Historical Society Archives, Little Falls, Minnesota
MnHS   Minnesota Historical Society
MnSC65   1865 Minnesota State Census
MnTC57   1857 Minnesota Territorial Census
MorCC   Morrison County Courthouse Records, Little Falls, Minnesota
MtHS   Montana Historical Society
TCC   Todd County Courthouse Records, Long Prairie, Minnesota

Preface

1. Extended absence of a husband, as well as his death, could thrust nineteenth-century women into the role of surrogate head of household. While Victorian family life has traditionally been viewed as staid and stable, in reality many wives and children found themselves coping with responsibilities at home in the absence of husbands and fathers who were at war, in the merchant marine, or away on business matters. While wives married to soldiers or sailors expected to be left and usually benefited from support systems attendant upon their husbands' positions, wives of westering men were often surprised to find themselves suddenly left in charge of affairs at home. They were forced to develop their own support systems, typically by networking with family members or other women with absent husbands.

2. The omission of women's stories in the chronicle of the westward movement is hardly surprising, since the American frontier experience has traditionally been viewed in an exclusively white male framework. Those mythmakers who did add a feminine figure to the western scene tended to cast her in stereotypical roles—"gentle tamer," "soiled dove," or "madonna of the prairie." Only recently have we begun to broaden our understanding of the frontier experience and demythologize

our view of the western woman. Studies of women on the overland trails and of women homesteaders have shown that their experiences were significantly different from those of men, centered as they were in cooking, cleaning, and raising children and not in the adventure of exploring and conquering new lands.

For an overview of recent scholarship, see Sandra L. Myres, "Women in the West," in *Historians and the American West,* ed. Michael P. Malone (Lincoln: University of Nebraska Press, 1983), 369–86. See also John M. Faragher, *Women and Men on the Overland Trail* (New Haven: Yale University Press, 1979); Julie Roy Jeffrey, *Frontier Women: The Trans-Mississippi West, 1840–1880* (New York: Hill and Wang, 1979); Sandra L. Myres, *Westering Women and the Frontier Experience, 1800–1915* (Albuquerque: University of New Mexico Press, 1982); Lillian Schlissel, *Women's Diaries of the Westward Journey* (New York: Schocken Books, 1982); Susan Armitage and Elizabeth Jameson, eds., *The Women's West* (Norman: University of Oklahoma Press, 1987).

3. Laurel Thatcher Ulrich, *Good Wives: Image and Reality in the Lives of Women in Northern New England, 1650–1750* (New York: Alfred A. Knopf, 1982), 46. Useful parallels can be drawn between the experiences of nineteenth-century women and those of colonial wives serving as deputy husbands, a phenomenon examined by Ulrich.

4. Lillian Schlissel, "Diaries of Frontier Women: On Learning to Read the Obscured Patterns," in *Woman's Being, Woman's Place: Female Identity and Vocation,* ed. Mary Kelley (New York: G. K. Hall, 1979), 61.

5. Housed in three collections in two archives, the James Fergus Papers contain more than two hundred letters written by James and Pamelia from 1860 to 1864, the four-year period in which Pamelia stayed in Little Falls while James tried his luck in the goldfields of present-day Colorado and Montana. They also contain letters the couple exchanged during other periods of separation; letters to and from the Fergus children, other relatives, and business and personal friends; and numerous daybooks, journals, account books, and memorandums that supplement and clarify the information found in the letters.

Similar complete sets of correspondence are rare, and this lack has hampered our research into the experiences of women in waiting. As a rule, families at home tended to keep the letters sent by westering husbands and fathers, while, for various reasons, men on the frontier seldom kept the letters their wives sent to them. Not surprisingly, families have tended to value letters detailing life on the frontier more than those recording day-to-day activities at home, and until recently historians have held with that judgment. Only with the recent increased interest in family and women's history has the scarcity of the female half of correspondence been seen for the great loss it is. Elizabeth Hampsten has suggested that interest in women's diaries and letters has lagged because "it is generally assumed that what is worth keeping is what has historical value, and because historical value is measured by discrete events . . . which men are more likely to participate in and to describe, the writings of men are likely to be kept and to find their way to permanent archives" (*Read This Only to Yourself: The Private Writings of Midwestern Women, 1880–1910* [Bloomington: Indiana University Press, 1982], xi). J. S. Holliday's *The World Rushed In: The California Gold Rush Experience* (New York: Simon and Schuster, 1981) is one of the few works containing letters from men and women at home.

6. Sandra L. Myres suggests that the educated, middle-class women whose diaries she explores in *Westering Women* were fairly typical of westering Americans in the nineteenth century, since the westward movement was "primarily a middle-class activity; few of the very poor or the very rich undertook the move to the frontier" (*Westering Women*, xvii). This assertion seems valid, since the very rich had less incentive to give up what they had and gamble on the possibilities farther west and the very poor lacked the resources to move a family across the plains. There is evidence to suggest, however, that a significant number of men who were "very poor" may have made the trip west, leaving their indigent families behind them. The Fergus letters allow us to examine the experiences of some of those poorer families.

7. In addition to Pamelia, three other women eventually joined their husbands in the West, where one was literally widowed and another deserted. Of those women who never made the journey, two welcomed home husbands no richer for their venture, one waited in vain for her husband to return or send for her, and one came to know true widowhood when her husband died in a mine cave-in.

8. Julie Roy Jeffrey has also — reluctantly — concluded that the frontier experience itself was not usually liberating for women (*Frontier Women*, xv–xvi). Paula Petrik's examination of the experiences of women in Helena, Montana, during the late nineteenth century, led her to a more complex interpretation: "On the one hand, it seems clear that first generation westering women did not use the frontier as a springboard to self-fulfillment; on the other hand, it is evident that the frontier thrust these women into situations that fundamentally altered their lives. Frontier women, in short, redefined womanhood, but they did it reluctantly and only when confronted with an environment antithetical to their sensibilities. To look for liberation is to look to the second generation on the frontier" (*No Step Backward: Women and Family on the Rocky Mountain Mining Frontier, Helena, Montana, 1865–1900* [Helena: Montana Historical Society Press, 1987], 96).

CHAPTER 1. Beginnings

1. In the flush of excitement surrounding the Pikes Peak discovery, Little Falls gave its founding father a hero's send-off. But not all the world saw the Pikes Peakers in a complimentary light. Letters of a contemporary settler in Iowa give a different view of the men who rushed to the goldfields. J. H. Williams of Homer, Iowa, in writing to his son of the stampede to Colorado in the spring of 1859, denigrated the characters and belittled the chances of men who left home to find fortunes in the goldfields: "The persons that are going, will make nothing even if there is gold there in abundance. It is not got without hard Labor and exposure working in rain, cold, mud, and watter. . . . All that are going from here are reckless" (J. H. Williams to son James, February 27, 1859, in John Kent Folmar, ed., *"This State of Wonders": The Letters of an Iowa Frontier Family, 1858–1861* [Iowa City: University of Iowa Press, 1986], 24–25). Williams's letters gave periodic reports of neighbors who left for Pikes Peak; he found the news of their departure "encourageing, as it gives room for better [people] to come in" (J. H. Williams to son James, April 1, 1860, in Folmar, *"State of Wonders,"* 74).

2. Others from the area who went west during this period were David Bentley, Charley Campbell, Peter Cardinell, Robert Ells, Alexander Gammell, C. H. Klein, Bill Mitchell, William and George Moore, Jonathan Pugh, Andrew Shea, Hugh Thompson, and William Wright. Names of the miners were derived from letters in the James Fergus Papers in the Mansfield Library Archives, University of Montana, Missoula (FPUM); the James Fergus Papers in the Montana Historical Society Archives, Helena (FPMtHS); and the Oscar Mueller Collection in the Montana Historical Society. See, for instance, James Fergus to Pamelia Fergus, May 6 and May 14, 1861; July 10, 1861; August 11, 1862; July 15, 1863 — all in FPUM. The names of miners from the area who joined the Fisk expedition of 1862 were also gleaned from Helen McCann White's *Ho! For the Gold Fields: Northern Overland Wagon Trains of the 1860s* (St. Paul: Minnesota Historical Society, 1966), 264–66. Though White lists David Bentley as a resident of Otter Tail County at the time of his departure, he was a former resident of Little Falls. White lists a "Peter Cardinell" and gives an alternate spelling as "Caldwell." In a letter written in 1863, James Fergus referred to "Cardinell the quarter breed that went out with Sturgis," but a turn-of-the-century article authored by Fergus spells the name "Cardwell." (JF to PF, July 15, 1863, FPUM; James Fergus, "Early Mining Life at Bannack and Alder Gulch," *Rocky Mountain Magazine* 1 [1900–1901]: 265.) Hugh Thompson changed his name to Charley Dodge once he arrived in Colorado Territory; such name changes were common among emigrants in the West. (JF to William Butler, March 20, 1875, FPUM.)

3. In his biography of James Fergus, Robert Horne recognized and gave passing mention to the phenomenon of women left waiting by westering husbands. "Perhaps James should never have crossed the plain at all, for he did risk his family's well-being in quest of highly uncertain wealth. In that position, however, he did not act alone, for in the mid-nineteenth century the women stayed behind — a task in many ways more difficult than the hardships experienced by their Argonaut husbands" (Robert Horne, "James Fergus: Frontier Businessman, Miner, Rancher, Free Thinker" [Ed.D. diss., University of Montana, Missoula, 1971], 39). Lillian Schlissel called for a study of temporary role transfers between husbands and wives but admitted that "entries concerning the periods when the women ran the households are ambiguous or missing" ("Diaries of Frontier Women," in *Woman's Being,* ed. Kelley, 62). The present authors published the beginnings of their research in "Women in Waiting in the Westward Movement: Pamelia Dillin Fergus and Emma Stratton Christie," *Montana the Magazine of Western History,* Spring 1985, p. 2–17.

4. Mary Paul to JF, January 10, 1861, and PF to JF, July 18, 1861 — both in FPUM.

5. The Ferguses were persistent correspondents, and most of the letters they wrote over the four-year period of their separation eventually reached their destination. Eagerly read and carefully preserved, those letters provide a fairly complete picture of Pamelia's life as woman in waiting, as well as of James's adventures as westering husband. The letters of James and Pamelia, plus many other letters written by friends and relatives that are cited in this work, reside in the James Fergus Papers (FPUM and FPMtHS) and in the Oscar Mueller Collection (MtHS). Unless otherwise indicated, all quotations are true to the original punctuation and spelling. Full citations appear in the source notes.

6. Mrs. S. C. Gilpatrick, "Biographical Sketch of Mrs. James Fergus," *Contribu-*

tions to the Historical Society of Montana 4 (1966): 188–91. In a letter of March 3, 1917, to her cousin Burritt McHose (FPMtHS), Luella Fergus Gilpatrick passed along conflicting information received from another cousin (George W. Dillin), who said that Mahala "was adopted by a Baptist preacher at Albany, New York," possibly by the name of West. Conceding that this might well be the case, since Mahala's retention of her birth name made it difficult to trace her "adoption," Luella suggested that perhaps the adoptive parents, not the birth parents, were close friends of the Browns and thus Mahala named her eldest daughter for General Brown's wife.

7. These names were derived from context in letters of Pamelia and James Fergus, FPUM, FPMtHS. Since William shared his father's first name, the family frequently referred to him as Thomas, his middle name, though letters in his own hand are signed "William."

8. Gilpatrick, "Biographical Sketch," 189. The family moved around 1842. (James Fergus, "Biographical Notes on Pamelia Fergus," unpaginated manuscript, FPMtHS.)

9. Luella Fergus Gilpatrick to Burritt McHose, February 19, 1917, FPMtHS; Horne, "James Fergus," 7–8; JF to father, October 20, 1854; JF to father, August 30, 1853; JF to father, March 8, 1856—all in FPUM. In a letter to his father, James alluded to his earlier mistreatment and implied that he had been physically beaten by his father. Yet that same letter notes that he and Pamelia had chosen to name their new baby Andrew, presumably after James's father, though they were also honoring Scottish tradition by naming their first son Andrew. (Andrew James Fergus to Peavy and Smith, August 22, 1988.) They expected to have to come up with a suitable second name for the baby, since, James confessed, "Andrew or any name with an R . . . [is] rather hard for me to pronounce plain" (JF to father, August 30, 1853, FPUM). The ambivalence expressed toward his father in this letter is indicative of that James apparently felt throughout his life, for his actions and his comments reveal his need to prove himself worthy of the Fergus name, even as he rejected many of his father's precepts.

10. JF to Collins Gilpatrick, October 11, 1898, FPUM.

11. Fergus was declared a naturalized citizen of the United States in October 1842. (Copy of citizenship papers from Jackson County, Iowa, and Memorandum of an Agreement, November 27, 1847—both in Legal Documents, 1841–1900, FPUM.)

12. Luella Fergus Gilpatrick to Burritt McHose, February 19, 1917, FPMtHS. Luella noted that "some of the nicest people in Moline were at their wedding."

13. William Cole to JF, April 17, 1845, FPUM.

14. Hazel Fergus Bubar, "Biographical Sketch of Pamelia Dillin Fergus," FPUM. Hazel Fergus is the widow of Andrew Fergus and daughter-in-law of James and Pamelia Fergus. Allis B. Stuart, wife of Montana pioneer Granville Stuart and a neighbor of the Ferguses during their years at the ranch on the Armells, described the courtship of James Fergus and Pamelia Dillin in this way: "The gentle dignified young girl charmed him at once and their friendship soon ripened into love" ("James Fergus," biographical sketch, July 13, 1942, MtHS).

15. JF to brother Charles, September 6, 1845, FPUM.

16. Stuart, "James Fergus," MtHS; JF to N. B. Buford, October 21, 1853, FPUM.

17. Family tree provided by Hazel Fergus (Pamelia's daughter-in-law), Andrew James Fergus (Pamelia's grandson), and Stephen F. Gilpatrick (Pamelia's great-grandson).

18. George Stephens to JF, August 16, 1853; Daniel Berry to JF, November 19, 1854, December 30, 1855, March 9, 1856; JF to George Stephens, February 25, 1880 — all in FPUM. James Dillin's name also appears in the early Fergus household account books (Financial Records, 1842–1885, FPUM).

19. Jonathan Huntoon to JF, February 24, 1875, FPUM.

20. JF to N. B. Buford, February 22, 1854, and JF to father and brothers, July 17, 1853 — both in FPUM. The railroad was later called the Chicago, Rock Island & Pacific.

21. Financial Records, 1842–1885, FPUM.

22. JF to father, July 17, 1853, FPUM.

23. JF to Dr. E. A. Wood, December 25, 1886, FPUM.

24. Agreements between S. W. Wheelock and JF, March 4 and March 28, 1856, Legal Documents, 1841–1900, FPUM.

25. JF to Wilbur F. Sanders, undated, circa 1892, FPUM.

26. JF to PF, undated, 1853, FPUM. According to Andrew James Fergus, Andrew's son, Andrew often repeated a story concerning a scar on the back of one of his hands. When Andrew was little more than a toddler, his mother left him in the charge of his sisters and went to visit with a neighbor. Summoned by his screams and those of Luella and Mary Agnes, she returned to find his hand caught in the wood-burning stove. He had apparently inserted his hand into the damper hole with the fingers extended, but when he felt the heat from the firebox, he instinctively closed his fist and was therefore unable to withdraw his hand without his mother's help. (Andrew James Fergus to Peavy and Smith, August 22, 1988.)

27. PF to JF, July 16, 1853, FPUM.

28. JF to PF, July 12, July 22, and July 26, 1853, FPUM. According to Carl Degler, nineteenth-century fathers tended to take very seriously the notion of child rearing. Although the actual care of children was generally left to mothers, fathers felt constrained to offer advice — especially medical advice. (Carl N. Degler, *At Odds: Women and the Family in America from the Revolution to the Present* [New York: Oxford University Press, 1980], 78–79.)

29. JF to PF, August 10, 1853, FPUM.

30. PF to JF, July 24, 1853, FPUM.

31. As Degler has noted, one of the hallmarks of early-nineteenth-century family life was the sharply differentiated roles society assigned to husbands and wives. People spoke of "separate spheres," and a woman was often referred to as "the angel of the home." Predictably, the privilege of being elevated to a status that normally eliminated the necessity of working outside the home was not without its price tag. Women were expected to be true to what Barbara Welter and others have called "the cult of true womanhood," a code that prescribed piety, domesticity, submissiveness, and passivity and that stood in stark contrast to the worldly ways of the "manly" code followed by most men of the era. The more closely a married woman adhered to the cult of true womanhood, the higher her husband rose in the eyes of his colleagues. For a fuller discussion of gender expectations in the nineteenth century, see Degler, *At Odds,* especially p. 26–65; Joan Kelly's "Family and Society," in

Women, History, and Theory: The Essays of Joan Kelly (Chicago: University of Chicago Press, 1984), 110–55; and Barbara Welter's "The Cult of True Womanhood: 1820–1860," *American Quarterly* 18 (Summer 1966): 151–74.

32. PF to JF, August 24, 1853, FPUM.

33. JF to father, August 30, 1853, FPUM.

34. Undated fragment concerning terms of sale of paper mill, January 31, 1854, Financial Records, 1842–1885, and Thomas Muscatine to JF, February 24, 1854—both in FPUM.

35. Minnesota Historical Records Survey Project, WPA, 1940, Benton County Inventory, MnHS. Dakota lands west of the Mississippi River in what was to become the state of Minnesota were ceded in the treaties of Traverse des Sioux and Mendota on July 23 and August 5, 1851. (William Watts Folwell, *A History of Minnesota*, rev. ed., vol. 1 [St. Paul: Minnesota Historical Society, 1956], 280–81, 284–86, 305.)

36. *Minnesota Pioneer* (St. Paul), July 29, 1852.

37. As Carl Degler has pointed out, married women of Pamelia's era were not the primary decision makers: "Marriage has been many things, but at all times it has been a relationship of power, however muted or disguised it may be in any particular case. . . . Certainly in the 19th century, when a husband was acknowledged by all to be the head of the family, there can be no doubt that power or the making of decisions was unequally distributed" (Degler, *At Odds*, 29).

38. *The Una* was published in Providence, Rhode Island, between February 1853 and October 1855. Among its subscribers were some of the most influential feminists of the era—including Susan B. Anthony and Elizabeth Cady Stanton. The James Fergus Papers contain an undated letter in Pamelia's hand addressed to Mrs. Paulina Wright Davis, editor of *The Una*, and noting that "In the March No of the Una was published the names of those who subscribed with me for that gem of literature Mrs N. Ewing H. Scott and H. Anderson." Pamelia's papers had arrived on schedule, but the others had not received theirs, and she wrote this letter on their behalf. Though the handwriting is hers, the diction and spelling show the help of her three friends, and it is intriguing to think of the bravado that moved the four women to compose the letter's flamboyant closing: "We who live in the far distant West value the Una much And warmly is it welcomed as it comes with truth and light beaming from its pages kindling the smoldering fires of liberty in the breast of down trodden woman and triumphing over long established error and oppression" (PF to Mrs. Davis, circa summer 1854, FPUM). Intellectual awareness was one thing, but the realities of day-to-day life quite another. Years would pass before "the smoldering fires of liberty" in Pamelia's breast would flare against the "error and oppression" in her own life.

39. *The Una*, March 1854. This is the issue in which Pamelia and her three friends are listed as new subscribers.

40. Pamelia's association with Mary J. Colburn helped give her the background she needed to cope with medical emergencies on the Minnesota frontier, during the overland journey, and in the Montana wilderness. In later life, Luella Fergus Gilpatrick recalled that her mother assisted Mrs. Colburn at a Moline birthing. This was the same Mrs. Colburn who later sent written advice to Pamelia concerning the abscessed breast she suffered in Little Falls. (Mary Colburn to PF, April 22, 1859, FPUM; Gilpatrick, "Biographical Sketch," 190.)

41. *The Una,* March 1854.

42. Daniel Berry to JF, November 24, 1855, FPUM.

43. JF to father, January 6, 1855, FPUM. James's letter to his father is actually dated January 6, 1854, but internal evidence indicates that the letter was written during the first week of the new year, and James simply misdated it.

44. Dan Jones invoice, August 8, 1854, Financial Records, 1842–1885, FPUM.

45. Platted in 1849, the village of St. Anthony was incorporated as a city in 1855, only to be united with its more rapidly expanding neighbor, Minneapolis, in 1872. (Lucile M. Kane, *The Falls of St. Anthony: The Waterfall That Built Minneapolis* [1966; reprint, St. Paul: Minnesota Historical Society Press, 1987], 19, 28, 29, 38, 40, 60.)

46. JF to father, January 6, 1855, FPUM.

47. Draft of Agreement, 1854, Legal Documents, 1841–1885, FPUM.

48. A native of Connecticut, Tuttle had pioneered in the St. Croix Valley, then returned briefly to his former home in Alton, Illinois, before moving to St. Anthony in 1846. (Lucius F. Hubbard and Return I. Holcombe, *Minnesota in Three Centuries, 1655–1908,* Semi-Centennial ed., vol. 3, *Minnesota as a State: 1858–1870* [Minneapolis: Publishing Society of Minnesota, 1908], 42; JF to father, January 6, 1855, FPUM.)

49. Warren Upham, *Minnesota in Three Centuries, 1655–1908,* Semi-Centennial ed., vol. 1, *Descriptions and Explorations* (Minneapolis: Publishing Society of Minnesota, 1908), 65–74; JF to father, January 6, 1855, FPUM. Like other entrepreneurs of his day, James Fergus saw the land and river as things to be mastered in the name of progress. To be of use, virgin territory must be transformed into something else. The idea that progress demanded conquest of land, water, and forests has been described by Annette Kolodny as a particularly masculine way of looking at a new land. (Annette Kolodny, *The Lay of the Land: Metaphor as Experience and History in American Life and Letters* [Chapel Hill: University of North Carolina Press, 1975].)

50. JF to PF, October 6, 1854, FPUM.

CHAPTER 2. Early Little Falls

1. Between 1855 and 1857, seven hundred towns in Minnesota Territory were platted into more than three hundred thousand lots — providing enough homesites for 1.5 million people. According to historian William Watts Folwell, "The whole urban population was more or less infected with the virus of speculation" (Folwell, *History of Minnesota,* 1:362–63 [quotation on 363]).

2. Return I. Holcombe, *Minnesota in Three Centuries, 1655–1908,* Semi-Centennial ed., vol. 2, *Early History—Minnesota as a Territory* (Minneapolis: Publishing Society of Minnesota, 1908), 507–8.

3. Elliott Coues, ed., *The Expeditions of Zebulon Montgomery Pike to Headwaters of the Mississippi River, through Louisiana Territory, and in New Spain, during the Years 1805-6-7,* vol. 1 (New York: Francis P. Harper, 1895), 105.

4. *Sauk Rapids Frontierman,* June 7, 1855. In *Minnesota Geographic Names,* Warren Upham notes that the fall is eleven feet in three-quarters of a mile. The Ojibway called the area "Kakabikansing," meaning "the place of the little squarely cut-off rock" and referring to the quartz fragments left by ice-age inhabitants. (*Minnesota Geographic Names: Their Origin and Historic Significance* [1920; reprint, St. Paul: Min-

nesota Historical Society, 1969], 353.) Upham's source for the derivation of the Indian name was J. V. Brower's monograph *Kakabikansing* (vol. 5 of *Memoirs of Explorations in the Basin of the Mississippi* [St. Paul: H. L. Collins Company, 1902]), 33. Nathan Richardson ascribes a different meaning to the word, citing an Indian narrative that indicates "Keke-bicauge" means "Great Rock." (Nathan Richardson, "The History of Morrison County," mimeographed copy of *Little Falls Transcript* articles published in 1876, MCHS, 48.)

The main falls was in the west channel, with a difficult rapids in the east channel. Pike's journal entry of October 15, 1805, notes "a fall . . . of the river over a bed of rocks, through which we had two narrow shoots [rapids] to make our way the next day" (Coues, *Expeditions,* 104).

5. Clara Fuller, *History of Morrison and Todd Counties, Minnesota,* vol. 1 (Indianapolis: B. F. Bowen and Company, 1915), 181; Richardson, "History," 14–15; James Green Papers, MCHS; Henry M. Rice Papers, MnHS. The five investors were John R. Irvine, a St. Paul merchant; J. B. S. Todd and N. J. J. Dana, captains at Fort Ripley construction site; and fur traders Henry M. Rice of St. Paul and Allan Morrison of Crow Wing.

6. *Minnesota Democratic Weekly,* May 27, 1851.

7. Mortgage of William and Rosanna Sturgis to H. M. Rice, May 28, 1852, BenCC; agreement between Sturgis, Tuttle, and Fergus, February 5, 1855, Legal Documents, 1841–1900, FPUM.

8. Richardson, "History," 27–28. Richardson, a New Yorker who settled in Little Falls in the spring of 1855, was chosen town historian and produced a history of the area for the nation's centennial in 1876. (Richardson, "History," 18.)

9. Hubbard and Holcombe, *Minnesota,* 3:42; Warren Upham and Rose Barteau Dunlap, comps., *Collections of the Minnesota Historical Society,* vol. 14, *Minnesota Biographies, 1655–1912* (St. Paul: Minnesota Historical Society, 1912), 798. Tuttle and Fergus had known each other earlier; Tuttle later recalled their first meeting as having taken place on Fergus's wedding day in Moline, Illinois. (C. A. Tuttle to JF, February 13, 1898, FPUM.)

10. JF to PF, March 25, 1860, FPUM; agreement between Fergus, Sturgis, Tuttle, February 5, 1855, Legal Documents, 1841–1900, FPUM; JF to *Fergus Falls Weekly,* September 19, 1889; deeds from Little Falls Manufacturing Company records, MCHS.

11. Richardson, "History," 18.

12. Mary Logan Sweet, *William Sturgis: First in Cedar Falls* (Cedar Falls, Iowa: Cedar Falls Historical Society, 1981), 16–17; John Hartman, ed., *History of Black Hawk County,* vol. 1 (Chicago: S. J. Clark Publishing Company, 1915), 37.

13. Mortgage Deed, Benton County, May 28, 1852.

14. Sweet, *William Sturgis,* 17.

15. Although Richardson's history says that Little Falls was surveyed in 1855 by S. M. Putnam, the two plats done in that year do not bear Putnam's name. (Richardson, "History," 16.) Putnam did sign the plat map completed and filed in May 1856. (William Sturgis to JF, February 24, 1856; JF to father, March 8, 1856 — both in FPUM; plat map of Little Falls, Minnesota, May 21, 1856, surveyed by Samuel Putnam, MorCC.)

16. JF to father, September 30, 1857, FPUM. By James's own count, twenty-five persons lived in that house in the fall of 1857. The 1857 Minnesota Territorial Census indicates fifteen nonfamily occupants of the Fergus house. In addition to the immediate family and Pamelia's brother, James Dillin, the household consisted of William Algans, mason; John Crist, laborer; Moses LaFond, Ben Nickerson, Timothy Huxley, James Horn, C. S. Rockwell, and Orson J. Rockwell, farmers; Alexander Chisholm, blacksmith; Johanna Restell and Sarah H. Bumsted, probably housekeepers; Charles E. Garden, Arthur Garden, and Charles Knowlton, machinists; Charles Freeman, land agent.

17. MnTC57. In August 1988 the O. A. Churchill store was finally demolished, having been declared unsafe by building inspectors. The oldest part of the building featured seventeen-inch-by-one-inch boards, probably from the mill run by the Little Falls Manufacturing Company. (Jan Warner, director, MCHS, to Peavy and Smith, August 19, 1988.)

18. *Sauk Rapids Frontierman,* October 4, 1855.

19. Education was a major focus of the American dream being pursued by families across the frontier, and schools were generally established early in a community's development. Soon after James Fergus arrived in Little Falls, he wrote to friends in Moline asking for help in recruiting a teacher. By early fall of 1855, Helen M. Nichols, whom George Stephens called "a glorious fine young woman," had made the trip upriver, moved in with the Fergus family, and opened a school. (George Stephens to JF, December 26, 1855, and April 6, 1856, FPUM.) Within a year, Miss Nichols had resigned her post to marry G. T. K. Smith, a carpenter from Maine who was working for the Little Falls Manufacturing Company, and by the close of 1856 she had given birth to her first child. (Helen M. Smith to JF, March 2, 1860, FPUM; MnTC57.)

20. Richardson, "History," 16, 18. Built by W. B. Fairbanks and Nathan Richardson around 1855, the Northern was purchased by John and Margaretha Ault shortly thereafter. (Richardson, "History," 18; *Northern Herald,* August 19, 1857.)

21. *Sauk Rapids Frontierman,* June 7, 1855.

22. L. M. Ford to JF, April 22, 1856, FPUM.

23. The other two physicians were Zachariah Jodon of Maryland and R. L. Metcalf of Kentucky. (Richardson, "History," 39; MnTC57.)

24. Named for Allan Morrison and his brother William—who claimed to be the first white man to see Lake Itasca, the headwaters of the Mississippi River—Morrison County was formed from Benton and Stearns counties on February 25, 1856. (Bruce Mellor, MCHS archivist, to Peavy and Smith, September 27, 1988; Upham, *Minnesota,* 1:316.)

25. Richardson, "History," 16; certified testimony, Legal Documents, 1841–1900, FPUM.

26. C. A. Tuttle to JF, February 24, 1856, FPUM. For more details on the decline of the company, see Horne, "James Fergus," 18–29.

27. William Sturgis to JF, January 15, 1856, FPUM.

28. Williams Heald & Co. of Moline to JF, March 31, 1856, FPUM.

29. JF to brother (probably Charles), January 12, 1857; George Stephens to JF, February 11, 1857—both in FPUM; Richardson, "History," 19. In a letter written in August 1858, James Fergus invited his brother William to come to Little Falls,

adding, "One thing I would advise you to bring a wife with you. Young women are scarce here" (JF to William Fergus, August 1, 1858, FPUM). A handwritten copy of an advertisement placed in the *Northern Herald* at about this same time reads: "Wanted by some half a disen good looking young men (who are tired of living alone) an Equal number of young women to accompany them through the journey of life. Aplicants will call at the Store of Gravel & Butler at the office of John L. Metcalf Esq or at the tin shop of Robert Hamilton where all nessacary information can be had. Terms easy. Applicants mus be good looking" (undated, handwritten advertisement, Speeches and Writings, FPUM). Though Richardson cites C. E. French as the newspaper's founder, the printing was likely done by E. C. Church, a printer from Massachusetts. (*Daily Minnesotian,* November 18, 1856, and MnTC57).

30. Allan Morrison to JF, August 22, 1856; JF to Allan Morrison, August 22, 1856—both in FPUM. Sloan's Indian wife, known as Mary, was alternately listed in the census as "Odishquaw" (MC60) and "Swuagamequa" (MnSC65) Sloan. According to Bruce Mellor, MCHS archivist, her Ojibway name was also spelled Odishquahgahmequay and Equayzainceshish. The surname of her first husband was Chaboillez, and they had one daughter, Margaret, who was thirteen at the time Sloan left. Her two sons by Sloan were six-year-old John, Jr., and ten-year-old William. Sloan abandoned Odishquaw to marry Mary Ann Jane Morrison, Allan Morrison's daughter. (Bruce Mellor to Peavy and Smith, September 27 and October 5, 1988; MC60.)

As the town matured and the gender ratio of the population began to improve, more and more Indian women were abandoned in like fashion. In a letter to her father in December 1863, Luella Fergus noted, "all the squaw men are getting married" (Luella Fergus to JF, December 27, 1863, FPUM). For an excellent discussion of intermarriage between American Indian women and white men, see Glenda Riley's *Women and Indians on the Frontier, 1825–1915* (Albuquerque: University of New Mexico Press, 1984).

31. In his latter-day reminiscences, William H. Fletcher, who moved to Little Falls as a sixteen-year-old in 1858, recounted a scene he observed with horror shortly after his arrival in town. Attracted by the booming of drums, he joined a crowd that watched a triumphant Ojibway war party waving Dakota scalps in a victory dance performed near the Northern Hotel. (Mimeographed copy of William H. Fletcher, "Reminiscence of Little Falls," February 1925, p. 3, in William H. Fletcher Papers, MnHS.)

32. Philo Farnham Probate Papers, Probate No. 226, TCC; John H. Sheets, A. H. Hendrickson, and O. B. DeLaurier, *Todd County Histories, Containing Reproductions of the Original Histories of Todd County* (Long Prairie, Minnesota: Todd County Historical Society, 1976), 304, 388. Though these histories indicate that the Indian attacks were associated with the disturbances in 1862, Farnham's probate indicates that they took place in 1858.

33. JF to Dr. E. A. Wood, December 25, 1886, FPUM.

34. Richardson, "History," 16; Little Falls Manufacturing Company agreements, Financial Records, 1842–1885, FPUM.

35. Throughout Minnesota Territory, inflation was rampant; land that had been purchased for $1.25 an acre in 1854 was bringing $5.00 an acre. In actuality, the boom

was drawing to a close, for the three years of greatest immigration during the territorial period were 1855, 1856, and 1857. (Holcombe, *Minnesota,* 2:507–13.)

36. Richardson, "History," 1, 28; Holcombe, *Minnesota,* 2:437–38; Minutes of Morrison County Commissioners, 1856–1857, MCHS; Fuller, *History,* 73–74.

37. Though the town was surveyed and platted as Elk City and though Rosanna Sturgis herself called it Elk City, it was popularly referred to as Little Elk. (Plat of Elk City by Samuel M. Putnam, filed February 20, 1857, Register of Deeds, MorCC.)

38. November 1856 entry, Little Falls Manufacturing Company records, MCHS; Richardson, "History," 43; Bruce Mellor, MCHS archivist, to Peavy and Smith, August 8, 1987.

39. *Northern Herald,* January 14, 1857.

40. MnTC57; Sweet, *William Sturgis,* 9. Young John Sturgis was likely living with Catherine Sturgis Adams, his paternal aunt.

41. O. A. Churchill to JF, January 16, 1857, FPUM.

42. *Northern Herald,* August 19, 1857.

43. Sturgis note dated July 15, 1858, for debts incurred between November 1856 and March 1857, Financial Records, 1842–1885, FPUM.

44. William Sturgis to Amos Sturgis, November 12, 1857, p. 405; William Sturgis to Lydia Kidder, December 12, 1857, p. 452; William Sturgis to Margaret Steele, December 12, 1857, p. 434—all in Record of Deeds, Book A, MorCC.

45. JF to father, September 30, 1857, FPUM.

46. JF to father, November 1, 1857, FPUM; Miscellaneous Records, MorCC; *Pioneer Democrat Weekly,* November 19 and November 26, 1857.

47. Folwell, *History of Minnesota,* 1:363–64.

48. JF to father, November 1, 1857. In his letter of September 30, 1857, Fergus had predicted that the nation would face economic problems due to a trade imbalance caused by heavy importation to meet American demands for "too much high living too many silk dresses, too much broadcloth and other extravagances in proportion" (JF to father, September 30, 1857, FPUM).

49. Folwell, *History of Minnesota,* 1:363–64. The 1857 Minnesota Territorial Census lists 336 citizens in Little Falls, while the 1860 U.S. manuscript census schedules list 216.

50. James Fergus, "Reminiscence," undated, Oscar Mueller Collection, MtHS. Fergus informed his father that his property had been worth fifty thousand dollars and was now worth less than ten thousand dollars—"of what use is the property of yesterday if it will not buy a dinner today?" (JF to father, November 1, 1857). Land sales decreased drastically from 1856 to 1860, reaching rock bottom in 1860 when only seven thousand acres of land changed hands in all of Minnesota. (Alvin C. Glueck, Jr., *Minnesota and the Manifest Destiny of the Canadian Northwest* [Toronto: University of Toronto Press, 1965], 117 n. 94.)

51. Although Horne's biography indicates that there is no record that Fergus served in the Constitutional Convention, he received a letter of congratulation from S. Croswell, secretary of the convention, noting that he had been the unanimous choice of the Republican party in the primary. Apparently, Sturgis defeated him in the general election. Two of the three partners in the Little Falls Manufacturing Company were integrally involved in shaping the destiny of the nation's thirty-

second state—Calvin Tuttle also served in the Constitutional Convention. (Hubbard and Holcomb, *Minnesota*, 3:42–43; S. Croswell, secretary of Constitutional Convention, to JF, May 21, 1857; political flyer, October 13, 1857, Speeches and Writings, FPUM; Horne, "James Fergus," 30.)

52. Fuller, *History*, 74; Miscellaneous Records, MorCC; MnTC57. The gristmill may not have been added until after the flood of 1858 washed out Sturgis's first sawmill on the Little Elk River. (Richardson, "History," 41.)

53. Minutes, Morrison County Commission, May 2, 1856, MCHS.

54. John Ault first appeared on the 1857 Minnesota Territorial Census as a thirty-five-year-old lumberman from Canada; Margaretha is listed as thirty-two years old, keeping house. In the 1860 U.S. manuscript census schedules, Margaretha's age has increased—she is listed as forty—and John is listed as hotelkeeper.

55. *Northern Herald*, January 14, 1857.

56. April 13, 1857, notice of mortgage default by John and Margaretha Ault to James Napier, Miscellaneous Records, MorCC.

57. O. A. Churchill to JF, January 16, 1857, FPUM; *Northern Herald*, October 28, 1857.

58. JF to O. A. Churchill, December 1859, FPUM.

59. Robert Hamilton to JF, June 8, 1863; Francis Gravel to JF, May 6, 1863—both in FPUM.

60. MnTC57; Fletcher, "Reminiscence," 2. The support system for the bridge proved faulty, and it was blown down "by a heavy wind" nine years after its erection. (Richardson, "History," 17 [quotation]; Fuller, *History*, 159.)

61. Fletcher, "Reminiscence," 4; Richardson, "History," 41.

62. Fletcher, "Reminiscence," 4; Richardson, "History," 41.

63. Richardson, "History," 7–8; Fletcher, "Reminiscence," 5–6.

64. Richardson, "History," 8.

65. Fletcher, "Reminiscence," 7.

66. JF to C. A. Freeman, January 28, 1859, FPUM.

67. JF to directors and stockholders of Little Falls Manufacturing Company, February 12, 1859, Little Falls Manufacturing Company Correspondence, 1859–1886; JF to James Hall, February 9, 1859—both in FPUM.

68. JF to directors and stockholders of Little Falls Manufacturing Company, February 12, 1859, Little Falls Manufacturing Company Correspondence, 1859–1886, FPUM.

69. Samuel Hidden, 1859 Committee Report of Little Falls Manufacturing Company, Legal Documents, 1841–1900, FPUM.

70. C. A. Tuttle to JF, August 12 and October 5, 1859, FPUM.

71. JF to brother Andrew, September 29, 1859; George Stephens to JF, October 28, 1858—both in FPUM.

72. JF to Aldrich, a company director, September 12, 1859; C. A. Tuttle to JF, February 23, 1860—both in FPUM.

73. Richardson, "History," 17.

74. Mimeographed copy of W. H. Fletcher, "A Bit of Family History, Prepared by W. H. Fletcher for the Information of the Children and Grand Children of Mary A. Everest," 1924, p. 1, in William H. Fletcher Papers, MnHS.

75. William Butler and Francis X. Gravel were two of a number of French Canadians who had emigrated to Little Falls by 1857. Butler, who came to Little Falls in 1855, shortly thereafter became a clerk in Churchill's store. Gravel arrived around 1856 and by 1857 he and Butler had gone into partnership and opened a store of their own. Butler is typical of many emigrants who anglicized their names. He appears as Butolier in the 1857 Minnesota Territorial Census but as Butler in the 1860 U.S. manuscript census schedules and thereafter. Likewise, Joseph Batters appears as Better in 1857, a rough English translation of Le Mieux, the name he reclaimed in the 1860 census. He appears as Batters in the 1865 Minnesota State Census and thereafter. (MnTC57, MC60, MnSC65, MC70; Richardson, "History," 18; interview by Linda Peavy with Billy Batters Bennett, Little Falls, March 26, 1988.) For an excellent overview of French Canadian immigration to Minnesota Territory, see Sarah P. Rubinstein's "The French Canadians and French," in *They Chose Minnesota: A Survey of the State's Ethnic Groups,* ed. June Drenning Holmquist (St. Paul: Minnesota Historical Society Press, 1981), 36–54.

76. Financial Records, 1842–1885, FPUM. The 1860 U.S. manuscript census schedules show that Eliza Holmes, Temperance's sister; storekeeper Joseph LeSage; and teamster Patrick Hays were sharing the Churchill home.

77. JF to father, April 25, 1858; JF to *Fergus Falls Journal,* September 19, 1889 — both in FPUM.

78. George Stephens to JF, December 21, 1859, FPUM.

79. Horne, "James Fergus," 23; JF to PF, March 22, 1860, FPUM.

80. C. A. Tuttle to JF, December 21, 1859, FPUM.

81. JF to James Hall, February 9, 1859, FPUM; Bruce Mellor, MCHS archivist, to Peavy and Smith, September 28, 1987. James Fergus had studied single- and double-entry bookkeeping in Scotland and had worked as a bookkeeper for other business ventures before he took over the books of the Little Falls Company. (JF to brother Andrew, February 20, 1874, FPUM.) Nonetheless, he tended to ignore the rules of good bookkeeping and to lump all enterprises under a single umbrella, thereby making it extremely difficult to track specific transactions and determine their impact. As early as February 1857, Tuttle had complained, "I never did like your system of amalgamation in keeping Books" (C. A. Tuttle to JF, February 8, 1857, Oscar Mueller Collection, MtHS).

82. A part of Kansas Territory at the time of the 1859 gold strike, the Denver area became Jefferson Territory in late 1859, before finally being designated Colorado Territory in February 1861. Though no gold was discovered for some time within sixty miles of Pikes Peak, "the first reports located the diggings near that mountain, and 'Pike's Peak' — one of those happy alliterations which stick like burs in the public memory — was now the general name for this whole region" (Albert D. Richardson, *Beyond the Mississippi: From the Great River to the Great Ocean* [Hartford, Connecticut: American Publishing Company, 1867], 178).

83. In his decision to go west, James was likely influenced by his Moline friend George Stephens, who had written that there was "great excitement about the gold being discovered in Kansas and there is a good many going from our town to try their luck. . . . I would like to go but cannot. . . . Can you go?" (George Stephens to JF, January 4, 1859, FPUM).

84. JF to brother William, June 23, 1859; Mary Colburn to PF, April 22, 1860—both in FPUM. Dr. Smith had actually been only intermittently in town since early 1858. Contemporary historian Nathan Richardson reported that after 1858 Morrison County had no practicing physician except the Fort Ripley post doctor. (Richardson, "History," 39.) According to the William H. Fletcher family history, there was no doctor in town in the fall of 1858, for the Fletchers were forced to take an injured child to Fort Ripley for treatment by the doctor on duty there. (Fletcher, "A Bit of Family History," 2.)

85. After presenting their claims, both Fergus and the board felt they each owed about forty thousand dollars; therefore they canceled each other's debts. However, to reduce debts and improve the Little Falls operations, the company began issuing stock assessments. As a major stockholder, Fergus found his debts to the company rising with every assessment. (Horne, "James Fergus," 34.)

86. A daybook kept by Fergus indicates that by late January 1860 he was buying supplies for the Pikes Peak venture; subsequent entries indicate the provisions purchased up to Fergus's March departure date. (James Fergus Day Book entry, January 23, 1860, FPMtHS.) In a January 1858 letter to his father, James noted that his wife's brother "about 20 years old . . . has been brought up in our family" (JF to father, April 25, 1858; MnTC57; MC60).

87. MnTC57; MC60; JF to brother William, March 14, 1860, FPUM.

88. Sheets et al., *Todd County Histories*, 314. Bosworth was one of a number of settlers who had come to the Little Falls area from Maine, thinking to pursue familiar work in logging and lumbering. (MC60.)

89. The U.S. manuscript census schedules of 1860 list Bosworths and Farnhams as adjoining households. Farnham is alternately spelled Farnam, appearing on census rolls and in county histories in both forms.

90. JF to brother William, March 14, 1860, FPUM.

91. JF to PF, March 25 and March 28, 1860, FPUM.

92. JF to PF, March 28, 1860, FPUM.

93. *Northern Herald* notice, October 28, 1857; MnTC57; MC60; JF to PF, March 28, 1860, FPUM. Freeman was a native of New York, his wife a native of Ohio. Their son, Freddie, was born in Little Falls in early March 1860.

94. A native of Vermont, James Hall had come to Little Falls around 1855 after a sojourn in Iowa, where he was rumored to have made a small fortune in undisclosed dealings. He was thirty-five years old when James Fergus left for Pikes Peak in 1860. (William Butler to JF, February 21, 1868, FPUM; MC60.)

95. JF to PF, March 25, 1860; Power of Attorney, March 22, 1860, Legal Documents, 1841–1900—both in FPUM.

96. JF to PF, March 28, 1860, FPUM.

97. JF to PF, March 28, 1860, FPUM. William Fletcher had died early in 1860, shortly after getting his mill into operation and without repaying the debt he had incurred in buying lumber from the Little Falls Manufacturing Company. Emma Fletcher maintained the business partnership with Samuel Hays, and she eventually married him. (Fletcher, "Reminiscence," 7.)

98. JF to PF, March 28, 1860, FPUM.

99. JF to PF, March 31, 1860, FPUM. James's request seems to indicate that the primary reason for saving his letters was to keep a record of business matters

therein, yet he saved Pamelia's letters as well—often under very difficult circumstances and without regard to their business content. Thousands of families experienced separation during the westward movement, and though many were literate and did write letters during the husband's absence, of that number, relatively few double sets of letters seem to have been preserved. The survival of both James's and Pamelia's letters and of so many Fergus journals, notebooks, and legal documents would indicate that James saw himself as a man whose accomplishments were worth noting and remembering. Furthermore, his children and their spouses agreed enough with his assessment to preserve and cherish the large collection, even when doing so became, at times, a hardship.

100. References to "Kansas streams" and "Kansas plains" reflect the fact that Colorado was a part of Kansas Territory when gold was first discovered there. "The Pike's Peaker's Farewell to his Wife and Children," found in James's hand in the Fergus Papers at the University of Montana, has long been attributed to Fergus himself by family members. (Speeches and Writings, 1850–1864.) Biographer Robert M. Horne concurred with that judgment. While the Fergus papers contain a number of unattributed poems written in James's own hand and presumed to be his own compositions, it is quite possible that some of them, including "The Pike's Peaker's Farewell," were merely copied by Fergus from contemporary periodicals and altered to express his own sentiments.

101. JF to brother William, December 1, 1861, Oscar Mueller Collection, MtHS.

CHAPTER 3. Colorado Quest

1. At the time James Fergus left for Pikes Peak, Pamelia's mother, Mahala Dillin, was fifty-six and a widow of several years' standing. In a January 1856 letter to James Fergus, Mahala's son Thomas discussed the disposition of his father's estate: "Mother would jus as sone let it [the farm] to a stranger—I spoke to the girls [his sisters] about leting me have their share of land" (William Thomas Dillin to JF, January 20, 1856, FPUM). The 1850 U.S. manuscript census schedules for Illinois show William Thomas Dillin, Mahala's son, as the eldest male in the Dillin household.

2. JF to PF, March 29 and March 30, 1860, FPUM.

3. MC60; Richardson, "History," 39. On July 9, 1856, Timothy Smith purchased twelve pieces of land in Benton County under the Military Bounty Land Act of March 3, 1855; the following day he transferred all twelve pieces to a James Winslow of Cincinnati, perhaps in payment for debts incurred in Ohio. Deed Record Book B, 778–85, BenCC.

4. C. A. Tuttle to JF, February 18, 1858, FPUM; A. Bowers Barton versus T. M. Smith, July 17, 1860, Judgment Docket Book C, MorCC.

5. JF to PF, April 4, 1860, FPUM.

6. JF to PF, April 4 and April 6, 1860, FPUM.

7. JF to PF, April 8, 1860, FPUM.

8. JF to brother William, December 17, 1861, and March 14, 1860, FPUM. James indicated in a letter to his brother that he planned to travel "by steamboat and Railroad [and] overtake them on the Missourri River."

9. JF to Mary Agnes Fergus, April 13, 1860, FPUM; JF to brother William, December 1, 1861, Oscar Mueller Collection, MtHS. The wagon load described by James was definitely an overload; most wagons could carry efficiently only about three thousand pounds. Indeed, in his later instructions to Pamelia for her trip west, James advised that she plan on carrying no more than three thousand pounds in any of her wagons. (JF to PF, November 22, 1863, FPUM.)

10. JF to Mary Agnes Fergus, April 13, 1860, FPUM.

11. JF to John Currie, April 15, 1860; JF to PF, April 29, 1860—both in FPUM.

12. JF to PF, April 29, May 12, and May 25, 1860, FPUM.

13. PF to JF, April 17, 1860, FPUM.

14. JF to PF, May 25, 1860, FPUM.

15. JF to PF, May 25, 1860, FPUM. The surcharge was dropped by early fall. James noted to Pamelia, "We have a U. States mail now and the letters cost no more than in the states" (JF to PF, September 28, 1860, FPUM).

16. PF to JF, May 20, 1861, FPUM.

17. PF to JF, March 30, 1861, FPUM.

18. JF to father, March 16, 1860, FPUM. James contrasted the down-to-earth look of the middle-aged man in the 1860 picture with the pretentious look of the nineteen-year-old boy he had been when he left Scotland in a sleeved waistcoat and moleskin pants, intent on making his fortune in the new world.

19. JF to father, March 16, 1860, FPUM. James's comments in this letter concerning the children's picture he sent to Scotland are an early indication of the extent to which he valued appearances:

> The likeness to the left is my eldest daughter Mary Agnes, 13 years old. It is a very bad one and does not do her justice. She was not in a good humor, and there is an unusual expression of dislike about the features. The central figure is Frances Luella my second daughter 11 years old, and a very fair likeness. The little boy to the right is Andrew 9 years old and our only son. He is small of his age, but makes it up in hardihood and activity. His position in the middle is not good, he sits in an awkward careless manner and is too much shaded, but such as they are, I send them to you with the promise of a better likeness of the young folkes, together with a likeness of my wife and youngest child, when a better opportunity offers.

Yet Fergus was equally concerned with integrity, noting that the children were dressed "in their usual day attire on their way from school, so you have the whole just as they appear at home. No dressing or ornaments, no deception."

20. PF to JF, May 8, 1860; Mary Agnes Fergus to JF, April 22, 1860—both in FPUM. Pamelia's letters mention each of the children and describe their separate interests and activities, and her devotion to them is clear. Caught up as he was in business affairs, James, too, took time to discuss the needs and concerns of each of his four children. The Freeman and Russell letters cited elsewhere in this work also reflect the typical middle-class nineteenth-century interest in the child as an individual, an aspect of family life explored by Carl Degler in *At Odds,* 66–110.

21. PF to JF, April 17, 1860, FPUM.

22. Mary J. Colburn to PF, April 22, 1860, FPUM.

23. PF to JF, April 17, 1860, FPUM.

24. Currie had been called in response to James's nagging worries about the possibility of fire. Currie was to "sweep the chimney down about every 6 weeks" and to "set up a ladder from the back porch to the roof, and then fasten one from there to the top of the house, so as to be able to get up quick in case of fire and also so your insurance will be good" (JF to PF, April 8, 1860, FPUM).

25. PF to JF, April 17, 1860, FPUM. Though letters in the Fergus Papers tend to paint Tuttle as somewhat of a villain, Nathan Richardson's 1860 history of Morrison County noted: "Though he has grown unfortunate, his honor and integrity have never been questioned. . . . If there is any one man deserving the kindest regards and sympathies of the people of Little Falls and Morrison County, Calvin A. Tuttle is that man" (Richardson, "History," 29).

26. C. A. Freeman to JF, April 23, 1860, FPUM. In March 1898, at age eighty-nine, C. A. Tuttle wrote a letter of reconciliation to James Fergus, noting that he never had questioned James's "acuracy in book keeping" but only objected to "the conglomerate method of putting so many distinct kinds of our business all into one." And he added, "I have never seen the books since you left [Little Falls]" (C. A. Tuttle to JF, March 18, 1898, FPUM).

27. PF to JF, April 17 and April 24, 1860; Mary Agnes Fergus to JF, April 22, 1860 — all in FPUM. According to Pamelia, Mahala's trip from Geneseo took six days. (PF to JF, April 24, 1860, FPUM.)

28. PF to JF, May 8, 1860, FPUM.

29. PF to JF, June 10, 1860, FPUM; C. A. Freeman to JF, June 10, 1860, FPUM; Richardson, "History," 17.

30. PF to JF, June 9 and June 10, 1860, FPUM.

31. PF to JF, June 10, 1860, FPUM.

32. PF to JF, September 3, 1860, FPUM.

33. JF to PF, June 10 and June 17, 1860, FPUM.

34. JF to PF, November 23, 1860, FPUM.

35. JF to PF, July 22, 1860, FPUM.

36. PF to JF, July 4, 1860, FPUM.

37. Francis Gravel to JF, July 27, 1860, FPUM.

38. C. A. Freeman to JF, July 27, 1860, FPUM.

39. PF to JF, May 1860, FPUM. According to Bruce Mellor, MCHS archivist, a Dakota raid on the Ojibway took place around May 10 or 11, 1860; the Dakota dug up the body of Ojibway leader Hole-in-the-Day (Pugonageshig) and scattered his bones. The dead leader's son, Hole-in-the-Day the Younger, and his band of warriors caught up with the Dakota at Maine Prairie (in Stearns County), collected a few scalps, and turned north, celebrating in Little Falls on their way back home. (Bruce Mellor to Peavy and Smith, September 27, 1988.)

40. PF to JF, May 1860, FPUM.

41. PF to JF, June 30, 1860, FPUM.

42. JF to PF, July 1, 1860, FPUM.

43. JF to PF, June 10, 1860, FPUM.

44. JF to PF, May 12, 1860, FPUM.

45. JF to PF, June 17, 1860, FPUM.

46. JF to PF, June 17, 1860, FPUM.

47. JF to PF, July 30, 1860, FPUM.

48. JF to PF, June 10, 1860, FPUM.

49. JF to PF, June 17, 1860, FPUM.

50. JF to PF, June 10, 1860, FPUM.

51. Timothy Smith to JF, June 28, 1860, FPUM.

52. PF to JF, July 4, 1860, FPUM.

53. Timothy Smith to JF, June 28, 1860, FPUM.

54. Census records from 1850 (MC50), 1857 (MnTC57), and 1860 (MC60) list Stone as farmer, manufacturer, and hotelkeeper, but never judge. That title was likely a carry-over from his stint as "judge of election" during the vote for Minnesota statehood in 1858. Early in 1855, he had been one of a group appointed to lay out the territorial road from St. Cloud to Minneapolis, and he had served as Benton County's representative to the Seventh Territorial Legislature in 1856. (William Bell Mitchell, *History of Stearns County, Minnesota* [Chicago: H. C. Cooper, Jr., and Company, 1915], vol. 1, 48, 93, 441.)

55. Lewis Stone was still in Little Falls as late as April 11, 1860, when he and Elizabeth sold Lot 2, Block 40, in Little Falls Township to Clara Hall for two hundred dollars, double the price they had paid for it four years earlier. (Morrison County Deed Books, April 11, 1860, 232; MC60, Benton County.) The Platte River of Minnesota, which originates in the northeast corner of Morrison County and empties into the Mississippi in the northwest corner of Benton County, is not to be confused with the Platte River along whose banks so many pioneers crossed Nebraska. Though Pamelia and most of her friends still referred to the settlement by its original name, Platte River, it was officially known as Langola. Totally destroyed by a flood in 1867 and never rebuilt, it was later referred to as the "lost village of Langola" (Frank B. Logan, "Historical Sketches of Royalton and Vicinity," reprinted on June 14, 1930, from the *Royalton Banner* of February, March, April, and May 1930, p. 13–15; Harold Fisher, *The Land Called Morrison,* 2d ed. [St. Cloud: Volkmuth Printing Company, 1976], 73–74).

56. PF to JF, July 4, 1860, FPUM.

57. PF to JF, July 4, 1860, FPUM.

58. PF to JF, August 9, 1860, FPUM.

59. As Carl Degler indicates in *At Odds,* nineteenth-century women were expected to make raising the children and maintaining the home a full-time job. Even so, they did not have the final say in domestic matters, since the father was clearly the head of the family. (Degler, *At Odds,* 29.)

60. By the mid-nineteenth century, the duties deemed "suitable" for wives in American households in well-developed areas such as the industrialized East and the antebellum South tended to be limited to "womanly" tasks within the home. Even in Moline, a city on the edge of the frontier in the late 1840s, Pamelia's duties had been fairly well limited to domestic affairs; during James's trip to the eastern seaboard, there is no indication that she was expected to handle any of his business affairs. However, once she moved to the Minnesota frontier, she found that women's work was, essentially, whatever needed to be done to sustain the family. In this respect, Pamelia and her neighbors were not unlike the colonial women whose lives Ulrich has described in *Good Wives.* A woman of that era was expected to act as "deputy husband," to stand in, "should fate or circumstance prevent the husband from fulfilling his role." Thus almost any task was considered suitable for

a woman, "as long as it furthered the good of her family and was acceptable to her husband" (Ulrich, *Good Wives,* 36, 38).

Living in relative isolation, the women of Little Falls had to rely on gardens and livestock for food items city dwellers bought at corner markets. With husbands heavily involved in activities outside the home (lumbering, milling, construction, and often several of these activities at once), these frontier wives played an active role in farming and in caring for and butchering livestock. Between 1855 and 1860, Pamelia had often been left to handle general household affairs during James's not infrequent trips to St. Cloud, St. Anthony, and St. Paul, and it is likely she had also handled small business transactions on such occasions.

However, not until her husband's departure for Pikes Peak was she asked to assume responsibility for all business as well as personal affairs. Property that had once been in James's name had been transferred to Pamelia's as a safeguard against attachment during the troubled years of the Little Falls Manufacturing Company, yet only after James left for the West did she have the burdensome responsibility for paying taxes on "her" property and making decisions regarding its upkeep and sale.

61. PF to JF, July 4, 1860, FPUM.
62. JF to PF, July 1, 1860, FPUM.
63. JF to PF, July 1, 1860, FPUM.
64. JF to PF, July 8, 1860, FPUM.
65. JF to PF, July 30, 1860, FPUM.
66. JF to PF, June 17, 1860, FPUM.
67. William Butler to JF, June 12, 1860, FPUM.
68. JF to PF, June 10, 1860, FPUM.
69. JF to PF, July 8, 1860, FPUM.
70. JF to PF, July 8, 1860, FPUM.
71. JF to PF, June 10, 1860, FPUM.
72. JF to PF, July 1, 1860, FPUM.
73. C. A. Freeman to JF, June 10, 1860; JF to PF, July 22, 1860—both in FPUM.
74. PF to JF, July 26, 1860, FPUM.
75. PF to JF, July 16, 1860, FPUM.
76. C. A. Freeman to JF, July 27, 1860, FPUM.
77. PF to JF, July 26, 1860, FPUM.
78. JF to PF, July 22, 1860, FPUM.
79. PF to JF, July 26, 1860, FPUM.
80. PF to JF, August 25, 1860, FPUM.
81. PF to JF, August 25 and August 28, 1860, FPUM. Charles Freeman confirmed the bounty of crops in 1860: "I don't think there is a state in this union that has ever raised such crops as Minnesota has this season. I never saw the like in all my life. . . . There is no danger of starving this year" (C. A. Freeman to JF, September 9, 1860, FPUM).
82. PF to JF, November 22, 1860, FPUM.
83. PF to JF, August 18, 1860, FPUM.
84. JF to PF, September 28, 1860, FPUM.
85. PF to JF, August 25, 1860, FPUM.
86. PF to JF, August 18, 1860, FPUM.

87. PF to JF, August 28, 1860, FPUM.

88. JF to PF, undated, circa summer 1860; PF to JF, August 28, 1860—both in FPUM. The household at that time consisted of Pamelia, the four children, Mahala Dillin, Jane Dillin, and sometimes one of the hired men.

89. PF to JF, July 26 and August 26, 1860, FPUM.

90. PF to JF, October 23, 1860, FPUM.

91. PF to JF, November 11, 1860, FPUM.

92. JF to PF, July 30, 1860, FPUM.

93. JF to PF, July 8, 1860, FPUM. "To have seen the elephant" was a nineteenth-century phrase implying that one had "seen it all" and found it wanting. The phrase was commonly associated with those miners and homesteaders who gave up and returned home after trying their luck in the West.

94. JF to PF, July 22, 1860, FPUM.

95. PF to JF, August 18, 1860, FPUM.

96. JF to PF, July 8 and July 30, 1860. The mountain Fergus climbed was, by his estimate, six miles high and one mile straight above Blue River. Since the highest peak in Colorado is just over 14,200 feet, the estimate is another Fergus exaggeration. Upon hearing of the climb, Freeman sent a message to his agnostic friend by way of Pamelia: "Tell Fergus he had bettr staid on the top of that hgh mountain for you must have been very near heaven and he is afraid you will never get so near again" (PF to JF, August 18, 1860, FPUM).

97. JF to PF, July 30, 1860, FPUM.

98. JF to PF, August 17 and September 15, 1860, FPUM.

99. PF to JF, August 18, 1860, FPUM.

100. PF to JF, September 8, 1860, FPUM.

101. C. A. Freeman to JF, September 9, 1860, FPUM.

102. PF to JF, September 9, 1860, FPUM.

103. PF to JF, September 8, 1860, FPUM.

104. PF to JF, September 8, 1860, FPUM.

105. PF to JF, September 8, 1860, FPUM.

106. Sheets et al., *Todd County Histories,* 337; MC50.

107. Alexander Paul mortgaged 160 acres to Ovid Pinney on March 24, 1860. (Deed Book C, 497, BenCC.)

108. MC50, MnTC57, MC60.

109. The Russell family contends that Janet was the first white child born in Benton County, a claim not documented, yet not disproved. (*A Genealogical Register of the Descendants of Robert and Agnes (Leitch) Russell,* compiled by their grandchildren [North St. Paul, Minnesota, and Bismarck, North Dakota: Nelson and Robert Flint, 1923], 5–6; hereafter, this publication is referred to as the Russell Register.)

110. Russell Register, 10.

111. PF to JF, September 8, 1860, FPUM.

112. PF to JF, September 23, 1860, FPUM.

113. C. A. Freeman to JF, September 9, 1860, FPUM.

114. Caroline Bosworth to Daniel Bosworth, undated fragment, circa November 1860, FPUM. Caroline's letter also contained a note from her mother, Sarah Farnham, describing the same gathering of the widows. (Sarah Farnham to Daniel Bosworth, undated fragment, circa November 1860, FPUM.)

115. Caroline Bosworth to Daniel Bosworth, undated fragment, circa November 1860, FPUM. Despite the closeness of the widows, they did not always appreciate the tendency of their wayfaring husbands to rely upon James Fergus as the bearer of news: "I learned by Mr Ferges letter that you had bought a clame and some one had jumped it. . . . Why don't you tell mee such things [or] do you think hee [Fergus] tells it and it is of no youse to write [to me]" (Caroline Bosworth to Daniel Bosworth, undated fragment, circa November 1860, FPUM).

116. C. A. Freeman to JF, July 27, 1860, FPUM.

117. JF to PF, August 3, 1860, FPUM.

118. PF to JF, August 18, 1860, FPUM.

119. PF to JF, October 23, 1860; Mary Agnes Fergus to JF, September 15, 1860 — both in FPUM.

120. PF to JF, October 23, 1860, FPUM.

121. PF to JF, September 8, 1860, FPUM.

122. Luella Fergus to JF, July 1860, FPUM.

123. Mary Agnes Fergus to JF, September 23, 1860, FPUM.

124. Mary Agnes Fergus to JF, September 15, 1860, FPUM.

125. JF to PF, September 28, 1860, FPUM.

126. JF to PF, September 28, 1860, FPUM.

127. JF to PF, September 28, 1860, FPUM.

128. Note signed by T. M. Smith on September 21, 1860, in Mountain City, owing James Fergus twenty dollars, FPUM.

129. PF to JF, September 8, 1860, FPUM.

130. JF to PF, August 3, 1860, FPUM.

131. JF to PF, August 17, 1860, FPUM.

132. JF to George Stephens, August 17, 1860, FPUM.

133. George Stephens to JF, September 2, 1860, FPUM.

134. PF to JF, September 8, 1860, FPUM.

135. PF to JF, September 23 and September 15, 1860, FPUM.

136. PF to JF, October 9, 1860, FPUM.

137. Mary Agnes Fergus to JF, November 25, 1860, FPUM.

138. The girls' expenses for the trip totaled $15.92, not counting the stage from Little Falls to St. Anthony. In addition, Pamelia had been able to spare twelve dollars for their incidental expenses in Moline. (Undated memorandum, FPUM.)

139. PF to JF, November 11, 1860, FPUM.

140. PF to JF, November 11, 1860, FPUM.

141. PF to JF, October 23, 1860, FPUM.

142. PF to JF, October 23, 1860, FPUM.

143. PF to JF, October 23, 1860, FPUM.

144. PF to JF, November 22, 1860, FPUM.

145. PF to JF, November 11, 1860, FPUM.

146. PF to JF, November 11, 1860, FPUM. There was evidently some family relationship between the Smiths and the Stones. Timothy Smith at times refers to Judge Stone as "Uncle Lewis," though the term might merely have been one of respect. (Timothy Smith to JF, August 31 and November 1, 1861.)

147. C. A. Freeman to JF, December 11, 1860, FPUM.

148. Timothy Smith to JF, December 4, 1860, FPUM.

149. C. A. Freeman to JF, December 11, 1860, FPUM.
150. PF to JF, November 11, 1860, FPUM.
151. PF to JF, December 23 and December 28, 1860, FPUM.
152. JF to PF, November 25, 1860, FPUM.
153. C. A. Freeman to JF, December 11, 1860, FPUM.
154. PF to JF, October 9, 1860, FPUM.
155. PF to JF, July 4, 1860, FPUM.
156. PF to JF, November 11, 1860, FPUM.
157. PF to JF, December 23, 1860, FPUM.
158. C. A. Freeman to JF, September 9, 1860, FPUM.
159. JF to PF, September 28, 1860, FPUM.
160. JF to PF, October 10, 1860, FPUM.
161. Pamelia may well have drawn strength and inspiration from a visiting lecturer who provided a role model for Minnesota women thrown on their own resources. Jane Grey Swisshelm, who had come to Minnesota with her young daughter after leaving an unhappy marriage, was editor and publisher of the *St. Cloud Democrat* and an ardent abolitionist and feminist. Having drawn a capacity crowd upon her first appearance in Little Falls some eight months earlier, Swisshelm returned in December 1860 to sound again the call for equality of the sexes. (Jan Warner, "Which Sixties Are We Talking About: The Lives of Morrison County Women," delivered at the Morrison County Historical Society women's history conference, "As Good As Gold: The Value of Women's Work on the Frontier," March 15–26, 1988, Little Falls, Minnesota; Abigail McCarthy, "Jane Grey Swisshelm: Marriage and Slavery," in *Women of Minnesota: Selected Biographical Essays,* ed. Barbara Stuhler and Gretchen Kreuter [St. Paul: Minnesota Historical Society Press, 1977], 34–54.)
162. MnTC57.
163. PF to JF, September 23 and December 23, 1860, FPUM.
164. PF to JF, December 23, 1860, FPUM.
165. PF to JF, December 23, 1860, FPUM.
166. PF to JF, December 23, 1860, FPUM.
167. PF to JF, December 23, 1860, FPUM.
168. JF to PF, October 10, 1860, FPUM.
169. PF to JF, November 11, 1860, FPUM.
170. C. A. Freeman to JF, September 9, 1860, FPUM.
171. C. A. Freeman to JF, September 9, 1860, FPUM.
172. C. A. Freeman to JF, June 10, 1860, FPUM.
173. PF to JF, June 9, 1861; C. A. Freeman to JF, December 11, 1860—both in FPUM.
174. PF to JF, March 3, 1861.
175. C. A. Freeman to JF, September 9, 1860; William Butler to JF, June 12, 1860—both in FPUM. John Ault was apparently a bit of a Falstaff, as attested to by this riddle that appeared in the January 14, 1857, edition of the *Northern Herald:* "Why is John Ault, Esq. Like one of Shakespeare's prominent heroes?"
176. Francis Gravel to JF, December 30, 1860; PF to JF, March 3, 1861—both in FPUM.
177. PF to JF, November 11, 1860, FPUM.

178. Mary Agnes Fergus to JF, December 20, 1860, FPUM. Elisha Kane, M.D., was much feted by the British and American public for his two voyages into the polar regions. Though Kane himself had died some four years before the lecture Agnes wrote of, she noted that his dog and his gun were featured in the show. (*Encyclopedia Americana,* vol. 16 [New York: Encyclopedia Americana Corporation, 1958], 290–91.)

179. PF to JF, December 23, 1860, FPUM.

180. C. A. Freeman to JF, September 9, 1860, FPUM.

181. A family legend describes Andrew's hunting with an Indian friend whose shoulder he used to steady the gun as he fired. The family later learned that the Indian was deaf in one ear as an adult. (Agnes Quigley Miedema, daughter of Andrew Fergus, to Peavy and Smith, fall 1986; Pamelia Fergus Pittman, daughter of Andrew Fergus, to Peavy and Smith, fall 1986.) The Indian boy was likely one of the two sons of Sloan and his Indian wife, Odishquaw.

182. JF to PF, November 8, 1860, FPUM.

183. JF to PF, December 1, 1860, FPUM.

184. C. A. Freeman to JF, December 11, 1860, FPUM.

185. PF to JF, September 8, 1860, FPUM. In that letter, Pamelia noted that Lillie "says at the table she wants good tea as well as I . . . she does not want milk and watter and throughs her spoon with a vengence."

186. C. A. Freeman to JF, December 11, 1860, FPUM.

187. C. A. Freeman to JF, July 27, 1860, FPUM.

188. PF to JF, September 9, 1860, FPUM.

189. Infant deaths were not uncommon on the frontier, and the Freemans were not the only Little Falls couple to lose a child in 1860. In June Charles Freeman himself had written James that "Halls folks buried their youngest yesterday in fumiation on the brain I believe was the cause of the death it lived about 20 hours after it was taken sick" (C. A. Freeman to JF, June 30, 1860, FPUM).

190. C. A. Freeman to JF, December 11, 1860, FPUM.

191. Francis Gravel to JF, December 30, 1860, FPUM. Pamelia hinted at the pregnancy in a letter to James, noting euphemistically that Abby had been sick "but it may fall in her arms" (PF to JF, December 23, 1860, FPUM).

192. PF to JF, December 23, 1869; Abby Freeman to PF, February 8, 1863 — both in FPUM.

193. PF to JF, December 28, 1860, FPUM.

194. Luella Fergus to JF, December 23, 1860, FPUM.

195. JF to PF, November 23, 1860, FPUM.

196. PF to JF, November 11, 1860, FPUM.

197. JF to PF, December 1 and December 12, 1860, FPUM.

198. PF to JF, December 28, 1860, FPUM.

199. PF to JF, November 11, 1860, FPUM. Pamelia reminded James that the nutgall remedy was "what cured you in a short time when you were in Rock Island."

200. JF to PF, December 1, 1860, FPUM.

201. PF to JF, December 3, 1860, FPUM.

202. PF to JF, December 28, 1860, FPUM.

203. Hamilton/Fergus account sheet for 1860, Financial Records, 1842–1885, FPUM.

204. C. A. Freeman to JF, December 11, 1860, FPUM. On December 28, Pamelia noted that when Bosworth arrived on the stage "yesterday," Caroline "had just been gone three days out to long prairie her Fathers folks are gone on to their clame" (PF to JF, December 28, 1860, FPUM). Francis Gravel reported December 29 as Bosworth's arrival date. (F. X. Gravel to JF, December 30, 1860, FPUM.) Despite this confusion of dates, all three correspondents agreed that Bosworth was furious to find that Caroline had moved to Long Prairie with her family and was not in Little Falls to meet him.

205. PF to JF, December 28, 1860, FPUM.

206. Daniel Bosworth to O. J. Rockwell, January 3, 1861.

207. In all the Fergus papers, there is only one account of extensive drinking by James. During a Robert Burns Centennial dinner in St. Paul, he drank punch containing old Scotch whiskey. Many toasts were given, and the festivities did not end until nearly 5:00 A.M. James himself gave the last toast to the Scottish poet: "May he live till the day of judgment, and play his bagpipes in response to the Angel Gabrail." Whether or not he described his night of revelry to Pamelia, he wrote about it in some detail to Freeman and likely bragged a bit to others, once he returned to Little Falls. By his own account, James had sat near the biggest punch bowl and the president of the Robert Burns group "took good care to fill my glass as often as Empty, which unfortunately to be fashionable in such a gathering was not seldom, and to tell the truth I drank more than I have in many years and probably as much as any man there. A few could not navigate when I left and I was as sober as a judge, and stranger still next morning I had no head ache and have had none since" (JF to C. A. Freeman, January 28, 1859, FPUM).

208. Daniel Bosworth to O. J. Rockwell, January 3, 1861, FPUM.

209. JF to PF, September 27, 1863; PF to JF, December 12, 1863—both in FPUM.

210. PF to JF, December 28, 1860, FPUM.

211. PF to JF, February 11, 1861, FPUM.

212. Daniel Bosworth to O. J. Rockwell, January 3, 1861, FPUM. According to Pamelia, all work on the dam had stopped, since the workers had quit after being denied promised wages. (PF to JF, December 3, 1860, FPUM.)

213. F. X. Gravel to JF, December 30, 1860, FPUM. The mill on the Little Elk was the only gristmill in Morrison County at that time. (Richardson, "History," 41.)

214. William Sturgis to JF, January 13, 1861, FPUM.

215. PF to JF, January 7, 1861, FPUM.

216. PF to JF, January 19, 1861, FPUM.

217. PF to JF, February 11, 1861, FPUM.

218. PF to JF, April 23, 1861, FPUM. While James tolerated Pamelia's sending kisses from Lillie, he did not otherwise tolerate sentimentality in her letters: "Write me sensible letter[s]," he admonished Pamelia once. "Don't write about lovy dovy as you did about some girl of James [Dillin's] but let your letters contain good sound sense" (JF to PF, undated, circa summer 1860, FPUM).

219. JF to son Andrew, March 19, 1861, FPUM. Like many other nineteenth-century husbands and fathers whose wives were providing most of the income necessary to the family's survival, James Fergus liked to remind himself and his children of his importance as provider. Though Pamelia earned money by making butter, not by writing books, her situation as actual, if not perceived, breadwinner mir-

rors that of the "literary domestics" described in Mary Kelley's *Private Women, Public Sphere* (New York: Oxford University Press, 1984).

220. PF to JF, April 23, 1861, FPUM.

221. Mary Agnes Fergus to JF, January 6 and February 3, 1861, FPUM.

222. Luella Fergus to JF, February 3 and January 6, 1861, FPUM.

223. Mary Agnes Fergus to JF, January 6, 1861, FPUM.

224. George Stephens to JF, February 5, 1861, FPUM. Luella was not unaware of her social successes: "I got ten valentines this year Agnes got one I rather beat Agnes on that point" (Luella Fergus to JF, March 3, 1861, FPUM).

225. Mary Agnes Fergus to JF, February 3, 1861, FPUM.

226. George Stephens to JF, February 5, 1861, FPUM.

227. JF to PF, February 10, 1861, FPUM.

228. PF to JF, February 11, 1861, FPUM.

229. PF to JF, October 23, 1860, FPUM.

230. PF to JF, December 11, 1860, FPUM.

231. PF to JF, February 11, 1861, FPUM.

232. PF to JF, February 22, 1861, FPUM.

233. PF to JF, February 1, 1861, FPUM.

234. PF to JF, February 1, 1861, FPUM.

235. JF to PF, February 11, 1861, FPUM. With James, Mary Agnes, and Luella far from home, the holiday season had been lonely for Pamelia, and she had confessed, "I did not anticipate of being quite so lonely" (PF to JF, December 23, 1860, FPUM).

236. PF to JF, February 22, 1861, FPUM.

237. PF to JF, February 1, 1861, FPUM.

238. JF to PF, March 14, 1861, FPUM.

239. Pamelia's complaints were temporarily stifled by a passage from James that was meant to put her feelings of frustration in proper perspective. "You can see now when the little business I left with you caused you so much trouble," he wrote, "[how such pressure could account for] my peculearities of temper and disposition amidst such a press of business and losses that I had to bear at Little Falls" (JF to PF, October 10, 1860, FPUM). When she read those words, Pamelia hastened to reply, "You speak of your peculieraites and temper and losses and crosses while at Little Falls [and about how] I had ought to [have overlooked them in view of the pressure you were under] and did in a meshur and can do [so even] more next time, [for] our [personal] troubles are all forgotten and forgiven now a hundred fold" (PF to JF, November 11, 1860, FPUM).

240. PF to JF, April 7, 1861, FPUM.

241. PF to JF, March 3, 1861, FPUM.

242. PF to JF, March 16, 1861, FPUM.

243. Luella Fergus to JF, March 3, 1861, FPUM.

244. PF to JF, April 14, 1861, FPUM.

245. PF to JF, March 16, 1861, FPUM.

246. PF to JF, March 30, 1861, FPUM.

247. JF to PF, April 10, 1861, FPUM.

248. JF to PF, February 10, 1861, FPUM.

249. PF to JF, March 27, 1861, FPUM.

250. PF to JF, November 11, 1860, FPUM.

251. PF to JF, February 11, 1861, FPUM. In October, Pamelia had reported that "Mrs Smith is expecting the Doctor soon now He [said he] would start the first of Oct and should keep money enough right in his breetches pocket to fetch him home" (PF to JF, October 9, 1860, FPUM).

252. PF to JF, February 11, 1861, FPUM.

253. PF to JF, March 27 and April 23, 1861, FPUM.

254. PF to JF, April 14, 1861, FPUM.

255. JF to PF, April 10, 1861, FPUM.

256. Mary Paul to JF, January 10, 1861, FPUM.

257. PF to JF, March 3, 1861; JF to PF, March 14, 1861 — both in FPUM.

258. PF to JF, February 11, 1861, FPUM.

259. PF to JF, April 14, 1861, FPUM. At the time Mary Paul was considering moving to St. Cloud, the town had a population of one thousand, was known as one of the most enterprising in Minnesota, and would have offered ample opportunity for work as housemaid, laundry woman, or cook. (Henrietta L. Memler, "A History of St. Cloud, Minnesota, 1861–65" [undated typescript, MnHS], 3–5.)

260. PF to JF, February 11, 1861, FPUM.

261. PF to JF, February 22 and April 14, 1861, FPUM.

262. JF to PF, March 14, 1861, FPUM.

263. Russell Register, 6–7; JF to PF, April 10, 1861, FPUM. While Russell family memoirs admit that Robert "frequently drank to excess" and "in common with the majority of the men of [his] race and time" was "addicted to the use of liquor," they add tempering notes — he "never touched liquor except when in company with kindred spirits" and his drinking "did not interfere with" his "adhering to the harsh creed of the Presbyterian faith" (Russell Register, 7).

264. JF to PF, April 4 and April 10, 1861, FPUM.

265. PF to JF, April 30, 1861, FPUM.

266. PF to JF, March 16, 1861, FPUM.

267. PF to JF, April 7, 1861, FPUM.

268. PF to JF, May 11, 1861, FPUM.

269. PF to JF, April 7, 1861, FPUM.

270. PF to JF, April 14, 1861, FPUM.

271. PF to JF, April 23, 1861, FPUM.

272. PF to JF, May 11, 1861, FPUM.

273. Rosanna's mother, Margaret Steele, and her younger brother and sister were also absent from the household, having moved down to Swan River. (MC60.)

274. PF to JF, May 11, 1861, FPUM.

275. PF to JF, January 19, 1861, FPUM.

276. PF to JF, February 1, February 11, and April 14, 1861, FPUM.

277. PF to JF, April 30, 1861, FPUM.

278. PF to JF, April 23, 1861, FPUM.

279. PF to JF, April 30, 1861, FPUM. Augusta Byers appeared on the 1857 Minnesota Territorial Census as a fifteen-year-old from Germany, living at Ault's hotel. Augusta was eighteen and Orlando Churchill thirty-six when she had his child. (MnTC57; MC60.) By 1860, she and Churchill's baby were living in St. Paul, and

he was bragging about taking her to California with him. (PF to JF, March 30, 1860, FPUM.)

280. PF to JF, May 11, 1861, FPUM. The tone of Pamelia's comments concerning the Churchill affair suggests the gossipy nature of the town's discussions of this topic. Sober citizens like Freeman had no patience with Churchill's behavior and predicted, "He is going just where he ought to go and where any man would go that has got no more honesty or principle than he has" (C. A. Freeman to JF, December 11, 1860, FPUM).

281. PF to JF, July 1, 1861, FPUM. Pamelia dated this letter June 31, 1861, and family members altered the date to June 30; in reality, it was written on July 1, 1861, for it was written on a Monday. (PF to JF, June 9, 1861, FPUM; MC60.)

282. "Register of School taught in Sub-District No. [blank] of School District Little Falls, in the County of Morrison and State of Minnesota, for the term commencing on the 4th day of March, A.D. 1861," signed by P. H. Taylor, MCHS; PF to JF, May 6, 1861, FPUM.

283. PF to JF, April 14, 1861, FPUM.

284. PF to JF, April 30, 1861, FPUM.

285. PF to JF, May 20, 1861, FPUM.

286. PF to JF, June 2, 1861, FPUM.

287. PF to JF, May 6, 1861, FPUM.

288. PF to JF, September 9, 1863, FPUM.

289. PF to JF, May 20, 1861, FPUM. Even older men were rushing to enlist, for Pamelia reported that Judge Stone's forty-five-year-old brother, George, had "enlisted fainted away the first time [he] went to drill then [they] picked him up [moved] him into the house [and] sent him home This may seem to some like a laugh[ing] matter but when you know it is so and know that men get crazy [over war] its no joke" (PF to JF, June 19, 1861, FPUM).

290. Mary Agnes Fergus to JF, May 15, 1861, FPUM.

291. PF to JF, June 19, 1861, FPUM.

292. PF to JF, May 11 and May 20, 1861, FPUM. The rumor concerning William's enlistment was apparently false.

293. PF to JF, September 6, 1861. Hiram Dillin served with General George McClelland and was taken prisoner for a few months in 1862. (Hiram Dillin to PF, August 9, 1861, Oscar Mueller Collection, MtHS; PF to JF, July 28, 1862, FPUM.)

294. PF to JF, June 19, 1861, FPUM.

295. PF to JF, July 8, 1861, FPUM.

296. JF to PF, May 6, 1861, FPUM.

297. JF to PF, no date, FPUM.

298. PF to JF, May 20, 1861, FPUM. Pamelia seems to have known her husband well enough to know he would find fault with her letters. Earlier, she had noted, "I suppose you have hard work sometimes to read my scratches but you are not plagued very much nowadays by us" (PF to JF, September 9, 1860, FPUM). And while James tended to be overly critical, he did write one letter of real praise: "Dear wife I received your Excellent letter of March 3 by last mail. All the letters I get from the States lately are so well composed and well written that I am getting ashamed of mine" (JF to PF, April 4, 1861, FPUM).

299. PF to JF, April 23, May 6, and June 2, 1861, FPUM.

300. PF to JF, May 11, 1861, FPUM.

301. PF to JF, May 11, 1861, FPUM.

302. PF to JF, July 8, 1861, FPUM.

303. PF to JF, July 18, 1861, FPUM.

304. PF to JF, June 19 and June 9, 1861, FPUM.

305. PF to JF, July 18 and June 9, 1861, FPUM.

306. PF to JF, April 23, 1861; George Stephens to PF, April 23, 1861 — both in FPUM.

307. Mary Agnes Fergus to JF, May 14, 1861, FPUM.

308. George Stephens to PF, April 23, 1861, FPUM.

309. JF to PF, April 25, 1861, FPUM.

310. JF to PF, April 4, 1861, FPUM.

311. Fergus apparently felt Paul should have followed Russell's example and worked for wages. (JF to PF, April 25 and April 10, 1861, FPUM.)

312. JF to PF, April 25, 1861, FPUM.

313. PF to JF, June 2, 1861, FPUM.

314. Robert Russell to Agnes Russell, June 22, 1861, Russell Register, 37–38. The child was eventually named John Higgins Russell, after the kindly neighbor who had been Agnes's mainstay during her husband's absence. Found in the Russell Register, this series of letters from Robert, dated June 22, 1861, has been edited and transcribed by family members and stands in stark contrast to the unedited letters of Robert Russell found in the Fergus Papers at the University of Montana and quoted elsewhere in this work. While the misspellings found in the unedited letters are a constant reminder of the writer's lack of formal education, the quaint but descriptive phrases and keen observations therein are those of a sensitive, intelligent man.

315. Robert Russell to son Robert, June 22, 1861; Robert Russell to daughter Agnes, June 22, 1861; Robert Russell to Jennie Russell, June 22, 1861 — all in the Russell Register, 37–38. Robert Russell's tone in addressing his wife and children suggests that he was a caring husband and father who held high expectations for his children. Apparently, he was a stern disciplinarian as well, for in later years, his eldest son noted that he was "unduly severe in his discipline," yet hastened to add that "he dearly loved his children" (Russell Register, 7).

316. Robert Russell to son Robert, June 22, 1861, Russell Register, 37.

317. JF to PF, January 6, 1861; JF to PF, May 6, 1861 — both in FPUM.

318. PF to JF, June 9, 1861, FPUM.

319. PF to JF, April 14, 1861, FPUM. As close as she was to the Freemans, Pamelia was annoyed by Abby's tendency to act as if she knew a great deal about business matters: "You know she talks about Fergus not doing as he agreed I know nothing about [it] nor she much more so." Whereas Abby tended to pretend a knowledge she did not have, Pamelia kept silent, noting, "It is better to sit still than to rise up and fall." Over the years Pamelia had "learnt" that Abby knew "less evry day . . . it spoils folks sometimes to know to much" (PF to JF, April 23, 1861, FPUM).

320. PF to JF, April 23, 1861, FPUM.

321. PF to JF, May 20, 1861, FPUM.

322. PF to JF, June 9, 1861, FPUM. A month later Pamelia wrote about the taxes

again: "Now Fergus I do not know what to say about your business here in your town. Our county taxes are not payed yet nor wont be if I do not watch it. . . . You had better come home and do something with this property it is good for nothing as it [is]. . . . The taxes are forty dolers . . . and the whole thing is not worth [that] . . . amount" (PF to JF, July 8, 1861, FPUM).

323. PF to JF, July 8, 1861, FPUM.

324. JF to PF, July 25, 1861, FPUM.

325. PF to JF, June 19, 1861, FPUM.

326. JF to PF, May 6, 1861, FPUM.

327. JF to brother William, December 1, 1861, FPMtHS.

328. JF to brother William, December 1, 1861, FPMtHS.

329. PF to JF, May 20, 1861, FPUM. Between mid-May and July 10, there is but one letter extant in James's hand.

330. PF to JF, June 25, 1861, FPUM.

331. PF to JF, June 2, 1861, FPUM.

332. PF to JF, June 2, 1861, FPUM.

333. PF to JF, June 3, 1861, FPUM.

334. PF to JF, June 19, 1861, FPUM.

335. PF to JF, July 1, 1861, FPUM.

336. PF to JF, July 18, 1861, FPUM.

337. PF to JF, May 11 and June 2, 1861, FPUM.

338. Timothy Smith to JF, August 31, 1861, FPUM.

339. JF to PF, May 14, 1861, FPUM.

340. PF to JF, September 6, 1861, FPUM.

341. Timothy Smith to JF, November 1, 1861, FPUM.

342. Timothy Smith to JF, November 1, 1861, FPUM.

343. JF to PF, July 10 and August 20, 1861, FPUM.

344. JF to PF, July 24, 1861, FPUM.

345. JF to PF, July 25, 1861, FPUM.

346. JF to PF, July 10, 1861, FPUM.

347. PF to JF, July 8, 1861, FPUM.

348. PF to JF, April 23, May 6, and June 2, 1861, FPUM. Jane had taught one season at Platte River in September 1860. (Mary Agnes Fergus to JF, September 15 and September 23, 1860, FPUM.)

349. PF to JF, July 8 and July 18, 1861, FPUM.

350. PF to JF, July 18, 1861, FPUM.

351. PF to JF, July 18, 1861, FPUM.

352. PF to JF, July 1, 1861, FPUM.

353. PF to JF, July 8, 1861, FPUM.

354. JF to PF, August 4, 1861, FPUM.

355. JF to PF, August 25, 1861, FPUM.

356. JF to PF, August 25, 1861, FPUM.

357. PF to JF, September 11, 1861, FPUM.

358. PF to JF, September 6 and August 20, 1861, FPUM.

359. PF to JF, September 11, 1861, FPUM.

360. PF to JF, July 8 and September 6, 1861, FPUM. Katherine Freeman was born on May 12, 1861. (PF to JF, May 20, 1860, FPUM.)

361. JF to PF, August 16, 1861, FPUM.

362. Camp Weld was located within the present southern city limits of Denver. (Leroy Hafen and Ann Hafen, *The Colorado Story* [Denver: Old West Publishing Company, 1960], 206.)

363. JF to PF, July 24, 1861, FPUM.

364. JF to PF, September 1, 1861, FPUM.

365. JF to PF, September 1, 1861, FPUM.

366. PF to JF, September 11, 1861, FPUM. According to a March 18, 1862, entry in his ledger, James Fergus himself was instrumental in taking in a second boarder, Agnes Russell's eldest son, Robert, who was working "in Little Falls at building boom piers" in the spring of 1862. (Robert Russell entry, James Fergus Ledger, 1859–1862, FPMtHS.) According to Russell's memoirs, he "boarded with a Mr. Ferguson [*sic*] who was an old friend of Father's." While Russell made a common error in his recollection of the Fergus name, he remembered well James's generosity: "When I wanted to pay my bill he told me that when my father came home with the $40,000 that he had promised to get he would take the money, but until then 'No.' " (Russell Register, 10).

367. PF to JF, May 11, 1861, FPUM.

368. Robert Hamilton served as postmaster from March 13, 1861, to February 18, 1864. The first postmaster of Little Falls had been William Sturgis, who served from June 25, 1852, until June 30, 1854, when the office was discontinued. Upon its reestablishment on April 3, 1855, James Fergus was named postmaster. He was followed, a year later, by O. A. Churchill, who served until March 27, 1857, when James Hall took office. Hall was succeeded by Hamilton's immediate predecessor, Charles Garden, on July 30, 1859. (U.S. Post Office records, MCHS.)

369. George Stephens to JF, September 1, 1861, FPUM.

370. In early December, Fergus received a letter mailed to Little Falls from David Heron, Jr., of Wide Awake City in the Colorado mines. That letter indicates that Heron had received a letter from Fergus postmarked October 28, 1861, saying that he (Fergus) was back in the States. Though Fergus might have posted that letter in Moline, or even Omaha, rather than in Little Falls, a letter to his brother written December 1, 1861, mentions that he had been home "over a month," so his return can be marked between October 28 and mid-November. The Little Falls daybook in which he had made a final entry in March 1860, just before his departure to Pikes Peak, bears a November 14 entry, indicating that he was back at work soon after his return to Minnesota. (FPMtHS.)

CHAPTER 4. The Interim

1. JF to brother William, December 1, 1861, FPMtHS. James Fergus was less than accurate in these statements. Mahala Dillin had actually returned home in July 1861, rather than earlier in the spring. Moline is only some nine hundred miles from Denver, depending upon the route traveled.

2. JF to PF, September 8, 1861, FPUM.

3. Timothy Smith to JF, November 1, 1861, FPUM.

4. Robert Russell to JF, December 8, 1861, FPUM.

5. Robert Russell to JF, January 5, 1862, FPUM.

6. Robert Russell to JF, June 8, 1861, FPUM.

7. PF to JF, July 8, 1861, FPUM.

8. Margaretha Ault obituary, *Little Falls Weekly Transcript,* March 13, 1896; Margaretha Ault to Robert Hamilton, January 29, 1872, FPUM.

9. JF to William Wood, publisher of the *Minnesota Union* (St. Cloud), June 8, 1862, FPUM.

10. William Fergus to JF, January 29, 1862, FPUM. One pound sterling equaled about five dollars in U.S. currency in 1857. (Horne, "James Fergus," 28.)

11. JF to brother William, March 5, 1862, FPUM.

12. JF to brother William, March 5, 1862, FPUM.

13. S. O. Crawford to JF, January 6, 1862; JF to Maury Drake of St. Louis, May 29, 1862—both in FPUM.

14. Robert Russell to JF, January 5, 1862, FPUM.

15. Robert Russell to JF, January 26, 1862, FPUM.

16. Robert Russell to JF, May 18 and June 8, 1862, FPUM.

17. Robert Russell to JF, June 8, 1862, FPUM.

18. Robert Russell to JF, June 8, 1862, FPUM.

19. George Stephens to JF, January 26, 1862, FPUM.

20. James Dillin to JF, March 1, 1862, FPUM.

21. *Congressional Record,* 37th Cong., 2d sess., 1862, vol. 56, pt. 1, 505; White, *Ho!,* 35. The first of the Salmon River gold strikes in what was soon to become Idaho Territory took place in August 1860.

CHAPTER 5. Montana Gold

1. The railway route had been surveyed in 1853 by Isaac I. Stevens, an early governor of Washington Territory. (Theodore C. Blegen, *Minnesota: A History of the State* [Minneapolis: University of Minnesota Press, 1975], 193; James L. Fisk, *Expedition from Fort Abercrombie to Fort Benton,* 37th Cong., 3d Sess., 1862–63, Ex. Doc. 80, vol. 8 [Serial 1164], p. 4.) The nine were John Ault, Robert Ells, and C. H. Klein of Fort Ripley; Peter Cardinell and William Sturgis of Elk City (Little Elk); and David Bentley, James Fergus, O. J. Rockwell, and William Wright of Little Falls. (White, *Ho!,* 31, 264–66; JF to PF, August 11, 1862, and July 15, 1863, FPUM.)

2. White, *Ho!,* 265–66; JF to PF, July 9, 1862, FPUM.

3. PF to JF, June 30, 1862, FPUM.

4. William Sturgis to JF, June 14, 1862, FPUM.

5. C. A. Freeman to JF, July 13, 1862, FPUM.

6. JF to PF, June 22, 1862, FPUM.

7. JF to PF, June 22, 1862, FPUM.

8. The Mr. Rice referred to was most likely George F. Rice, who appears on the 1860 U.S. manuscript census schedules as a painter; JF to PF, June 22, 1862, FPUM.

9. JF to PF, June 22, 1862, FPUM.

10. JF to PF, July 6, 1862, FPUM.

11. JF to PF, July 9, 1862; PF to JF, June 30, 1862, FPUM.

12. Fisk, *Expedition,* 6.

13. JF to PF, July 6, 1862, FPUM.

14. JF to PF, July 6, 1862, FPUM.

15. JF to PF, July 6, 1862, FPUM.

16. JF to PF, July 9, 1862, FPUM.

17. Having missed his St. Cloud rendezvous after "his oxen got away" and had to be rounded up again, John Ault had set out for Fort Abercrombie. En route, further trouble with some of the oxen and the heavily loaded wagon drove the three Fort Ripley men to drastic measures: "[Ault] and Dutch Henry cut their wagon in two. Ault and Ells taking the fore wheels and making a cart of it and Henry the hind wheels." That feat accomplished, the Fort Ripley contingent caught up with the Fisk expedition on July 8, while they were camped on the Cheyenne River. (PF to JF, July 1, 1862, and JF to PF, July 9, 1862, FPUM.)

18. JF to PF, July 9, 1862, FPUM. Helen McCann White quotes Samuel R. Bond, expedition clerk, as saying there were 117 men, 13 women, and 53 wagons on the 1862 expedition; no children were noted. (White, *Ho!*, 31.) Dr. W. D. Dibb, expedition physician, set the total at 130, including 10 women and "some eight (8) or ten (10) children" ("Report of Dr. Dibb" in Fisk, *Expedition*, 28). According to Dr. Dibb's diary of 1862, he attended Mrs. Josephus (Mary Jane) Stark's delivery of a son on August 8 of that year ("Diary of Dr. William D. Dibb, 1862," in White, *Ho!*, 60.) Samuel Bond reported that the new baby was "added to our list of emigrants." Bond also described a wedding ceremony performed during the journey, "with the moon shedding a bright, chaste light over the scene" ("Report of Samuel R. Bond" in Fisk, *Expedition*, 9–10, 19).

19. PF to JF, June 30, 1862, FPUM. Lillie's adjustment to James's absence was not unlike the adjustments made by many nineteenth-century children whose fathers were soldiers, sailors, or traveling businessmen. However, for the children of westering men, periods of separation often stretched into years, during which time there were no benefits such as those provided for the families of soldiers, sailors, or merchant mariners and no steady income such as that sent by salesmen working away from home. For the families of westering men, periods of absence were often periods of deprivation. And of uncertainty, since these families not only awaited the return of the absent father but also lived in anticipation (or dread) of a letter telling them to load up their belongings and prepare themselves for the move west.

20. PF to JF, July 1 and June 30, 1862, FPUM.

21. PF to JF, July 1, 1862, FPUM.

22. PF to JF, July 1, 1862, FPUM.

23. JF to PF, August 11, 1862, FPUM.

24. JF to PF, August 11, 1862, FPUM.

25. JF to PF, August 11, 1862, FPUM. Fergus's letter of July 15, 1863, identifies Cardinell as the half-breed. (JF to PF, July 15, 1863, FPUM.)

26. JF to PF, August 11, 1862. Deer Camp was the early name for present-day Deer Lodge, Montana. Between 1848 and 1864, various parts of the state of Montana belonged, at different times, to Oregon, Nebraska, Washington, Dakota, Idaho, and Montana territories. (Dave Walter, "Prior Governmental Jurisdictions over Montana Land," in "Visual History of Montana," manuscript, [Helena: Office of Public Instruction, 1976], 190–91.)

27. Russell Register, 7. There is no extant letter from Pamelia or James relaying the news or in any way mentioning the death.

28. JF to PF, September 6, 1862, FPUM.

29. PF to JF, July 28, 1862, FPUM.

30. PF to JF, July 28, 1862, FPUM.

31. PF to JF, July 28, 1862, FPUM.

32. JF to William Butler, March 20, 1875, FPUM; Fergus, "Early Mining Life," 265. At least one Union general saw draft dodging as a prime motivating factor for men going west during the Civil War years: "Why will the government continue to act so foolishly, sending out emigrant trains at great expense? Do they know that most of the men that go are persons running away from the draft?" (General Alfred Sully, as quoted in Hiram M. Chittenden's *History of Early Steamboat Navigation on the Missouri River*, vol. 2 [New York: Francis P. Harper, 1903], 270).

33. *St. Paul Press*, March 19, 1863, in White, *Ho!*, 35. While popular literature has painted a romantic picture of westering males as gallant heroes who established a new order in the wilderness, James's description of the men who populated the Fisk expedition of 1862 is probably closer to the truth. The West seemed to offer a chance for a new start to those with a checkered past, and there is some validity to the assessment by one woman of Montana pioneer stock: "Everybody who came out here back then was probably running from something" (response from audience member to presentation by Linda Peavy, Denton, Montana, February 1985).

34. Fisk, *Expedition*, 26; JF to PF, September 6, 1862, FPUM.

35. JF to PF, September 6, 1862, FPUM.

36. JF to PF, September 25, 1862, FPUM. James returned to the Prickly Pear region early in 1863 and again in 1865. (PF to JF, May 3, 1863, and April 1865, FPUM.)

37. JF to PF, September 25, 1862, FPUM.

38. The annuity payments made in the form of provisions and money were partial payment for lands in southwestern Minnesota the Indians had ceded to the government in a treaty signed eleven years earlier. (Kenneth Carley, *The Sioux Uprising of 1862* [St. Paul: Minnesota Historical Society, 1976], 2–6; this work offers a detailed and reliable account of the conflict.)

39. Carley, *Sioux Uprising*, 1.

40. Governor Ramsey's telegram of September 6, noting, "This is not our war; it is a national war," finally moved Lincoln to action. (Carley, *Sioux Uprising*, 27–31, 59–60.)

41. "Hole-in-the-Day," *Harper's New Monthly Magazine*, 26 (January 1863): 186–91; Folwell, *History of Minnesota*, 2:374–82.

42. Richardson, "History," 5.

43. Rosanna Sturgis to William Sturgis, October 8, 1862. This letter has most likely been edited for spelling and punctuation, and it was erroneously dated 1869 by family members. (The letter is taken from a typed transcript in the William Sturgis Collection, MtHS; a copy is in the Sioux Uprising Collection, MnHS.)

44. WPA Memories of Marie Farnham, No. 1105, MCHS.

45. Russell Register, 12.

46. James Fergus, "Biographical Notes on Pamelia Fergus," mimeographed, FPMtHS.

47. In an undated note to her father, Luella Fergus noted, "Mother has written

you in her other letters about the Indian war." That same note listed among the casualties John Whitford, "the old scotch man at Fergus Falls." Whitford, who had surveyed Fergus Falls for James in the late 1850s, was supposedly "killed by the Souix Indians" (Luella Fergus to JF, undated fragment, circa October 1862, FPUM).

48. Captain Fisk's report noted that the emigrant train was unaware of the fighting "until met in the mountains by an express from Walla-Walla, giving news how narrowly we had escaped the terrible raid of the Sioux" (Fisk, *Expedition,* 2).

49. JF to PF, November 2, 1861, FPUM. Rampant but unfounded rumors purported that the Ojibway were uniting with their age-old enemies, the Dakota, to take back their lands from the whites.

50. JF to PF, November 2, 1862, FPUM. James did not even mention the Indian crisis until he had written five pages of general news. Perhaps he was putting off writing about something he found disturbing or perhaps he wondered whether he should admit having heard the news, since he did not plan to start home at once.

51. JF to PF, November 2, 1862, FPUM.

52. JF to PF, December 13, 1862, FPUM.

53. JF to PF, February 5, 1863, FPUM. In addition to receiving detailed letters from home, James had likely read a January 1863 *Harper's* article on Hole-in-the-Day's offensive, for he had instructed Pamelia to have his favorite journals and newspapers routed to him at Deer Lodge or at the Beaverhead diggings. (JF to PF, May 24, 1863, FPUM.)

54. William Butler to JF, January 11, 1863, FPUM.

55. PF to JF, August 30, 1863, FPUM. According to Pamelia, when Reverend Dada left that morning, he "lookd meaner than our little dog . . . that we used to call rover [did] when he was whiped." Richardson notes that Dada "made haste to get himself at a safe distance from Hole-in-the-day's horde of scalpers . . . thus leaving his flock to look out for themselves as best they could" (Richardson, "History," 33).

56. Robert Hamilton to JF, January 26, 1863, FPUM.

57. JF to PF, June 15, 1863, FPUM.

58. Rosanna Sturgis to William Sturgis, October 8, 1862, William Sturgis Collection, MtHS.

59. Rosanna Sturgis to William Sturgis, October 8, 1862, William Sturgis Collection, MtHS. According to Pamelia, "Mr Amos Sturgis has been here and stayed two weeks . . . I suppose he came to see about the Indian trouble . . . if their [had been further trouble] . . . all of Sturgis family [was] to come down their to Michigan" (PF to JF, October 9, 1862, FPUM).

60. PF to JF, October 9, 1862, FPUM.

61. Luella Fergus to JF, October 1862, FPUM. Luella is likely mistaken as to the given name of her teacher, for a Morrison County school register, Little Falls District, April 27, 1861, is signed "P. H. Taylor," not Edward. On June 19, 1861, Pamelia had written to tell James that Taylor, whom she called "a very intresting young man," was engaged to be married to "a young girl that lived to Mr Ayrs" (PF to JF, June 19, 1861, FPUM).

62. Luella Fergus to JF, October 9, 1862, FPUM.

63. Luella Fergus to JF, October 9, 1862, FPUM.

64. PF to JF and Luella Fergus to JF, October 9, 1862, FPUM.

65. Luella Fergus to JF, October 9, 1862, FPUM.

66. PF to JF, October 1862, FPUM.

67. PF to JF, October 1862, FPUM. In June 1863, Pamelia had still not received any turnips from Mr. Paul, who had, by that time, gone to Fort Ripley. (PF to JF, June 14, 1863, FPUM.)

68. PF to JF, October 9, 1862, FPUM.

69. PF to JF, October 9, 1862, FPUM.

70. JF to PF, September 6, 1862, FPUM.

71. PF to JF, October 9, 1862, FPUM.

72. JF to PF, January 27, 1863, FPUM.

73. JF to PF, October 16, 1862, FPUM.

74. JF to PF, November 2, 1862, FPUM.

75. Bannack was named for the Bannock Indians, though the name was misspelled.

76. JF to PF, November 2, 1862, FPUM.

77. JF to PF, December 13, 1862, and January 4, 1863, FPUM; Sweet, *William Sturgis*, 20.

78. JF to PF, January 27, 1863, FPUM. According to the memoirs of one Montana pioneer, Ault's tavern was the first building in Bannack to have "a real floor." He had "a puncheon floor," suitable for dancing. (Sarah Wadams Howard, "Reminiscences of a Pioneer," as told to Mrs. F. C. McFadden, printed in *Souvenir Booklet Commemorating Bannack Pageant, August 15, 1854*, Renne Library, Montana State University, Bozeman.)

79. JF to PF, January 4, 1863, FPUM.

80. JF to PF, December 13, 1862, FPUM.

81. JF to PF, November 2, 1862, FPUM.

82. PF to JF, December 18, 1862, FPUM.

83. PF to JF, December 18, 1862, FPUM. Anson Northup, who served as senator in the first state legislature, had led a lynching party five years earlier that seized and killed three Indians accused of robbing a German peddler. Contemporary historian Nathan Richardson's account reflects a prevalent attitude toward justice for Indians: "A tree that held up one end of the pole on which they were hung was hauled to the writer and sold with other small trees for wood, and was recognized and laid aside to be kept in remembrance of the good it had done the human race" (Richardson, "History," 5–6). Nearly 2,000 Indians were taken captive in the wake of the 1862 war. Of that number 392 were brought to trial under a five-man military commission, which convened on September 28, 1862, and handed down its last decision on November 5, 1862. In what historian Kenneth Carley described as "a travesty of justice," 307 men were sentenced to death and 16 given prison terms. Ultimately Abraham Lincoln approved death sentences for only 39 of those convicted. On December 26, 1862, 38 Dakota Indians were hanged in "America's greatest mass execution." (Carley, *Sioux Uprising*, 67–75; quotations on 69, 75.)

84. PF to JF, November 28, 1862, FPUM.

85. Mary Agnes Fergus to JF, November 28, 1862, FPUM.

86. PF to JF, November 28, 1862, FPUM.

87. PF to JF, December 18, 1862, FPUM. Rounding up the milk cow was apparently Andrew's job, and in later life he recounted an incident during the conflict of 1862 when he was sent to retrieve the cow from a clump of trees in which he was

sure Indians were lurking. His arrival flushed pheasants, whose flight so frightened him that his hair stood on end. (Andrew James Fergus [Andrew's son] to Peavy and Smith, August 22, 1988.)

88. PF to JF, November 28, 1862, FPUM.

89. C. A. Freeman to PF, February 8, 1863, FPUM.

90. Abby Freeman to PF, February 8, 1863, FPUM.

91. William Garcelons to JF, April 26, 1862, FPUM.

92. Russell Register, 7, 14.

93. PF to JF, September 9, 1863, FPUM.

94. PF to JF, December 18, 1862, FPUM.

95. Margaretha Ault obituary, *Little Falls Weekly Transcript,* March 13, 1896; PF to JF, January 25, 1863, FPUM.

96. PF to JF, January 25, 1863, FPUM.

97. PF to JF, November 7, 1863, FPUM.

98. Rosanna Sturgis to William Sturgis, October 8, 1862, William Sturgis Collection, MtHS.

99. Rosanna Sturgis to William Sturgis, October 8, 1862, William Sturgis Collection, MtHS.

100. PF to JF, December 18, 1862, FPUM.

101. PF to JF, January 25, 1863, FPUM.

102. JF to PF, December 13, 1862, FPUM.

103. PF to JF, April 5, 1863, FPUM; Emma Fletcher to PF, February 21, 1863, FPUM. After her husband's untimely death in 1860, Emma Fletcher had faced heavy odds, and by 1863 her luck and her money had run out.

104. PF to JF, January 25, 1863, FPUM.

105. JF to PF, September 6 and June 1, 1862, FPUM. All during James's Pikes Peak sojourn, Hall had "talk[ed] strong" of going west, but his wife's pregnancies prevented his going until 1862. (PF to JF, February 1, 1861, FPUM.)

106. JF to PF, December 13, 1862, FPUM.

107. JF to PF, June 4, 1863, FPUM.

108. PF to JF, March 11, 1863, FPUM.

109. PF to JF, December 18, 1862, FPUM.

110. JF to PF, February 5, 1863, FPUM.

111. PF to JF, April 5, 1863, FPUM.

112. PF to JF, December 18, 1862, FPUM. The girls, too, wrote news of their general health and well-being. In contrast to twentieth-century teen-agers, young women of the 1860s were proud of their "fleshiness," and Luella boasted, "I weight one hundred and thirty pounds Agnes weighs one hundred and twenty six" (Luella Fergus to JF, January 25, 1863, FPUM).

113. PF to JF, March 11, 1863, FPUM.

114. JF to PF, March 24, 1863, FPUM.

115. JF to PF, June 1, 1863, FPUM.

116. JF to PF, December 13, 1862, FPUM.

117. Fergus, "Early Mining Life," 266.

118. JF to PF, January 27, 1863, FPUM.

119. JF to PF, January 27, 1863, FPUM. In the 1880s, Fergus's friend and neighbor Granville Stuart campaigned against Indian hunting rights in Fergus County. While

Fergus did not oppose Stuart in that incident, he did take the Indians' part in a similar controversy over hunting and fishing rights near Helena. In a letter to Indian agent Peter Ronan, he noted: "I am sorry . . . you called the Indians back to their reservation. They had a right to hunt and fish and ought to have been protected against all comers" (JF to Peter Ronan, November 7, 1885, FPUM). Fergus also wrote his old friend Ignatius Donnelly of Minnesota that "If the treaties made with the Indians were honorably and faithfully carried out, we would hear of fewer massacres, and our government would be at less expense on Indian accounts" (JF to Ignatius Donnelly, August 31, 1864, Donnelly Papers, MnHS). Ironically, if the treaty of 1855 had been honored by the government, James Fergus would not have been able to ranch in central Montana in the 1880s.

120. JF to PF, December 13, 1862, FPUM.

121. JF to PF, December 13, 1862, FPUM.

122. JF to PF, December 13, 1862, FPUM.

123. PF to JF, January 25, 1863, FPUM.

124. JF to PF, March 24, 1863, FPUM. William H. Fletcher called David Bentley "one of the down and outers at Little Falls," but noted that he was "prosperous in Montana" and owned a large mercantile store in Helena in 1866. (Fletcher, "Reminiscence," 9.)

125. JF to PF, March 7, 1864, FPUM.

126. In a November 1862 letter, James had described Ard Godfrey as "the first millwright who came to St. Anthony to build the big mills there and owns mills now at the mouth of Minnehaha Creek where his family are" (JF to PF, March 24, 1863, and November 2, 1862, FPUM). Godfrey was one of many Minnesotans in the Bannack and Virginia City area. On January 4, 1863, Fergus claimed that "nearly half of the population here [Bannack] are Minnesotians" (JF to PF, January 4, 1863, FPUM).

127. Ann Sturgis to William Sturgis, January 3, 1863, William Sturgis Collection, MtHS.

128. Mary Agnes Fergus to JF, undated, 1863, FPUM.

129. PF to JF, May 3, 1863, FPUM.

130. PF to JF, March 11, 1863, FPUM.

131. PF to JF, May 3, 1863, FPUM.

132. PF to JF, April 5, 1863, FPUM.

133. PF to JF, March 30, 1861; William Butler to JF, June 12, 1860; Robert Hamilton to JF, June 8, 1863; PF to JF, April 5, 1863 — all in FPUM. In turn, the Churchills moved in above Morse's store, which Orlando had purchased "for the sum of two hundred and fifty [dollars]" (PF to JF, April 5, 1863, FPUM).

134. Francis Gravel to JF, May 6, 1863; PF to JF, April 5, 1863 — both in FPUM.

135. PF to JF, April 5, 1863, FPUM.

136. JF to PF, May 3, 1863, FPUM.

137. JF to PF, May 24, 1863, FPUM.

138. JF to PF, May 24, 1863, FPUM.

139. PF to JF, April 5, 1863, FPUM.

140. Luella Fergus to JF, April 5, 1863, FPUM.

141. In early May, Pamelia described her sister's death in greater detail: "She bid them all farewell without a strugle and when her little baby four months was

brought she seemed dispossessed and hug[g]ed and kissed over it seemed she could not give it [up] told Jane to take good care of Mothers bird and said *Mother must leave it.*" Overcome by the recounting of the scene, she broke off with "I cannot write any more now" (PF to JF, May 3, 1863, FPUM).

142. PF to JF, May 3, 1863, FPUM.

143. PF to JF, June 7, 1863, FPUM.

144. JF to PF, May 27, 1863, FPUM.

145. PF to JF, June 14, 1863, FPUM.

146. PF to JF, July 14, 1863, FPUM.

147. JF to PF, July 15, 1863, FPUM.

148. Luella Fergus to JF, April 5, 1863, FPUM.

149. PF to JF, June 14, 1863, FPUM.

150. PF to JF, August 19, 1863, FPUM.

151. Luella Fergus to JF, August 19, 1863, FPUM.

152. PF to JF, September 9, 1863, FPUM.

153. PF to JF, September 22, 1863. Though reconciled to remaining in Little Falls rather than going to Illinois, Pamelia was not yet reconciled to the loss of her sister: "Saturday evening we wer surprised by a satchel come in the express it contained some of sister Mary's clothses they wer very nice and a likeness of her in health I do not see . . . [that it] looks like her but the girls say that it is like her exactly and I am glad that they saw her when she was in health and so gay for it does me good to think how lively she use to [be] and [I] always thought I should see her [again] but she is no more and has got rid of a great deal of trouble but O how we hate to spare her" (PF to JF, October 5, 1863, FPUM).

154. Mary Agnes Fergus to JF, undated, 1863, FPUM. Luella gave a fuller description of the courses the girls were taking: "We all go to school to Miss Camp Agnes studies Robinsons Practical Arithmetic, Warrens Geography, Greens Grammar I study the same except the addition of Robinsons Mental Arithmetic which Agnes does not study. Andrew studies Arithmetic, Geography, Reading Spelling Writing" (Luella Fergus to JF, September 22, 1863, FPUM).

155. PF to JF, August 30, 1863, FPUM.

156. PF to JF, August 30, 1863, FPUM.

157. PF to JF, August 1, 1863, FPUM. Andrew may have been fishing while his sisters were at Sabbath school, since he was basically inclined to share his father's opinion of religion. Perhaps his attitude was evident to those who instructed him, for some months earlier he had come home from church complaining, "Mama I have been so many Sundays [yet] Mr Elwell does not choose to give your *heathen a bible* nor he wont sell him one so I think I will go fishing" (PF to JF, June 7, 1863, FPUM). Sometime before the Fergus family left Little Falls, Pamelia herself gave Andrew a leather-bound Bible, which he took with him on the overland trail and treasured all his life. (Andrew James Fergus to Peavy and Smith, August 22, 1988; Agnes Fergus Miedema to Peavy and Smith, July 27 and August 4, 1988.)

158. PF to JF, July 14, 1863, FPUM.

159. PF to JF, August 19, 1863, FPUM.

160. Luella Fergus to JF, August 19, 1863, FPUM.

161. PF to JF, August 19, 1863, FPUM. Apparently, Ed Grady disapproved of the

young woman's plans, for Pamelia noted, "Ed say[s] she shall not Janett says she will if she can get it."

162. JF to PF, undated, circa 1863, FPUM.

163. Luella Fergus to JF, October 5, 1863, FPUM.

164. JF to PF, undated, circa 1863, FPUM.

165. Mary Agnes Fergus to JF, undated, circa 1863, FPUM. When children were needed at home, school was simply ignored for the day. Aware of this fact, Miss Camp had adjusted her sessions so that the children had a free day on Mondays, rather than Saturdays.

166. PF to JF, July 14, 1863, FPUM. As noted earlier, Pamelia's considerable knowledge of tourniquets and sutures came, most probably, from her association with Mary J. Colburn, who practiced the healing arts in Moline during the years the Fergus family lived there. According to family members, Pamelia was known for her medical skills in Little Falls, where she once assisted a doctor during a surgical procedure. (Mary Colburn to PF, April 22, 1859, FPUM; Gilpatrick, "Biographical Sketch," 190.)

167. Luella Fergus to JF, July 14, 1863, FPUM. Mrs. Dow is likely Mary E. Dow, wife of William Dow, a millwright who lived down by the slough. (MC60.) Upon hearing of Luella's accident, James noted that he had lost an old ax in the slough a few years back and that might well have been what Luella cut her foot on. (JF to PF, August 14, 1863, FPUM.)

168. PF to JF, June 14, 1863, FPUM.

169. PF to JF, June 27, 1863, FPUM.

170. JF to PF, May 10, 1863, FPUM.

171. JF to PF, June 4, 1863, FPUM.

172. JF to PF, May 27, 1863, FPUM.

173. JF to PF, June 4, 1863, FPUM.

174. Dick Pace, *Golden Gulch: The Story of Montana's Fabulous Alder Gulch* (Virginia City, Montana: Virginia City Trading Company, 1962), 7–15.

175. JF to PF, June 15, 1863, FPUM. Henry Edgar, one of the discoverers of gold in Alder Gulch, was elected recorder.

176. JF to PF, June 15, 1863, FPUM.

177. Pace, *Golden Gulch*, 15–17. On July 5, 1863, James wrote Pamelia: "My last letter was dated at Verona [*sic*], but the[y] have changed the name of the place to Virginia City, because it was named after Jefferson Davis' wife" (JF to PF, July 5, 1863, FPUM).

178. JF to PF, June 15, 1863, FPUM.

179. JF to PF, July 15, 1863, FPUM.

180. JF to PF, July 19, 1863, FPUM.

181. JF to PF, August 14, 1863, FPUM. According to a letter written to a friend years after the fact, Fergus eventually realized eight thousand dollars in dust. (JF to E. A. Wood, December 25, 1886, FPUM.) Apparently he made enough money during his first season of mining in Montana to interest the United States government in his tax position. Under tax laws enacted by Congress as an emergency measure during the Civil War, the government tried to collect 3 percent of his profits from his Bannack and Virginia City claims. Fergus fought the assessment, noting "As we were in this country in '63 [men] very often carried their whole kits on their backs

and seldom put themselves to the trouble of carrying books." He cited that as reason enough for his failure to keep up with his earnings for tax purposes. "But I acknowledge an income from a placer claim in 1863 over and above all the expenses of the sum of 3018 on which I am willing after deducting the $600 allowed by law to pay a . . . tax of 3 pct collectable by the law . . . under protest." His protest was then duly stated: (1) During his time at Bannack, the government had sent no soldiers or other officers to protect him and his fellow miners from the Indians; (2) there had been no tax assessors in Bannack in 1863 to collect the taxes, hence he would not pay the 5 percent penalty the government wished to assess; and (3) the money made by the southern miners who had since gone to their respective states had not been taxed. (JF to Charles Farmer, July 15, 1865, FPUM; PF to JF, October 5, 1863, FPUM.)

182. JF to PF, July 5, 1863, FPUM. Sent in early May, the gold dust carried by Charles Miles of St. Anthony did not arrive until October. And when Pamelia and Robert Hamilton went down to St. Anthony to collect it, they were shocked to find that she lost thirty dollars in converting one hundred dollars' worth of gold dust into currency.

183. PF to JF, August 30, 1863, FPUM.

184. PF to JF, August 1 and October 5, 1863, FPUM.

185. JF to PF, December 28, 1863, FPUM.

186. JF to PF, May 10, 1863, FPUM.

187. Eastern Montana was a part of Dakota Territory and the western portion of Montana a part of Washington Territory when James arrived in the area in 1862. The goldfields became a part of Idaho Territory when that entity was created in March 1863. From 1854 to 1861, eastern Montana was part of Nebraska Territory. (Walter, "Prior Governmental Jurisdictions," 190–91.) In the letters James had sent Pamelia since his arrival in the area, he had instructed her to write him at Washington Territory, Dakota Territory, and Idaho Territory. (JF to PF, August 11 and October 16, 1862, FPUM.)

188. JF to PF, August 14, 1863, FPUM.

189. PF to JF, June 14, 1863, FPUM.

190. PF to JF, January 25, 1863, FPUM.

191. JF to PF, May 27, 1863, FPUM.

192. JF to PF, undated, circa 1863, FPUM.

193. JF to PF, November 22, 1863, FPUM.

194. JF to PF, July 19, 1863, FPUM.

195. JF to PF, July 5, 1863, FPUM.

196. JF to PF, July 5, 1863, FPUM. In 1863 there were ten thousand people in the fourteen-square-mile Alder Gulch area. (Michael P. Malone and Richard B. Roeder, *Montana: A History of Two Centuries* [Seattle: University of Washington Press, 1976], 51.)

197. JF to PF, July 15, 1863, FPUM.

198. JF to PF, July 5, 1863, FPUM.

199. JF to PF, July 19, 1863, FPUM.

200. JF to PF, July 15, 1863, FPUM.

201. JF to PF, July 19, 1863, FPUM.

202. JF to PF, July 19, 1863, FPUM.

203. JF to PF, July 15, 1863, FPUM.
204. Luella Fergus to JF, August 19, 1863, FPUM.
205. PF to JF, March 11, 1863, FPUM.
206. PF to JF, August 30, 1863, FPUM.
207. PF to JF, June 27, 1863, FPUM. Because of the Indian unrest, the second Fisk expedition was very different in character from the first. The entire train comprised sixty men, and thirty-six of those were employed by Fisk. Following a more northerly route, the 1863 expedition did, in fact, reach Fort Benton with no hostile Indian encounters. (White, *Ho!*, 78, 80.)
208. PF to JF, September 22, 1863, FPUM.
209. PF to JF, August 30 and August 19, 1863, FPUM. A sign of the times, tax sales had become a very common means of transfer of property. Even the indigent could manage an occasional purchase; Agnes Russell was high bidder—at $1.26—on a tract of land in 1865. (Record Book D, 317, BenCC.)
210. PF to JF, August 19, 1863, FPUM.
211. PF to JF, September 22, 1863, FPUM.
212. PF to JF, August 30, 1863, FPUM.
213. PF to JF, August 30, 1863, FPUM.
214. Robert Hamilton to JF, June 8, 1863, FPUM.
215. Robert Hamilton to JF, June 8, 1863, FPUM.
216. PF to JF, June 7 and September 9, 1863, FPUM.
217. Robert Hamilton to JF, January 26, 1863, FPUM.
218. Robert Hamilton to JF, September 9, 1863, FPUM.
219. PF to JF, September 9, 1863, FPUM.
220. PF to JF, July 14, 1863, FPUM; Philo Farnham to JF, December 20, 1863—both in FPUM. The Union Army, according to Pamelia, had been nearly destroyed by a new Confederate general: "This new general they have [in the] South is doing the work May be you inquire who [he is] Why it is general *Starvation* that is what they say them selves" (PF to JF, July 14, 1863, FPUM).
221. PF to JF, August 1, 1863, FPUM. In 1863 the United States passed its first nationwide federal conscription. The law was grossly unfair to the poor, since it allowed a man to purchase exemption for three hundred dollars or to hire a substitute. In New York City, a draft protest in 1863 led by Irish Americans turned into a riot that lasted several days and claimed over five hundred lives. (Thomas A. Bailey, *The American Pageant: A History of the Republic* [Boston: D. C. Heath and Company, 1961], 444.)
222. Robert Hamilton to JF, August 16, 1863, FPUM. Because of the turmoil and anxiety caused by the Indian conflict, the draft in Minnesota was postponed until November 10, 1862. According to Robert Hamilton and Pamelia Fergus, no draft touched Little Falls until August 1, 1863. However, an order of August 14, 1862, said that no man was to leave the state without a pass from the attorney general or to leave the county without a pass from the sheriff. (PF to JF, August 1, 1863, FPUM; Folwell, *History of Minnesota*, 2:103–5.)
223. PF to JF, September 9, 1863, FPUM.
224. PF to JF, October 8, 1863, FPUM.
225. Recalling John Currie's reasons for joining the army, she wondered whether her former handyman had "seen enough of country and places . . . [He] wanted

to see Washington and if Uncle Sam did not pay his expences he feared he never should I think they have all seen the elipant poor boys" (PF to JF, September 9, 1863, FPUM).

226. PF to JF, August 1, 1863, FPUM. James Dillin, who had married in late spring of 1863, served for the duration of the war on cavalry posts in the West and then moved to Detroit. (PF to JF, June 7, 1863, FPUM.) Far from the war, James Fergus and the other miners felt its effects less directly. "We had no [Fourth of July] celebration here We have too many seccessionists and southerners, but we all live together peaceably and have nothing to say about politics or the war" (JF to PF, July 15, 1863, FPUM).

227. Luella Fergus to JF, April 5, 1863; PF to JF, July 14, 1863 — both in FPUM; Folwell, *History of Minnesota,* 2:289.

228. PF to JF, September 9, 1863, FPUM.

229. PF to JF, September 22, 1863, FPUM.

230. PF to JF, November 7, 1863, FPUM.

231. Sweet, *William Sturgis,* 21; JF to PF, July 15, 1863, FPUM.

232. PF to JF, August 19, 1863, FPUM.

233. PF to JF, September 9, 1863, FPUM.

234. PF to JF, October 5, 1863, FPUM.

235. The town was called Gallatin City, later Three Forks. Book 70, Deeds, Etc., 1862–1865, Gallatin County Courthouse.

236. PF to JF, October 8, 1863, FPUM. James's reply of December 10, 1863, showed a competitive streak: "If Mrs Ault has more things there than you I have more money here than Ault to balance it" (JF to PF, December 10, 1863, FPUM).

237. PF to JF, November 7, 1863, FPUM.

238. PF to JF, August 30, 1863, FPUM.

239. JF to PF, December 13, 1862; PF to JF, November 7, 1863 — both in FPUM.

240. PF to JF, June 7 and November 7, 1863, FPUM. The severity of the drought is evident in letters from Pamelia and Luella. In August, Pamelia wrote of how bored she was without a garden to tend: "The times are very dull here and lonesome If we had any gardens or crops we could spend some time in looking at them and we [would have] something to eat. . . . People will not get their seed back this year Here in this part of the country [there] has not been rain enough to wet the potatoes since they wer[e] planted" (PF to JF, August 1, 1863, FPUM). Luella later noted, "We have not dug our few potatoes yet our turnips are no bigness still The largest is not as big as my fist" (Luella Fergus to JF, October 5, 1863, FPUM).

241. PF to JF, September 22, 1863, FPUM.

242. JF to PF, August 14, 1863, FPUM.

243. JF to PF, September 27, 1863, FPUM. James had earlier described Bosworth as "a first rate fellow honorable and honest to a fault . . . a friend when friends are needed" (JF to PF, March 7, 1861, FPUM).

244. Philo Farnham to JF, December 20, 1863, FPUM; MC70, Todd County. Philo Farnham and his wife Sarah were apparently considering the long trip themselves, for he asked Fergus, "Is such old hulks as we are worth the trouble by fetching so far for the sake of living with our children and . . . giving them a chance to make something to help themselves when we are gone" (Philo Farnham to JF, December 20, 1863, FPUM).

245. JF to PF, August 14, 1863, FPUM.
246. JF to PF, March 24, 1863, FPUM.
247. JF to PF, August 14, 1863, FPUM.
248. JF to PF, undated, circa 1863, FPUM.
249. JF to PF, August 27, 1863, FPUM.
250. JF to PF, August 14, 1863, FPUM.
251. JF to PF, undated, circa 1863, FPUM.
252. JF to PF, October 18, 1863, FPUM.
253. JF to PF, September 27, 1863, FPUM.
254. PF to JF, October 8, 1863, FPUM. She seemed to dismiss the money as lost, but Pamelia did not give up on it entirely. She wrote the postmaster to find out whether a D. D. Hackett actually resided in Troy, Minnesota. Though he did have a home there, his family reported that they had not seen him since he went west and had not heard that he had started for home. (PF to JF, November 11, 1863, FPUM.)
255. PF to JF, November 15, 1863, FPUM. Tearing down houses and rafting the lumber to St. Cloud was a practice that continued for several years—until, by 1874, Little Falls had fewer than half its original houses. (A. L. Randall to JF, April 24, 1864, FPUM.)
256. JF to PF, September 27, 1863, FPUM.
257. JF to PF, September 27, 1863, FPUM.
258. JF to PF, September 27, 1863, FPUM.
259. In an earlier letter, James had promised: "I intend to buy you a good sewing machine to bring out with you" (PF to JF, undated, circa spring 1863, FPUM).
260. PF to JF, December 11, 1863, FPUM.
261. Philo Farnham to JF, December 20, 1863, FPUM. Among those who read the notice of James Fergus's success at Virginia City was Helen M. [Nichols] Smith, the young woman who had come to Little Falls as a teacher and stayed to marry carpenter G. T. K. Smith. On December 18, 1863, Helen Smith asked James Fergus several astute questions concerning the chances her husband might have in the gold-fields and difficulties he might face in making the trip across the plains. She noted, "I am urging my Husband to go to the mines himself [even] if he does not take us He seems loth to go [and] thinks if business starts [up here] he could make as much here." She mentioned that the baby, who was six months old, was crying and she must close her note. (Helen M. Smith to JF, December 18, 1863, FPUM.) Unfortunately, carpenter Smith did not take his wife's advice but remained in Little Falls "drink[ing] woefully." By April 1864, a scant four months after she wrote to James, Helen Smith was dead and William Butler reported that her husband had "misused his wife very much while she was Sick" (William Butler to JF, June 7, 1864, FPUM).
262. PF to JF, December 11, 1863, FPUM. In actuality, Pamelia's cellar was not well-enough insulated to withstand what she later described as one of the coldest winters she could remember: "Our well froze up on Christmas night [and] we have not been able to get any watter out of it since. . . . Some of our apples [and] Some potatoes in the celler [froze]" (PF to JF, January 10, 1864, FPUM).
263. PF to JF, December 7, 1863, FPUM.
264. PF to JF, November 7, 1863, FPUM.
265. PF to JF, December 7, 1863, FPUM.

266. Mary Agnes Fergus to JF, November 15, 1863, FPUM. The friend was Sarah Elwell and, according to Mary Agnes, "Her intended is mr Stately Mary Stately the squaws husband Mary is dead so he would like to get married again."

267. PF to JF, December 11, 1863, FPUM.

268. PF to JF, December 27 and December 7, 1863, FPUM.

269. Luella Fergus to JF, December 27, 1863, FPUM.

270. PF to JF, December 27, 1863, FPUM.

CHAPTER 6. The Crossing

1. JF to PF, November 15 and August 14, 1863, FPUM.

2. JF to PF, November 15, 1863, FPUM.

3. PF to JF, November 15, 1863, FPUM.

4. Mary Agnes Fergus to JF, November 15, 1863; Luella Fergus to JF, February 1864—both in FPUM.

5. JF to PF, March 7, 1864; Luella Fergus to JF, February 1864—both in FPUM.

6. PF to JF, December 27, 1863, FPUM. By December 1863 the Farnhams and the Bosworths had moved back into Little Falls and were living in Hall's former home. (PF to JF, December 27, 1863, FPUM.)

7. Philo Farnham to JF, December 20, 1863; Francis Gravel to JF, November 28, 1863—both in FPUM. While Gravel had his doubts about taking his wife and children west, Pamelia noted that "Mrs Gravel is anxious to come if he does" (PF to JF, November 15, 1863, FPUM). If the whole family went west, Gravel faced the problem of what to do with his house, a substantial structure that cost him one thousand dollars and would not bring nearly that amount on the depressed market. He decided to lease the house, knowing that "a good many houses have gone to St Cloud," rafted downriver to be sold as lumber. (PF to JF, December 18, 1863, FPUM.) Leasing also gave him the option of returning to Little Falls, should his business not do well in the West.

8. Pamelia was certainly not the only woman whose destiny was out of her own hands. As Lillian Schlissel notes in her introduction to *Women's Diaries of the Westward Movement*, between 1840 and 1870 a quarter-million Americans emigrated from their homes in the East and Midwest to the unsettled lands beyond the Mississippi. "Women were part of the journey because their fathers, husbands, and brothers had determined to go. They went West because there was no way for them *not* to go once the decision was made" (Schlissel, *Women's Diaries*, 10).

9. JF to PF, November 15, 1863, FPUM.

10. JF to PF, November 15, 1863, FPUM.

11. PF to JF, January 10, 1864, FPUM.

12. Robert Hamilton to JF, January 5, 1864, FPUM.

13. Mary Agnes Fergus to JF, January 5, 1864, FPUM.

14. PF to JF, January 10, 1864, FPUM.

15. PF to JF, January 10, 1864, FPUM.

16. PF to JF, January 10, 1864, FPUM.

17. JF to PF, November 21, 1863, FPUM.

18. JF to PF, November 21, 1863, FPUM. In a letter to Dr. E. A. Wood of Sabula,

Iowa, Fergus noted that he spent three thousand dollars getting his family to Montana — with a year's worth of supplies. (JF to E. A. Wood, December 25, 1886, FPUM.)

19. JF to PF, November 21, 1863, FPUM.

20. JF to PF, November 21, 1863, FPUM.

21. List in letter from JF to PF, November 21 and December 4, 1863, FPUM. James repeated his instructions a few weeks later, in case the first letter was lost.

22. JF to PF, November 22, 1863, FPUM.

23. JF to PF, November 22, 1863, FPUM.

24. JF to PF, November 22, 1863, FPUM. From this point onward, Pamelia and James refer to William Thomas Dillin by his middle name. Thirty-one years old in 1864, Thomas was still living in Henry County, Illinois, on his father's farm, and Mahala lived with him when she was not visiting her other children. (MC50.)

25. PF to JF, January 30, 1864, FPUM.

26. PF to JF, January 30, 1864, FPUM.

27. PF to JF, January 31, 1864, FPUM.

28. PF to JF, March 8, 1864, FPUM. A Fergus tax receipt from Morrison County, January 27, 1864, shows payment of $504 in back taxes on lots 1, 2, 3, and 4 of Block 14. (Financial Records, 1842–1885, FPUM.)

29. PF to JF, January 31, 1864, FPUM.

30. JF to PF, December 28, 1863, FPUM.

31. JF to PF, December 28, 1863, FPUM.

32. JF to PF, December 28, 1863, FPUM.

33. Luella Fergus to JF, February 1864, FPUM.

34. Luella Fergus to JF, January 10, 1864, FPUM.

35. Luella Fergus to JF, February 1864, FPUM.

36. Luella Fergus to JF, February 1864, FPUM.

37. Luella Fergus to JF, February 1864, FPUM.

38. James Dillin to JF, February 10, 1864, FPUM.

39. PF to JF, February 1864, FPUM. Though Pamelia had been bartering with Emma Fletcher concerning William Fletcher's old debt, she had to leave Little Falls without closing the deal. Ultimately, it was O. J. Rockwell who "settled with Mrs Fletcher got a cow [and] a yoke of small steers . . . and 20$ out of the mill" (PF to JF, March 26, 1864, FPUM).

40. PF to JF, March 8, 1864, FPUM.

41. William Butler to JF, June 7, 1864, FPUM.

42. Gilpatrick, "Autobiographical Sketch," as told to A. J. Noyes, November 20, 1923, p. 1, FPUM.

43. PF to JF, March 8, 1864, FPUM.

44. PF to JF, September 22, 1863, FPUM.

45. Apparently Pamelia had not carried through with her earlier plan to have the children vaccinated the summer before during the smallpox outbreak in Little Falls. (PF to JF, June 14, 1863 and March 8, 1864, FPUM.)

46. PF to JF, March 8, 1864, FPUM.

47. PF to JF, March 8, 1864, FPUM.

48. PF to JF, March 26, 1864, FPUM.

49. James Dillin to JF, February 10, 1864, FPUM.

50. Simon Stein to JF, April 8, 1864, FPUM.

51. Margaretha Ault to JF, April 20, 1864, FPUM.

52. PF to JF, March 26, 1864, FPUM. According to Pamelia, Gravel's wagon was to be "load[ed] with clothing principaly Robrt [Hamilton] with tin" (PF to JF, January 31, 1864, FPUM).

53. PF to JF, March 26, 1864, FPUM.

54. In *Good Wives* Laurel Ulrich demonstrates the extent to which women are burdened by duties in a primitive society in which families are more or less self-sufficient. Though the eastern seaboard states were becoming industrialized by the early 1800s, communities on the western frontier were fairly well removed from the influence of that society. Indeed, Glenda Riley has demonstrated that women on the Iowa frontier between 1830 and 1870 assumed domestic duties fully as burdensome as those of the colonial women Ulrich studied. (Ulrich, *Good Wives,* 13–34; Glenda Riley, " 'Not Gainfully Employed': Women on the Iowa Frontier, 1833–1870," *Pacific Historical Review* 49 [May 1980]: 237–64.)

55. Women were not alone, of course, in their interest in establishing schools and churches, Dee Brown's assertions notwithstanding. (Dee Brown, *The Gentle Tamers: Women of the Old Wild West* [New York: G. P. Putnam's Sons, 1958].) For a broadened picture of the roles women played in the settling of the West, see Joan M. Jensen and Darlis A. Miller's "The Gentle Tamers Revisited: New Approaches to the History of Women in the American West," *Pacific Historical Review* 49 (May 1980): 173–213.

The extent to which women did lead efforts to establish social, cultural, educational, and religious institutions in frontier communities has yet to be documented, though initial studies of the contributions made by members of women's organizations would suggest that women were indeed the "molders and shapers" of western society. Recent research has shown that women were integrally involved in establishing communities, yet generally received less credit than did men for their community service, thereby reinforcing the idea that men primarily operated outside the home, women within. (See Elizabeth Jameson, "Women as Workers, Women as Civilizers: True Womanhood in the American West," in *The Women's West,* ed. Armitage and Jameson, 145–64; Karen Blair, *The Clubwoman as Feminist: True Womanhood Redefined, 1868–1914* [New York: Holmes and Meir Publishers, 1980]; Ann Firor Scott, "Women's Voluntary Associations in the Forming of American Society," in *Making the Invisible Woman Visible* [Chicago: University of Illinois Press, 1984], 279–94; and Laurie Mercier et al., *Molders and Shapers, Montana Women as Community Builders: An Oral History Sampler and Guide* [Helena, Montana: Molders and Shapers Collective, 1987].)

56. The idea that moving west freed a man to live life on his own terms stems largely from Frederick Jackson Turner's emphasis on the ways in which the wilderness environment fostered the abandonment of eastern customs and conventions. Historians are only now beginning to examine whether women, too, found new freedoms in the West. (See Paula Petrik's *No Step Backward,* for instance.) Such an exploration is long overdue, for, as Joan Kelly has suggested, "Feminist historiography has . . . disabused us of the notion that the history of women is the same as the history of men, and that significant turning points in history have the same impact for one sex as for the other" (Kelly, *Women, History, and Theory,* 3). In view of

the added domestic duties that fell to women who moved away from "civilization" and into frontier settlements lacking the educational, religious, medical, and social amenities of their former homes, it seems highly unlikely that the westward movement was as liberating for women as it has been purported to be for men.

57. PF to JF, March 26, 1864, FPUM.

58. PF to JF, March 26, 1864, FPUM.

59. Simon Stein to JF, April 8, 1864, FPUM. Though Luella Fergus Gilpatrick's reminiscence indicates an April 6 departure from Grinnell, Stein's letter is dated April 8, and his contemporary date is likely the correct one. (Gilpatrick, "Autobiographical Sketch," 1.)

60. PF to JF, April 23, 1864, FPUM.

61. Diary Consolidation, Oscar Mueller Collection, MtHS.

62. PF to JF, April 23, 1864, FPUM.

63. PF to JF, April 23, 1864, FPUM.

64. PF to JF, April 23, 1864, FPUM.

65. Diary Consolidation, Oscar Mueller Collection, MtHS.

66. PF to JF, April 23, 1864, FPUM. The pony Andrew rode was one Emma Fletcher had given to Pamelia in partial payment of William Fletcher's old debt to James. (PF to JF, January 10, 1864, FPUM.)

67. PF to JF, April 23, 1864, FPUM.

68. PF to JF, April 23, 1864, FPUM.

69. Gilpatrick, "Autobiographical Sketch," 1.

70. JF to PF, March 7, 1864, FPUM. There were times when James could exchange a greeenback for less than ninety cents. Though at the time of this letter there was near parity in the exchange rate between gold and greenbacks, James knew that the rate had been more favorable to gold and trusted that it would be so again.

71. PF to JF, May 13, 1864, FPUM.

72. PF to JF, May 13, 1864, FPUM.

73. Bill from Megeath, Bro., and Co., Dealers in Staple and Fancy Dry-Goods, Omaha, 1864, Financial Records, 1842–1885, FPUM.

74. PF to JF, May 13, 1864, FPUM.

75. PF to JF, May 13, 1864, FPUM.

76. PF to JF, May 13, 1864, FPUM. On July 4, 1864, Pamelia's brother James echoed her sentiments concerning Rockwell: "I was well satisfied they would not get along well with Rockwell as he is too pasionate for any use" (James Dillin to JF, July 4, 1864, Oscar Mueller Collection, MtHS).

77. PF to JF, May 13, 1864, FPUM.

78. PF to JF, May 22, 1864, FPUM.

79. PF to JF, May 22, 1864, FPUM.

80. PF to JF, May 22, 1864, FPUM. According to Glenda Riley, "Migrants readily blamed American Indians for any misfortune or irregularity that occurred [on the trail]" (Riley, *Women and Indians,* 90).

81. Gilpatrick, "Autobiographical Sketch," 2.

82. PF to JF, June 17, 1864, FPUM.

83. PF to JF, June 17, 1864, FPUM.

84. JF to PF, December 28, 1863, FPUM. In giving his directions, James Fergus may have confused some names. It is more likely that the party, having struck the

Missouri, or at least the headwaters of that river, at Gallatin City—now Three Forks—would have followed the Madison rather than the Jefferson south.

85. PF to JF, June 17, 1864, FPUM.

86. PF to JF, June 17, 1864, FPUM.

87. PF to JF, June 17, 1864, FPUM.

88. PF to JF, June 17, 1864, FPUM.

89. PF to JF, June 17, 1864, FPUM.

90. PF to JF, June 17, 1864, FPUM; Diary Consolidation, Oscar Mueller Collection, MtHS; Dorothy Johnson, *The Bloody Bozeman* (New York: McGraw-Hill, 1971). According to Luella Fergus Gilpatrick, a party that left the fort just after Rockwell's train opted to take the Bozeman Trail. One man in that train was killed in an Indian attack. (Gilpatrick, "Autobiographical Sketch," 1.)

91. Diary Consolidation, Oscar Mueller Collection, MtHS.

92. The Stinking Water River is now known as the Shoshone River.

93. Diary Consolidation, Oscar Mueller Collection, MtHS.

94. Luella Fergus to JF, July 31, 1864, FPUM. Erysipelas is an inflammation of the skin caused by a bacterial infection.

95. Halfway through her overland journey, Pamelia's destination was altered by a May 26, 1864, act of Congress that created Montana Territory. The territory became the State of Montana on November 8, 1889.

CHAPTER 7. The Settling

1. Henry N. Blake estimated that by 1864 "at least 10,000 and probably 15,000 persons" lived in the Alder Gulch area. (Tom Stout, ed., *Montana: Its Story and Biography* [Chicago: American Historical Society, 1921], vol. 1, 220.)

2. Although Fergus praised the vigilantes for their actions during the winter of 1863–64, he disapproved of their continued activity after law and order had been established. In a letter to the "Gentlemen of the Vigilante Committee," he noted that the time for vigilante justice had passed and reminded the committee that "American Citizens claim the right to be tried by the laws of their country, in open court and by a jury of their country men and the power that deprives them of that right is a tyrant and a usurper be it one or many" (JF to Gentlemen of the Vigilante Committee, September 10, 1864, Speeches and Writings, FPUM). However, in later years and in a more primitive environment, he was once again to champion vigilante action.

3. Advertisements in the *Montana Post,* September 10 and September 17, 1864.

4. *Montana Post,* August 27, 1864. See also *Montana Post* issues of February 18, January 21, and January 28, 1865.

5. Margaretha Ault to JF, April 20, 1864, FPUM.

6. Margaretha Ault to JF, April 20, 1864, FPUM. For an excellent treatment of gender-related fears of Indian assaults, see Glenda Riley's *Women and Indians on the Frontier.* James Fisk did, in fact, attempt to lead another expedition across the plains in 1864, but the journey came to a disastrous end when the train was attacked by Dakota Indians in the southwestern corner of present-day North Dakota. There were twelve fatalities among the emigrants. (White, *Ho!,* 115.)

7. Margaretha Ault to JF, April 20, 1864, FPUM.

8. James Dillin to JF, July 4, 1864, Oscar Mueller Collection, MtHS. Fort Lyon, Colorado, was located about thirty miles west of present-day Las Animas, Colorado.

9. The acting governor of Idaho Territory had appointed James Fergus county commissioner for Madison County the previous February, and James was again appointed county commissioner when the county became a part of Montana Territory in May 1864. (Horne, "James Fergus," 93.)

10. Fergus bill from Hamilton's store, September 12, 1864 through March 6, 1865, for a total of $107, Financial Records, 1842–1885, FPUM.

11. Gilpatrick, "Autobiographical Sketch," 2–3. Rev. Thomas J. Dimsdale held the first Episcopal services in Virginia City and ran the first school there as well. The *Montana Post,* August 27, 1864, contains a notice of Dimsdale's school. A March 4, 1865, entry in one of James Fergus's daybooks shows tuition payments to Dimsdale for Andrew and Lillie. (Account Book in Mining Records, Grasshopper Diggings, 1862–1869, FPUM.)

12. According to the cult of "true womanhood," a phrase in frequent use in the popular literature of the day, a nineteenth-century woman was judged—by her husband, her neighbors, and society—by the degree to which she exhibited four cardinal virtues: piety, purity, submissiveness, and domesticity. (Welter, "Cult of True Womanhood," 152.) By James's account here, Pamelia had failed to meet any of the standards of true womanhood.

13. JF to PF, undated, FPUM.

14. JF to PF, undated, FPUM.

15. JF to PF, undated, FPUM.

16. William Butler to JF, June 7, 1864, FPUM. Butler would have sold Dillin's house as lumber, for his letter of June 7 noted, "The only Show to sell any property here is to have it torn'd down and taken to St. Cloud" (William Butler to JF, June 7, 1864, FPUM). Pamelia had earlier described the practice of rafting lumber to St. Cloud. (PF to JF, November 15, 1863, FPUM.) And in his 1876 history of Morrison County, Nathan Richardson estimated that one-third of the town was rafted to St. Cloud during the early 1860s. (Richardson, "History," 18.)

17. JF to PF, undated, FPUM.

18. JF to PF, October 10, 1860, FPUM.

19. Johnson, *Bloody Bozeman,* 150–52. The *Montana Post* gave but nine lines to the April 9 surrender at Appomattox in its April 22, 1865, issue, while it gave liberal coverage to the flour raids. (*Montana Post,* April 22, 1865.)

20. *Montana Post,* January 14, 1865.

21. *Montana Post,* April 15, 1865.

22. *Montana Post,* April 15, 1865.

23. PF to JF, April 1865, FPUM. Further proof of Pamelia's thriving boarding business is seen in records from Robert Hamilton's store. Bills for Fergus food items suggest that there were far more people to feed than the immediate family, and bills for such tableware items as new sets of spoons would suggest that she had plenty of customers. (Hamilton bills to Fergus, September 12, 1864, through March 6, 1865, Financial Records, 1842–1885, FPUM.)

24. PF to JF, April 1865, FPUM.

25. Luella Fergus to JF, April 1865, FPUM. Luella bordered the four pages of the letter in black. Though Lincoln was shot on April 14, the *Montana Post* did not carry news of the assassination until April 29, 1865. (Johnson, *Bloody Bozeman,* 154.)

26. Helena was established on October 30, 1864. Edgerton County, established in February 1865, became Lewis and Clark County on December 20, 1867. (Dennis Lutz, *Montana Post Offices and Postmasters* [Rochester, Minnesota: Johnson Printing Co., 1986], 86, 108.)

27. PF to JF, May 3, 1865; Robert Hamilton to JF, May 13, 1865—both in FPUM.

28. Robert Hamilton to JF, May 13, 1865, FPUM.

29. Robert Hamilton to JF, May 13, 1865, FPUM.

30. Robert Hamilton to JF, October 22, 1865, FPUM.

31. O. J. Rockwell to JF, February 24, 1866, FPUM.

32. Robert Hamilton to JF, December 26, 1865, FPUM.

33. William Butler to JF, June 7, 1864, FPUM. Butler's letter referred to James Fergus's earlier report of a slump in the mining activities in Virginia City. Though the slump occurred several months before Francis Gravel arrived in Virginia City with his load of clothing and other merchandise, Butler was correct in assuming that the drop in mining activity would mean a depressed economy that would make it difficult for Gravel to succeed as a merchant.

34. Public Notice, April 25, 1865, Legal Documents, 1841–1900, FPUM.

35. Charles Rumley, Assayer, to JF, December 27, 1865, FPUM. Robert Hamilton had earlier and prematurely congratulated his father-in-law for striking a rich lode in the gulch: "I am Glad you have found So good a Lode you have looked Long for it and I hope you have found it at last" (Robert Hamilton to JF, October 22, 1865, FPUM).

36. Public Notice, December 20, 1865, Legal Documents, 1841–1900, FPUM.

37. Robert Hamilton to JF, December 26, 1865, FPUM. Six years earlier James had written his brother William that he had "thought rather seriously of Engaging in farming on a large scale, particularly the raising of stock and sheep, but so far I have not been able to obtain any land to suit me that I could buy having no money" (JF to William Fergus, September 29, 1859, FPUM).

38. O. J. Rockwell to JF, February 24, 1866; George Stephens to JF, February 11, 1866; James McGuire to JF, January 1, 1866—all in FPUM.

39. Organized in June 1866, Montana became Argenta in February 1871. (Lutz, *Montana Post Offices,* 6, 36, 60.)

40. Sweet, *William Sturgis,* 21–22; notarized authorizations for and reports on construction of toll roads by Beaverhead Wagon and Road Company, owned by William Sturgis and James Ryan, March 11, 1866, William Sturgis Collection, MtHS.

41. Sweet, *William Sturgis,* 22. The post office at Sturgis was established on January 31, 1868, with William Sturgis as postmaster, but a year later the town was renamed Ryan, for Sturgis's road-building partner, and Ryan took over as postmaster. (Lutz, *Montana Post Offices,* 43, 48.)

42. Public Notice, January 10, 1866, Legal Documents, 1841–1900, FPUM; Bill of Sale, JF to Stephen C. Gilpatrick, February 29, 1866, L&CCC. Gilpatrick was a native of Maine who had lived in Wisconsin before coming to Alder Gulch in 1864. (S. C. Gilpatrick obituary, *Helena Daily Independent,* September 5, 1934, p. 10.)

43. Gilpatrick bought a quartz claim in April 1866, but soon thereafter he decided

on a merchant's career and gave up both his mining and his 160-acre ranch. (S. C. Gilpatrick to Charles Scoll, April 16, 1866, Deed Book E, 109, L&CCC.)

44. Robert Hamilton to JF, March 4 and July 18, 1866, FPUM. The Hamilton baby was born on March 1, 1866. (Christine Kloezeman, "Hamilton Genealogy Chart," July 1989.)

45. Robert Hamilton to JF, July 18 and September 15, 1866, FPUM. Kloezeman's chart gives October 11, 1866, as the baby's death date.

46. JF to Mary Agnes Hamilton, August 23, 1866, FPUM.

47. JF to Robert Hamilton, August 23, 1866, FPUM.

48. Robert Hamilton to JF, September 15, 1866, FPUM.

49. Robert Hamilton to JF, October 1, 1866, FPUM.

50. George Stephens to JF, February 11, 1866; Robert Hamilton to JF, March 22, April 22, April 27, and June 9, 1866; William Staines of Salt Lake City to JF, June 19, 1866; William Thomas Dillin to James Fergus, March 18, 1866 — all in FPUM. With his letter, William Dillin sent "a few appel Seeds" from some "splendi[d] appels," adding a note: "I hope you will live to Eat appels from these seeds but [I] Fear [you will] not."

51. JF to Robert Hamilton, September 9, 1866; Wells Fargo bill to JF, June 7, 1873 — both in FPUM.

52. William Butler to JF, August 31, 1866, FPUM.

53. William Butler to JF, October 12, 1866, FPUM.

54. William Butler to JF, October 12, 1866, FPUM.

55. John Ault to JF, December 28, 1866, FPUM. Ault's inquiry about the Bailey lode was in regard to the new goldfields of the Lead-Deadwood area in what is now South Dakota. James Fergus corresponded with H. B. Bailey through 1866 and 1867 regarding mining prospects there. (H. B. Bailey to JF, August 12 and September 15, 1866; March 21, July 7, September 21, and November 3, 1867 — all in FPUM.)

56. James Dillin to PF, January 28, 1868; James Dillin to JF, September 4, 1866 — both in FPUM.

57. William Sturgis to JF, September 23, 1866, FPUM.

58. William Butler to JF, October 12, 1866, FPUM.

59. Probate Records, Benton County, September 26, 1867.

60. Marriage Records, Lewis and Clark County, Book A, 64; Gilpatrick to Lloyd Brown, February 7, 1867, Deed Book D, 106 — both in L&CCC.

61. Robert Hamilton to JF, January 7, 1867, FPUM. According to his biographer, James Fergus eventually simply abandoned his investments in Virginia City and Deer Lodge County. (Horne, "James Fergus," 94.) In 1866 E. Melvin Trask wrote Fergus that his cabin at Bannack had been torn down for firewood. (E. Melvin Trask to JF, January 21, 1866, FPUM.)

62. Sweet, *William Sturgis,* 22; Rosanna Sturgis to William Sturgis, May 11, 1867, William Sturgis Collection, MtHS. The two oldest Sturgis girls did not make the trip. Jeanette had married and remained in Minnesota. Jennie, aged eighteen, was likely with relatives in Sturgis, Michigan.

63. Margaretha Ault to JF, April 14, 1867, FPUM.

64. Rosanna sailed on the *Luella,* which left St. Louis on April 25, 1867. ("Statement of Steamers Making the Trip from St. Louis to Fort Benton and the Upper Missouri

River," in *Collections of the State Historical Society of North Dakota,* vol. 2 [Bismarck: Tribune State Printers and Binders, 1908], 372–74.)

65. A ticket from St. Louis to Fort Benton on a river steamer averaged $150. (Betty M. Madsen and Brigham D. Madsen, *North to Montana!* [Salt Lake City: University of Utah Press, 1980], 153.)

66. More and more steamers set out for Fort Benton each season, but not all of them made it there. Though three feet of water was sufficient to float a 150-ton steamer, as the season wore on the Missouri grew more shallow and vessels were forced to put in at the mouth of the Marias River, ten miles from Fort Benton, or at Cow Island, some 125 miles east of Fort Benton. (C. W. Howell and J. N. Macomb, "Obstacles to Navigation in the Missouri River in 1867," in *Collections of the State Historical Society of North Dakota,* 2:379–91.) The year of Rosanna's passage marked the peak port activity at Fort Benton. Forty-three vessels left St. Louis for Fort Benton and thirty-seven made it all the way there, two more making it as far as Cow Island. (Howell and Macomb, "Obstacles to Navigation," 387–88.)

67. Rosanna Sturgis to William Sturgis, May 11 and May 16, 1867, William Sturgis Collection, MtHS.

68. William Sturgis obituary in the *Dillon Examiner,* April 24, 1901, p. 1; "Statements of Steamers," 373.

69. Having emigrated to Montana in 1864 on the same train that carried Pamelia west, Johnson had worked as a bartender in several saloons and had fallen in love with Isabella "Curly" Gross, a popular prostitute in Blackfoot, Montana. Insanely jealous, he had accosted one of her customers and was shot in the ensuing scuffle. (*Weekly Independent,* November 2, 1867, p. 1.)

70. William Butler to JF, October 20, 1867, FPUM. Butler's letter states that Johnson's two sons, John and Jacob, were to be sent back to Minnesota, implying that they were in Montana with their father, having either made the journey with him in 1864 or crossed the plains sometime thereafter. (MC60.)

71. William Butler to JF, October 20, 1867, and February 21, 1868, FPUM.

72. Probate No. 2468, Book E, 36, MorCC, gives Temperance Churchill's death date as August 18, 1868; MC70. Predictably, Orlando had not given himself over to prolonged grieving. By 1870 he was married to an Englishwoman from St. Paul. (William Butler to JF, December 2, 1870, FPUM.)

73. MC70; William Butler to JF, December 2, 1870, FPUM.

74. Deeds, March 18, 1876 and April 23, 1878, in Legal Documents, 1841–1900, FPUM.

75. JF to son Andrew, March 10, 1872; restaurant license to James Fergus, May 1 through November 1, 1872, Financial Records, 1842–1885—both in FPUM. Records in FPUM show that the stage station served detachments from Forts Benton, Baker, Ellis, Maginnis, Missoula, and Shaw. In addition, those forts also purchased potatoes and other produce from Fergus.

76. Hotel license, June 1 through September 1, 1875. The license was renewed until March 1880, at which time the Ferguses sold the stage station.

77. JF to William Butler, March 20, 1875; election records, Montana Territory, October 1864, and certified bill of election, Fairweather Mining District, September 2, 1864, in Legal Documents, 1841–1900; bill of appointment, February 6, 1864, in Licenses, Citations, and Appointments; JF to Stephen Gilpatrick, January 29,

1866 — all in FPUM. In December 1867 Edgerton County became Lewis and Clark County.

78. JF to Robert Hamilton, May 13, 1899, FPUM.

79. Gilpatrick, "Biographical Sketch," 190–91.

80. Vawter and Company of Helena, weekly butter order sent to Pamelia Fergus, December 16, 1874, FPUM; Gilpatrick, "Biographical Sketch," 189.

81. JF to Daughter, undated, FPUM.

82. Virginia City, the territorial capital since 1865, had been steadily losing its population and influence to Helena. Three disputed elections eventually brought the "capital question" into the courts. In 1875 Helena was finally proclaimed the capital city. (Malone and Roeder, *Montana,* 84–85.)

83. Robert Hamilton to JF, July 31, 1873, FPUM. In addition to the baby who died in Virginia City in 1866, the Hamiltons had two daughters, Mary Agnes and Nellie Luella, and three more sons — Robert Emmett, Thomas Moore, and Robert Stavely, Jr.

84. Sweet, *William Sturgis,* 22.

85. William Sturgis to JF, June 7, 1873, FPUM.

86. Sweet, *William Sturgis,* 22.

87. Rosanna Sturgis left a married daughter behind her again. Twenty-year-old Ann had married Eugene Trask and remained in Montana. (Con Bray to JF, December 4, 1873, FPUM.) Sturgis kept the Beaverhead property and, over the next few years, returned to Montana every spring to work the ranch.

88. A. L. Randall to JF, April 24, 1874, FPUM. Lewis Randall had boarded briefly with Pamelia in the spring of 1865, before settling in Whitehall.

89. Margaretha Ault to Robert and Mary Hamilton, January 29, 1872, FPUM.

90. Margaretha Ault to Robert and Mary Hamilton, January 29, 1872, FPUM.

91. Margaretha Ault to Robert and Mary Hamilton, January 29, 1872, FPUM.

92. Ault Probate, Probate Records, Gallatin County, Montana, Book D, 464; JF to William Butler, March 20, 1875, FPUM. John Ault died on December 30, 1874. (John Ault obituary, *Bozeman Avant Courier,* January 1, 1875, p. 3.)

93. William Butler to JF, April 9, 1875, FPUM. Butler added some news of his own, possibly gained from Margaretha's "enemies" in Verona: "[Ault's] wife was married to another man some 2 years ago so we heard. She must have married prior to his death."

94. Memorandum of June 20, 1874, in James Fergus Day Book, 1872–1878, FPUM; Horne, "James Fergus," 118. In a letter to his brother Robert late in 1879, James noted that he had just made "an enumeration of the value" of his property so as to give Andrew one-fourth of it as a reward for his contributions to the Fergus estate. "Our total valuation if sold at private sale will reach $30,000 which will give him $7500 but to make everything sure we call it $6500, not bad for a man of 27 to begin with" (JF to Robert, December 16, 1879, FPUM).

95. Frank Maury's father changed the family name from Mauriano to Maury upon emigrating from Saxy, Belgium, around 1850, with his wife and four young sons. Frank and four younger siblings were born in Utica, New York, where the Maurys lived before moving to Key West, Iowa, a small French settlement eight miles south of Dubuque. (M. E. Wareham to Margaret Bristol, March 15, 1862, Margaret Bristol personal files.)

96. When James Fergus wrote Frank Maury to ask why he had not married Lillie

in the spring of 1876, Maury replied, "The reason that Lillie did not come with me in the Spring is that I intended to come & buy & then go back to stop in Montana one year to work to earn enough to go to work on our own place & not be oblige to work on any others Farm but we made a mistake in the first place so now we will be oblige to pay for it & do the best we can" (F. H. Maury to JF, October 14, 1876, FPUM).

97. Lillie's wedding date is taken from Book A, 165, L&CCC.

98. The baby was likely born on September 15, 1876, for on January 15, 1877, Lillie informed her mother that "baby is four months old to-day." However, he may have arrived on September 19, for in a letter begun May 18, 1877, she wrote, "May 19th To day is some ones birthday 8 months old." In a letter written February 22, 1877, Lillie says the baby is "going on six month," which makes the birth date late August or early September. Named Marion Maurice Maury, the boy was called Maurice until he was a year or so old, and Marion thereafter. (Lillie Fergus Maury to PF, January 15, 1877, FPUM.)

99. Lillie Fergus Maury to PF, February 22, 1877, FPUM. Even after she was safely in Iowa, Lillie received reports from Pamelia of suggestive comments made by curious neighbors. "I think Mrs Clark is pretty inquisitive and had better pay her [own] debt[s]," she wrote upon hearing one report.

100. Lillie Fergus Maury to PF, April 7, 1877, FPUM.

101. JF to William Fergus, October 20, 1884, FPUM. Lillie would not even write her father's name at first—telling her mother, "O yes I havent written to—Yes I did write you" (Lillie Fergus Maury to PF, March 30, 1877, FPUM).

102. F. H. Maury to JF, February 12, 1877, FPUM. Though Pamelia had apparently chosen to keep Lillie's pregnancy from Mahala Dillin and the other relatives in Illinois until after the wedding, by April 1877 she was urging Lillie to write to her grandmother, tell her of the marriage, and invite her for a visit. Unwilling to assume that responsibility by herself, Lillie replied, "I have started to write to Grandma so many times; but I surely will write as soon as she gets your letter—that I have a baby" (Lillie Fergus Maury to PF, April 7, 1877, FPUM).

103. Andrew kept a journal of this trip, and he notes the names and addresses of the relatives he was to visit before and after the exhibition. (Andrew Fergus Journal, begun on departure date, September 29, 1876, FPUM.)

104. Luella Fergus Gilpatrick to Andrew Fergus, March 5, 1888, FPUM.

105. Bill for stereopticon and pictures from H. M. Parchen & Company of Helena to James Fergus, June 23, 1875; bill from Kinna and Jack of Helena for seventy-five feet of one-and-one-quarter-inch pipe for gaslights, 1875; bill from S. E. Larabie & Company for two pedigreed horses for three thousand dollars, September 29, 1877—all in Financial Records, 1842–1885, FPUM.

106. Lillie Fergus Maury to PF, June 22, 1877, FPUM.

107. Lillie Fergus Maury to PF, March 30, 1877, FPUM. Lillie had three more children—Claude, Elsie, and Merle.

108. Mining Records, Grasshopper Diggings Journal, 1862–1869, p. 74, 57, 76, FPUM.

CHAPTER 8. Endings

1. L. B. Lyman to JF, May 6, 1873, FPUM.

2. Stuart, "James Fergus," biographical sketch, 1942, MtHS. T. C. Powers, Granville Stuart, and Henry Brooks were already on the plains by this time. (Horne, "James Fergus," 118.)

3. Nearly forty years earlier James had written to Dr. E. A. Wood, a friend from his Canadian days: "I want to be with you in the west. . . . I want more elbow room than there is here more freedom more generosity more wages for work bigger souls" (JF to E. A. Wood, November 6, 1841, FPUM). Those who knew him well were not surprised to hear of the proposed move. A. L. Randall, who had been with him at Little Falls, Pikes Peak, and Bannack, noted later, "I suppose Mr. Fergus is satisfied now he has got off down in that wild lonesome country. . . . [He] will go there and work as long as he can get one foot before the other" (A. L. Randall to unknown person—possibly S. C. Gilpatrick—September 5, 1880, FPUM).

4. Reminiscences by JF of the early cattle industry of Lewistown, Montana, FPUM. Lewistown was settled in 1881 as Reed's Fort, a trading post. When it was incorporated as a town, its name was changed to Lewistown. (Roberta C. Cheney, *Names on the Face of Montana: The Story of Montana's Place Names* [Missoula: University of Montana Publications in History, 1971], 138.)

5. Luella Fergus Gilpatrick to PF, August 9, August 20, and August 30, 1880, FPUM.

6. Bill from M. Silverman, wholesaler, Helena, September 18, 1880; bill of sale from Fort Benton, October 8, 1880—both in Financial Records, 1842–1885, FPUM. James Fergus soon had use for his guns—not against Indians, but against cattle rustlers and horse thieves who roamed the Judith Basin in the early 1880s. Granville Stuart led a vigilante group in a number of raids that left several rustlers dead and others wounded. Too old and weak to go out himself, Fergus helped to finance and organize the vigilante raids and took pride in Andrew's participation in them. Though he had earlier decried the continued vigilante activity in Virginia City, he justified his participation now by explaining, "Now as the country don't protect us, the army don't protect us, there is no way left but to protect ourselves" (Horne, "James Fergus," 165–69; JF to *Rocky Mountain Husbandman,* August 16, 1884, FPUM).

7. Bill of sale, October 8, 1880, Financial Records, 1842–1885, FPUM.

8. JF to son Andrew, December 16, 1880, and January 4, 1881, FPUM.

9. JF to son Andrew, December 5, 1880, FPUM.

10. Andrew Fergus to JF, December 23, 1880, FPUM.

11. JF to son Andrew, January 24, 1881, FPUM.

12. Andrew Fergus to PF, January 11, 1881, Oscar Mueller Collection, MtHS.

13. Luella Fergus Gilpatrick to Andrew Fergus, April 3, 1881, Oscar Mueller Collection, MtHS. James returned to the Armells ranch on March 21, 1881, according to a diary entry he made that day. (JF Notebook, November 15, 1880, through July 18, 1882, FPMtHS.)

14. JF Notebook, April 4, 1881, FPMtHS.

15. JF Notebook, November 15, 1880, through July 18, 1882, FPMtHS; James Fergus, undated memoir to his children, Oscar Mueller Collection, MtHS. The Armells ranch remained isolated at least through 1888, for in July of that year James

described their home as "3 miles from a neighbor, thirteen from a post office, 27 from the county seat" (JF to George Stephens, July 28, 1888, FPUM).

16. Gilpatrick, "Biographical Sketch," 189.

17. JF to Robert Mills, May 7, 1883, FPUM.

18. JF in an undated letter to a Mrs. Harding, probably late 1887, shortly after Pamelia's death, FPUM.

19. James Fergus was not only the typical nineteenth-century entrepreneur, he also represented the risk-taking spirit of the American frontier. For those who went west, risk-taking, financial and otherwise, was a way of life.

20. Memorandum about money matters, James Fergus Day Book, 1882-1883, FPMtHS. In the early 1880s, as Pamelia and James were settling on the Armells ranch, Lyman Signor, the register of deeds of Morrison County, Minnesota, quietly went about buying up all the Fergus and Little Falls Manufacturing Company property remaining in Little Falls. His offer of fifty dollars per lot was endorsed as fair by William Butler. (Lyman Signor to JF, April 22, 1878; May 17, May 25, June 21, June 23, July 7, and August 8, 1881; March 2, April 11, June 9, July 13, and September 7, 1882; February 5, May 30, June 27, September 18, and December 21, 1883 — all in FPUM.)

21. According to Hazel Fergus, widow of Andrew Fergus, at the time of James Fergus's death, the library at the ranch held over 2,500 volumes. (Hazel Fergus Bubar to Larry Barsness, December 31, 1962; titles from Fergus library list dated 1888-1894, Miscellany — both in FPUM.)

22. Certificate of election, November 17, 1884, Legal Documents, FPUM. Margery Brown, "Metamorphosis and Revision: A Sketch of Constitution Writing in Montana," *Montana the Magazine of Western History* 20 (Autumn 1970): 11. His was a laissez-faire brand of politics: "The people of the United States are governed too much and taxed too much." That philosophy was evident in his record; his vote was more frequently no than yes, and he introduced few bills. (Horne, "James Fergus," 212-14; JF to W. F. Sanders, June 6, 1890, FPUM.) Known for his brilliant oratory and his penchant for using the stump as a platform for his agnosticism, he fought against blue laws. (Horne, "James Fergus," 189-215.)

23. JF to son Andrew, January 14, 1884, FPUM.

24. JF to son Andrew, January 27, 1884, FPUM.

25. JF to son Andrew, February 2, 1884, FPUM.

26. JF to son Andrew, February 15, 1884, FPUM.

27. JF to brother Andrew, December 18, 1885, FPUM. In fact, Fergus did not vote against the bill that created Fergus County, but abstained. (Horne, "James Fergus," 206).

28. JF to Mrs. D. P. Shafer of Cottonwood, 1887, Speeches and Writings, FPUM.

29. Luella Fergus Gilpatrick to JF, March 22, 1887, FPMtHS.

30. PF to son Andrew, April 28, 1887, Oscar Mueller Collection, MtHS.

31. Luella Fergus Gilpatrick to JF, May 21, July 12, and July 30, 1887, FPMtHS. In a letter of July 25, 1887, Dr. W. L. Steele assured James, "I do not think the breast will ever bother her any more [but] she must not expect to recuperate like a younger person." Dr. Steele's instructions for injecting morphine were contained in that letter: "Enclosed find the syringe & medicine when you wish to use it put syringe in warm water until it tightens up then pinch up the skin shove the needle in under

the skin avoiding the veins give about 10 minins of the sol[ution] repeating again in an hour if necessary. The minins are marked on syringe After drawing the fluid in the syringe turn it up and shove the piston up until the liquid commences to flow out that excludes all the air. Then introduce the needle & inject slowly as soon as done wipe the needle dry and insert the wire as very little rust will close it" (W. L. Steele to JF, July 25, 1887, FPMtHS).

32. During the time Pamelia spent at home, James wrote to Dr. Steele, who noted, "The cancer may be breaking out in the liver or some of the internal vicera" and advised wine, whisky, or brandy and morphine. (W. L. Steele to JF, September 12, 1887, FPMtHS.) During Pamelia's final months, James requested and received advice on cancer treatments from relatives and friends. Lillie wrote from Dilley, Oregon—where the Maurys had moved a few years before—in early June to tell him she had heard of a doctor who applied plasters to a woman's breast cancers and cured her. (Lillie Fergus Maury to JF, June 9, 1888, FPUM.) Nathan Richardson sent James a cancer "recipe" he bought from an old man in Little Falls. In return, James was to send him a quitclaim deed for a Little Falls town lot to which James held one-third title. Richardson wrote again soon thereafter to say he had omitted the "blood root," an herb known for its cleansing properties, from the recipe. (Nathan Richardson to JF, August 12 and August 28, 1887, FPMtHS.)

33. Most likely, Fergus drove Pamelia to Billings to catch the Northern Pacific. No other rail route to Helena would have been available to him in early October 1887. (Dave Walter, reference librarian, Montana Historical Society, to Peavy and Smith, May 20, 1988.) While James could have driven her all the way to Helena by horse and buggy, a distance of around two hundred miles, the trip would have been slower and rougher than her journey by rail. Also, Fergus obviously felt he had time to attend to several matters at the ranch before joining her in Helena.

34. W. L. Steele to JF, October 4, 1887, FPMtHS.

35. JF draft of a letter to a correspondent in Glascow, Scotland—probably Janet Simpson, a daughter of his "closest cousin," circa 1888, FPUM.

36. Lillie was already en route to Helena by train when her mother died. She later told Andrew that she heard their mother calling her the evening of her death and knew that she had passed away. (Lillie Fergus Maury to Andrew Fergus, October 12, 1887, Oscar Mueller Collection, MtHS; Andrew Fergus to JF, October 1887, FPUM.)

37. Sanders eulogy as printed in the *Helena Daily Herald,* October 12, 1887. James's description of Pamelia's funeral, as printed in the *Mineral Argus,* noted, "In compliance with the wishes of the deceased, no religious services were held" ("A Friend" to the *Mineral Argus,* October 11, 1887). Yet there is no way of knowing whether Pamelia might have preferred religious services, were it not for James's agnosticism. Pamelia did, after all, send the children to Sabbath school quite regularly in Little Falls and sometimes went to church herself, though she likely found churchgoing more of a social than a spiritual experience. (PF to JF, June 7 and August 2, 1863, FPUM.)

James's will, drafted only months before her death, had eulogized Pamelia in its own way, making her his sole heir in recognition of the fact that she had "done her full share towards raising our family, procuring a living and acquiring what property we possess. I deem it but just and right if she survives me that she should have the use, benefit and Enjoyment of the whole of our common property during her natural life" (James Fergus will, August 8, 1887, Legal Documents, 1841–1900, FPUM).

38. JF to "daughters and friends," October 1887, FPUM. In a letter written a dozen years later, Luella noted, "Her energies of brain and muscle went in her work had she had the time to use her brain in other directions without so much muscular or physical labor she would have been remarkable in some other line but she did what she was given to do and did it abley" (Luella Fergus Gilpatrick to JF, March 24, 1899, FPMtHS).

39. JF to W. F. Saunders, circa 1892, FPUM.

40. JF to son Andrew, July 1, 1893, FPUM.

41. JF to Nathan Richardson, as printed in the *Little Falls Weekly Transcript,* September 17, 1897, MCHS.

42. JF to editor of *Fergus County Argus,* as reprinted in the *Little Falls Weekly Transcript,* December 10, 1897, MCHS.

43. Though James Fergus himself never made it to Alaska, he staked a grandson's prospecting venture and so had a vested interest in the action there. Collin Gilpatrick's case is not unlike that of James Fergus: he was married when he left for the goldfields, and he left his wife behind with little financial support. (Collin Gilpatrick to JF, November 3, 1897; February 19 and March 14, 1899; and June 13, 1901, FPUM.) Though James ultimately gave up his dream of trying his luck in the goldfields of the far north, he never gave up his quest for Montana gold. A month before the turn of the century, at age eighty-six, he staked a claim at Voltaire Lode in the Cone Butte District of Fergus County, and in January and April of the following year he staked two additional claims in that area. (Fergus Claim Records, November 24, 1899; January 22 and April 14, 1900 — both in Legal Documents, 1841–1900, FPUM.)

44. James Fergus obituary, *Fergus County Argus,* July 2, 1902. Upon Andrew's death on July 18, 1928, the Fergus Livestock and Land Company, which owned ten thousand acres, was dissolved. (*Lewistown Democrat News,* July 19, 1928, p. 3.) Mary Agnes and Robert Hamilton eventually left Helena for a ranch on the Fergus spread, where Agnes died of pneumonia on January 29, 1920. (Mary Agnes Fergus Hamilton obituary, *Helena Daily Independent,* January 30, 1920, p. 5.)

Luella Fergus Gilpatrick lived out her life in Helena, dying there on February 27, 1931. (Luella Fergus Gilpatrick obituary, *Helena Independent,* February 27, 1931, p. 5.) In 1912 Frank Maury died in Dilley, Oregon, where he and Lillie had lived since they moved from Iowa. Sometime thereafter, fifty-five-year-old Lillie married Scott Sparks of Forest Grove, Oregon, ignoring the family's comments that she was "too old to be married a second time." She outlived her second husband and died of a stroke in January 1930 at age seventy-three. (Margaret Maury Bristol to Peavy and Smith, May 22, 1988; Lillie Fergus Maury Sparks obituary, *Lewistown Democratic News,* February 9, 1930.)

45. The letters of William Butler to James Fergus, the primary source of news and once-lengthy reports of Little Falls happenings, gradually became one-paragraph business memorandums and ended completely in November 1887, a month after Pamelia's death. It was from Butler that the Ferguses learned that Orlando Churchill had left Little Falls, moving first to St. Paul with his second wife, whom he

abandoned there in 1875 in order to go "to California with a bad woman" (William Butler to JF, April 9, 1875, FPUM). Mathilda Churchill filed for divorce shortly thereafter, but by 1878 the couple had remarried, returned to Little Falls, and moved into the apartment over Butler's store that Orlando had once shared with Temperance. (William Butler to JF, January 30, 1878, FPUM.) It was Butler who kept the Ferguses apprised of the resurgence of Little Falls, of the long-anticipated coming of the railroad, and of new investments in lumbering that had sent the town into another boom period. In 1890 Charles A. Weyerhaeuser and R. D. Musser established the Pine Tree Lumber Company in Little Falls.

William H. Fletcher noted that Nathan Richardson, Butler, Gravel, the Batters family, Moses LaFond, William Dow, and John Workman were among the few "who remained in or near the town during its long Rip Van-winkle sleep and witnessed its resurrection and rehabilitation some fifteen years later" (Fletcher, "Reminiscence," 10).

46. Russell Register, 7.

47. Probate Records, TCC.

48. *Todd County Argus,* August 18, 1882. Bosworth completed the log drive in 110 days.

49. Sheets et al., *Todd County Histories,* 314. The Bosworths lost one son, Willie, to diphtheria and another, Parker, to "a disease of the spine." If Caroline is buried beside her husband and sons, there is no marker to attest to that fact. (Tombstones in Bosworth plot, Evergreen Cemetery, Long Prairie, Minnesota.)

50. Margaretha Ault obituary, *Little Falls Weekly Transcript,* March 13, 1896.

51. William Sturgis to JF, February 25, 1884, FPUM. Later that same year, Nathan Richardson, who had called on Sturgis while visiting in Michigan, reported to Fergus that William was "down near the bottom of the ladder yet and will likely remain so . . . old Bill is . . . as hard up as ever" (Nathan Richardson to JF, August 25 and September 29, 1884, FPUM). Despite his fear of another failure, Sturgis apparently did try his entrepreneurial skills again—first in the sheep business in Kansas and later in real estate in Socorro, New Mexico. (Luella Fergus Gilpatrick to JF, August 8, 1889, FPUM; William Sturgis obituary in the *Sturgis Democrat* [Sturgis, Michigan], as reprinted in the *Little Falls Daily Transcript,* April 23, 1901, MCHS.)

52. Arthur J. Sturgis drowned in 1893 and Annie Sturgis Trask died in Butte, Montana, in 1894. (William Sturgis to JF, February 18, 1898, FPUM; Rosanna Sturgis obituary in the *Sturgis Democrat,* as reprinted in the *Little Falls Herald,* May 27, 1898, MCHS.)

53. Rosanna Sturgis obituary in the *Sturgis Democrat* as reprinted in the *Butte Miner,* June 2, 1898, MtHS. The obituary noted, "Her life was devoted to the performance of her duties as wife and mother and loving service to her family and friends."

54. Nathan Richardson to JF, March 4, 1898, FPUM.

55. William Sturgis obituary in the *Sturgis Democrat,* as reprinted in the *Little Falls Daily Transcript,* April 23, 1901, MCHS.

Index

Fort Shaw, 285n75
Fourth of July, celebrated, 61, 66, 116,
117, 119; ignored, 275n226
Freeman, Abby, 38, 73, 77, 109, 114, 134,
224
Freeman, Charles, 5, 242n16; business in-
terests, 38, 47, 58, 71, 72, 73, 96; as cor-
respondent, 44, 50, 57, 62, 74, 76,
252n81, 260n280; as parent, 76–77;
plans to go west, 108–9; on trip west,
114; in West, 134, 224
Freeman, Freddie, 38, 77, 134
Freeman, Kate, 103, 114, 262n360
French, Col. C. E., publisher, 22
French Canadians, 246n75
Frontier experience, as liberating in-
fluence, 235n8, 251n60; views of,
240n59. *See also* Crossing the plains
Fuller, Mary B., 146
Funk, Eric, composer, xiiin1

Gallatin City, Mont., 187, 280n84
Gallatin Claim Club, 159
Gallatin Valley, 175
Gammell, Alexander, miner, 236n2
Garden, Arthur, machinist, 83, 242n16
Garden, Charles, machinist, 242n16,
263n368
Gender ratio, in frontier towns, 22–23,
242n29, 243n30
Gender role expectations, *see* Cult of
true womanhood; Patriarchal house-
holds; Separate spheres in marriage
Gender role reversals, 194. *See also* "Dep-
uty husband"; Surrogate head of
household; "Women in waiting"
Gilpatrick, Collins, 211, 218, 223, 291n43
Gilpatrick, Frances Luella Fergus, *see*
Fergus, Frances Luella
Gilpatrick, Frank, 211, 218, 223
Gilpatrick, George, 211, 218, 223
Gilpatrick, James, 211, 218, 223
Gilpatrick, Stephen Collins, 194, 198,
202, 204, 206, 208–9, 223, 226;
depicted, 206
Godfrey, Ard, 141, 143, 270n126
Gold rush, Colorado, 34, 36, 246n82;
Montana, 119, 121; Klondike, 228–29,
231, 291n43; Idaho, 264n21. *See also*

Colorado goldfields; Idaho goldfields;
Klondike gold strikes; Montana
goldfields
Gould, Betsy, 65
Gould, Chessman, 91
Grady, Edward, miller, 116, 127, 135–36,
141, 142, 158, 271n161
Grasshoppers, plagues, 25
Gravel, Clara, 142, 175, 183
Gravel, Emilie, 142, 175, 183
Gravel, Francis X., 5, 68, 77, 291n45;
merchant, 4, 32, 41, 142, 201, 209; busi-
ness interests, 69, 70, 74, 114, 136, 168;
plans to go west, 140–41, 142, 156, 166,
175; on trip west, 177, 178, 180, 183, 184.
See also Butler and Gravel's store
Gravel, Frankie, 142, 175, 183, 187, 201
Gravel, Hermine, 142, 175, 177, 178, 183,
209, 277n7
Gravel family, 181
Green, James, millowner, 15
Gregory Diggings, Colo., depicted, 53
Gros Ventres Indians, 120
Gross, Isabella, prostitute, 285n69

Hackett, D. D., miner, 161–62
Hall, Clara, gold rush widow, 5, 54,
136–37, 209, 251n55
Hall, James, attorney, 4, 38, 82–83; plans
to go west, 5, 109; debts, 48, 54, 57, 73,
100, 107; luck in west, 136–37; death,
209
Halliday, Robert, artist, 132
Hamilton, James Lincoln, 202, 286n83
Hamilton, Mary Agnes Fergus, *see*
Fergus, Mary Agnes
Hamilton, Mary Agnes, 286n83
Hamilton, Nellie Luella, 286n83
Hamilton, Robert, 79, 93, 135, 148, 156,
273n182; boarder, 104–5, 120, 134, 137,
155; tinsmith, 104, 155, 193, 242n29;
postmaster, 104, 155, 263n368; draft status, 120, 156, 157; as correspondent,
126, 162, 167; shopkeeper, 155, 193;
plans to go west, 156, 163; courtship,
164, 167, 173; on trip west, 178–79, 181,
183, 184, 189; wedding, 179; as husband, 179, 183, 193, 198, 199, 211, 223;
advises James Fergus, 200, 201, 203;

Picture Credits

The photographs and other illustrations used in this book appear through the courtesy of the institutions and individuals listed below. The names of the photographers, when known, are given in parentheses, as is additional information about the source of the item.

The text and display faces of this book were set in Bembo by Stanton Publication Services, Minneapolis. Printing and binding were performed by Thomson-Shore, Inc., Dexter, Michigan, with the cloth edition Smyth sewn for durability. Judi Rettich designed the book's cover and interior, and Alan Ominsky drew the maps.

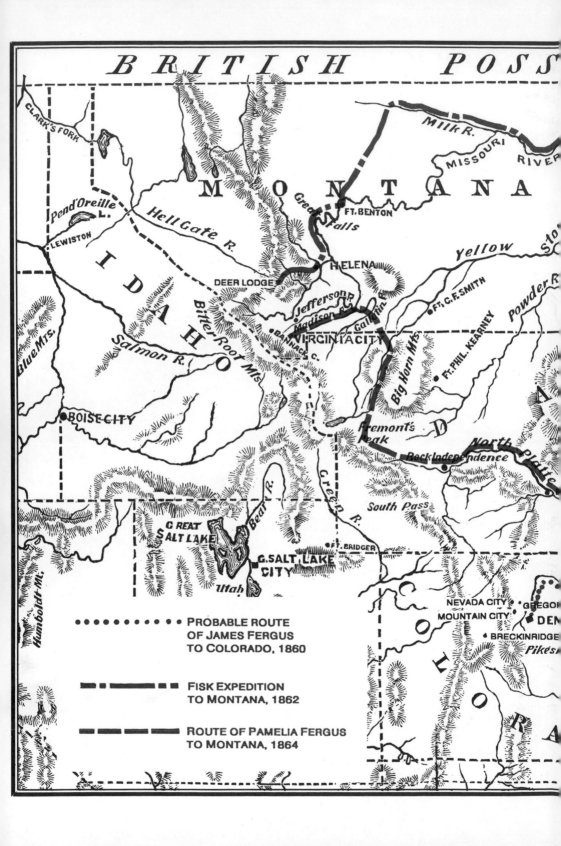

PROBABLE ROUTE
OF JAMES FERGUS
TO COLORADO, 1860

FISK EXPEDITION
TO MONTANA, 1862

ROUTE OF PAMELIA FERGUS
TO MONTANA, 1864